Building Splunk Solutions

Grigori Melnik
Dominic Betts
Matthew Tevenan
David Foster
Brian Schutz
Liying Jiang

Foreword by Stephen Sorkin

Building Splunk Solutions

Splunk Developer Guide

2nd edition

ISBN: 978-1-5146-1574-4

Library of Congress Control Number: 2015915374
CreateSpace Independent Publishing Platform, North Charleston, SC

Printed in the United States of America.

In memory of David Carasso,

Splunk's Chief Mind

Contents

Foreword

For many years, Splunk was primarily an engine for searching and exploring IT data (that is, Google for your log files). It was aimed at helping system and network administrators aggregate and analyze the data needed to run and troubleshoot large computing infrastructures. Splunk has since evolved into a highly-efficient platform for all types of machine generated data. While being very powerful out of the box, it's more of a blank slate — there is a lot of additional value that Splunk can offer through the apps that extend and enrich the capabilities of the core Splunk platform. The target users now include security and business analysts, marketing experts and developers.

The Splunk Developer Platform is open and extensible. It provides a diverse set of services and APIs to support Splunk apps both in standalone and distributed deployments. It includes execution and search services with support for your custom UIs as well as data services (for data ingestion and data access), persistence and identity services. These not only power our own products, but also allow you to build your own custom apps that analyze machine data from any system. The platform also comes with tools to make Splunk development more like modern Web development, reconciled with the idioms of your language of choice (be it Python or C#, JavaScript or Ruby, Java or PHP). Notably, a lot of your skills building Web apps can be reused effectively. We want to give you all the right building blocks and tools to make you successful on our platform.

Developers have told us that it has been hard to know where to start and have an all-around picture of the Splunk extensibility surface area. Fortunately, this authoritative developer's guide fills that gap and offers guidance on how to build comprehensive Splunk apps. It follows a Splunk software engineering team on their journey to build a solution with a partner, focusing on the real world use case and learning objectives to showcase various technologies of the Splunk Developer Platform. Like a documentary, it captures their story from envisioning a product and user experience prototyping to development, packaging and deployment. It includes diverse perspectives of developers and testers, administrators and product owners, security experts and release engineers. It presents architectural discussions, performance crossroads, tradeoff analyses, retrospectives from user experience design sessions, bug triages, security reviews, app certification - all analyzed and presented in the form of lessons learned. The guidance is written by developers for developers: no fluff, only pragmatic stuff.

I highly recommend you use this guide in concert with studying the source code of the reference apps and the associated tests. The corresponding code repos are open (in fact, you can see and replay the code in motion, as it was developed). The code is built with good and proven practices in mind. We encourage you to reuse and learn from it. I can assure you that if you work through the reference apps and this guide, you will see how easy it is to create comprehensive, multifaceted, powerful apps.

I must commend the authors for their effort in putting together such a comprehensive set of guidance targeting developers and helping them make a real business impact with Splunk solutions. Writing this guide involved a lot of work. I mean a LOT OF WORK!

Importantly, we plan to make a continuous investment in keeping this guidance regularly updated and improved. This is where we look forward to your contributions. Feel free to submit your feedback or even code pull requests. We welcome your participation!

So... let's get started! Read on, learn, code, and liberate your data with the help of Splunk and Splunk apps!

Stephen Sorkin
Chief Strategy Officer
Splunk

May 2015
San Francisco, USA

The Team Who Brought You This Guide

This guide was not a small undertaking with many people contributing to both the reference apps and the written guidance.

- Vision and Product Management: **Grigori Melnik** (Splunk).
- Business Requirements: **Randy Hammelman** and **Dave Weir** (Conducive Consulting), **Eugenio Pace** and **Matias Woloski** (Auth0).
- Project Management: **Ari Brown** (Splunk).
- Development: **David Foster**, **Satoshi Kawasaki, Grigori Melnik**, and **David Poncelow** (Splunk), **Brian Schutz, Randy Hammelman** and **Praveen Pohar** (Conducive Consulting), **Eugenio Pace** and **Sebastian Iacomuzzi** (Auth0).
- User Experience: **Peter Stern** (Blink Interactive), **Brian Carlos Reyes** (Splunk).
- Testing: **Liying Jiang** (Splunk).
- Documentation: **Dominic Betts** (Content Master Ltd.), **Grigori Melnik**, **Matthew Tevenan, David Foster**, and **Liying Jiang** (Splunk).
- Edit, Post-Production and Release: **RoAnn Corbisier** (Independent), **Chris Burns** (Independent), **Stephanie Coffaney**, **Franck Curier**, and **Matthew Tevenan** (Splunk).

Many thanks to the following people who provided meaningful feedback and support:

- Our customers – **Bernie Macias** of Zillow, **Kate Engel** of Morgan Stanley, **Brad Newman** of ViewPost, **Mika Borner** of LC Systems-Engineering, and **Serdar Sutay** of Chef – for beta testing the reference app and reviewing our technical guidance.
- Our colleagues – **Chris Bauer**, **Dritan Bitincka**, **Brent Boe**, **Dennis Bourg**, **Jack Coates**, **Macy Cronkrite**, **Damien Dallimore**, **Mark Groves**, **Oleg Izmerly**, **Alex James**, **Satoshi Kawasaki**, **Edward Kostowski**, **Divanny Lamas**, **David Maislin**, **David Noble**, **Sanford Owings**, **David Poncelow**, **Michael Porath**, **Hal Rottenberg**, **Michael Szebenyi**, **Eric Woo**, **Brian Wooden**, **Simeon Yep**, and **Dmitrii Zakharov** – for providing feedback on the project and reviewing our technical guidance.
- **Stephen Sorkin**, Splunk's Chief Strategy Officer for being a trusted advisor, our project sponsor, and a strong advocate for the developer ecosystem.
- **Mark Groves** for letting us loose, yet providing important suggestions and steering the project.

- **Glenn Block** for diligent review of the questions backlog, validating the HTTP Event Collector scenarios and implementation, continuing advocacy of the project among customers, and thoughtful doc reviews.
- **Jack Coates** and **Adrian Hall** for insights on extensibility and various aspects of compliance to the Common Information Model.
- **David Carasso** and **Alex Raitz** for validating our approach, asking questions, and providing pointers to capabilities of Splunk we didn't know existed.
- **Matt Elting**, **Siegfried Puchbauer**, **Nick Filippi**, and **Carl Yestrau** for consulting with us on the particulars of the UI framework and custom alert actions.
- **Clint Sharp** for many insights on using and troubleshooting eventgen.
- **Sanford Owings** for the valuable real-world insights on the distributed deployment considerations.
- **Denis Gladkikh** for conducting code reviews and providing ideas for improvements.
- **Jon Rooney**, **Misty Gibbs**, and **Erick Mechler** for marketing and communication support.
- **Fred Wilmot** for security review, identifying a vulnerability, and helping come up with a better implementation.
- **Randy Young**, **Amrit Bath**, **Margaret Lee**, and **Alex Munk** for supporting and deploying the PAS app to the Splunk Cloud Sandbox.
- **Alex Prokhorenko** and **Terry Martin** for support in publishing and certifying the reference apps.
- **Christopher Gales** for guiding our documentation adventures.
- **Paddy Griffin** and **Rick Roberts** for the metaphors and diagrams that help explain Splunk concepts.
- **Ashwin Kedia** for the initial facilitation of the partnership with Conducive.
- **Ji-Hyun Park** for legal support, **Patricia Iorg**, **Rendi Miller**, and **Dee Bender** for administrative support.
- **Manish Sainani** for validating our approach to anomaly detection.

The authors and the development team thank our executive team for their leadership and ongoing support of our effort: **Godfrey Sullivan**, **Stephen Sorkin**, **Guido Schroeder**, **Doug Merritt**, **Steve Sommer**, **Snehal Antani**, **Shay Mowlem**, **Markus Zirn**, **Krishna Tammana**, **Carola Thompson**, and **Colin Savage**.

We gratefully recognize participants of SplunkLive!, Splunk Partner Summits, .conf, and other conferences who provided feedback and suggestions.

Thank you!

Companion Resources

Understanding the code is the key to getting the most from this guide, we encourage you to download and explore as you read through the chapters.

dev.splunk.com	**Splunk's main developer hub**
dev.splunk.com/goto/devguide	**Online version of the guide**
github.com/splunk/splunk-ref-pas-code	**Splunk Reference App - PAS code repo**
github.com/splunk/splunk-ref-pas-test	**Splunk Reference App - PAS test repo**
github.com/auth0/splunk-auth0	**Splunk Reference App - Auth0 code repo**
github.com/splunk	**Other open-source Splunk projects**
splunk.com/getsplunk/onlinesandbox	**Splunk Cloud Trial (comes with the PAS app pre-installed)**
dev.splunk.com/page/developer_license_sign_up	**Request a free developer license**
answers.splunk.com	**Community forums**
splunkbase.splunk.com	**Public repo of Splunk apps and add-ons**

Part I
JOURNEY

1

Planning a journey

This chapter introduces the companies that will collaborate on this journey, the people from those companies who will come along with us, and most importantly the Splunk apps that we intend to build as the goal of our journey. This chapter outlines some of the key features and functionality that we plan to include in the finished apps and introduces some of the issues we are considering right at the start of our journey. The chapters that follow enable you to follow along as we continue on this journey to build our Splunk apps.

A JOURNEY

This guide describes the journey undertaken by the project team and is intended to give you an insight into how to set about developing Splunk apps, to recommend some good and proven practices, and to provide a useful reference when you come to build your own Splunk apps. However, like on any real journey, we make mistakes, have arguments, and change our minds along the way; so in addition to showing you how best to do things, we highlight the pitfalls and issues that we encounter, and the solutions we find. We do not intend this guide to cover everything related to developing Splunk apps, it focuses on the specific issues we faced in building our two sample apps. However, our two sample apps are representative of the typical apps Splunk customers do build.

The primary objective of our journey is to deliver applied engineering guidance along with Splunk apps that act as reference implementations. We hope this guidance will help to lower the entry barrier, reduce the time to market, and decrease the risk for you, our Splunk customers and partners. The following five principles characterize our guidance philosophy:

We're planning a journey, and like any real journey we need to know who's coming with us, have an idea of where we want to get to, and what some of the choices along our way will be. We need to make some plans before we start. This journey is not a journey to a place, but the journey we took to learn how to build Splunk® apps in the real world.

- ***Proven:*** based on real-world experience, and validated by field engineers and partners.
- ***Authoritative:*** offers the best available advice, in context.
- ***Accurate:*** technically validated and properly tested.
- ***Actionable:*** provides the steps to success.
- ***Relevant:*** addresses a real world problem.

Each chapter of this guide covers a specific theme such as UI design orgdata onboarding and follows the basic chronology of the journey as we develop our apps. The chapters also include commentary from various experts, descriptions of some of the team's working practices where they shed light on what happened, and discussions about why we made particular decisions. We hope this guide will mature through a dialog with you, our audience of Splunk app developers.

OUR ORGANIZATIONS

Three different companies collaborate on this journey: Splunk, Conducive, and Auth0. Conducive already uses Splunk Enterprise and has previously developed Splunk apps; Auth0 is new to Splunk Enterprise. Both Conducive and Auth0 have ideas about how they can use Splunk apps to add value to their own products and services and want to partner with Splunk to pursue those plans further. This means that the journey includes two separate development projects for two separate Splunk apps: one for Auth0 to enable insights into how users are interacting with the Auth0 service, and one for Conducive to build a Splunk app to assist in monitoring secure document repositories (for more information, see Our apps below). We built both of these Splunk apps using Splunk simple XML. The next chapter Platform and tools: a kitbag for our journey discusses why we chose this specific technology in more detail.

Conducive

Conducive is a system integrator with one of the focus areas being standards compliance. Their user audience includes business managers, compliance officers, auditor, and investigators.

Some of the specific goals that the Conducive team has for their involvement in the project are to learn how to:

- Extend the Common Information Model.
- Develop highly configurable advanced visualizations and user interactions.
- Implement auto complete drop downs that can lazy load a large number of options.
- Perform form validation prior to running a search.
- Use pivots that enable a user to use drag and drop to manipulate the columns displayed on a dashboard.
- Detect deviations from the norm across multiple variables.
- Incorporate predictive and statistical analytics.

- Handle outliers.
- Design an app and dashboards that enable non-technical users to create reports and configure alerts.

Auth0

Auth0 is an Identity-as-a-Service infrastructure provider. Their user audience is primarily developers.

Some of the specific goals Auth0 has for their involvement in this journey are to enhance their monitoring and reporting functionality with a Splunk app.

Their learning objectives include:

- Understanding a structure of a Splunk app.
- Using the Splunk *search processing language* (SPL™).
- Building and testing modular inputs.
- Performing data validation when configuring a modular input.
- Utilizing Simple XML to build a basic set of panels and dashboards and to refine them iteratively.
- Packaging and publishing a Splunk app.

OUR PANEL OF EXPERTS

A panel of experts from a number of roles follow the journey, and the following chapters include their comments on the development effort. The roles these experts perform are:

A developer, expert in using Splunk and developing Splunk apps. He wants to see a well written Splunk app that follows proven practices.

An architect who wants to see a well-architected solution.

A UX designer who wants to see an engaging, intuitive, easy-to-use UI for the app.

A tester who wants to ensure the highest possible quality for the reference implementations.

A system administrator who wants to know how to deploy and monitor the apps, and understand how to configure them.

A representative of the business who knows how the apps will be used and their expected benefit to the business.

A release manager who wants to ensure that the apps are packaged in a way that makes them easy to deploy and to update in the future.

A security expert who wants to ensure that the apps comply with any security requirements in the target environment.

A performance tester who wants to ensure that the apps performance is acceptable with production loads.

OUR APPS

During the journey, the team develops two apps, one with Conducive and one with Auth0. This book focuses primarily on the Conducive app but discusses the Auth0 app where it provides a contrast or highlights different issues. The following two sections in this chapter provide overviews of the apps as we envision them at the start of the project.

ADM

If you're planning to list your app on the Splunk Apps web site, you should follow the naming guidelines at dev.splunk.com/goto/namingguide**.**

Pluggable Auditing System (PAS)

The PAS Splunk reference app is intended to enable an organization to monitor a fleet of document repositories such as ones hosted on Box.com or SharePoint. Conducive wants the organization to use the app to see who has looked at, updated, modified, deleted, or downloaded documents in the repository. The app should enable the organization to be both reactive and proactive in its approach so that in addition to being able to see what happened, the app notifies the organization of potential security issues when it detects unusual behavior associated with either a user or a document.

Potential users of the app include anyone with responsibility for protecting sensitive data. We expect the end users of the app to be non-technical business users such as:

- An investigator assigned to protect data or to discover the identity of someone who is stealing data. An investigator is typically from the compliance or auditing side of the business.
- A manager who needs to know what his or her employees are doing. This is not necessarily to monitor productivity but to identify unusual behavior.

BUS

These end user roles are typically non-technical, and they should be able to use the app without technical help: an intuitive UI is important.

In addition to the end users, there is a technical role for configuring the app with rules for triggering alerts specific to the organization and its requirements. Some organizations may configure these rules once when they deploy the app, others may have the requirement to be able to update these rules in response to changes in the business environment or to emerging threats. This may require some basic technical knowledge of Splunk Enterprise. The app should include a set of basic default rules to get started.

SEC

The app should define an access policy. Splunk Enterprise supports role-based access control with a user given access to a resource or action based on the permissions given to the role(s) to which that user belongs.

The app should include the following five key elements:

- An *Overview Dashboard* to provide summary details of most reports and to highlight areas that require further investigation.
- A *Reactive Analysis* capability to determine the activities of one or more users of the document repository and the geographic location where they performed those activities. The app should also be able to correlate those activities across different users, documents, or data sets.
- A *Rules-based Proactive Analysis* capability to apply a set of predetermined and custom rules to the audit logs and reference data to search for potentially malicious activity. The organization can add custom rules as required to search for evolving and newly identified undesirable behaviors, or to filter out changes in behaviors that the organization no longer considers to be undesirable.
- A *Statistical Proactive Analysis* capability to apply statistical analysis to the audit and reference data to establish various behavioral norms. This capability should include the functionality to apply weighting factors to the different data elements in order to differentiate false positives and noise from normal behavior.
- A *Workflow Solution* with capabilities such as triggering incidents for review, categorizing them by type, assigning tasks to the relevant personnel, capturing details relevant to the investigation in an unalterable manner, and escalating incidents.

BUS

These were our goals at the start of the journey. The finished apps do not incorporate everything we envisaged, primarily because we ran out of time and resources needed to implement everything in our backlog.

Auth0

At the start of the project, Auth0 is using Splunk Enterprise to monitor some basic events related to users of the Auth0 services. For example, whenever a new user signs up with Auth0, the Auth0 service sends event data to a Splunk REST endpoint. This event data includes information such as the event type, the target app, the client IP address, and the userid. Auth0 then display this information in a simple dashboard.

Auth0 would like to build a Splunk app that will replace the current solution and have the following features:

- Identifying and tracking 'slipping away' users. Auth0 assign all users a status (new, active, very active, slipping away, all but deleted) and they send out a boilerplate email to slipping away customers asking why they are leaving. Auth0 would like to use rules in Splunk Enterprise to identify slipping away users.
- Sending emails to all users of a specific connection type. For example, if Facebook make a change to one of their APIs, Auth0 wants to send a notification to all users of the Auth0 Facebook connector.

Auth0 are also considering making a Splunk app available to their customers to enable them to track business metrics such as:

- If the customer has a portfolio of applications, who is accessing which ones?
- Which users are encountering problems?
- Suspicious log-ins and other anomalies.

ARCH

You check the details of your Splunk Enterprise license if you are planning to provide your customers with reports and data from your Splunk Enterprise installation.

BUS

The app should display this information in way that's attractive to customers.

BEGINNING OUR JOURNEY

The following chapters describe what happened on our journey, with each chapter focusing on a high level theme. Each chapter covers the issues the team encountered in tackling the various stories and use cases, how they resolved those issues, the decisions they made, and the lessons they learned. You'll also learn more about the specifics of the Splunk apps we have introduced in this chapter. Some chapters will also include sections that describe how the team works or arrives at particular decisions.

The following flowchart illustrates the typical workflow for developing a Splunk app. Not all projects will follow these steps exactly, but they provide a rough outline of the key stages for most Splunk app projects:

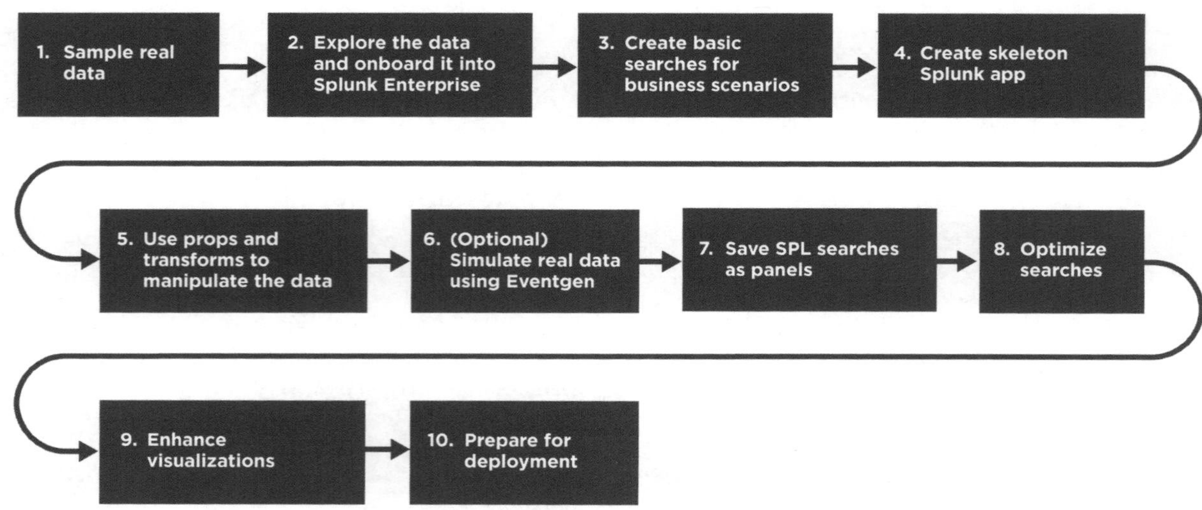

1. To start, look at a sample of the real business data and begin to understand what information is available.
2. Then you must work out how to get that data into Splunk. Options include, using file monitors, open ports, scripted inputs, or modular inputs. The chapter "Working with data: where it comes from and how we manage it" discusses these options for the PAS and Auth0 apps.
3. Determine the basic business scenarios your app will address by involving your business end users. Create some basic searches to support these scenarios. The chapter "Adding code: using JavaScript and Search Processing Language" describes an example of this.
4. Create a skeleton app using the Splunk Enterprise web UI or the command-line tools. You can then add dashboards and visualizations to this app. This is discussed in the chapter "Platform and tools: a kitbag for our journey."
5. Use Splunk Enterprise features such as transforms to manipulate the incoming data to make it easier to search. The chapter "Working with data: where it comes from and how we manage it" discusses these options.
6. Optionally, during the development process use simulated data so you are not reliant on a third-party system while you are building the app. Typically, this helps you develop and test faster. The chapter "Platform and tools: a kitbag for our journey" discusses this.
7. Run the basic searches and add them as panels to the dashboards in your skeleton app. This is discussed in the chapter "Platform and tools: a kitbag for our journey."
8. Optimize the searches (see the chapter "Adding code: using JavaScript and Search Processing Language") and consider using a data model (see the chapter "Working with data: where it comes from and how we manage it").
9. Enhance the visualizations and add polish to the UI. These are discussed in the chapters "UI and visualizations: what the apps look like" and "Adding code: using JavaScript and Search Processing Language"
10. Prepare your app for deployment by adding features such as user roles and permissions. The chapter "Packaging and deployment: reaching our destination" discusses these options.

Our team has a variety of technical skills relevant to the project that include:

- JavaScript, XML and knowledge of Model-View-Controller web development. These are all relevant to building our apps.
- C# and Python. These are relevant to building our tests and connectors/modular inputs.

Some of the team also have experience of building Splunk apps using technologies such as Splunk SPL and the simple XML development model for apps.

PRODUCTION NOTES

Note that code samples and screenshots shown in the following chapters do not necessarily match the code and UI in the completed apps. The samples show the code and UI at that particular point in the journey, and in some cases they may be modified at a later stage in our journey. In particular, some screenshots and code sample refer to the **warum** app; this was our original internal code name for the app that was changed near the end of the project to **pas**.

The majority of the screenshots in this guide were taken on a Windows machine, in some cases where there is a significant difference we show a *nix screenshot as well.

MORE INFORMATION

For an introduction to developing Splunk apps and using various Splunk APIs, see Get Started (dev.splunk.com/goto/getstarted) on the Splunk Dev web site.

For additional information about Conducive Consulting, see conducivesi.com.

For additional information about Auth0, see auth0.com.

2

Platform and tools: a kitbag for our journey

OUR DEVELOPMENT AND TEST ENVIRONMENTS

Splunk® apps are typically client-side web applications that may also include server-side components, it's also possible for a Splunk app to consist purely of server-side components. You can use a wide variety of different web technologies to build them such as XML, JavaScript, HTML, CSS, Python, C#, Java, and Ruby. Therefore, you can choose the development tools you are most comfortable with: a good programmer's text editor is essential, you'll also need to know how to debug your scripts and access any log data your app generates. If you are using JavaScript, you should learn how to use the developer tools in your browser: most browsers enable you to debug JavaScript, view the resources a page uses (such as stylesheets, images, and JavaScript files), and examine the effect of any CSS files on your formatting and layout. The following screenshot shows the Chrome browser developer tools open on the **Summary** page in the Pluggable Auditing System (PAS) app, with the JavaScript code paused at a breakpoint:

This chapter focuses on the preparations for our journey and describes some of the tools, techniques, and approaches we use for developing and testing the apps.

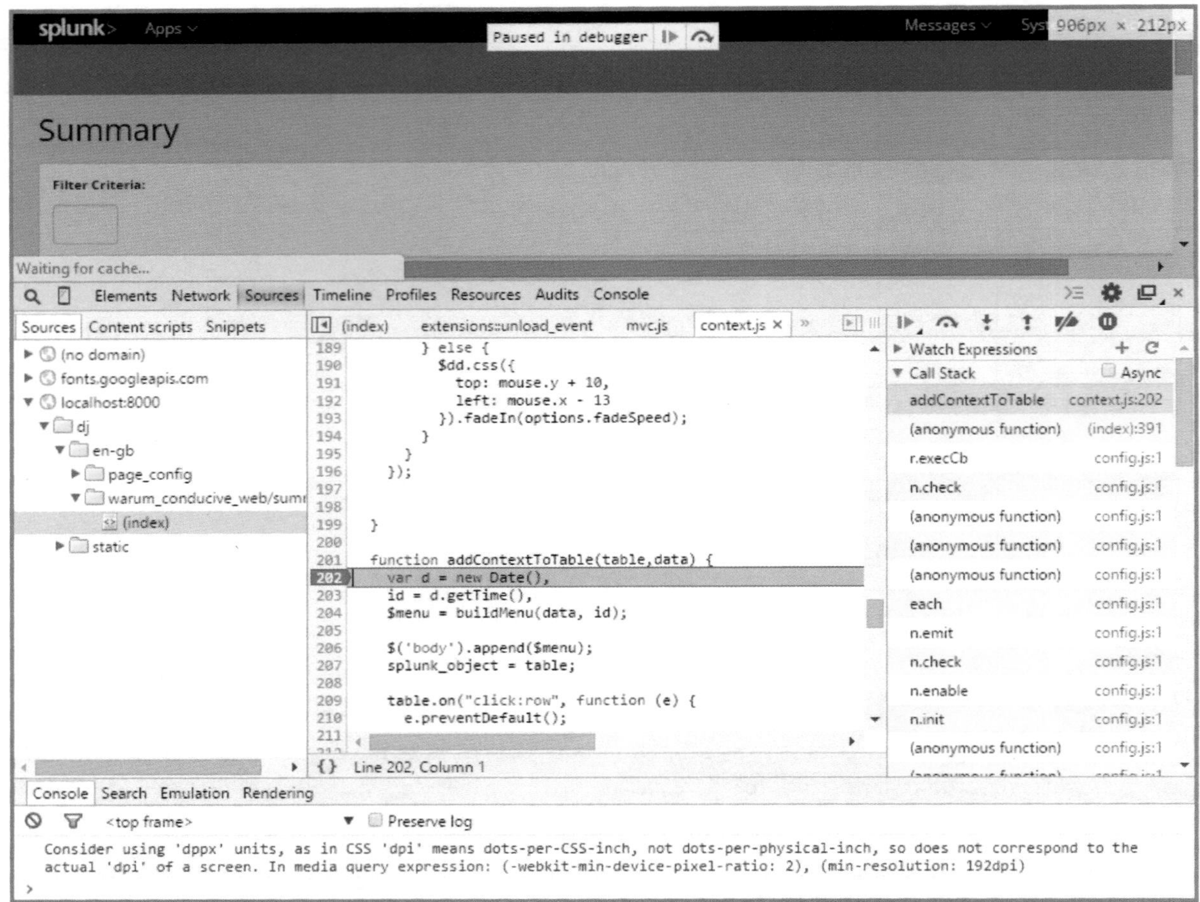

TEST

Splunk Enterprise itself generates log data that you can query and analyze using Splunk Enterprise. You can do so by specifying `index=_internal` **in the default Splunk search app. For more information about Splunk instrumentation, introspection and various troubleshooting techniques, see** "What Splunk logs about itself." **For Splunk crash log analysis, see:** "Community:Troubleshooting Crashes."

The approach we are taking to develop the PAS app is to:

- Begin by understanding what the app must display and (along with our UX designer and business user) sketch out a design of the dashboard. This includes the panels, visualizations, drilldowns, and page navigation.
- For each panel, understand the data requirements: where does the data come from, how we should interpret it, and do we need to implement features such as field extractions and lookups. Then we can define the searches.

- Optimize the solution. For example, we might decide to build a data model to abstract the underlying data and then refactor the searches.

DEV

When the team started developing the PAS app they used sample data and had some control over the format and content of the data they were using, enabling them to focus more on the UI and the visualizations. In a real project with real data, you would analyze the available data to determine what types of questions you could ask which, in turn, would inform you of the types of visualizations you could use. Therefore in a real project, you would consider both the underlying data and the visualization requirements in parallel.

Overall, we will take a modular approach to the development of the apps, focusing on one particular dashboard or even just one particular panel at a time. Each panel is typically self-contained, but Splunk Enterprise does include capabilities that enable panels to share data if necessary.

ARCH

The team found that it doesn't make sense to build the data models before they get a good idea of what the app looks like and what searches it requires. Your dashboard and search requirements feed in to your data model design.

The focus of much of the testing will be on the UI, so we are using Selenium as a browser automation tool. It includes a selection of drivers for automating the most commonly used web browsers to enable cross-browser testing and there are bindings for a variety of languages such as C#, Java, JavaScript, Ruby, and Python. To run these automated user acceptance tests we've chosen a Python solution, and the familiarity of the test team and other Splunk Enterprise developers with this platform is one of the main reasons for adopting it. A test sends commands to the browser to simulate a user interaction, such as clicking on a button, and then captures the Document Object Model (DOM) content in the browser to enable us to verify the expected output. One challenge we face is how to test the graphical output in the Splunk app: the visualization libraries we plan to use generate Scalable Vector Graphics (SVG) code for the graphics, so we need to learn how to parse and extract the information we need from the SVG code embedded in the generated app web page.

TEST

If you are using Selenium, be sure to check which versions of the browsers you are using it supports. Selenium is not always updated immediately to support the very latest versions.

We also initially planned to use the Splunk Python SDK to connect to Splunk Enterprise beneath the UI and access data directly in some test scenarios, but decided not to do so as we rely on the correctness of search execution by the core product.

In the methodology adopted for this project, the test team defines a set of acceptance test scenarios for each story we implement, and the developers then implement the code with those test scenarios in mind. The test team then completes writing a collection of automated user acceptance tests to verify that the code complies with those test scenarios. Note that for this project, we are not following a full Test-Driven Development methodology, although this is definitely something we will consider in the future.

Walkthrough: How we worked with a UX designer to mock up the PAS app

When we set out to build the reference app, we started with a backlog of questions we wanted our guidance to address. The resulting backlog was rather comprehensive and included 60+ questions such as:

- What does a typical Splunk app architecture look like?
- How should I set up my dev environment to be productive with Splunk Enterprise?
- What are the different ways to integrate a Splunk app with existing systems?
- How do I generate sample data to test my app?
- What are the distributed deployment considerations?
- How do I package an app? How do I deal with app versioning and updates?

In parallel, we worked with our partner to identify high-priority use cases for the app.

UX

By building a real-world app that delivers real value to its users, we would achieve the high-level objective of learning and documenting the various architectural and technological aspects of building solutions on the Splunk platform.

To build a real app that delivered real value, the team needed to reconcile the questions backlog with the proposed business use cases. This was done iteratively for each sprint when we demoed progress made to the business owner and prioritized new development stories for the next sprint. The developers would then take the verified designs and approved stories and start making them a reality.

We had engaged with a UX designer early in the process to iteratively build mockups for the application. In the figures below, you can see the progress of our UX mockups for the Summary dashboard with the increasing fidelity. Many valuable insights originated from team brainstorming and whiteboarding sessions with the designer. We were able to have a fast turnaround because the designer was available to join the team on site. Our partner (business owner) was able to provide feedback on the designs early and frequently. These discussions brought many usability issues to light early in the process.

Below you see how we mapped various learning objectives to the specific use cases and visual elements of the reference app.

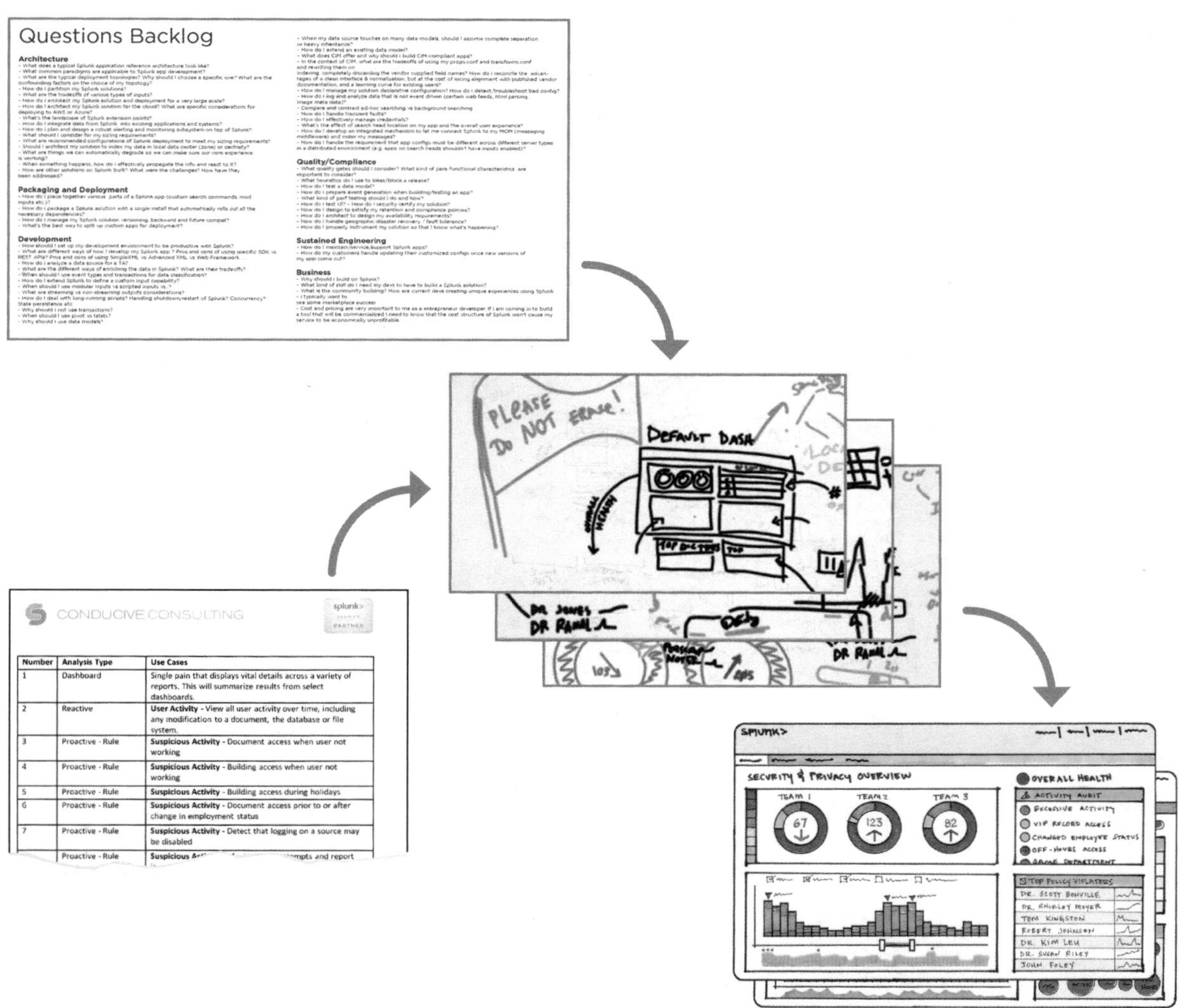

Questions Backlog

Architecture
- What does a typical Splunk application reference architecture look like?
- What common paradigms are applicable to Splunk app development?
- What are the typical deployment topologies? Why should I choose a specific one? What are the confounding factors on the choice of my topology?
- How do I partition my Splunk solutions?
- What are the tradeoffs of various types of inputs?
- How do I architect my Splunk solution and deployment for a very large scale?
- How do I architect my Splunk solution for the cloud? What are specific considerations for deploying to AWS or Azure?
- What's the landscape of Splunk extension points?
- How do I integrate data from Splunk into existing applications and systems?
- How do I plan and design a robust alerting and monitoring subsystem on top of Splunk?
- What should I consider for my sizing requirements?
- What are recommended configurations of Splunk deployment to meet my sizing requirements?
- Should I architect my solution to index my data in local data center (zone) or centrally?
- What are things we can automatically degrade so we can make sure our core experience is working?
- When something happens, how do I effectively propagate the info and react to it?
- How are other solutions on Splunk built? What were the challenges? How have they been addressed?

Packaging and Deployment
- How do I piece together various parts of a Splunk app (custom search commands, mod inputs etc.)?
- How do I package a Splunk solution with a single install that automatically rolls out all the necessary dependencies?
- How do I manage my Splunk solution versioning, backward and future compat?
- What's the best way to split up custom apps for deployment?

Development
- How should I set up my development environment to be productive with Splunk?
- What are different ways of how I develop my Splunk app ? Pros and cons of using specific SDK vs REST APIs? Pros and cons of using SimpleXML vs Advanced XML vs Web Framework
- How do I analyze a data source for a TA?
- What are the different ways of enriching the data in Splunk? What are their tradeoffs?
- When should I use event types and transactions for data classification?
- How do I extend Splunk to define a custom input capability?
- When should I use modular inputs vs scripted inputs vs..?
- What are streaming vs non-streaming outputs considerations?
- How do I deal with long-running scripts? Handling shutdown/restart of Splunk? Concurrency? State persistence etc
- Why should I not use transactions?
- When should I use pivot vs tstats?
- Why should I use data models?
- When my data source touches on many data models, should I assume complete separation or heavy inheritance?
- How do I extend an existing data model?
- What does CIM offer and why should I build CIM-compliant apps?
- In the context of CIM, what are the tradeoffs of using my props.conf and transforms.conf and rewriting them on indexing, completely discarding the vendor supplied field names? How do I reconcile the advantages of a clean interface & normalisation, but at the cost of losing alignment with published vendor documentation, and a learning curve for existing users?
- How do I manage my solution declarative configuration? How do I detect/troubleshoot bad config?
- How do I log and analyze data that is not event driven (certain web feeds, html parsing, image meta data)?
- Compare and contrast ad-hoc searching vs background searching
- How do I handle transient faults?
- How do I effectively manage credentials?
- What's the effect of search head location on my app and the overall user experience?
- How do I develop an integrated mechanism to let me connect Splunk to my MOM (messaging middleware) and index my messages?
- How do I handle the requirement that app configs must be different across different server types in a distributed environment (e.g. apps on search heads shouldn't have inputs enabled)?

Quality/Compliance
- What quality gates should I consider? What kind of para-functional characteristics are important to consider?
- What heuristics do I use to bless/block a release?
- How do I test a data model?
- How do I prepare event generation when building/testing an app?
- What kind of perf testing should I do and how?
- How do I test UI? - How do I security certify my solution?
- How do I design to satisfy my retention and compliance policies?
- How do I architect to design my availability requirements?
- How do I handle geographic disaster recovery / fault tolerance?
- How do I properly instrument my solution so that I know what's happening?

Sustained Engineering
- How do I maintain/service/support Splunk apps?
- How do my customers handle updating their customized configs once new versions of my app come out?

Business
- Why should I build on Splunk?
- What kind of skill do I need my devs to have to build a Splunk solution?
- What is the community building? How are current devs creating unique experiences using Splunk
- I typically want to see some marketplace success
- Cost and pricing are very important to me as a entrepreneur developer. If I am coming in to build a tool that will be commercialized I need to know that the cost structure of Splunk won't cause my service to be economically unprofitable.

CONDUCIVE CONSULTING

splunk> PARTNER

Number	Analysis Type	Use Cases
1	Dashboard	Single pain that displays vital details across a variety of reports. This will summarize results from select dashboards.
2	Reactive	**User Activity** - View all user activity over time, including any modification to a document, the database or file system.
3	Proactive - Rule	**Suspicious Activity** - Document access when user not working
4	Proactive - Rule	**Suspicious Activity** - Building access when user not working
5	Proactive - Rule	**Suspicious Activity** - Building access during holidays
6	Proactive - Rule	**Suspicious Activity** - Document access prior to or after change in employment status
7	Proactive - Rule	**Suspicious Activity** - Detect that logging on a source may be disabled
	Proactive - Rule	**Suspicious Ac**[illegible]mpts and report

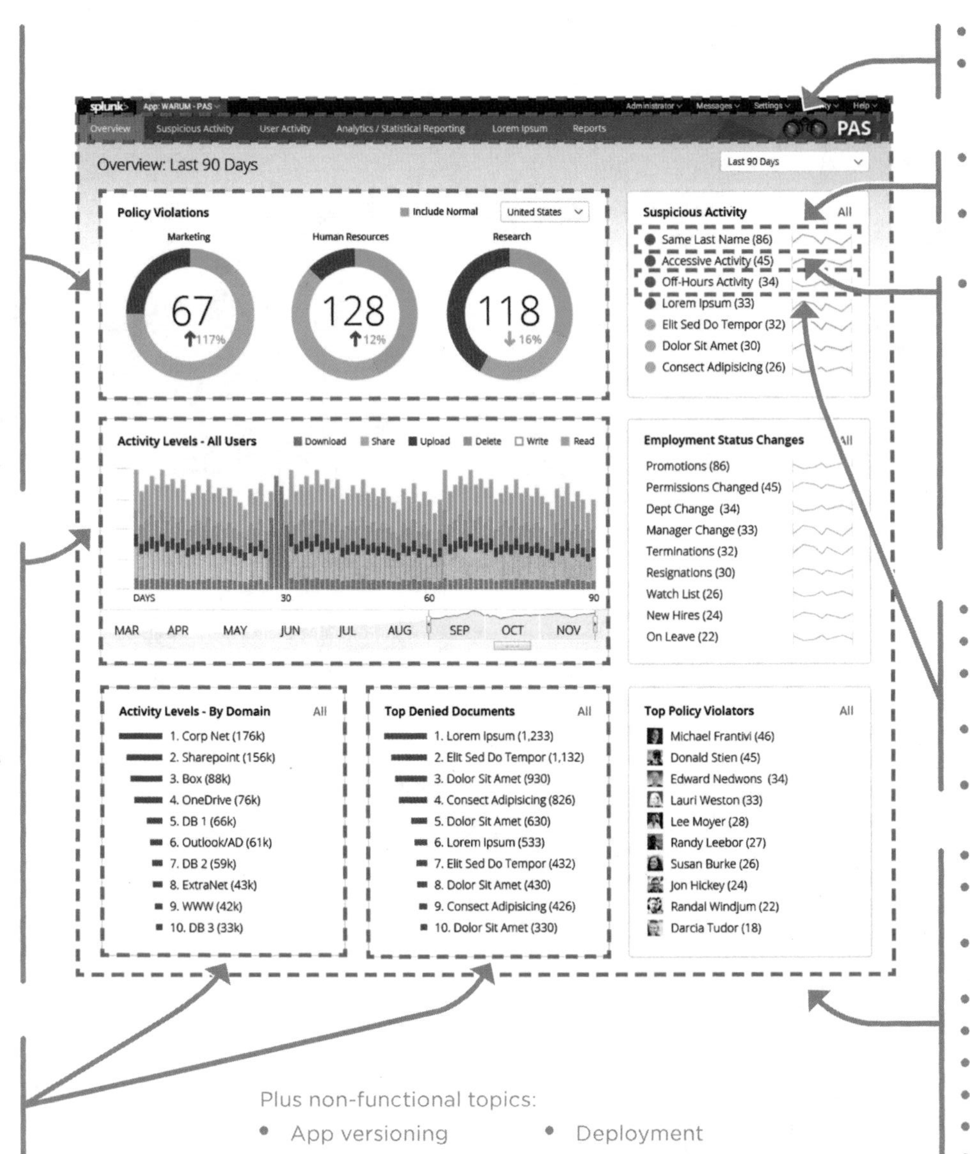

- Data
  - Search language
  - Aggregating siloed metrics intomeaningful KPIs
  - Data manipulation
  - Data normalization
  - Sub-searches
  - Config-driven
  - Persistence with KV store
  - Macros
- Viz:
  - Dynamic scaling
  - Customizing in-the box viz controls

- General search patterns
- Search optimizations
- Ux Prototyping
- Adapting 3rd party viz library
- Composite charts with interactions
- Dealing with high-volume data sets
- Troubleshooting perf issues
- Post-process or not-post-process – deployment implications
- Automated UI testing (with Selenium)

- Post-processing
- Integrating with 3rd party component
- Unit testing (with Mocha)
- Persisting state (per user)

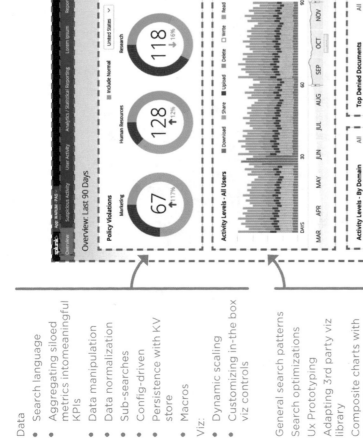

- Custom nav
- Ux activities permeating all dev

- Using sub-searches to correlate data
- Troubleshooting searches

- Data mining:
  - Exploration
  - Preparation: filtering/deduping/bucketing
  - Using advanced statistics functions
  - Threshold-based anomaly detection
  - Evaluating goodness/accuracy

- Data modeling
- Using lookups
- Building a baseline lookup table
- Windows of time/Custom time ranges
- Overlaying time data

- Setting the stage
- Overall Splunk app structure
- UI technology selection: Simple XML vs SplunkJS
- Modularity
- Dev & test env
- Dev workflow
- Modularity
- Data onboarding
- CIM compliance
- Tools

Plus non-functional topics:

- App versioning
- Packaging Installation
- Security review
- Deployment
- Publishing to Splunkbase
- App certification

Engaging with a UX designer early provided the following benefits:

- Facilitating insightful discussions among project stakeholders.
- Making use cases more concrete and detailed, seeing how a potential solution would fit into target user's collection of tools, techniques, activities.
- Validating UI designs using low-fidelity prototypes.
- Identifying additional strategic opportunities for business.
- Delighting end users with usable dashboards.

UX design played a vital role in empathizing with our users and understanding our users' needs, iteratively designing and testing solutions, and communicating optimal solutions to the development team.

Walkthrough: How we initially created the PAS app

These are the steps we followed to create a new, empty app when we first began development on both the PAS and Auth0 apps. These steps will create a **barebones** app that you can use as the starting point for your own Splunk apps. Note that you can also create a **barebones** app using the Splunk Enterprise command-line interface (CLI).

1. In Splunk Enterprise, click the **Apps** link, and then choose **Manage Apps**.
2. On the **Apps** page, click **Create app** and complete the required information about your app. You should choose a name for your app that makes it easy to recognize, and you should adopt a naming convention for the folders you use to make it easy to locate the source files: we've chosen to use the project name, the organization name, and the individual app name.

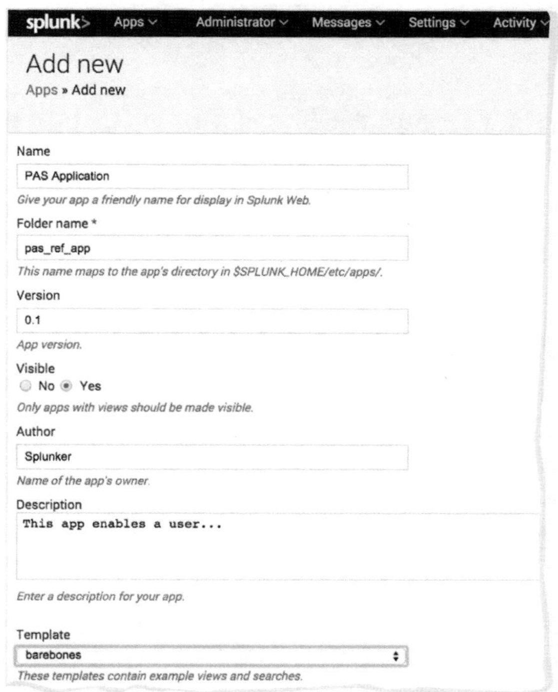

Notice how we've chosen the **barebones** template.

3. When we click **Save**, Splunk Enterprise creates a folder using the name we chose in the previous step in the Splunk `etc/apps` folder. This folder contains the following standard subfolders to organize the app resources: `bin`, `default`, `local`, and `metadata`. The app does not initially contain any views or dashboards.
4. You should add your app to your source code control system. We are using GitHub for our project. We first moved the folder that Splunk Enterprise created (in this example, `pas_ref_app`) from `etc/apps` to a more convenient location: in our case this was to a subfolder in our `home` directory in Linux, but if you are using Windows it could be to a subfolder in your `Documents` folder.
5. From the new location we performed the initial check-in to our GitHub repository.
6. Finally, we added a symbolic link from the `etc/apps` folder to our new location for the app source files. For more information about how and why we use symbolic links, see the section "Multiple projects in a single Git repository."

Workflows: Developing a Simple XML dashboard

Both apps use Simple XML dashboards to create the UI. This section describes the workflows we use when we create and edit a new Simple XML dashboard. The Splunk Simple XML Form Cheat Sheet is a useful quick reference if you are just starting out with Simple XML.

Creating a new Simple XML dashboard

We create new dashboards through the Splunk Enterprise UI. First we click **Dashboards** to access a list of dashboards in our app.

> **DEV**
>
> If you customize your app navigation, you may want to leave links such as the **Dashboards** link until you have added all your dashboards. Otherwise, you must remember the URL to get to your list of dashboards or find the list of views from the **Settings** menu.

Next we click **Create New Dashboard**:

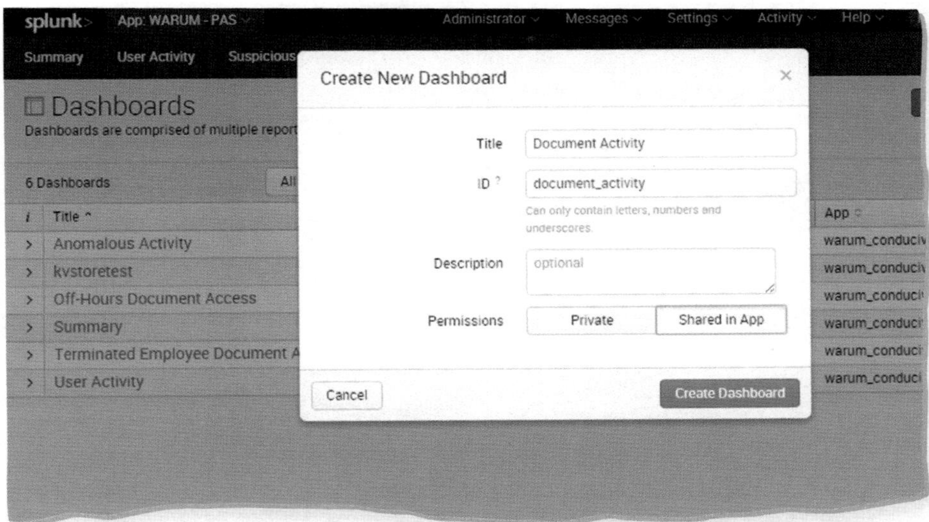

It's important to set the permissions to **Shared in App** to ensure that Splunk Enterprise adds the XML file within the app's folder in the Splunk **etc/apps** folder, and is then available to check into your source control system along with your other files. We can now see the **document_activity.xml** file if we look in the app's **local/data/ui/views** folder. For more information about managing the permissions of dashboards and other objects, see "Manage knowledge object permissions."

DEV

Permissions are the most common problem encountered when copying apps to a different location. If the permissions are not set to **Shared in App** or **Global**, the files will not be located in the app directory.

You can also create a new dashboard by creating a new XML file containing Simple XML markup in the `/default/data/ui/views` folder.

Editing the dashboard

After creating a new dashboard through the Splunk Enterprise UI, we continue to use the UI to develop the dashboard. when we click **Edit** on a Simple XML dashboard we have the choice of editing the panels or editing the XML source directly:

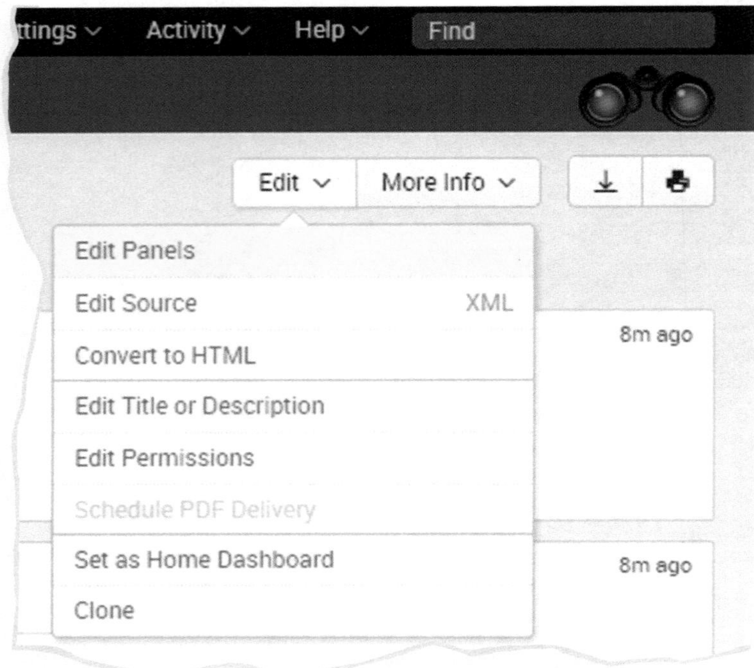

If we choose **Edit Panels** we can use a graphical editing environment to develop the dashboard, while **Edit Source** lets us edit the XML source code directly.

When we start working with the JavaScript extensions and use an external editor for our JavaScript files, our developers find it convenient to use an external editor for the Simple XML files as well and move away from the Splunk Enterprise visual editing environment. Typically, by this stage the dashboard UI is mostly complete, so any edits to the XML are minor tweaks rather major changes to content.

File locations and packaging

When we use the Splunk Enterprise UI to create and edit our dashboards, it follows the standard Splunk Enterprise convention and saves all the changes we make in the `local` folder within the app. For example, the dashboard we just created is saved in this location: `local/data/ui/views/document_activity.xml`. When we package the app for distribution, we should not have any files in the `local` folder, so we must copy any resources from the local folder to the `default` folder. Therefore, we should move our `document_activity.xml` file to `default/data/ui/views/document_activity.xml.`

It's possible that during development you accidentally end up with two copies of a dashboard XML file, one in **local** and one in **default**. In this case, Splunk Enterprise renders the version in the local folder. It's important that everyone knows which is the active file and, if they are using an external text editor, that they edit the correct version. You may want to choose a specific point in the lifecycle of developing a new dashboard to move the XML file into the **default** folder and at the same time switch from using the Splunk Enterprise visual editing environment to only using an external text editor.

SHIP

It's easy to forget during development that you've made a change that updates a file in the `local` folder that must be copied to the `default` folder. Be especially careful if you have configured your source code control system to ignore the `local` folder as this can cause you to forget to check in your updates. You should consider creating a script to perform the copy operation, especially if your solution consists of multiple apps.

DEV

You can also inadvertently save artifacts to other app context's `local` directory where the permission is global. So, be sure to watch out for these.

Test and sample data

Our test team needs predictable sample data in the index to ensure that tests are repeatable; for example, a test of a UI element might expect it to contain a specific value. To achieve this, we generate a large set of sample data to use in our automated tests. However, this sample data spans a fixed time range making it awkward to use by the developers for simple tests such as searching for recent events (such as for events in the last day). To meet this requirement for recent dynamic data, we also include a dynamic event generator in the app that produces a pseudo live stream of event data.

Sample data for automated UI testing

To perform automated UI testing, our business user has provided some sample log files containing almost one million records for us to work with. To facilitate using this test data, we have created a simple Splunk app that contains these sample log files and indexes them into a separate index. This app contains two folders: the **data** folder contains the sample log files, and the **default** folder contains the **.conf** files that define the Splunk app. The **app.conf** file contains a configuration setting to make this app invisible, and the **indexes.conf** file defines an index named *pas*. The following sample shows the definition of one of the three inputs in the **inputs.conf** file:

```
######################################
# linux configuration
######################################
[monitor://$SPLUNK_HOME/etc/apps/pas_sample_data/data/*]
disabled = false
followTail = 0
sourcetype = ri:pas:application
index = pas
######################################
# windows configuration
######################################
[monitor://%SPLUNK_HOME%\etc\apps\pas_sample_data\data\*]
disabled = false
followTail = 0
sourcetype = ri:pas:application
index = pas
```

Notice how we define the same input twice. The first definition works correctly if the app runs in a Linux environment, the second works correctly if the app runs in a Windows environment. This makes it easy for us to deploy this simple test app in different environments during development and test.

DEV

Don't forget to define the SPLUNK_HOME environment variable on your machine.

On *nix you can do so by using the "`export SPLUNK_HOME = <actual path>`**" command, adding that export statement to your** `.profile` **or** `.bashrc` **files, or by running the** `./setSplunkEnv`**. On Windows, adjusting the environment settings through the UI will do the trick. Alternatively, create a batch file using** `splunk envvars` **and then run that batch file as follows:**

```
splunk envars > setSplunkEnv.bat
setSplunkEnv.bat
```

While this data is useful during development and test, we will need larger data sets when we performance test our app. It's not always possible to work with real data during development and test. For example, real log files might contain sensitive information, or it may be difficult to find real log files that are a manageable size and that contain a full set of representative event data. We use the *Splunk Event Generator* utility described below to generate static log files for repeatable tests as well as to generate a pseudo live stream of data.

TEST

It's important that any fake test data is properly representative of the real-world log data your app will process. For example, the content of the fields, and the sequencing and pattern of the events should all be realistic.

Pseudo live stream of data

To generate a pseudo live stream of data for use in exploratory testing and demos, we use the open source Splunk Event Generator utility. You can find this utility on GitHub at dev.splunk.com/goto/eventgen.

DEV

There are several versions of this utility and we decided to use the most recent one we could find. This was the dev branch in the GitHub repository (dev.splunk.com/goto/eventgen).

SHIP

The latest version of the Splunk Reference App – PAS packages the latest version of the eventgen available at the time of this writing inside `appserver/addons`**. The install scripts would automatically create a symbolic link to it.**

Installing this version of the Splunk Event Generator is easy:

- We clone the code from GitHub, and add the contents of the **dev** branch (not the default **master** branch) to a folder named **eventgen** (the name of this folder is important) in the Splunk **etc/apps** folder.
- We then add configuration files to the PAS app that specify how to generate suitable sample data. These configuration files consist of an **eventgen.conf** file and a set of **.csv** and **.sample** files in a new **samples** folder in the root of the PAS app folder. The **eventgen.conf** file defines how the Splunk Event Generator generates the sample data using template events in the **.csv** files, and replaces tokens in the template events with values from the **.sample** files.
- We add a **metadata/default.meta** file to the PAS app that has the content shown below.

```
[eventgen]
export = system
```

DEV

Typically, you exclude the content of the `metadata` **folder when you check your code into your source code control system because the content is generated or modified whenever you install the app. We modified our** `.gitignore` **file to include this specific** `default.meta` **file in the check-in.**

For more information about how to use the **eventgen.conf** file, you should start by reading the tutorial included in the repository (dev.splunk.com/goto/eventgentut).

Multiple projects in a single Git repository

At the start of our journey, our GitHub repository contains three projects: the source for the PAS Splunk app, the source for the PAS Splunk sample data app, and a C# test project (that we later replaced with a Python script). To run the two Splunk apps when we check out the code, we need to remember to copy the source to the Splunk **etc/apps** folder. To run the Python tests, we can run the script from the check-out location.

To avoid having to remember to copy the Splunk app source to the correct location, we use symbolic links from the **etc/apps** folder to the location of the Git repository. In Windows, you can create symbolic folder links by using the `mklink /J` command at a command prompt. The following screen shot shows the symbolic links we created for our two Splunk apps:

```
Administrator: Command Prompt

c:\Program Files\Splunk\etc\apps>dir /AL
 Volume in drive C is OS
 Volume Serial Number is 021A-5AEB

 Directory of c:\Program Files\Splunk\etc\apps

12/09/2014  10:42    <JUNCTION>     conducive_sample_data [C:\Users\Dominic\Docu
ments\GitHub\warum-code-conducive\conducive_sample_data]
12/09/2014  10:40    <JUNCTION>     warum_conducive_web [C:\Users\Dominic\Docume
nts\GitHub\warum-code-conducive\warum_conducive_web]
               0 File(s)              0 bytes
               2 Dir(s)  45,609,816,064 bytes free

c:\Program Files\Splunk\etc\apps>
```

In a Linux or Mac OS environment, we can also create symbolic links. The following screenshot shows a **bash** shell with similar symbolic links that we created using the `ln -s` command:

```
dominic@dominic-Virtual-Machine: ~
drwxr-xr-x 6 dominic splunk  4096 Oct 14 10:20 gettingstarted
drwxr-xr-x 4 dominic splunk  4096 Oct 14 10:21 introspection_generator_addon
drwxr-xr-x 6 dominic splunk  4096 Oct 14 10:21 launcher
drwxr-xr-x 5 dominic splunk  4096 Oct 14 10:41 learned
drwxr-xr-x 3 dominic splunk  4096 Oct 14 10:21 legacy
lrwxrwxrwx 1 dominic dominic   49 Oct 31 08:24 ri_pas_sample_data -> /home/domi
ic/Documents/warum/ri_pas_sample_data/
drwxr-xr-x 6 dominic splunk  4096 Oct 14 10:21 sample_app
drwxr-xr-x 9 dominic splunk  4096 Oct 14 10:21 search
drwxr-xr-x 4 dominic splunk  4096 Oct 14 10:21 splunk_datapreview
drwxr-xr-x 4 dominic splunk  4096 Oct 14 10:20 SplunkForwarder
drwxr-xr-x 4 dominic splunk  4096 Oct 14 10:21 SplunkLightForwarder
lrwxrwxrwx 1 dominic dominic   42 Oct 31 08:25 TA-database -> /home/dominic/Do
ments/warum/TA-database/
lrwxrwxrwx 1 dominic dominic   42 Oct 31 08:25 TA-document -> /home/dominic/Do
ments/warum/TA-document/
lrwxrwxrwx 1 dominic dominic   38 Oct 31 08:25 TA-file -> /home/dominic/Documen
```

Now we can work directly with the files in our local Git repository and any changes we make are automatically reflected in the Splunk etc/apps folder.

DEV

We are not using a full IDE on this project. Instead, the development team is using a programmer's text editor that can do syntax highlighting for HTML and JavaScript.

Using .gitignore

In a local Git repository, you can use the **.gitignore** file to ignore changes to individual files or folders so that certain items (such as temporary, generated files) do not get checked in to the repository. The following shows the**.gitignore** file we use for the PAS app:

```
# OS X
.DS_Store

# Windows
Thumbs.db

# Python
*.pyo
*.pyc

# UI test automation generated files
test/unit-test/bin/Debug
test/unit-test/obj/Debug
test/pas-conducive-test.v12.suo

# Splunk app local files
local

# (Normally we'd exclude the entire "metadata" directory.
#  However we must preserve metadata/default.meta so that eventgen works.)
local.meta
```

This file tells Git to ignore some files generated by the operating system, compiled Python files, the files Visual Studio generates when we compile the test project, and the files that Splunk Enterprise generates at runtime in the **local** and **metadata** folders. There is no need to include any of these files in the repository because they are all generated when you run the app or the test project.

Restarting and reloading Splunk Enterprise

We have added some shortcuts to the list of favorites in our browser that make it easier to work with Splunk Enterprise while we are developing the apps. These shortcuts enable us to refresh our Splunk Enterprise environment when we make changes to our source code and configuration without the need to completely restart Splunk Enterprise, which can take time if you have lots of Splunk apps installed. The following is a list of the most useful URLs (you may need to change the port number and locale to reflect your local configuration):

- localhost:8000/en-US/_bump This flushes the client cache and is useful if you change a client-side JavaScript file, CSS file, or other static resource the **appserver\static** folder.
- localhost:8000/en-US/debug/refresh This refreshes almost all Splunk knowledge objects; it may take several minutes to run.
- localhost:8000/en-US/debug/refresh?entity=data/ui/views This refreshes just the UI views from the **default\data\ui\views** folder.
- localhost:8000/en-US/debug/refresh?entity=data/ui/nav This refreshes just the UI navigation from the **default\data\ui\nav** folder.
- localhost:8000/en-US/debug/refresh?entity=saved/searches This refreshes just the saved searches from the **savedsearches.conf** file.

DEV

To avoid having to remember to refresh the cache to see the change when you edit a static resource, you can simply disable cache when you are using the developer tools in the browser. In Chrome you check **Disable cache (while DevTools is open)** in **General Settings** in **Developer Tools.** In IE 11, click **Always refresh from server** on the **Network** panel in **Developer tools.**

DEV

You can find lots of useful information about your Splunk environment (including the URLs in the previous list) if you visit the Development services page at localhost:8000/en-US/info.

If you do need to restart Splunk Enterprise after you make a change, you can use the **splunk** command in the **bin** folder. For example, to get help about how to stop and start Splunk Enterprise services, execute the following at a command prompt or shell:

```
splunk help control
```

For example, you can request that Splunk Enterprise reload everything from the **static** folder (such as CSS or JavaScript files) by executing the following command:

```
splunk restartss
```

If you want to minimize effort and automate the restart of Splunk Enterprise services, you can also use the Splunk Enterprise development command-line interface (CLI) to help during development. You can install it through **npm install -g splunkdev-cli**. For more information about this Node.js package, see npmjs.org/package/splunkdev-cli. In addition to letting you stop, start, and restart Splunk Enterprise services, you can also use this tool to watch your local file system and automatically restart Splunk Enterprise services or reload configuration files when you make changes to your apps. Note that to use this tool depends on Node.js (a version of Node.js is included in a standard Splunk Enterprise installation).

DEV

We have seen customers who have efficiently automated their builds, Splunk Enterprise restarts, test runs and other tasks when code changes using tools such as Grunt and Chef.

The development environment for the Auth0 app

For the simpler Auth0 app, we have adopted a streamlined development methodology. In a standard Splunk Enterprise installation, the Splunk **etc/apps** folder contains a subfolder for each app that contains all the code, configuration, and other resources for that app. We have made this folder into a Git repository, so that we can directly check in to GitHub any changes we make to the app while we are developing it. The Auth0 app includes some server-side components implemented using Node.js. The following Windows screenshot shows the top-level of the Auth0 app including the hidden Git resources.

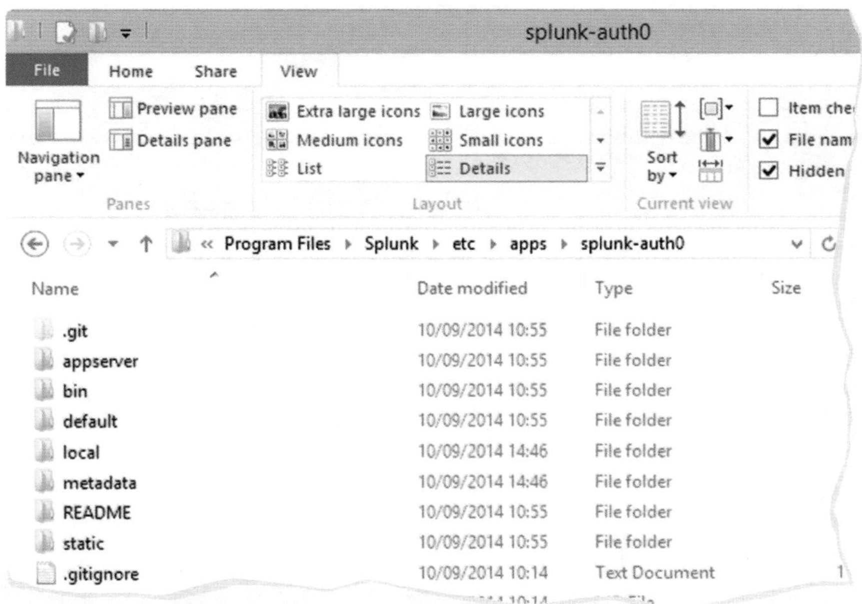

The `.gitignore` file includes a line to ignore the `node_modules` folder that contains the two installable node packages that the app uses (an **auth0** package and a **splunk-sdk** package).

DEV

This approach makes it very easy to edit the app and then immediately check in the code you changed. Don't forget to restart Splunk Enterprise using the appropriate URL (see the previous section) when you make a change. Doing a full restart of Splunk Enterprise is slow.

CHOOSING OUR PLATFORM: SIMPLE XML

Both apps are created using Simple XML, but use different parts of that framework. The Essentials guide that accompanies this description of our journey and online reference documentation include more details about the different options. We have chosen to use the Simple XML approach for building the Auth0 app, and a hybrid of Simple XML and Simple XML with SplunkJS Extensions for building the PAS app.

ARCH

The different technologies for building Splunk Enterprise apps are not necessarily mutually exclusive. It's possible to create an app that uses a mixture of approaches.

The following table summarizes the differences between the UI technologies we are using and some of their pros and cons. It also describes two options for extending the Simple XML model.

APPROACH	NOTES
Simple XML	You should start with this approach. It's easy to add the extensions later if you need them Lets you build simple dashboards. Splunk Enterprise includes interactive tools for creating and modifying dashboards and an XML editor that you can use to edit dashboard definition markup. This approach is ideal for simple apps that require only basic customization and that do not require complex navigation between different dashboards.
Simple XML with JS and/or CSS Extensions	Once you hit the limit of what you can achieve with Simple XML on its own, you can add JavaScript and CSS to the collection of tools. Extends the capabilities of Simple XML by adding more layout options, visualizations, and custom behaviors. This is useful for adding additional capabilities to a Simple XML dashboard, but it adds to the complexity of the app because your app now includes custom JavaScript and CSS resources. JavaScript libraries can include SplunkJS stack, third party libraries, or own your own JavaScript code.
Simple XML converted to HTML with custom JavaScript.	We don't recommend this approach because it will introduce maintenance issues in the future. Converts a simple XML dashboard to HTML with a lot of automated JavaScript code generation. This gives you full control of the rendering of the page. CAUTION: Maintainability concern: The generated dashboards end up being specific to the Splunk Enterprise version on which the dashboards have been generated and might not going to be future-compatible. Also, this is a one-way conversion (you can't go back to simple XML).

For the Auth0 app, its relatively simple requirements meant that we could use just Simple XML to build the UI and searches. The PAS app had more complex UI requirements so we used the JavaScript and CSS extensions on some of the dashboards.

Although on this project we chose not to use an IDE, if you choose to use one there are RelaxNG schemas available for Simple XML. You can use these schemas to validate your Simple XML documents and, if your IDE supports it, enable autocomplete functionality in the editor to speed up the development process. You can download the RelaxNG schemas and find out more about them if you navigate to localhost:8000/info in Splunk Enterprise.

In addition to the discussion of the Splunk Web Framework in the *Essentials* guide, the following resources on the Splunk developer and docs web sites provide detailed information about the framework:

- Splunk Web Framework Overview
- Simple XML
- SplunkJS Stack
- Splunk Web Framework Component Reference
- REST API Reference Manual

We also considered using the SplunkJS Stack to integrate Splunk Enterprise functionality into a standard web app hosted on a standard web server such as Apache or IIS. Although this option offers a very flexible approach, we can meet our requirements by creating Splunk apps to run in Splunk Enterprise. To learn more about reusing the SplunkJS libraries for features such as views and search managers, see Use SplunkJS Stack in your own web apps.

SPLUNK SDK FOR JAVASCRIPT

The Splunk SDK for JavaScript includes features that let you conveniently call much of the Splunk Enterprise REST API. You can use this SDK to enable your JavaScript code to interact programmatically with the Splunk engine. You can write both client-side and server-side JavaScript to interact with Splunk Enterprise through the SDK. The following resources provide more information about the JavaScript SDK and instructions on how to install it:

- Overview of the Splunk SDK for JavaScript
- Splunk SDK for JavaScript Reference

Initially, only the Auth0 application in its implementation of a Modular input uses the server-side component of JavaScript SDK. See the section "*Creating a Modular input*" in the chapter "Working with data: where it comes from and how we manage it."

TESTING TECHNIQUES AND APPROACHES

We have a selection of automated user acceptance tests in place for the dashboards and the features the development team has created. In this section, we highlight some of the techniques we have found useful in implementing our tests.

TEST

Some testing tools (such as the Selenium IDE) let you record a user session with a web application as a script that you can later refactor into a collection of tests. Because our app is relatively small, we've chosen to implement the user interactions with the app manually, writing code for each acceptance test scenario.

Identifying page elements

Originally, we used a C# project for our automated user acceptance tests, but in the final version of the project we use a Python script. In both cases we can use Selenium to help us automate the browser interactions. We chose to use Python rather than C# to make it easier for users to download and run the tests: in many case a developer or test workstation will have Python preinstalled.

Testing a web app typically requires us to be able to identify elements on a page (such as text boxes and buttons) and then simulate user interactions with those elements to drive a test case. The web pages rendered by Splunk Enterprise can be complex, especially those displaying charts that are rendered using SVG, so we have used a number of different techniques to programmatically locate elements on the page. Typically, we use the **Find** functions provided by Selenium to locate elements on the page. The **Find** functions can locate elements in a number of different ways such as by **Id**, by **ClassName**, by **LinkText**, and by **XPath** (**XPath** is particularly useful for parsing SVG data). Which particular technique we use depends on a careful analysis of the source of the rendered page (by using the view source feature in our web browser) to determine how to uniquely identify the specific element we need for our test. Due to the complexity of the web pages in our app, not all elements on the page are loaded immediately and we find it necessary to use repeated **Find** calls to locate an element reliably, as shown in the following code snippet that uses both the **find_element_by_tag_name** and **find_element** functions:

```
def WaitElementAppear(parentElement, byMethod, str, logMsg):
  if parentElement is None:
    parentElement = driver.find_element_by_tag_name('html')
  loaded = False
  stopTime = time.time() + timeoutThreshold
  startTime = time.time()
  ex = None
  result = None
```

```
  while not loaded and time.time()<stopTime:
    try:
      result = parentElement.find_element(byMethod,str)
      assert result! = None
      assert result.tag_name! = None
      loaded = True
      if logMsg:
        logstr = "{0}, {1}, {2}".format(time.time(), time.time() - startTime, logMsg)
        logs.append(logstr)
    except:
      ex = sys.exc_info()[0]
  ...
```

This example comes from a utility function named **StartWaitElementAppearTask** in our Python test script that we use to create an asynchronous wait for a specific element to appear on the page. The wait enables the script to run without failing if the web site is slow to respond. The following snippet shows an example of how we use this function:

```
def VerifySummaryPageElements():
  print "call VerifySummaryPageElements"

  #wait donut chart to show up
  ActionTask(VerifyDonutChart,"Verify DonutChart")

  #wait top - userstable show up
  userPanel = StartWaitElementAppearTask(driver, By.ID,"panel3").get()
  topUsersTask = StartWaitElementAppearTask(userPanel, By.CLASS_NAME,
                "shared-resultstable-resultstablerow","load summary page top-user table").get()

  #wait top-documents table show up
  documentPanel = StartWaitElementAppearTask(driver, By.ID,"panel4").get()
  topDocumentsTask = StartWaitElementAppearTask(documentPanel, By.CLASS_NAME,
              "shared-resultstable-resultstablerow", "load summary page top-documents table").get()
```

This snippet also makes use of the **ActionTask** to handle the asynchronous behavior. The following snippet shows the **ActionTask** function:

```
def ActionTask(action,logMsg = None):
  print "start to ActionTask({0})".format(action.func_name)

  pool = ThreadPool(processes = 1)
  starttime = time.time()
  task = pool.apply_async(TryAction(action))
  task.wait()
  stoptime = time.time()

  if logMsg:
    logstr = "{0}, {1}, {2}".format(time.time(), action.func_name, stoptime-starttime)
    logs.append(logstr)

  print "finish to ActionTask({0})".format(action.func_name)
```

Many of our tests require us to simulate a user interaction with the Splunk time range picker control, so we have created a set of wrapper functions such as **ChangeTimeRange** for this control that we can reuse from multiple tests. This is particularly useful where the outcome of the test depends on us selecting a specific set of events from a sample log files.

Automating advanced controls

Some controls require special techniques to automate them in a test. For example, on the **User Details** dashboard you can zoom in the time range by dragging the sliders. The following screenshot shows the sliders after a user has moved them to zoom in on the period **Sat Aug 9** to **Sun Aug 10**:

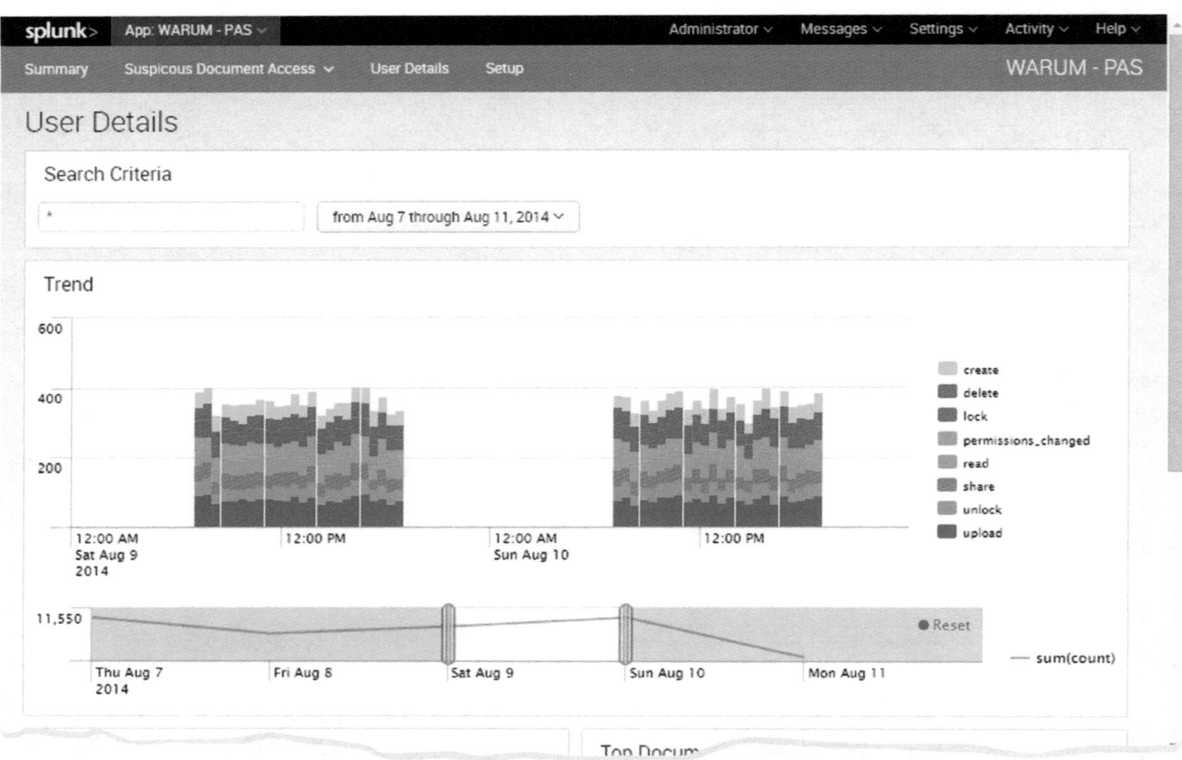

The following code snippet shows how we automate this zooming behavior in a test:

```
def VerifyUserPageZoomChart():
  zoomChart = StartWaitElementAppearTask(driver, By.ID,"zoom_chart").get()
  zoomchartTask = StartWaitElementsAppearTask(zoomChart, By.CLASS_NAME,
                "highcharts-axis-labels", "load userdetailspage zoomchart")
  zooms = zoomchartTask.get()

  startdate = "{0} {1}{2}".format(searchRangeStartTime.strftime("%b"), searchRangeStartTime.
day,searchRangeStartTime.year)
  enddate = "{0} {1}".format(searchRangeEndTime.strftime("%b"), searchRangeEndTime.day)

  assert startdate in zooms[0].text
  assert enddate in zooms[0].text

  #zoom out the zoomchart series
  highchartsGroup = StartWaitElementAppearTask(zoomChart, By.CLASS_NAME,
                "highcharts-series-group").get()
  highcharts = StartWaitElementAppearTask(highchartsGroup, By.CLASS_NAME,"highcharts-series").get()
  path = StartWaitElementsAppearTask(highcharts, By.TAG_NAME,"path").get()
  path = path[0]
  d = path.get_attribute("d");
  moveFrom = GetSvgLineCoordinates(d)[1];
  moveTo = GetSvgLineCoordinates(d)[3];
  ActionChains(driver).move_to_element_with_offset(path, moveFrom[0], moveFrom[1]).perform()
  ActionChains(driver).drag_and_drop_by_offset(path, moveTo[0]-moveFrom[0], 0).perform();

  #verify the "reset" shows up when the swim windows is selected.
  driver.find_element_by_class_name("icon-minus-circle")
```

This code first uses a series of nested searches to locate the SVG elements within the chart that have an HTML **div** element with an Id of **zoom-chart**. It then uses the Selenium **ActionChains** class to drag and drop the two **path** elements to new locations to set the zoom.

TEST

The Selenium **ActionChains** class is very useful for simulating mouse-based user interactions such as clicks and drag-and-drop.

Instrumenting our tests

Our test project captures timing information as the basis for collecting performance data from the app by writing timing information to a log file to capture information about the tests. The following shows some sample data from the log file collected over the course of several test runs. The timings show how long in seconds a given test item takes to run:

```
09/16/14 16:35:04, ============================== New Test Run Start ==============================
09/16/14 16:35:44, 1. Load App page = 20.1652754
09/16/14 16:36:09, 2. Load Summary page Center Chart = 3.854182
09/16/14 16:36:28, 3. Load Document Details page = 18.8270169
09/16/14 16:37:01, 2. Load Summary page Center Chart = 3.0892958
09/16/14 16:37:20, 4. Load User Details page = 18.4391709
09/16/14 16:37:42, 2. Load Summary page Center Chart = 4.3207587
09/16/14 16:38:11, 2. Load Summary page Center Chart = 2.8340855
09/16/14 16:38:16, ============================== End Test Run ==============================
09/16/14 20:27:54, ============================== New Test Run Start ==============================
09/16/14 20:28:27, 2. Load Summary page Center Chart = 4.5750334
09/16/14 20:28:54, 2. Load Summary page Center Chart = 4.0135587
09/16/14 20:29:16, 2. Load Summary page Center Chart = 3.8203631
09/16/14 20:29:35, 3. Load Document Details page = 19.3844841
09/16/14 20:29:55, 2. Load Summary page Center Chart = 2.9488817
09/16/14 20:30:15, 4. Load User Details page = 18.4408812
09/16/14 20:30:47, 1. Load App page = 15.1469081
09/16/14 20:30:49, ============================== End Test Run ==============================
09/16/14 20:37:24, ============================== New Test Run Start ==============================
09/16/14 20:38:08, 1. Load App page = 18.3666046
09/16/14 20:38:31, 2. Load Summary page Center Chart = 4.0516422
09/16/14 20:38:54, 2. Load Summary page Center Chart = 2.8054817
09/16/14 20:39:19, 2. Load Summary page Center Chart = 4.1741535
09/16/14 20:39:37, 3. Load Document Details page = 18.4968156
09/16/14 20:39:55, 2. Load Summary page Center Chart = 2.8528058
09/16/14 20:40:15, 4. Load User Details page = 19.352799
09/16/14 20:40:17, ============================== End Test Run ==============================
```

We can use Splunk Enterprise to visualize this information and plot the results over time. First, we define a new data source for the performance log data file, and then we define some extracts for the item under test (**measured_item**) and the time taken (**perf_value**). We then create a search to extract the data from the log file, and plot it as shown in the following screenshot:

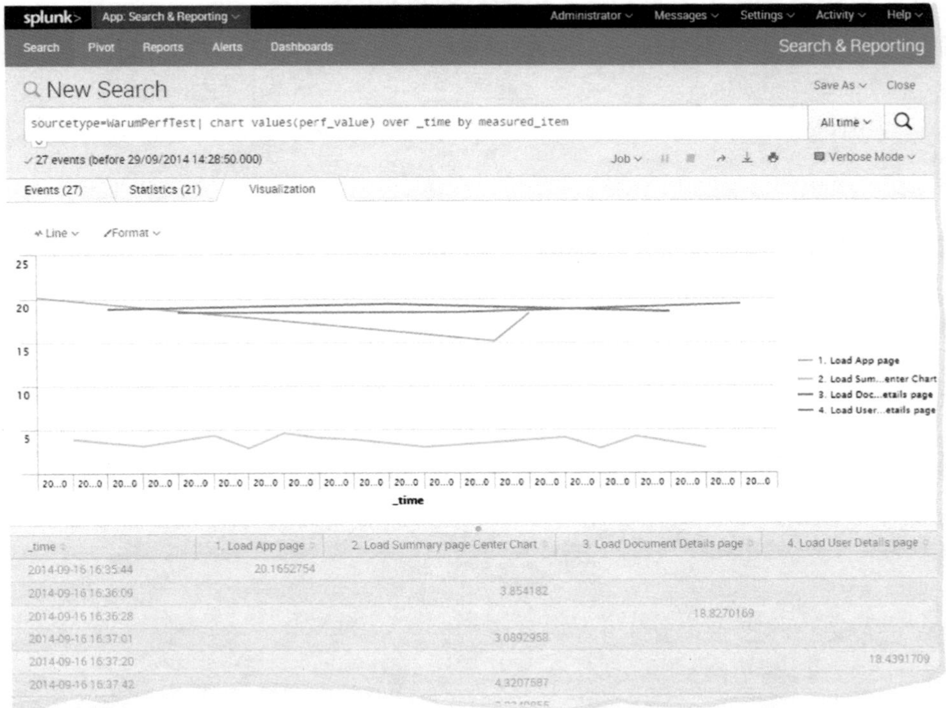

This lets us track how the performance of the items under test changes over time, and will allow us to measure the impact of any performance tuning we undertake in the future.

Monitoring search performance in Splunk Enterprise

At one point in our journey, our tests showed that it was taking some time for the **Summary** dashboard to finish loading, with the message "Waiting for data" displaying in the **Top Users** and **Top Documents** panels. It's possible to see how long individual searches take to complete by navigating to the list of completed **Jobs** from the **Activity** menu in Splunk Enterprise. The following screenshot shows that **summary_base_search** was taking almost four minutes to complete even though the dashboard eventually reported that no data was found:

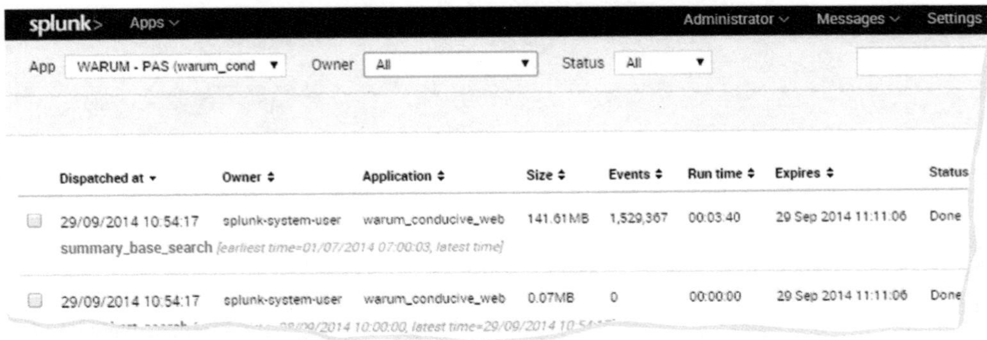

When we reviewed the code, we found that we had not set the time range for the query correctly so it was fetching all the data, before a filter on the table caused it not to display any of the returned data. After fixing the code by adding a time range filter to the original query, the **Summary** dashboard loaded significantly faster. The following screenshot shows the new search timings:

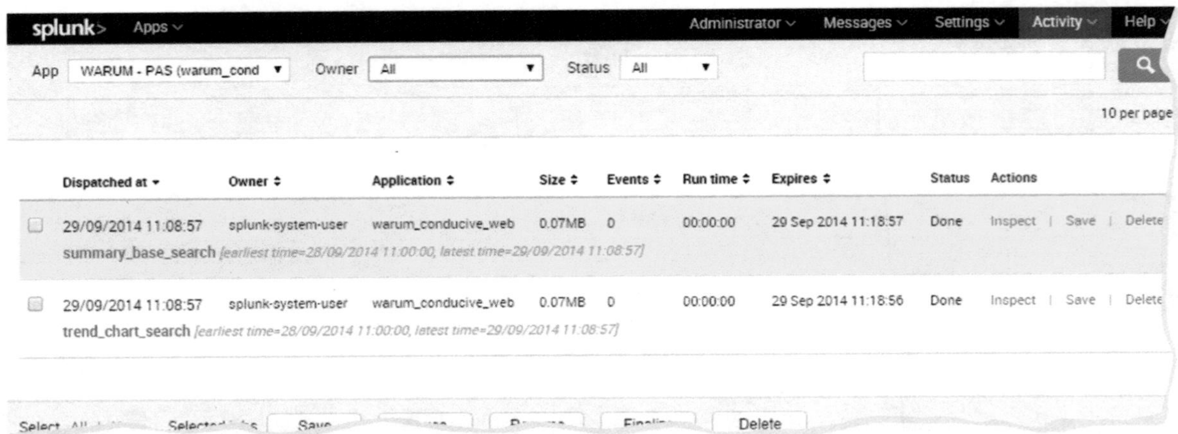

TEST

The Search Job Inspector tool (click the Inspect action) allows you to drill down into a particular search and troubleshoot its performance as well as help understand the behavior of the underlying knowledge objects such as tags, event types, lookups and so on. You will be able to evaluate the time spent parsing and executing the search (and subsearches) and setting up the data structures needed for it to run. This is broken down further for each command that is used. Thus, you can identify really expensive commands and begin your search optimizations.

DEV

Additional tips for fine-tuning your searches can be found at dev.splunk.com/goto/writebettersearches.

WHAT DID WE LEARN?

This section summarizes some of the key lessons learned from our preparations for the journey.

- It's quick and easy to set up a development environment for building Splunk apps.
- It's quick and easy to build a basic Splunk app using Simple XML.
- For an efficient development workflow, consider making your app folder in the Splunk **etc/apps** folder a Git repository so you can quickly check in changes when you update and test your code.
- Although we are not following a formal Test-Driven Development (TDD) methodology, it's still important for our test team and developers to identify the key test cases as early as possible (ideally, before development starts). In this way, the developers will have the test cases that their implementation must pass in mind as they develop the code, and the test team can begin writing the tests in parallel with the developers writing the code.
- We must ensure that we test the apps in both Windows and Linux environments to ensure that the configuration works correctly. For example, the application must work with the different path separators and environment variables on the two platforms.
- Creating user acceptance tests that automate UI interactions require a number of different techniques to reliably locate and interact with elements on the web page.
- Performance testing helps identify bottlenecks in the searches and devise optimization strategies. Budget sufficient time for this.

More information

For more information about Splunk instrumentation, introspection and various troubleshooting techniques, see "What Splunk logs about itself" at: dev.splunk.com/goto/tssplunklogs.

For Splunk crash log analysis, see the wiki page "Community:TroubleshootingCrashes" at: dev.splunk.com/goto/commtc.

For information about using Selenium as a browser automation tool, see: seleniumhq.org.

For an explanation the full test-driven development methodology, see: en.wikipedia.org/wiki/Test-driven_development.

A useful quick reference if you are just starting out with Simple XML is the Splunk Simple XML Form Cheat Sheet, available at: dev.splunk.com/goto/simplexmlcheatsheet.

For more information about managing the permissions of dashboards and other objects, see "Manage knowledge object permissions" at: dev.splunk.com/goto/managekoperm.

You can find the Splunk Event Generator utility on GitHub at dev.splunk.com/goto/eventgen.

For more information about how to use the **eventgen.conf** file, read the tutorial included in the repository (dev.splunk.com/goto/eventgentut).

For more information about the Node.js package, see npmjs.org/package/splunkdev-cli.

Tools to help automate your builds are available from Grunt (gruntjs.com) and Chef (chef.io/chef).

The following resources on the Splunk developer and docs web sites provide detailed information about the framework:

- Splunk Web Framework Overview at: dev.splunk.com/goto/webframeoverview.
- Simple XML at: dev.splunk.com/goto/simplexml.
- SplunkJS Stack at: dev.splunk.com/goto/splunkjsstack.
- Splunk Web Framework Component Reference at: dev.splunk.com/goto/webframeref.
- REST API Reference Manual at: dev.splunk.com/goto/restapi.

To learn more about reusing the SplunkJS libraries for features such as views and search managers, see Use SplunkJS Stack in your own web apps at: dev.splunk.com/goto/splunkjsintegrate.

The following resources provide more information about the JavaScript SDK and instructions on how to install it:

- Overview of the Splunk SDK for JavaScript at: dev.splunk.com/goto/javascriptsdkover.
- Splunk SDK for JavaScript Reference at: dev.splunk.com/goto/javascriptsdkref.

To learn about the Search Job Inspector tool, see: dev.splunk.com/goto/searchjobinsp.

3

UI and visualizations: what the apps look like

The primary skills our developers use when they work on the UI and visualizations are:

- XML
- HTML
- CSS
- JavaScript

Our developers have varying degrees of familiarity with the Splunk® Simple XML model. Simply re-using third-party JavaScript visualization libraries requires basic JavaScript skills; heavy customization of third-party JavaScript visualization libraries requires more in-depth JavaScript skills. Familiarity with the Splunk search processing language (SPL™) is useful in understanding how to format and manipulate data ready to display in a visualization.

A BRIEF INTRODUCTION TO TOKENS IN THE AUTH0 APP

One of the refinements we make to the Auth0 app is to let a user of the app to filter the information on the Simple XML dashboard by tenant. We do this in a Simple XML dashboard by using tokens to pass values from one control to another. The first step in this example is to define a dropdown to display on the dashboard that lets a user select from the list of available data sources. The following screenshot shows this dropdown:

In this chapter we focus on the UI of the apps and the processes we used to design and develop the various dashboards, forms, and visualizations that make up the PAS and Auth0 apps.

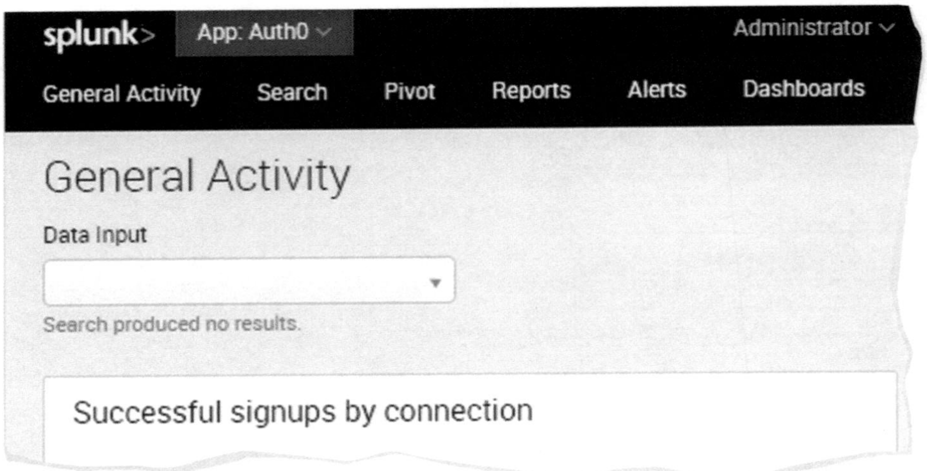

This code snippet from the `logins_dashboard.xml` file shows how we define this dropdown in Simple XML.

```
<fieldset submitButton = "false" autoRun = "true">
  <input type = "dropdown" token = "auth0_tenant" searchWhenChanged = "true">
    <label>Data Input</label>
    <selectFirstChoice>true</selectFirstChoice>
    <populatingSearch fieldForLabel = "source" fieldForValue = "source">
     | metadata type=sources | search totalCount &gt; 0 | table source</populatingSearch>
    <default>auth0://contoso</default>
  </input>
</fieldset>
```

Notice how we save the user's choice to the token named **auth0_tenant**, how we use the **searchWhenChanged** attribute to trigger a search when the user selects a new option, and how we use the **SelectFirstChoice** element to define a default choice.

Later, in the same dashboard file we use the **auth0_tenant** token when we construct a search string for one of the charts we display. Notice how the token name is delimited using the "**$**" character in the search string:

```
<chart>
  <title>Most frequent users</title>
  <searchString>source = $auth0_tenant$ | top limit = 10 user_name</searchString>
  ...
</chart>
```

DEV

In the Auth0 app, we spent more time fine-tuning our UI than we did developing the back-end code for the modular input discussed in the chapter "Working with data: where it comes from and how we manage it." **Tweaking and refining the UI can be addictive!**

AN INTRODUCTION TO THE PAS APP

The first use case the team has decided to tackle in the PAS app is creating a dashboard to view all user activity over time, including any modification to a document, the database, or file system. This part of the system lets investigators respond reactively by examining the history of a user's interaction with the system the PAS app is monitoring. This dashboard forms a part of the overall reactive analysis function envisioned for the system that will give an investigator the ability to determine which activities one or more users may have performed from any geographic location, and correlate that activity across different users, documents, or data sets.

Walkthrough of an early version of the app

The following screenshots, from an early version of the app lets you see the functionality we implemented for this story. We will then describe some of the issues we encountered and the solutions we implemented. Remember that this shows an early version of the app, and that it does change in subsequent iterations.

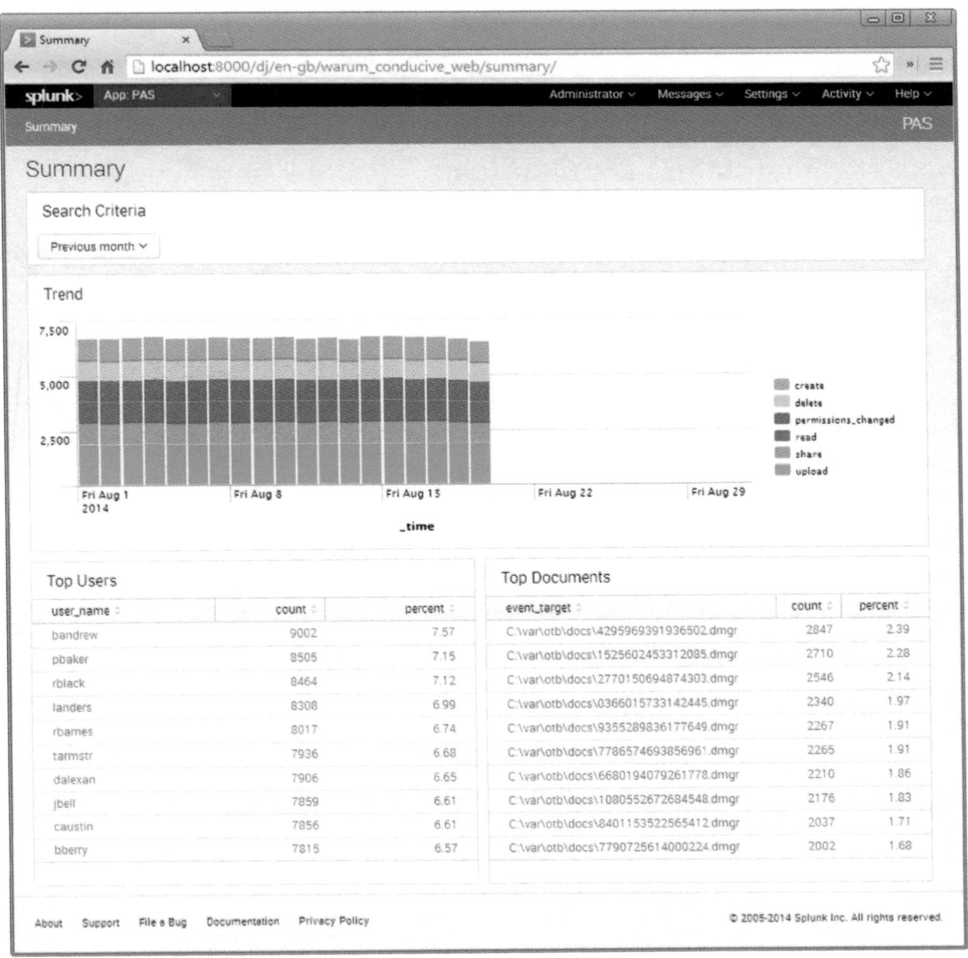

The screenshot shows a standard Splunk dashboard with panels, controls, visualizations, and tables. The user can specify a time range to view in the *Search Criteria* panel and this determines the data that the chart shows. For each interval in the time range, the chart shows the number of operations of different types (such as create, delete, and read) that took place. A user can view detailed information by hovering the mouse over the bars in the chart, and highlight operations by hovering the mouse over the chart legend. The tables show the most active users and documents over the time range, and the user can filter this information by clicking on a bar on the chart or on the legend.

Clicking on a user name in the list of top users takes the user to the following dashboard to display detailed information about that user. Similarly, clicking a document in the list of top documents takes the user to another with detailed information about that document.

ARCH

Remember the screenshots we show are from earlier versions of the PAS app to illustrate some of the issues we encountered as we started the journey and how we iterated on the implementation.

Issues discovered and proposed solutions

So far, this is a relatively simple Splunk app containing a set of dashboards that use standard Splunk Enterprise controls and visualizations, but we identified several interesting topics during the design and implementation of this story.

Using the Search element

Each of these dashboards displays three different sets of information: the chart and the two tables. We could define three separate **search** elements each with a complete standalone query, but this would mean the page would run three separate searches each returning the same data formatted slightly differently. The following snippets from the `summary.xml` file shows the solution we adopted to avoid this inefficiency:

```
<search id = "base_search">
  <query>
    | pivot ri_pas_datamodel Root_Event count(Root_Event) AS Count SPLITROW _time AS _time
      PERIOD auto SPLITROW user AS user
      SPLITROW command AS command SPLITROW object AS object
      FILTER command isNotNull $filter$ $exclude$ ROWSUMMARY 0 COLSUMMARY 0 NUMCOLS 0 SHOWOTHER 1
  </query>
</search>

...

<search id = "top_users_search" base = "base_search">
  <query>stats count by user | sort - count</query>
</search>

...

<search id = "top_documents_search" base = "base_search">
  <query>stats count by object | sort - count</query>
</search>
```

ARCH

At this point, do not worry about how the query is composed. We'll discuss the Splunk search language (SPL), data models and acceleration in the next chapter "Working with data: where it comes from and how we manage it."

This shows a **search** element called **base-search** that returns the data we need and two additional **search** elements that define post-process searches based on the data the **base-search** query returns. This means that the page only runs a single query, making it more efficient, while the post-process **search** elements manipulate the data into a suitable format and structure for the chart and the two tables to consume. Typically we don't recommend using post-process search instances for two reasons: first, they can only handle up to 10,000 events if they are filtering data, and second they do not provide any significant performance benefits in a distributed Splunk Enterprise deployment. However, in the scenario here, we are not using the post-process search instances to perform any additional filtering, they are just sorting and grouping the data from the base search instance. For more information about the **search** element, see the section "**Search element"** on Simple XML Reference.

DEV

Another benefit to using post-process searches is that they let you factor out the common prefixes of complex searches. This reduces duplication and makes the code more maintainable.

Navigation between dashboards

Clicking on a user name or document in the **Summary** dashboard does not perform the default drilldown action, but navigates to the **User Details** or **Document Details** dashboard and passes information about the selected user or document to enable the target dashboard to filter the data it displays. Although Simple XML enables drilldown functionality, we create some custom code to implement the feature on this page because we also want to include some custom filtering at the same location in the UI. At this point we are moving from using just Simple XML, to using Simple XML with JavaScript extensions to let us add this custom behavior (the chapter "Adding code: using JavaScript and Search Processing Language" includes more examples from the PAS app that show how to use JavaScript with Simple XML). The following code snippet from the **summary.js** file shows the click event handler for one of the tables on the dashboard:

```
document_table.on("click:row", function(e) {
     e.preventDefault();
     document_name = e.data["row.event_target"];
     earliest_time = tokens.get("earliest_time");
     latest_time = tokens.get("latest_time");
     window.location.href = "../document_details?document=" + document_name + "&earliest_time=" +
                               earliest_time + "&latest_time=" + latest_time;
});
```

Notice how this builds a URL with the appropriate parameter values from the tokens in order to pass the information to the **Document Details** dashboard. A much better approach is to use a standard JavaScript plugin to build the URL and this is something we implement later in the journey, replacing the code in the previous snippet with this approach using the jQuery plugin:

```
var queryParams = {
    "form.time.earliest": earliest,
    "form.time.latest": latest
};
queryParams["form." + field_name] = field_value;
window.open(page + "?" + $.param(queryParams), "_blank");
```

To read the parameter values on the target page we can use the jQuery **$.deparam** method. However, later in the journey we simplify the code that retrieves the querystring parameters and sets the token values on the page. The following code snippet comes from the **user_activity.js** file in the final version of the PAS app:

```
var submittedTokens = mvc.Components.get("submitted");
```

The **get** method of the **mvc.Components** class can retrieve the querystring parameters submitted to the dashboard by using the value **submitted** as a parameter. For more information about how we use this technique in the PAS app, see the section "Working with tokens in a custom component" in the chapter "Adding code: using JavaScript and Search Processing Language."

Outstanding issues

At this point, there are still some outstanding issues to address including:

- The chart type we used for the visualization is lacking some features.
- We are still querying the raw data in the log files and have not abstracted the data in any way.
- There are still some minor UI issues to address (such as the double backslashes you can see in the **Document Details** dashboard).
- We need to validate that our decision to use post-process search instances is a valid approach for optimizing performance.

HOW WE WORK #1: UI DESIGN PROTOTYPING

It's important that the UI design is appropriate for the compliance officers and investigators who will use the PAS app. A key part of the design will be to select visualizations for the dashboards that are easy to understand and intuitive to manipulate for these users. The requirements for the visualizations for the first use case include showing:

- The overall volume of activity for specific users and documents over time.
- The types and volumes of the different types of activity that were performed such as reads, writes, deletes, and downloads.
- A time scale that enables the user to zoom in and out. The range might be several days or just a few minutes.

During our meetings with business subject matter experts (SMEs), we discussed a number of options such as line charts, swim lanes, and stacked bar charts.

We considered line charts that can show a composite view of all activities, combined with a timeline and overall activity volume levels. For example:

We considered swim lane charts that can show each activity separately but stacked, combined with a timeline and overall activity volume level.

We also considered stacked bar charts that let the user see the relative volume of each activity combined with the overall activity volume and a scalable timeline in a single view. Also important for these charts is the ability to toggle the display of each activity type to let the user increase the visibility of the most important activities.

> **UX**
>
> **When the specific events you are looking for are relatively few in number compared to the majority of events in your data, it can be hard to spot them. It's a good idea to give the user the ability to toggle the display of certain categories of events on or off. For example, if the vast majority of events are read events, but you are interested in the infrequent delete or update events, you want to able to toggle the display of the read events off.**

For example, we considered the following stacked bar charts:

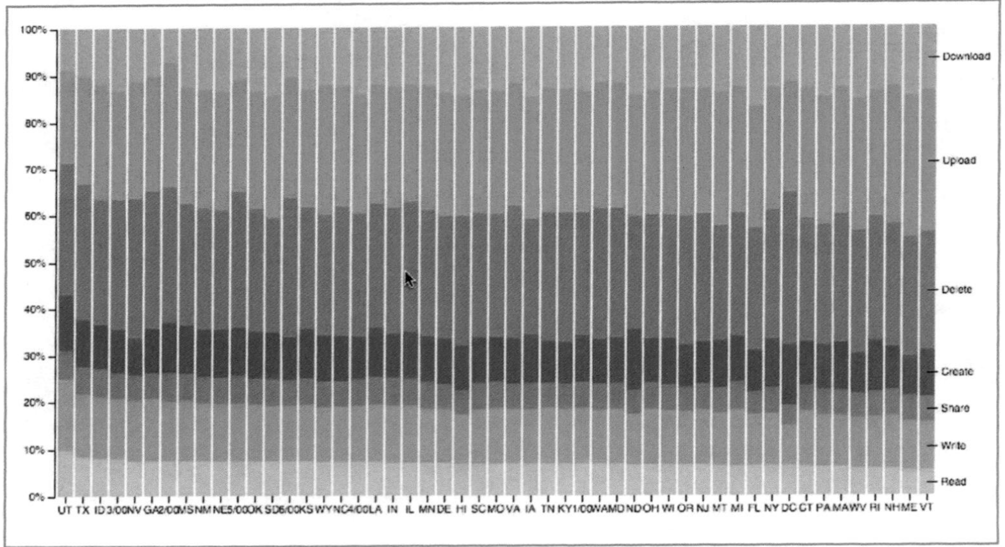

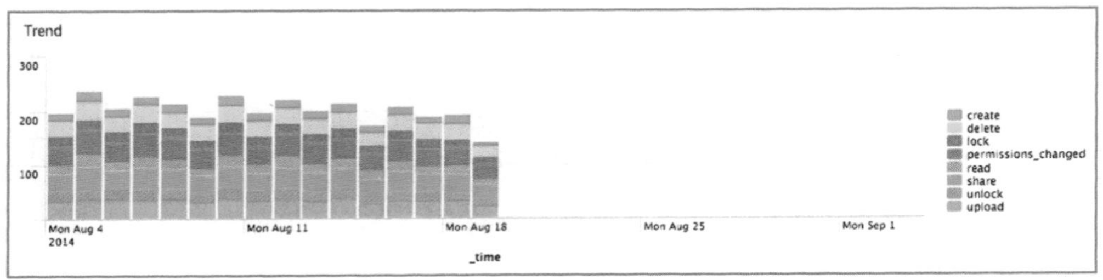

Our final choice was for a stacked bar chart with a scalable timeline below for zooming and panning because it provides the clearest way to see spikes in activity and makes it easy to identify suspicious or abnormal activity patterns. It also lets us use a single visualization to display the data and should therefore perform better than a solution that requires multiple visualizations to display the same information:

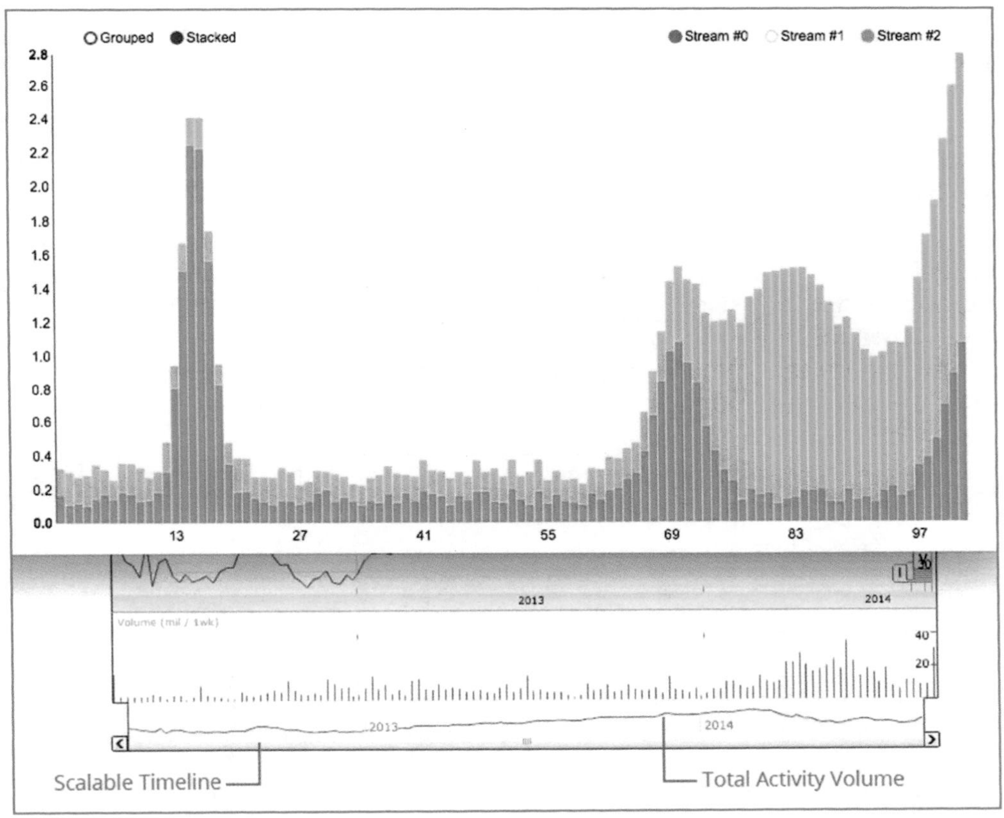

OPTIONS FOR IMPLEMENTING VISUALIZATIONS

If you are using Simple XML or the SplunkJS Stack you can chose from the many available built-in visualizations.

> **ARCH**
>
> **The Splunk 6.x Dashboard Examples app has numerous examples of how to visualize your data on a Simple XML dashboard. You can download the app from** dev.splunk.com/goto/dashboardexamples.

If you are using the Simple XML JavaScript extensions, you also have the option to integrate a third-party JavaScript visualization into your dashboard to expand your available choices. Not surprisingly, this is likely to involve more coding than using the standard Splunk Enterprise visualizations.

> **ARCH**
>
> **The Splunk Web Framework Toolkit contains examples of such advanced visualizations. Get it from** dev.splunk.com/goto/swft.

Refining the visualizations

During the initial stages of our journey, along with business subject matter experts at Conducive, we settled on using a stacked bar chart to enable a compliance officer to visualize the activities on a document repository over time. However when we began to implement this in the app, we discovered an issue with the way the visualization behaves when a user zooms in and out on the data. The following screenshot shows the visualization zoomed out to show the full range of sample data:

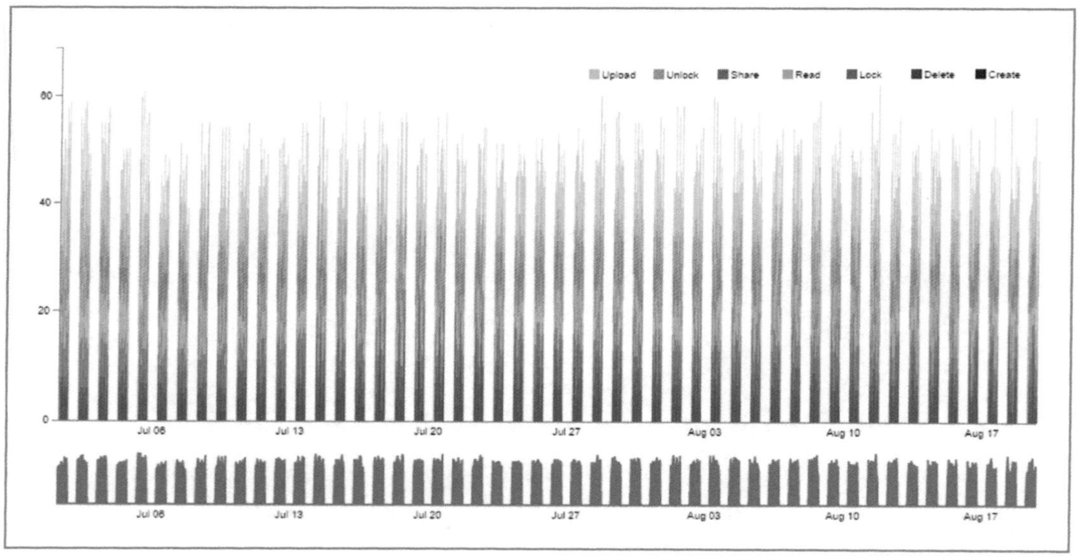

The narrowness of each individual bar makes it very hard to see the data, and the visualization does not aggregate the data into thicker vertical bars that summarize the activities over a wider time range. Note that the gaps in the chart are periods of time when there was no access to the document repository and therefore no log data. When a user zooms in by dragging with the mouse on the summary chart at the bottom to highlight a time range, the visualization looks like the following screenshot:

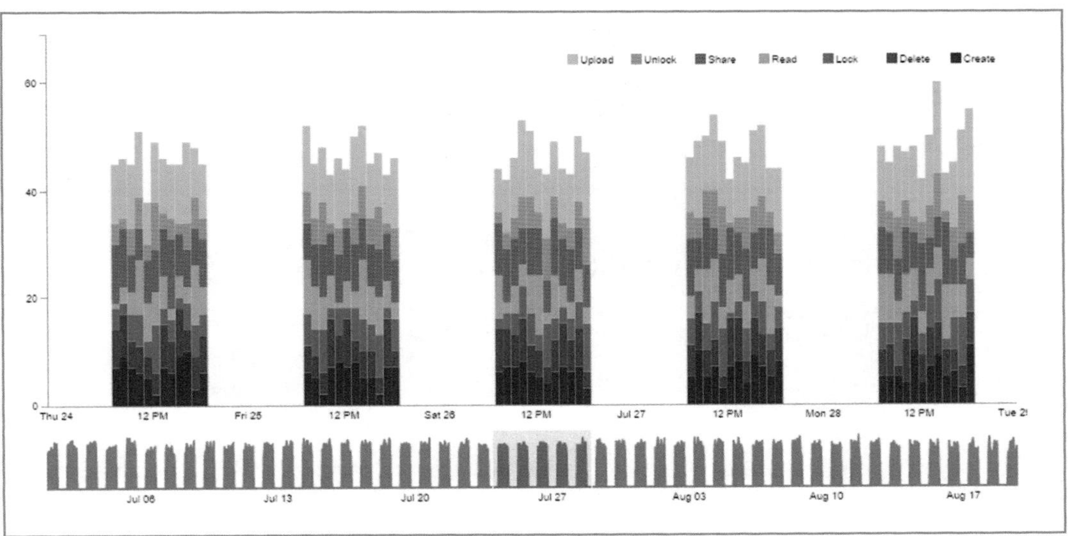

In this zoomed in version, a user can easily see the activities that took place every hour. We also implemented a small pop-up that can provide additional information when the user hovers the mouse over an area of the chart as shown in the following screenshot:

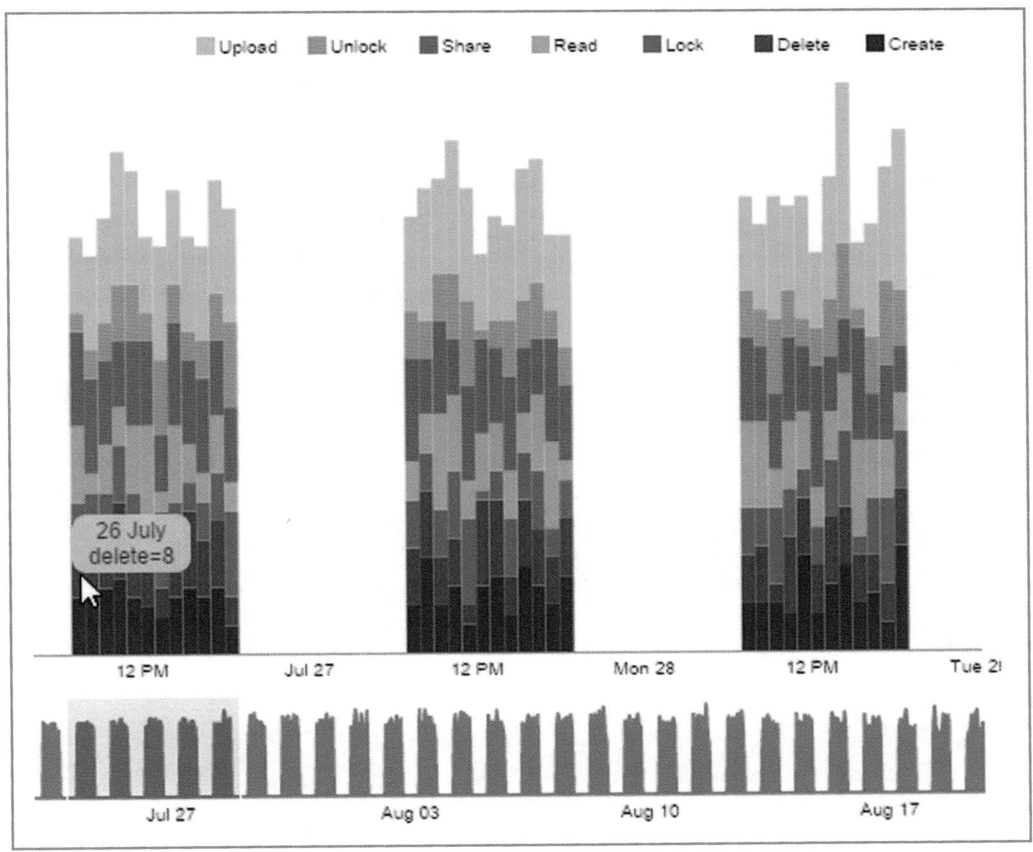

DEV

For this chart, the team is using the NVD3 chart library from NVD3.org **instead of one of the built-in Splunk Enterprise chart types.**

Using the third-party NVD3 chart visualization library

Attempting to use this third-party visualization in this dashboard raises a number of issues for us:

- When we implement it in our dashboard we discover that it does not display zoomed out data clearly.
- It requires complex JavaScript code (over 150 lines) to convert the data retrieved by a search into a format and structure that the visualization can use.
- There is a steep learning curve for using this third-party visualization.

Resolving the visualization issue

Because of the issue with the way the NVD3 chart renders the vertical bars when it is zoomed out, we revisited the built-in visualizations to see if it was possible to implement the zooming feature without the need to use complex third-party libraries. We discovered some new features in the latest release of Splunk Enterprise (version 6.1) in the form of the **Pan and Zoom Chart Controls**. The only documentation available to us at the time described how to use these controls in a Simple XML app that does not make use of the JavaScript extensions. However, it is possible to work out how to customize them using JavaScript by studying the rendered JavaScript from a Simple XML application (by viewing the source in a web browser), and by using a JavaScript debugger to examine the arguments passed in to the event handlers.

The following screenshots show an early version of the **User Activity** dashboard with a fully zoomed out view of the data and a zoomed in view. The line chart at the bottom acts as a zoom control, enabling the user to highlight the time of interest and redraw the remainder of the screen based on that time range selection.

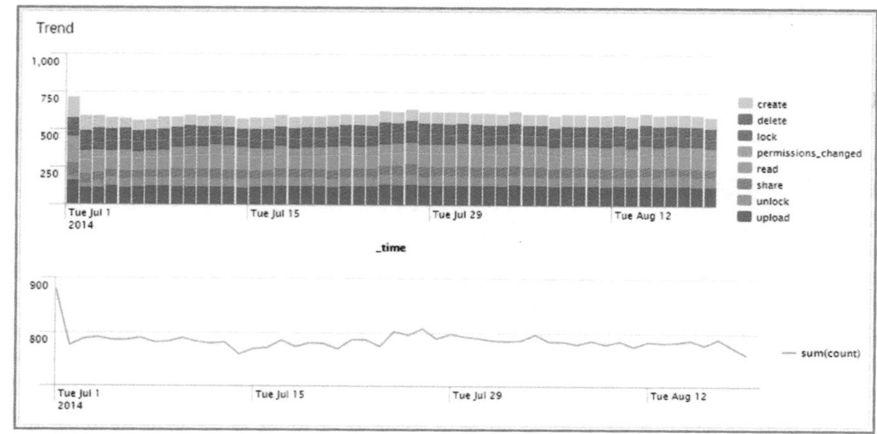

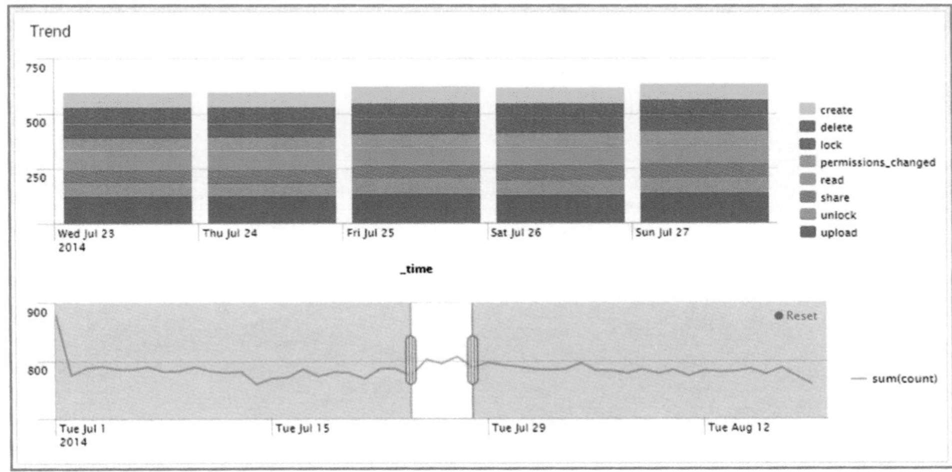

The following code snippet defines the stacked bar chart shown at the top in the screenshot:

```
<chart id = "trend_chart">
  <title>Trend</title>
  <search>
    <query>index=pas sourcetype=ri:pas:application user = $user$ | bucket span = 5m _time
    | stats count by _time event_name event_target | timechart sum(count) by event_name</query>
    <earliest>$trendTime.earliest$</earliest>
    <latest>$trendTime.latest$</latest>
  </search>
  <option name = "charting.chart">column</option>
  <option name = "charting.axisTitleX.visibility">collapsed</option>
  <option name = "charting.chart.stackMode">stacked</option>
  <option name = "charting.drilldown">none</option>
</chart>
```

The following code snippet defines the zoom control chart shown at the bottom in the previous screenshot:

```
<chart id = "zoom_chart">
  <search id = "zoom_search">
    <query>index = pas sourcetype=ri:pas:application user = $user$ | bucket span = 5m _time
           | stats count by _time event_name user | timechart sum(count)</query>
    <earliest>$time.earliest$</earliest>
    <latest>$time.latest$</latest>
  </search>
  <option name = "charting.chart">line</option>
  <option name = "charting.chart.nullValueMode">connect</option>
  <option name = "charting.axisTitleX.visibility">collapsed</option>
  <option name = "charting.axisTitleY.visibility">collapsed</option>
  <option name = "charting.drilldown">none</option>
  <option name = "height">100px</option>
</chart>
```

The JavaScript code in the following snippet shows how we update the range of data the upper trend chart displays in response to the user changing the selection in the lower zoom chart:

```
zoomChart.on("selection", function(e) {
  // Prevent the zoom chart from automatically zooming to the selection
  e.preventDefault();

  // Update trend chart's time range
  tokens.set({
    "trendTime.earliest": e.startValue,
    "trendTime.latest": e.endValue
  });
});
```

We are planning to continue using this approach for this particular visualization: the chart displays the information clearly, and it's much easier to implement than the NVD3 chart we looked at previously.

A SIMPLE EXAMPLE USING THE D3 THIRD-PARTY VISUALIZATION LIBRARY

BUS

The product owner asked for another view into the data, this time focusing on a customer whose personally identifiable information (PII) might have be accessed by someone in the organization. The visualization they requested provides a quick visual test of whether any inappropriate access took place.

The following screenshot of the **Customer Monitor** dashboard illustrates how we use the D3 dendrogram visualization to show which employees have accessed the records associated with a specific customer (in this example, Branden Morales). The dendrogram enables a user to drill down from the customer node, first to the departments, then to the divisions, and finally to the employees to see which employees have accessed documents relating to the customer. The panels at the top of the dashboard show summary figures: the total number of events that relate to the customer, the number of departments with employees who accessed the customer's documents, and the total number of employees who accessed the customer's documents.

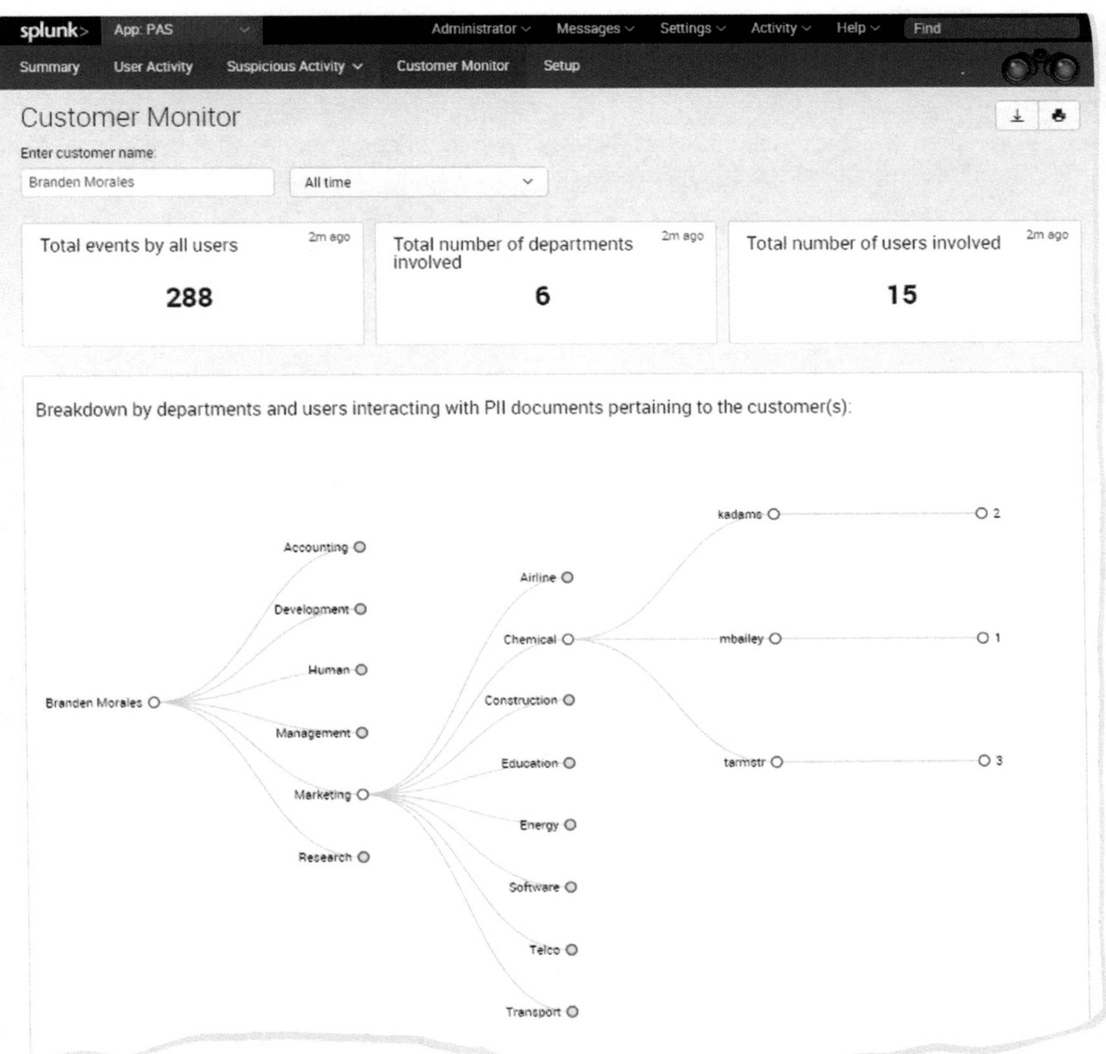

Originally, we did not create any custom JavaScript specifically for this dashboard (`customer_monitor.xml`), but the **form** element did reference a utility script named `autodiscover.js` that enables the autodiscovery and instantiation of components developed using the Splunk Django framework (see *"The recommended approach"* below for more information about how to avoid using this script). The implementation of the dendrogram visualization relies on the code in two folders:

- The D3 library elements are in the folder **appserver/static/components/d3**. You can learn more about D3 at d3js.org.
- The Splunk Enterprise specific wrapper code is in the folder **appserver/static/components/dendrogram**. We discuss this wrapper code in more detail below.

ARCH

Notice how we place these script files in their own folders in `appserver/static/components` **to indicate that this is library code rather than a script we created specifically for this app. This is not required, but it helps us organize our code better.**

The **customer_monitor.xml** file includes two **div** elements that define the dendrogram visualization. The first specifies the search that retrieves the customer data to display:

NOTE: This section describes our first pass at adding this visualization and does not show the recommended approach. The section "Tidying Up" below shows the recommended approach.

```
<div id = "dendrogram_search" class = "splunk-manager" data-require =
"splunkjs/mvc/searchmanager" data-options = '{
  "search": {
    "type": "token_safe",
    "value": "index = pas customer_name = $$customer$$| stats count by
              department department_group user "
  },
  "preview": true,
  "earliest_time": {
    "type": "token_safe",
    "value": "$$earliest$$"
  },
  "latest_time": {
    "type": "token_safe",
    "value": "$$latest$$"
  }
}'></div>
```

DEV

The `class, data-require,` and `data-options` **indicate that we are working with a component originally developed using the Django framework and that we must add the autodiscover.js file to ensure that autodiscovery works correctly. See "The recommended approach" for more information about the recommended way to avoid using these Django-related attributes.**

The search returns data in the correct shape for the visualization. The columns are in the order that we drill down through the levels: department, division (department group), user. Notice how the token that holds the customer name uses **$$** as a delimiter; this is because the search string is embedded within an HTML attribute value.

The second **div** element on the dashboard specifies how to render the dendrogram visualization:

```
<div id = "dendrogram" class = "splunk-view"
     data-require = "app/pas_ref_app/components/dendrogram/dendrogram" data-options = '{
        "managerid": "dendrogram_search",
        "root_label": {
          "type": "token_safe",
          "value":"$$customer$$"
        },
        "right": 600,
        "height": 600,
        "initial_open_lavel": 2,
        "node_outline_color": "#415e70",
        "node_close_color": "#b9d8eb"
     }'></div>
```

This element references the dendrogram wrapper code and the search definition in the previous **div** element. It then sets various configuration options such as **root_label** and **initial_open_level** that control the appearance and behavior of the visualization.

The wrapper code

The wrapper code that enables us to use the D3 dendrogram visualization is in the folder **appserver/static/components/dendrogram**. It consists of a JavaScript file (**dendrogram.js**) and a CSS file (**dendrogram.css**), and these files illustrate several important points about how to import and use a third-party visualization.

We create **dendrogram.js** from scratch by starting with the following template code:

```
define(function(require, exports, module) {
  var _ = require("underscore");
  var d3 = require("../d3/d3");
  var SimpleSplunkView = require("splunkjs/mvc/simplesplunkview");
  require("css!./dendrogram_basic.css");
  var Dendrogram = SimpleSplunkView.extend({
    className: "splunk-toolkit-chord-chart",
    options: {
      "managerid": null,
      "data": "preview"
    },
    output_mode: "json",
    initialize: function() {
      SimpleSplunkView.prototype.initialize.apply(this, arguments);
    },
    createView: function() {
      return true;
    },
```

```
    // Making the data look how we want it to for updateView to do its job
    formatData: function(data) {
      return formatted_data; // this is passed into updateView as 'data'
    },
    updateView: function(viz, data) {
    }
  });
  return Dendrogram;
});
```

Next we add the D3 code that creates the visualization to the **updateView** method. For this example, we can take the sample D3 code from bl.ocks.org/mbostock/4063570 and remove the lines that load sample data from the flare dataset that we don't need because we are using data from a Splunk Enterprise search:

```
updateView: function(viz, data) {
  this.$el.html("");
  var node_outline_color = this.settings.get("node_outline_color");
  var node_close_color   = this.settings.get("node_close_color");
  var node_open_color    = this.settings.get("node_open_color");
  var width  = this.$el.width();
  var height = this.settings.get("height_px");
  var m = [20, this.settings.get("margin_right"), 20, this.settings.get("margin_left")],
    w = width - m[1] - m[3],
    h = height - m[0] - m[2],
    i = 0;
  var tree = d3.layout.tree()
    .size([h, w]);
  var diagonal = d3.svg.diagonal()
    .projection(function(d) { return [d.y, d.x]; });
  var vis = d3.select(this.el).append("svg:svg")
    .attr("width", w + m[1] + m[3])
    .attr("height", h + m[0] + m[2])
    .append("svg:g")
    .attr("transform", "translate(" + m[3] + "," + m[0] + ")");
}
```

DEV

The most difficult part of using a third-party visualization is to get the data from a Splunk Enterprise search into the correct shape and format that the visualization control expects.

Next we need to format the search results in the shape the D3 control expects (often as a JSON object). In this example, we learned about the format of data expected by the visualization by looking at the sample D3 code from bl.ocks.org/mbostock/4063570. The following snippet shows the code in the **formatData** function that formats the results of the search:

```
formatData: function(data) {
  var height    = this.settings.get("height");
  var height_px = this.settings.get("height_px");
  this.settings.set("height_px", height === "auto" ? Math.max(data.length*30, height_px) : height);
  var nest = function(list) {
    var groups = _(list).groupBy(0);
    return _(groups).map(function(value, key) {
      var children = _(value)
        .chain()
        .map(function(v) {
          return _(v).rest();
        })
        .compact()
        .value();
      return children.length == 1 && children[0].length === 0 ? {"name": key} : {"name": key,
            "children": nest(children)};
    });
  };
  return {
    "name": this.settings.get("root_label"),
    "children": nest(data)
  };
},
```

This function creates a hierarchical dataset that models the hierarchy of data that the visualization displays.

You can learn more about this wrapper code at dev.splunk.com/goto/dendrowrap and by viewing the recording of the Splunk 2014 .conf session "I Want That Cool Viz in Splunk!"

You can also view another complete example that shows how to use the D3 Bubble Chart if you download and install the **Splunk 6.x Dashboard Examples** app.

The recommended approach

Our first-pass at implementing this visualization relied on the **autodiscover.js** file and some parts of the Django development framework. The approach shown here does require a small amount of custom JavaScript code but has fewer dependencies.

To make these changes, we remove the two **div** elements from the **customer_monitor.xml** file, we remove the **autodiscover.js** file, and we no longer have the confusing **$$** delimiters in the **customer_monitor.xml** file. In the final version of this dashboard, the Simple XML file contains the search and a placeholder **div** element as shown in the following snippet:

```
<search id = "dendrogram_search">
  <query>
    `pas_index` customer_name = $customer$
    | stats count by department department_group user
  </query>
</search>
...
<row>
  <panel>
    <html>
      <h2>Breakdown by departments ...</h2>

      <div id = "dendrogram"></div>
    </html>
  </panel>
</row>
```

DEV

We have left the search command in the Simple XML rather than moving it to JavaScript because it's easier to maintain there.

We now have the following code in the **customer_monitor.js** file to render the visualization:

```
require.config({
  paths: {
    "pas_ref_app": "../app/pas_ref_app"
  }
});
require([
  "splunkjs/ready!",
  "splunkjs/mvc/simplexml/ready!",
  "jquery",
  "pas_ref_app/components/dendrogram/dendrogram"
], function(
  mvc,
  ignored,
  $,
  DendrogramView
) {
  new DendrogramView({
    "managerid": "dendrogram_search",
    "root_label": mvc.tokenSafe("$customer$"),
    "right": 600,
    "height": 600,
    "initial_open_lavel": 2,
    "node_outline_color": "#415e70",
    "node_close_color": "#b9d8eb",
    "el": $("#dendrogram")
  }).render();
});
```

This code identifies the search and various options to configure the visualization. For more information about the **require.config** function, see the chapter "Adding code: using JavaScript and Search Processing Language."

Enhancing the visualization

In the final version of the app, we have modified the code in the `dendrogam.js` file to add count values to each node in the dendrogram visualization to provide more information to the user. All of these changes are in the **updateView** and **formatData** functions. The following screenshot shows the final version of the visualization:

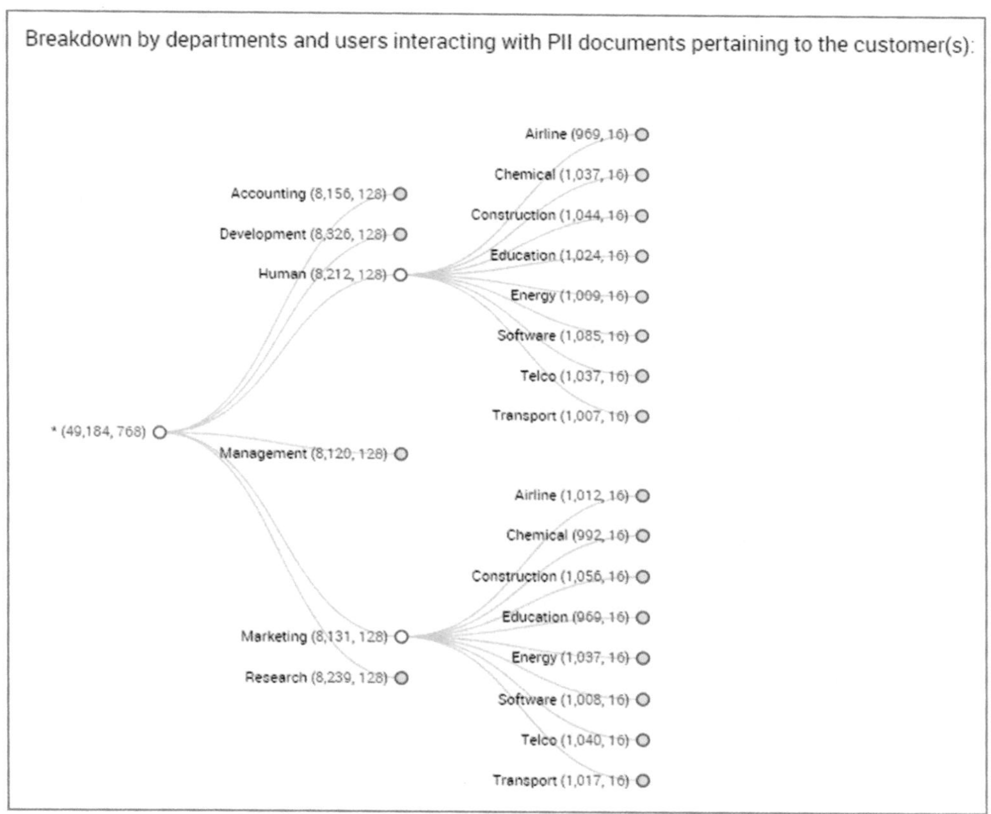

BUS

The first (red) number indicating the total number of notable events by all subnodes and the second (blue) number indicating the number of leaves (employees) associated with those event.

DEV

The clustered dendrogram implementation supports multiple levels of nesting.

A COMPLEX EXAMPLE USING THE D3 THIRD-PARTY VISUALIZATION LIBRARY

The previous section describes how we created a dendrogram visualization using the D3 library where we use a small amount of custom JavaScript code to insert the visualization on the page and the visualization is provided as a reusable control. At a later stage in the development of the PAS app we add the following **Policy Violations** panel to the **Summary** dashboard and construct the *donut* visualizations using the **D3.js** library (d3js.org/). That requires considerable more custom JavaScript because we are extensively modifying the basic visualization provided by the D3 library. Our approach is based on some pre-existing sample code using the D3 library to draw a donut that we then modified to meet our own specific requirements. We did consider using the HTML **canvass** element, but opted instead for an SVG vector graphics based approach over a raster-based approach. The advantages of the vector-based approach are that the graphics scale smoothly without pixilation as the user zooms in the browser, and our UI designers can use CSS to apply styles to the graphics elements independently of the code.

UX

All of our visualizations are implemented following the Reactive Design principles.

The following screenshot shows our donut visualization:

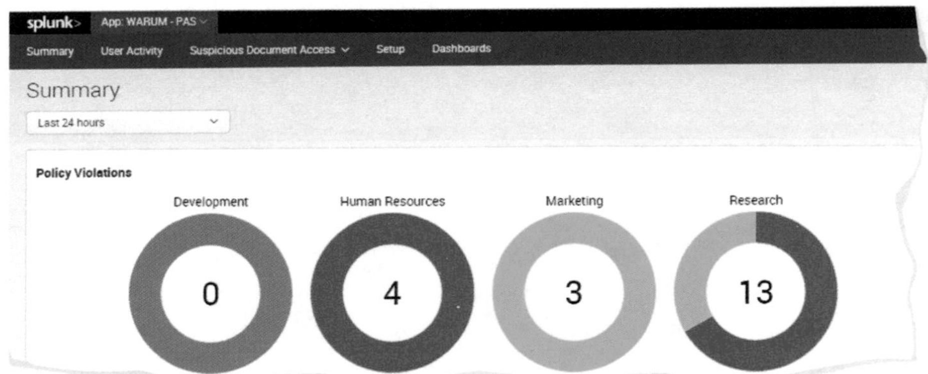

ARCH

You can mix and match different technologies for rendering views within the same dashboard. Different panels on the Summary dashboard use either built-in Simple XML controls or custom HTML.

We derive this visualization from a pie-chart sample found on the D3 web site and we add some automatic scaling to the panel and individual controls. The entire panel is data driven, so we pass as parameters to the panel the number of donuts, the labels, and the values to display. For the image in the previous screenshot, the panel uses the following data, passed as a JavaScript array, to build the display:

CENTERTEXT	DATA	TITLETEXT
0	color:gray, size:1	Development
4	color:red, size:1	Human Resources
3	color:orange, size:2	Marketing
13	color:red, size:2 color:orange, size:1	Research

ARCH

Behind the scenes, we retrieve the list of departments to display from data the user provides on the Setup dashboard and that is saved in the KV store.

In the **summary.js** file, the following JavaScript code passes this data to the view:

```
donutSeriesView.setData(donutSeriesData);
```

In **summary.js**, we define a class named **DonutSeriesView** to encapsulate the logic for the view. We instantiate the **donutSeriesView** instance in the previous code snippet as follows:

```
var donutSeriesView = new DonutSeriesView(
  d3.select(".donut_series"),
  200);
```

This code selects the **div** element on the page and sets its maximum height to be 200 pixels.

The **_renderDonutSeriesPanel** method in the **DonutSeriesView** class is responsible for rendering the view. It first calculates some dimensions based on the size of the view and the number of donuts, before adding each individual donut to the view as shown in the following code snippet:

```
_.each(data, function(donutData) {
  var donutContainer = container.append("span").attr("class", "donut");

  var donutSize = widthPerDonut - 2 * DONUT_SPACING;
  this._renderDonutChart(
    donutData.data,
    donutData.titleText,
    donutData.centerText,
    donutData.lowerText,
    donutContainer,
    donutSize,
    30/170 * widthPerDonut);

  donutContainer.node().style.marginLeft = DONUT_SPACING + "px";
  donutContainer.node().style.marginRight = DONUT_SPACING + "px";
}, this);
```

This code uses the **each** function from the **Underscore.js** library to iterate over the departments in our data and render each individual donut by calling the **_renderDonutChart** method.

Finally, the **_renderDonutChart** method uses the **D3.js** library to draw each donut. The method first defines an arc and a pie chart using the **D3.js** library as follows:

```
var TITLE_AREA_HEIGHT = 30;
var TITLE_TEXT_PX_HEIGHT = 14;
var radius = size / 2;
var arc = d3.svg.arc()
  .outerRadius(radius)
  .innerRadius(radius - thickness);
var pie = d3.layout.pie()
  .sort(null)
  .value(function(d) { return d.size; });
```

Next it defines an SVG container element to hold the SVG code that defines the donut:

```
var svg = container.append("svg")
  .attr("width", size)
  .attr("height", size + TITLE_AREA_HEIGHT)
  .append("g")
  .attr("transform", "translate(" + size/2 + "," + (size/2 + TITLE_AREA_HEIGHT) + ")");
```

Next it adds the text elements to the SVG to define the title and center text:

```
svg.append("text")
  .attr("class", "titleText")
  .attr("dy", (-(size / 2) - (TITLE_AREA_HEIGHT - TITLE_TEXT_PX_HEIGHT)/2) + "px")
  .style("text-anchor", "middle")
  .style("font-size", TITLE_TEXT_PX_HEIGHT + "px")
  .text(titleText);
svg.append("text")
  .attr("class", "centerText")
  .attr("dy", ".35em")
  .style("text-anchor", "middle")
  .style("font-size", size * 0.20 + "px")
  .text(centerText);
```

Finally, it draws the arcs that make up the donut, with one arc for each color:

```
svg.selectAll(".arc")
    .data(pie(data))
  .enter().append("g")
    .attr("class", "arc")
    .append("path")
    .attr("d", arc)
    .style("fill", function(d) { return d.data.color; });
```

DEV

Notice how the line starting with .enter() is unindented half a level. This is a D3 specific convention for indicating when the current node being acted upon changes during a sequence of calls.

In the final version of the PAS app we extract the code relating to the donut visualization into the files **policy_violations.js** and **policy_violations.css**. This makes it easier to maintain because all the code related to the custom panel is located in these two files. You can see how we include this code in the **summary.xml** file:

```
<form script = "summary.js,policy_violations.js"
  stylesheet = "summary.css,policy_violations.css,bootstrap-tagsinput.css">
```

While we were designing our donut visualization, we looked at the following resources for guidance and inspiration:

- highcharts.com/demo/pie-donut
- nvd3.org/examples/pie.html
- bl.ocks.org/mbostock/1346410
- bl.ocks.org/mbostock/3887193

Using dummy data during visualization development

We developed the donut control visualization before we developed the search that retrieves the data for the control. To manage this, we created a dummy data source that returns sample data in the same shape that we anticipated the real search would return. The following code snippet from the **summary.js** file shows how we retrieve the sample data from a CSV file and pass it to the donut visualization:

```
var dataSearch = new SearchManager({
  search: '| inputlookup example_violation_data.csv | lookup violation_info ViolationType |
    eval isYellow = if(ViolationColor="Yellow",1,0) | eval isRed = if(ViolationColor = "Red",1,0) |
    stats sum(isYellow) as NumYellows, sum(isRed) as NumReds, sum(ViolationWeight)
    as TotalWeight by Department
    | table Department, NumYellows, NumReds, TotalWeight'
});
dataSearch.data("results").on("data", function(resultsModel) {
  var rows = resultsModel.data().rows;

  // From the search results, compute what data the donut series
  // chart should display.
  var donutSeriesData = [];
  _.each(rows, function(row) {
    ...

    donutSeriesData.push({
      data: colorData,
      titleText: department,
      centerText: (totalWeight == null) ? "0" : totalWeight,
      // TODO: Compute % difference from last period
      lowerText: ""
    });
  });

  // Display the donut series chart
  donutSeriesView.setData(donutSeriesData);
```

DEV

Notice the "|" symbol at the start of the search string. It denotes a generating search command, which has no input. Such command is not searching over data from Splunk indexes. Instead, it is generating its own data. You need this to ensure that Splunk Enterprise executes the `inputlookup` command and does not do a keyword search for `inputlookup`!

DEV

When search is launched during onclick events, it may be useful to be able to cancel the search as follows: `dataSearch.cancel()`

DEV

If you generate a CSV file such as the one we use here (`example_violation_data.csv`) using Excel on a Mac, you must change the line endings from (CR) to (LF) so that Splunk Enterprise will recognize them correctly.

Later, when we developed the search that returns the real data, we replaced search in our code. see the section "Example: Combining multiple searches" in chapter "Adding code: using JavaScript and Search Processing Language."

ADDING CONTROLS IN SIMPLE XML MANUALLY

When we are editing the Simple XML directly and not using the graphical editing tools in Splunk Web, we place each control in its own **div** element to make it easy to reference the control from JavaScript. The following example comes from the **`setup.xml`** file:

```
<html>
  <form>
    <input id = "_key" type="hidden"></input>
    <div id = "departments">
      <h3>Departments to show on Summary dashboard: </h3>
      <div id = "departments_dropdown"></div>
      <p>
        <em>If the dropdown above has no choices then no events have been generated yet.</em>
      </p>
    </div>
    <hr/>
    <div id = "violation_types">
      <h3>Violation Types:</h3>
    </div>
    <hr/>
    <div id = "locations">
      <h3>Locations:</h3>
      <input type = "checkbox"/> Enabled<br/>
    </div>
    <hr/>
    <input id = "save" type = "button" class = "btn btn-primary" value = "Save"/>
  </form>
</html>
```

The following JavaScript code populates the content of the **departments_dropdown div** element:

```
var departmentsDropdown = new MultiDropdownView({
  managerid: "departments_search",
  labelField: "department",
  valueField: "department",
  el: $("#departments_dropdown")
}).render();
```

Note that we import the **MultiDropdownView** class from **splunkjs/mvc/multidropdown-view**.

DEV

You can still use the graphical editing tools in Splunk Enterprise after you have made changes to the source manually.

USING CUSTOM CSS WITH SIMPLE XML

We use the CSS extension feature of Simple XML to apply custom layout and styling to our dashboards. For example, in the **user_activity.xml** file we attach a **user_activity.css** file as shown in the following code snippet:

```
<form script = "user_activity.js" stylesheet = "user_activity.css">
```

This CSS file contains the following definitions:

```
#activity_levels_panel {
  width: 33% !important;
}
#trend_panel {
  width: 67% !important;
}
```

The Simple XML file references these definitions in some of its panel elements. For example:

```
<panel id = "activity_levels_panel">
...
<panel id = "trend_panel">
```

Notice how our naming convention makes it easy to identify all resources associated with a single dashboard: **user_activity.xml**, **user_activity.js**, and **user_activity.css**.

If you want to have a CSS (or JavaScript) file that's shared by multiple pages, you can add it to your Simple XML dashboard along with the page specific resources using the following notation:

```
<form script = "user_activity.js, utility.js" stylesheet = "user_activity.css, branding.js">
```

You can add as many resources as you need by using these comma separated lists for the **script** and **stylesheet** attributes.

If you want to automatically attach a JavaScript or CSS resource to every Simple XML page in your app, you can use the special files **dashboard.js** and **dashboard.css**. For example, you might want to check whether the app has been configured properly and automatically redirect to a setup screen if it is not or, you implement custom app licensing code that checks to see whether the app is licensed before letting you use the app. You don't need to add these files to the **script** and **stylesheet** attributes.

DEV

Adding such global checks to dashboard.js and dashboard.css is less error prone because you won't forget to add them when you create new dashboards.

In the PAS app we use the **dashboard.css** file to hide the editing buttons that normally show on all our dashboards by using the following CSS code:

```
.splunk-dashboard-controls .edit-btn { display: none; }
.splunk-dashboard-controls .more-info-btn { display: none; }
```

Customizing the heatmap visualization with CSS

An interesting use of CSS in the PAS app is where we hide the display of the next month on the standard heatmap control on the **User Activity** dashboard. This control normally displays the current and next month, but because we are displaying historical data there is never any data to display for the next month. To hide the next month, we simply set a fixed width for the panel that contains the heatmap control so there is only space for the current month. The following snippet from **user_activity.css** shows how we do this:

DEV

In practice, using dashboard.js is far more common than using dashboard.css.

```
#activity_levels_panel .panel-element-row {
  width: 250px;
  margin-left: auto; margin-right: auto;
}
```

Managing screen real estate with CSS

We also use CSS to modify the default dashboard layout to maximize the available screen real estate on some of our dashboards. The following screenshot shows the **User Activity** dashboard before we made the changes. As you can see, there is a lot of unused space next to the **User Activity** dashboard title text:

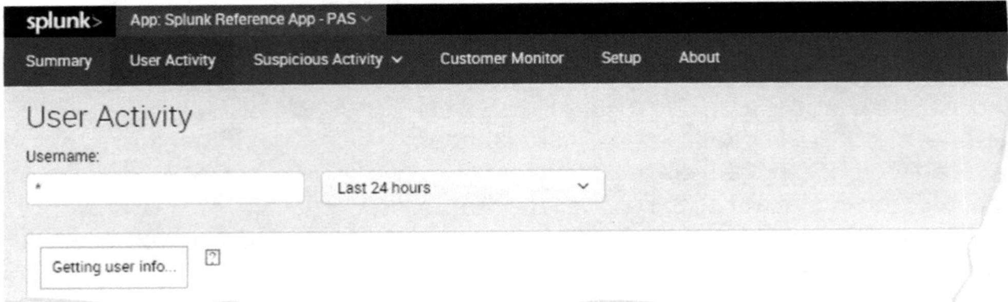

UX

Our Dashboards serve as information indicators and require high density.

We use CSS to adjust the layout as shown in the following screenshot:

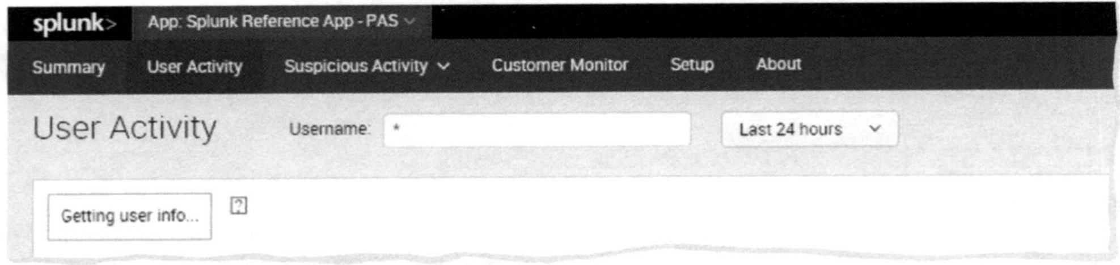

To achieve this result, our CSS moves the input fields up next to the title and shifts each row of the dashboard up to fill the empty space. The following snippet shows the relevant CSS code from the file **user_activity.css**:

```
.splunk-timerange {
  float: right;
  position: relative;
  left: 150px;
  top: -55px;"
 }
#input1 {
  position: relative;
  left: 250px;
  top: -55px;"
}
```

```
#input1 label {
  position: relative;
  left: -50pt;
  top: 19pt;
}
.dashboard-row {
  position: relative;
  top: -56px;
}
```

We have another example of using CSS to reclaim some space on the **User Activity** dashboard in the **Trend** panel. The following screenshot shows the layout before we make the changes:

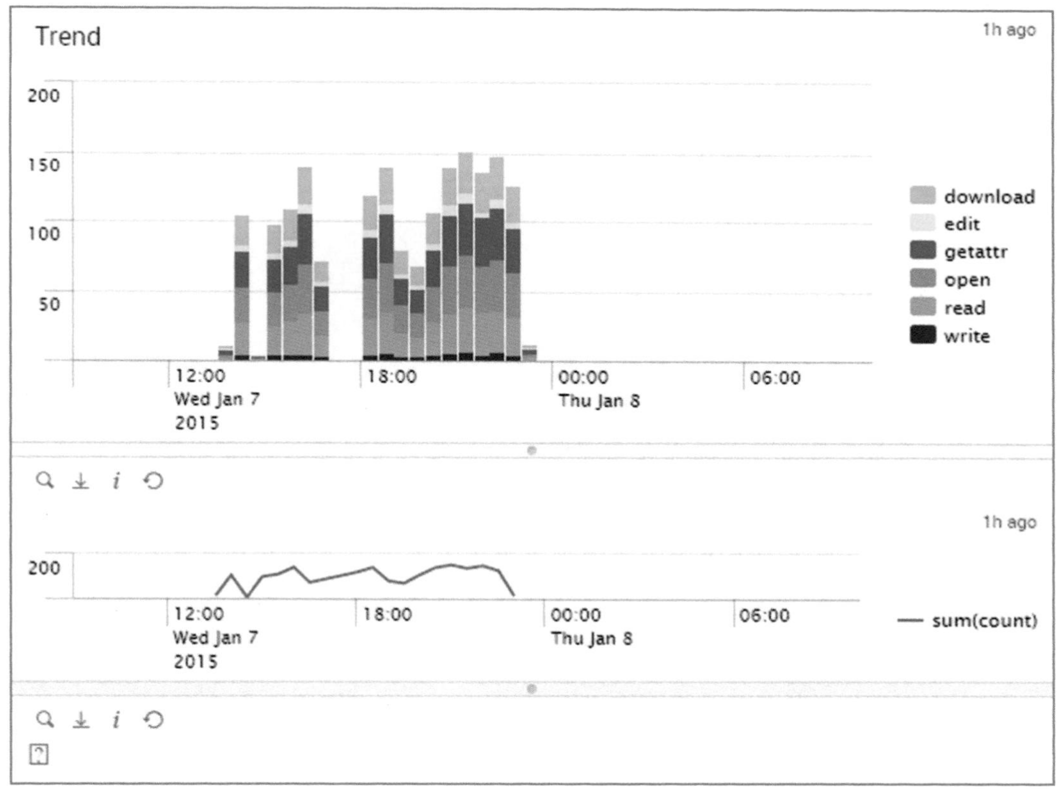

DEV

The techniques used to manipulate CSS are quite common in modern web development.

The next screenshot shows the results of our CSS changes where we hide the footer, the resize handles, and refresh time:

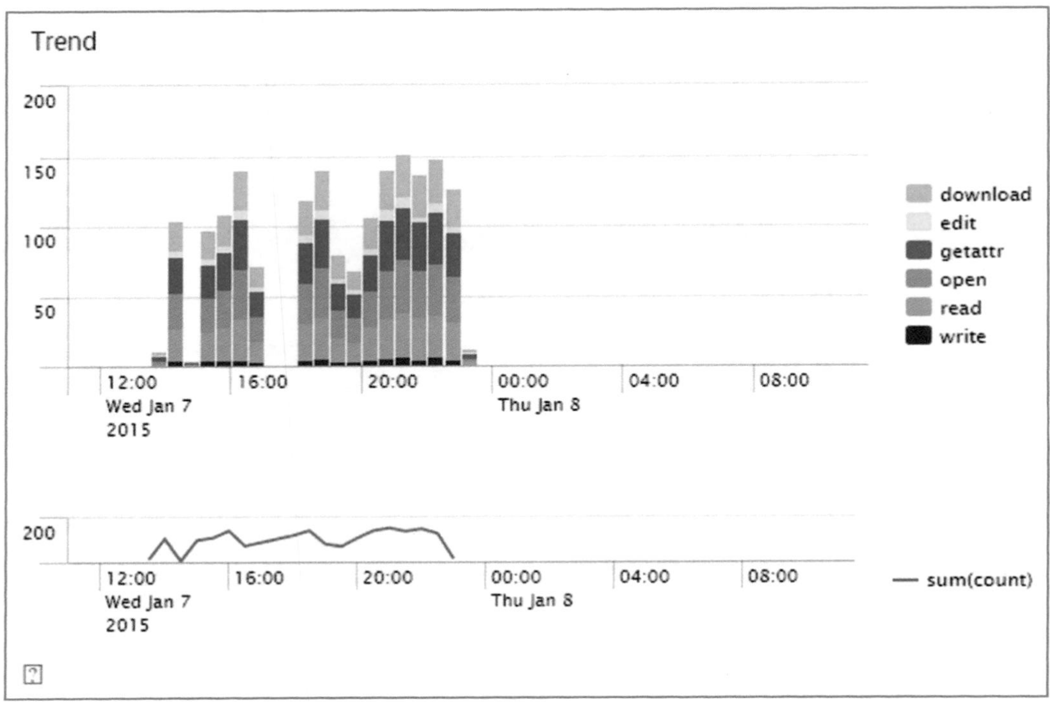

The following code snippet shows the relevant CSS code. Notice how we use a wildcard to identify the refresh time indicator that has a generated id:

```
div .ui-resizable-handle {
 display: none !important;
}

div .panel-footer {
 display: none !important;
}

div[id* = 'zoom_chart-refreshtime']{
 display: none !important;
}
```

USING A CUSTOM TABLE CELL RENDERER IN SIMPLE XML

On the **Summary** dashboard, in the **Suspicious Activity (Since Midnight)** panel we use the **CustomCellRenderer** class to add the colored dots in the first column:

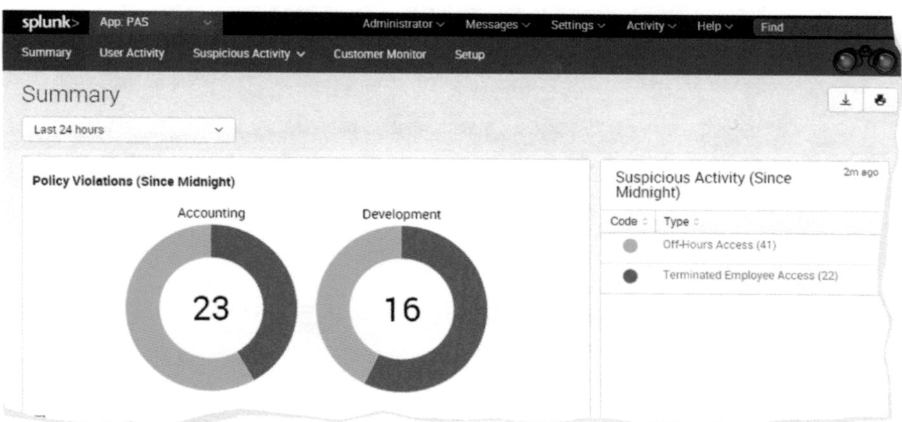

The following code snippet from the **suspicious_activity.js** file shows how we render custom content in the cell in the table view:

```
var CustomIconCellRenderer = TableView.BaseCellRenderer.extend({
  canRender: function(cell) {
    return cell.field === 'C';  // the color column
  },

  render: function($td, cell) {
    $td.html('<span style = "font-size: 3em; color: ' + cell.value + '">&#x25CF;</span>');
  }
});
```

Notice how this code uses the **TableView.BaseCellRenderer** class. In Simple XML, it is not straight forward to get access to a table view and it is necessary to access the view through the table element. The following code shows how we do this and then pass the view our custom cell renderer:

```
var tableElement = mvc.Components.getInstance('suspicious_activity_table');
tableElement.getVisualization(function(tableView) {
  tableView.table.addCellRenderer(new CustomIconCellRenderer());
  tableView.table.render();
});
```

For more information about custom cell renderers, see "How to create a custom table row renderer using SplunkJS Stack."

ADDING COLORS AND LOGOS

As a final set of changes to the PAS app at this stage in our journey we customize its appearance with a logo and some different colors. On the home page in Splunk Enterprise, the title bar for the PAS app in the list of installed apps now has a custom color:

We make this change by editing the **default/data/ui/nav/default.xml** file and adding the **color** attribute to the **nav** element:

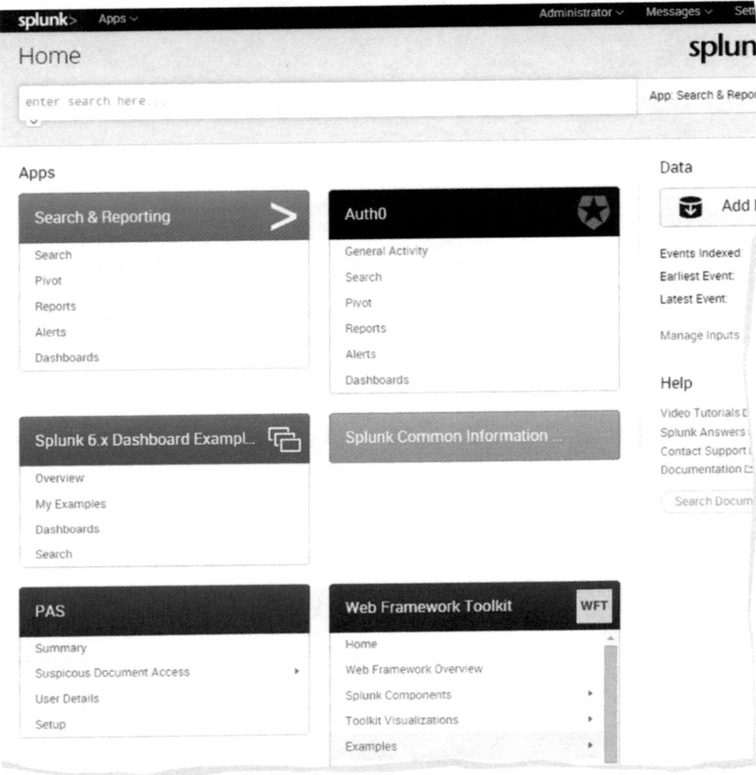


```
<nav color = "205365">
  <view name = "summary" default="true"/>
  <view name = "user_activity"/>
  <collection label = "Suspicious Document Access">
    <view name = "offhours_document_access"/>
    <view name = "terminated_employee_document_access"/>
    <view name = "anomalous_activity"/>
  </collection>
  <view name = "setup"/>
</nav>
```

We use the `default.xml` file to identify the **Summary** dashboard as the default dashboard for the PAS app.

We also add a logo to the top right of each dashboard:

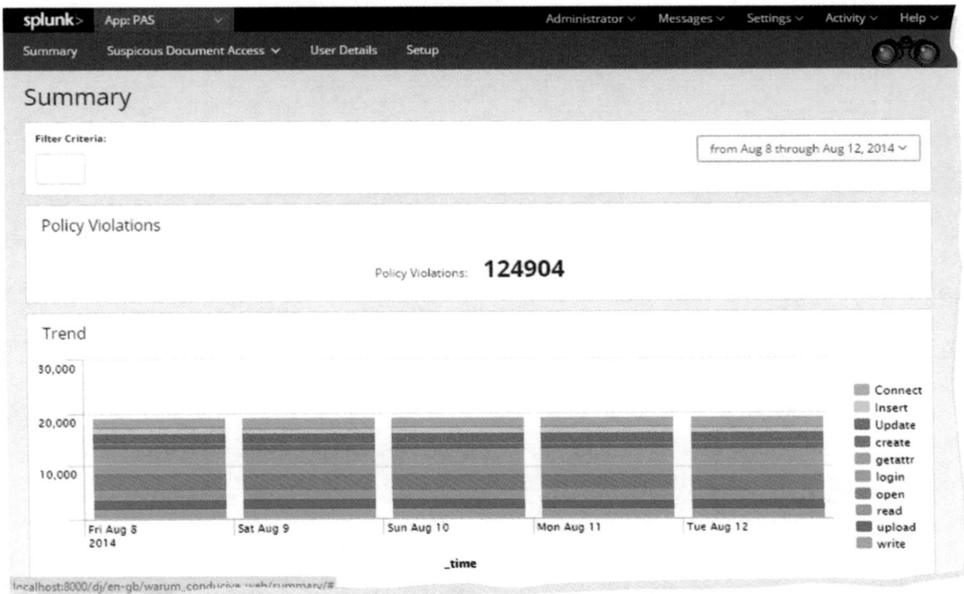

To add the logo, we add a `static/appLogo.png` file to the app.

HOW MUCH DETAIL SHOULD WE DISPLAY?

During the iterations on the design of the **User Activity Dashboard** for the PAS app, we received conflicting advice from the two subject matter experts (SMEs) we consulted over the level of detail to display on the form. One SME was in favor of including a panel that displays a raw feed of the log data, arguing that an auditor or compliance officer will want to get right into the data as soon as possible. The other SME argued that a raw feed was too detailed at this level and that a user would want some higher-level tools on the dashboard, but with the ability to drilldown when the need arises.

UX

It's common to encounter conflicting points of view when you are designing your dashboards. You need to get feedback from real end users about the usefulness of the alternative approaches.

WHAT DID WE LEARN?

This section summarizes some of the key lessons learned when we were building the UIs for our apps.

- Using **post-process** search instances on a dashboard can reduce the number of searches you need to perform and factor out common prefixes from complex searches in different places on the dashboard.
- To pass parameters between dashboards, you can implement your own mechanism using the request query string if you need to integrate it with other custom features. Otherwise, you can use the built-in drilldown capabilities and automatic population of token values from URL parameters provided by Simple XML.
- With minimal overhead, you can reuse visualization components from diverse libraries such as D3. The main effort would be in formatting the search results to meet the input requirements of the visualization component.
- Still, there is a two-fold risk associated with using third-party visualizations. The first element of risk is simply that it may take time to learn how to use the library effectively and be able to customize it to meet your requirements, many sophisticated visualizations are complex to use. The second element of risk is that third-party visualizations may require you to perform additional manipulations on your search results to get them into a suitable format for use with the visualization. For the next stories we tackle, we will focus first on an end-to-end solution using the built-in Splunk Enterprise visualizations. After we have the end-to-end solution working, we will then explore the options for beautifying our app by using suitable third-party visualizations.
- Our experience of trying to use the D3 visualization with our app illustrates how you can easily prototype ideas in Splunk Enterprise. In this case by trying to use a third-party visualization, we determined that it did not meet our requirements, so we looked for other another solution. This did not significantly affect the overall design of our app, our data model, or our searches.
- Customizing dashboard layouts can be challenging due the fact that Splunk Enterprise injects some CSS when it renders the page.

More information

For more information about the **search** element, see the section "**Search element"** on Simple XML Reference at: dev.splunk.com/goto/searchelem.

You can download the Splunk 6.x Dashboard Examples app from: dev.splunk.com/goto/dashboardexamples.

You can download the NVD3 chart library from: NVD3.org.

You can learn more about D3 from: d3js.org.

You can learn more about the wrapper code at: dev.splunk.com/goto/dendrowrap and by viewing the recording of the Splunk 2014 .conf session "I Want That Cool Viz in Splunk!" at: dev.splunk.com/goto/confviz.

The following resources were used for guidance and inspiration while designing the donut visualization:

- highcharts.com/demo/pie-donut
- nvd3.org/examples/pie.html
- bl.ocks.org/mbostock/1346410
- bl.ocks.org/mbostock/3887193

For more information about custom cell renderers, see “How to create a custom table row renderer using SplunkJS Stack” at: dev.splunk.com/goto/customtablerow.

4

Working with data: where it comes from and how we manage it

When working with data in the two apps, our developers make use of their knowledge of Splunk® Simple XML, Splunk search processing language (SPL™), and JavaScript. These all help in understanding how to make use of the data that Splunk Enterprise retrieves from the various sources.

GETTING DATA FROM THE AUTH0 SERVICE INTO SPLUNK ENTERPRISE USING A MODULAR INPUT

One of the first issues to address for the Auth0 app is how best to get the information collected by the Auth0 service into the Splunk app where it can be visualized and analyzed in real time. Both Auth0 and Splunk Enterprise are hosted services, so to enable viewing of real-time data from Auth0 in a Splunk app we must have some mechanism for transferring event data over the network. The initial approach we explored was to push data whenever anything interesting happened in the Auth0 service to an endpoint in Splunk Enterprise. Splunk Enterprise would then be able to index the incoming data and make it available to a dashboard in the Auth0 app. However, we identified the following potential issues with this solution:

- It is not robust. If the Splunk instance is not listening, or there are connectivity problems, then event data from Auth0 is lost.

The focus of this chapter is on how the apps access the data they use, and how we can manage the data.

- It is not efficient. Because of the way that the Auth0 service works internally, there is no opportunity for batching event data to send to the Splunk instance. For every interesting event in Auth0, the Auth0 service must make an HTTP call to the Splunk instance.
- It is not complete. Again, because of the way the Auth0 service works internally, it is only possible to push some event types to the Splunk instance. For example, the Auth0 service can send event data relating to successful logins, but not failures.
- It has limited reporting capabilities as you cannot get historical information. You can only pick up the new events that are sent to your Splunk instance.
- It is awkward to configure. You may need to configure firewall rules to allow the Auth0 service to push data to your Splunk instance.
- There is no easy deployment model. You need to add code to the Auth0 service to push data into your Splunk service.

However, the Auth0 service generates its own complete log files that contain all the detailed event data that the Splunk app requires. Copying log files on a schedule from the Auth0 environment to the Splunk Enterprise environment would not deliver the requirement for real-time information in the Splunk Enterprise dashboard. If the Splunk instance could request data from the Auth0 service every couple of seconds that would allow the dashboard to display sufficiently up-to-date information on all the events generated in the Auth0 service. It would also be more efficient, because the Splunk instance could request data in batches making it easier to configure since the Splunk service is calling a public endpoint in the Auth0 service to request data.

ARCH

A robust solution would be if the Splunk instance could keep track of the most recent event it received, and be able to resubmit a request if it failed to receive the data.

The model we chose also makes it easy for customers to deploy our solution because we can publish it as an app on the Splunk Apps site (dev.splunk.com/goto/auth0app). To implement this solution, we made changes to the Auth0 service and created a *modular input* using the Splunk SDK for JavaScript in the Splunk app (for more information, see "How to work with modular inputs in the Splunk SDK for JavaScript"). Splunk Enterprise also supports scripted inputs as an alternative to modular inputs. Scripted inputs are easier to write, however they are more complex to deploy and manage, especially if you need to support multiple operating systems. Scripted inputs also have limitations as compared to modular inputs. For example, scripted inputs:

- Do not support passing arguments in Splunk Web (which we require to pass in the Auth0 credentials).
- Do not provide validation feedback when you configure them.
- Do not support multiple instances (you would need two copies of the script if you had two Auth0 installations).
- Are less integrated with respect to logging to Splunk Enterprise's own internal logs.

ARCH

Although Auth0 was new to Splunk Enterprise, it took Auth0 just two weeks to get their basic Splunk app up and running along with making the necessary changes to their API.

Changes to the Auth0 service

DEV

Modular inputs configuration parameters can be managed through the Splunk REST API, which is really useful.

Our first challenge was how to retrieve data from the Auth0 service. We wanted to enable a modular input to continuously poll for data, but the Auth0 service itself did not have a suitable API. We determined that the best option was to create a new REST API in the Auth0 service that enables a client (such as a Splunk instance) to request the event data. This new API takes two parameters: **take** specifies the maximum number of log entries to return, and **from** specifies the log entry from which to start reading. This was a simple change to make in the Auth0 service and did not have an impact on any other features.

> **ARCH**
>
> **Auth0 uses MongoDB to store log data from the Auth0 service. Because MongoDB lets them assign incrementing IDs to log entries as they are written, it's easy to implement an API that reads a sequential set of log entries starting from a specified log entry.**

Creating a modular input

A modular input enables us to add a new type of custom input to our Auth0 Splunk application that behaves like one of the native input types. A user can interactively create and update the custom inputs using Splunk Enterprise, just as they do for native inputs (this would not be possible with a scripted input). The following screenshot shows the new custom Auth0 input type in the list of available input types in the Splunk Enterprise UI. This new Auth0 input type is defined in the **server.js** script that is discussed later in this section:

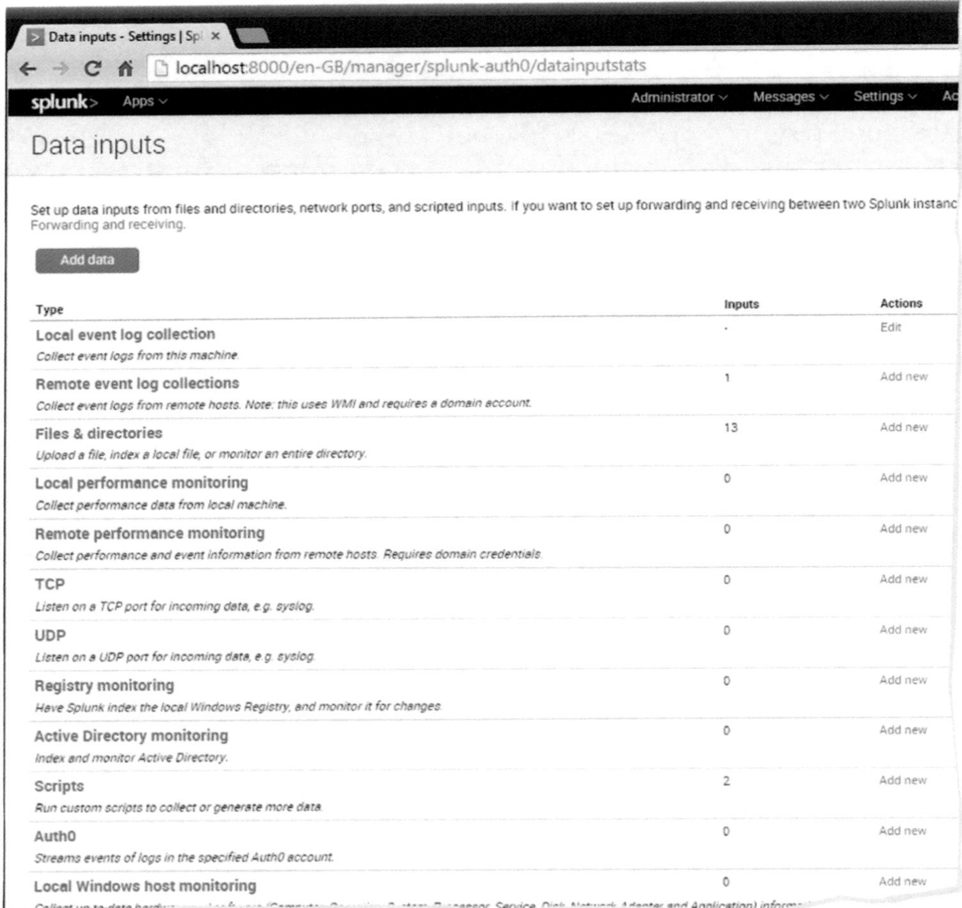

The next screenshot shows the Auth0 input type UI requesting details of the Auth0 service to which to connect:

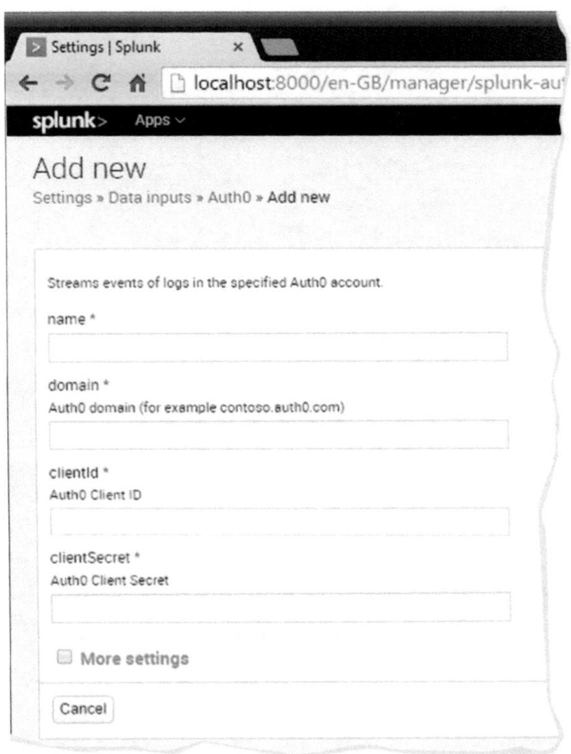

We choose to implement this modular input using the Splunk SDK for JavaScript as the team working on this app are experienced Node.js developers. Node.js is also a cross-platform development tool. It is just as easy to build a modular input using one of the other Splunk SDKs in a language of your choice. When you create a modular input using node.js, you define the input in a Node module that exports a standard set of functions. The following code snippets come from the **server.js** script in the **bin/app** folder in the app (there are also scripts called **auth0.cmd** and **auth0.sh** in the **bin** folder for launching the **server.js** script at startup for both Windows and Linux environments).

ARCH

Modular inputs are an alternative to scripted inputs. Where scripted inputs are quick and easy to implement, they may not be easy for an end user to use. Modular inputs require more upfront work by the developers, but are much easier for end users to use.

To implement a modular input, you must define a **Scheme** instance, which tells Splunk Enterprise about the arguments that a user configuring this input must provide. You then provide any optional validation logic for those arguments, as well as the logic for streaming the events back to Splunk Enterprise. The Auth0 input requires the user to provide credential information, it will then connect to the Auth0 service to validate the credentials, and then connect to the Auth0 service to begin retrieving the data that it streams into Splunk Enterprise. As you can see from the require calls below, the modular input relies on the Splunk JavaScript SDK for the modular input infrastructure as well as the Auth0 SDK for communicating with the Auth0 service:

```
(function() {
  var fs              = require('fs');
  var path            = require('path');
  var splunkjs        = require('splunk-sdk');
  var Auth0           = require('auth0');
```

The first section of the **server.js** script defines the **Scheme** instance for the input that displays in the UI of Splunk Enterprise for configuring the modular input. As you can see, we are exporting a **getScheme** function. The **Scheme** instance describes the input and provides its arguments. Notice how we set the property **useSingleInstance** to **false,** which causes the UI to display an optional **Interval** parameter to let a user specify how frequently the script should run. In this case, the parameter determines the polling interval for checking with the Auth0 service for new log data to request. For more information about creating modular inputs using JavaScript, see "How to work with modular inputs in the Splunk SDK for JavaScript."

```
exports.getScheme = function () {
  var scheme = new Scheme('Auth0');
  scheme.description = 'Streams events of logs in the specified Auth0 account.';
  scheme.useExternalValidation = true;
  scheme.useSingleInstance = false; // Set to false so an input can have an optional interval
                                    // parameter
  scheme.args = [
    new Argument({
      name:             'domain',
      dataType:         Argument.dataTypeString,
      description:      'Auth0 domain (for example contoso.auth0.com)',
      requiredOnCreate: true,
      requiredOnEdit:   false
    }),
    new Argument({
      name:             'clientId',
      dataType:         Argument.dataTypeString,
      description:      'Auth0 Client ID',
      requiredOnCreate: true,
      requiredOnEdit:   false
    }),
```

```
    new Argument({
      name:             'clientSecret',
      dataType:         Argument.dataTypeString,
      description:      'Auth0 Client Secret',
      requiredOnCreate: true,
      requiredOnEdit:   false
    })
  ];
  return scheme;
};
```

The remainder of this script is a JavaScript function that has been broken into chunks with commentary throughout so that you can follow along.

The first section validates that a checkpoint file can be created, and if one does not exist, creates it. This file is used to store the current seek location or last record seen during the polling of the Auth0 API. Splunk Enterprise provides a checkpoint folder for each input to store its checkpoint data.

```
exports.streamEvents = function (name, singleInput, eventWriter, done) {
  // Get the checkpoint directory out of the modular input's metadata
  var checkpointDir = this._inputDefinition.metadata['checkpoint_dir'];
  var checkpointFilePath  = path.join(checkpointDir, singleInput.domain + '-log-checkpoint.txt');
  var logCheckpoint = '';
  try {
    logCheckpoint = utils.readFile('', checkpointFilePath);
  }
  catch (e) {
    // If there's an exception, assume the file doesn't exist. Create the checkpoint file with
    // an empty string
    fs.appendFileSync(checkpointFilePath, '');
  }
```

Next, the script initializes the Auth0 object provided by the Auth0 module. This object will be used to retrieve log data from the Auth0 service.

```
  // Call Auth0 API
  var auth0 = new Auth0({
    domain:       singleInput.domain,
    clientID:     singleInput.clientId,
    clientSecret: singleInput.clientSecret
  });
```

The main body of the script uses an asynchronous loop to poll the Auth0 service for new log data. The **Async.whilst** method is from the Splunk SDK for JavaScript. The loop continues until there are no more logs or an error is encountered.

```
  var working = true;
  Async.whilst(
    function () {
      return working;
    },
```

In the body of the loop, we first use the Auth0 API to retrieve up to 200 new log entries, starting from the last checkpoint.

```
function (callback) {
  try {
    auth0.getLogs({
      take: 200, // The maximum value supported by the Auth0 API
      from: logCheckpoint
    },
```

We check for errors and if there are any remaining log entries to index. If there are none, **working** is set to false, which will then exit the whilst loop. We also use the Logger class from the SDK to record what happened.

```
    function (err, logs) {
      if (err) {
        Logger.error(name, 'auth0.getLogs: ' + err.message, eventWriter._err);
        return callback(err);
      }
      if (logs.length === 0) {
        working = false;
        Logger.info(name, 'Indexed was finished');
        return callback();
      }
      var errorFound = false;
```

Next, we loop over the log entries we retrieved from the Auth0 service. The **Event** and **EventWriter** classes from the JavaScript SDK are used to send data to Splunk Enterprise. We then record the most recent ID in the **logCheckpoint** variable.

```
      for (var i = 0; i < logs.length && !errorFound; i++) {
        try {
          var event = new Event({
            stanza:     singleInput.domain,
            sourcetype: 'auth0_logs',
            data:       JSON.stringify(logs[i]), // Have Splunk index our event data as JSON
          });

          eventWriter.writeEvent(event);
          logCheckpoint = logs[i]._id;
          Logger.info(name, 'Indexed an Auth0 log with _id: ' + logCheckpoint);
        }
```

If there are any errors, we log the error and save the most recent log entry id in the checkpoint file.

```
        catch (e) {
          errorFound = true;
          working = false; // Stop streaming if we get an error
          Logger.error(name, e.message, eventWriter._err);
          fs.writeFileSync(checkpointFilePath, logCheckpoint); // Write to the checkpoint file

          // We had an error, die
          return done(e);
        }
```

Finally, if everything worked, we save the id of the last log entry we indexed into the checkpoint file.

```
          fs.writeFileSync(checkpointFilePath, logCheckpoint);
          callback();
        });
      }
      catch (e) {
        callback(e);
      }
    },
    function (err) {
      done(err);
    }
  );
};
```

We designed this input based on the assumption that Splunk Enterprise will run a single instance at a given time, and fetch events by continually polling. Each time it fetches, it will pull down all available logs, send events back to the Splunk instance, and then the process is killed. The way intervals work in Splunk Enterprise, if the input is still collecting data when the interval timer expires, the Splunk instance does not launch a new instance of the input. The interval applies only when the input finishes its work. You can also configure the location where Splunk Enterprise stores the checkpoint file, but the default location is in the **$SPLUNK_HOME/var/lib/splunk/modinputs** folder. For more information, see "Data checkpoints."

DEV

You can create modular inputs using other languages such as Python and C#.

Refreshing an index with checkpoints

During our testing, we need to be able to delete our indexed data and start over. To do this, we followed this procedure:

1. Open Splunk Enterprise, click **Settings,** and then click **Data Inputs**. Click **Auth0** (the modular input we defined) and then select **Delete**.
2. Delete the log checkpoint file (that tracks the most recent event that Splunk retrieved from the Auth0 service) from the Splunk folder $SPLUNK_HOME`/var/lib/splunk/modinputs`.
3. Delete the content of the index by running the command **bin/splunk eventdata clean INDEX_NAME** in a shell or at a command prompt in Windows.

GETTING DATA INTO SPLUNK ENTERPRISE FOR THE PAS APP USING DATA MODELS AND SPLUNK COMMON INFORMATION MODEL EXTENSIONS

The PAS app currently uses log data from three different sources: a database, a document repository, and the file system. Each of these is defined as a separate *sourcetype*: **ri:pas:database**, **ri:pas:application**, and **ri:pas:file**. These three logs contain different types of event data with different formats from each other. Each of these types has different field names, which on first sight requires separate searches to pull the data. This is not ideal and introduces a potential maintenance issue if we add a new data source in the future (or if the format of one of the log files changes). We would like to make the log data from these three sources (and any data sources we define in the future) available in a normalized format to simplify the design of the searches in the app. We would also like to make it available for other apps to consume in a standardized format.

Fortunately, Splunk Enterprise offers a better solution. We can achieve the first of these goals by using *aliases* and *extracts* to translate and map the content of our log files into common field names, and by building data models based on the extracts and aliases. We can achieve the second of these goals by building a special model that maps and translates our log data into the structure defined in a Splunk *Common Information Model* (CIM).

A *data model* is a semantic mapping from a set of events that can be used for querying Splunk Enterprise. A data model specifies a set of fields with fixed data types and an agreed interpretation with respect to the events Splunk Enterprise is indexing that Splunk apps can use.

A Splunk CIM defines a core set of fields for a particular type of event that might come from multiple log sources. For example, there is a Change Analysis CIM data model with fields that describe **Create**, **Update**, and **Delete** activities, and there is an **Authentication** CIM data model with fields that describe login and logout activities. For more information about these and other Splunk CIM data models, see the section "Data Models" on the "Common Information Model Add-on Manual" page. In addition to the documentation, after you install the **Splunk Common Information Model Add-on**, you can browse the structure of the models from the **Pivot** page in the **Search & Reporting** app in Splunk Enterprise.

> **SHIP**
> **Splunk CIM is shipped as an add-on. Get it from** dev.splunk.com/goto/splunkcim.

ARCH

A CIM defines the lowest common denominator of the data associated with the activity such as change analysis, authentication, or intrusion detection. Browsing the model in Splunk Enterprise will give you more insight into the structure of the model.

A CIM focuses on normalizing data and making it interoperable with other apps. However, we also want to create a data model that is specific to our app, and that will define all of the rich data that we need to build our pivot reports. You can define multiple models for your data as CIM Extensions.

We also plan to accelerate our CIM PAS Extension data model to improve query performance, this will enable us to use commands such as **tstats** on the fields in our data model in our searches.

ARCH

Data model acceleration creates summaries for only those specific fields you and your Pivot Editor users are interested in and want to report on. To enable data model acceleration, follow these instructions: dev.splunk.com/goto/enabledatamodelacc. **While there, we highly recommend you review the restrictions on the kinds of data model objects that can be accelerated.**

DEV

You can manually generate accelerated namespaces and leverage the power of indexed fields to perform statistical queries without having to index fields. You do so by using the tscollect command.

Mapping to a Splunk Common Information Model

For the PAS app, we determined that the Change Analysis CIM data model was the most appropriate. After identifying the model to use, the next step is to map the existing fields in our data sources to the set of standard field names defined in the CIM to create a normalized view of the data. We begin by using a spreadsheet to document the mappings from our three data sources to the CIM and then implement the mappings using a combination of **aliases**, **extracts**, and static **evals** in the `props.conf` file for each data source. For example, we map the **SQLTEXT** field in the database log, use the static value "updated" for the document repository log, and map an extract field in the file log to the CIM field named **action**. Now a search can refer to the **action** field, regardless of the particular log file we are searching, and any other app that uses our data sources can expect to find the standard field names from the CIM. If our app needs to support another data source, we can perform a similar mapping operation and use search definitions that are very similar to our existing ones. Furthermore, if the format of a log file changes, we can accommodate those changes in our mappings without the need to modify any searches that depend on specific field names. The following table shows our initial set of mappings for our three data inputs:

DATABASE LOG ORIGINAL FIELD	DOCUMENT LOG ORIGINAL FIELD	FILE LOG ORIGINAL FIELD	CIM FIELD
SQLTEXT	"updated"	Extract	action
NAME *Enumerated values in log:* • *Connect* • *Insert* • *Update* • *Select* • *Delete* • *Quit* • *Grant* • *Revoke*	event_name *Enumerated values in log:* • *login* • *download* • *edit* • *read* • *create* • *upload* • *share* • *permissions_ changed* • *lock* • *unlock* • *delete*	Extract *Enumerated values in log:* • *getattr* • *read* • *open* • *write*	command
DOCUMENT		Extract	object
CONNECTION_ID		pid	object_id
IP	src_ip		src
USER	*user_id*	Extract	user
USER_ID		empid	user_id
	event_details		object_attrs
	event_id		event_id
	Extract		event_target
	"success"		status
	"application"		change_type

ARCH

For an event to show up in the Change Analysis CIM it must be tagged with the value change **as defined in the constraint in the Change Analysis data model. You must define a search that assigns this tag value to events from your data.**

Tagging our events

Tagging events lets us associate those events with a data model. This works with both Splunk Common Information Model and with our custom data model. To tag an event, we first define event types and then associate those event types with tags. The following screenshot shows the event types for our database provider add-on: you can view this page in the **Settings** section of Splunk Enterprise:

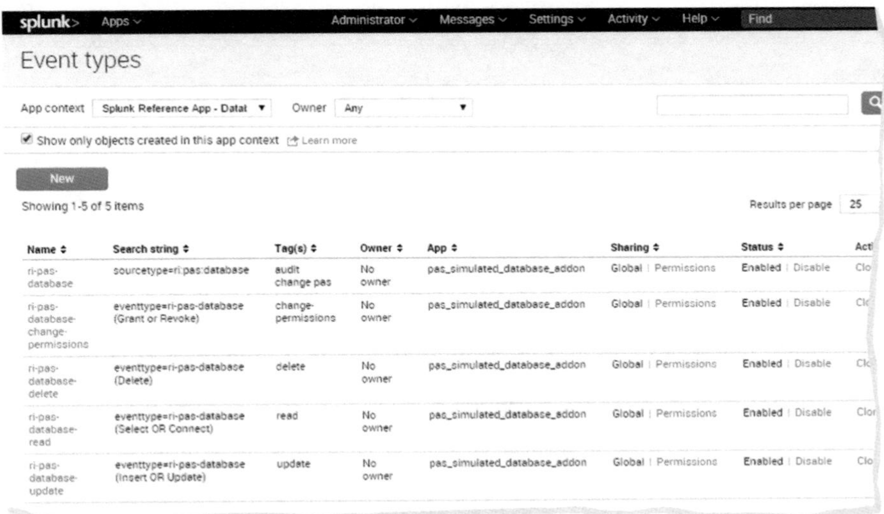

Name	Search string	Tag(s)	Owner	App	Sharing	Status
ri-pas-database	sourcetype=ri:pas:database	audit change pas	No owner	pas_simulated_database_addon	Global | Permissions	Enabled | Disable
ri-pas-database-change-permissions	eventtype=ri-pas-database (Grant or Revoke)	change-permissions	No owner	pas_simulated_database_addon	Global | Permissions	Enabled | Disable
ri-pas-database-delete	eventtype=ri-pas-database (Delete)	delete	No owner	pas_simulated_database_addon	Global | Permissions	Enabled | Disable
ri-pas-database-read	eventtype=ri-pas-database (Select OR Connect)	read	No owner	pas_simulated_database_addon	Global | Permissions	Enabled | Disable
ri-pas-database-update	eventtype=ri-pas-database (Insert OR Update)	update	No owner	pas_simulated_database_addon	Global | Permissions	Enabled | Disable

ADM

You should make sure that event type names are unique to each app, otherwise the definition in one app will overwrite the definition in another one.

Each event type has a search string that identifies the events and a set of associated tags. Notice how we reference the **ri-pas-database** event type in the subsequent definitions, and how some event types have more than one associated tags. You can also view the tags in the **Settings** section of Splunk Enterprise:

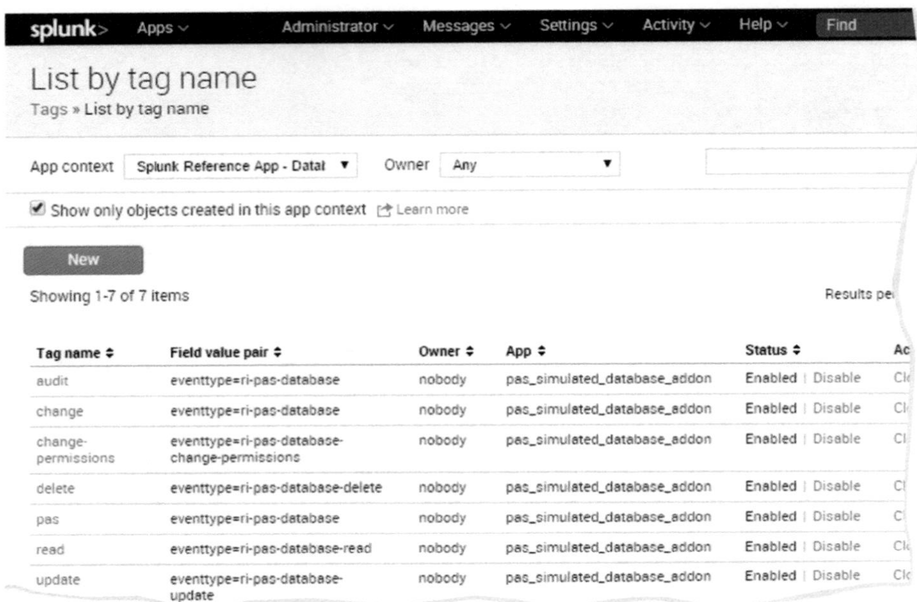

Some of these tags (**change_permissions**, **delete**, **read**, and **update**) are used to associate the events with the Change Analysis CIM, and some of these tags (**pas**, **change**, and **audit**) are used to associate events with our custom data model. The **pas** tag is intended to be unique to the PAS apps, while the other tags may be used by many other apps to identify events generically. In the **Google Drive** add-on app, we also define the tag **cloudstorage** that could be used in other similar apps such as add-ons for OneDrive or DropBox to indicate a category of data.

The files `eventtypes.conf` and `tags.conf` in each of the provider add-ons store these definitions.

Using tags

Searches in the PAS app can now use the tags instead of specifying an index to search. For example:

```
<search id = "dendrogram_search">
  <query>
    tag = pas tag = change tag = audit customer_name = $customer$
    | stats count by department department_group user
  </query>
</search>
```

The only place where we mention the **pas** index is the `authorize.conf` file in the main app (**Indexes** and **Access Controls** in **Settings**). In the **Access Controls** settings we specify **pas** as the default index for the users of the app. For more information about authorizations and permissions in the PAS app, see the "Packaging and deployment: reaching our destination" chapter in this guide. If you decide to create another add-on app for the main PAS app, if the add-on app has an `inputs.conf` file, that file will also refer to the **pas** index.

The following diagram summarizes the role of the Splunk knowledge objects related to tagging in the PAS app:

> **DEV**
> Not all our searches use tags, in some cases we search for events using more detailed criteria such as looking at the values in specific fields.

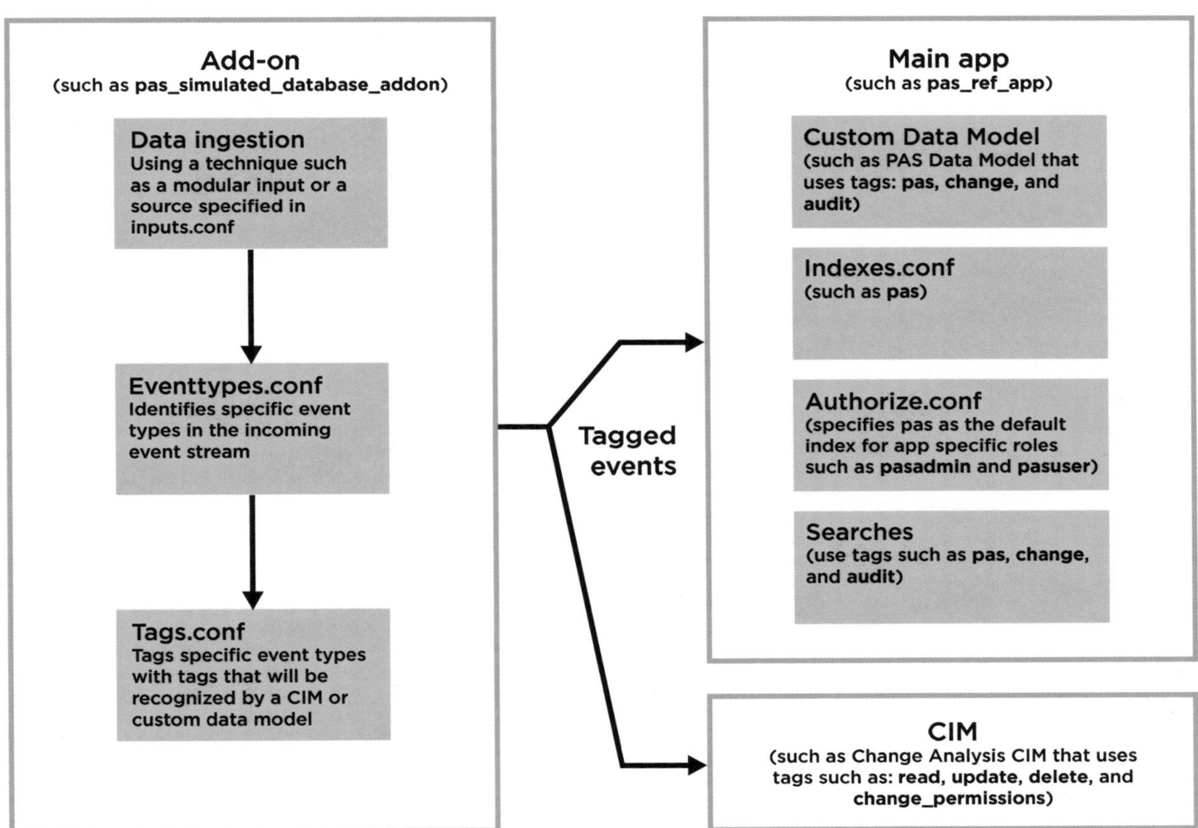

When we ship the PAS app it includes sample data provider add-ons, that together with the Eventgen app generate sample event data that is indexed in the **pas** index. When a customer deploys the app, they can use their own event data and indexes provided that:

- The events are tagged with the tags recognized by our data model.
- The **pasuser** and **pasadmin** roles are authorized to use the customer's index.

For more information about the **pasuser** and **pasadmin** roles, see the chapter "Packaging and deployment: reaching our destination" in this guide.

Defining a custom data model

In addition to mapping our log data to the Change Analysis CIM, we also defined our own custom data model within the app to support pivot-based searches on the app dashboards. A custom data model defines a set of fields (possibly organized hierarchically) and a constraint that identifies the events that the data model handles. This definition is expressed in JSON, and in our app the file is named **ri_pas_datamodel.json**. The app also contains a **datamodels.conf** file that contains metadata about the model such as whether it is accelerated.

ARCH

As a reminder, CIM is the least common denominator and not very rich. It makes sense to use other models or techniques as well. The key is to make sure that CIM is also covered when extracting data, so that the least common denominator can be relied on.

PERF

An accelerated model is equivalent to an indexed view in an Relational Database Management System (RDMS). Searches will be faster, at the expense of persisting and maintaining indexes.

The following screen shot from Splunk Enterprise shows the data model we defined for the PAS app:

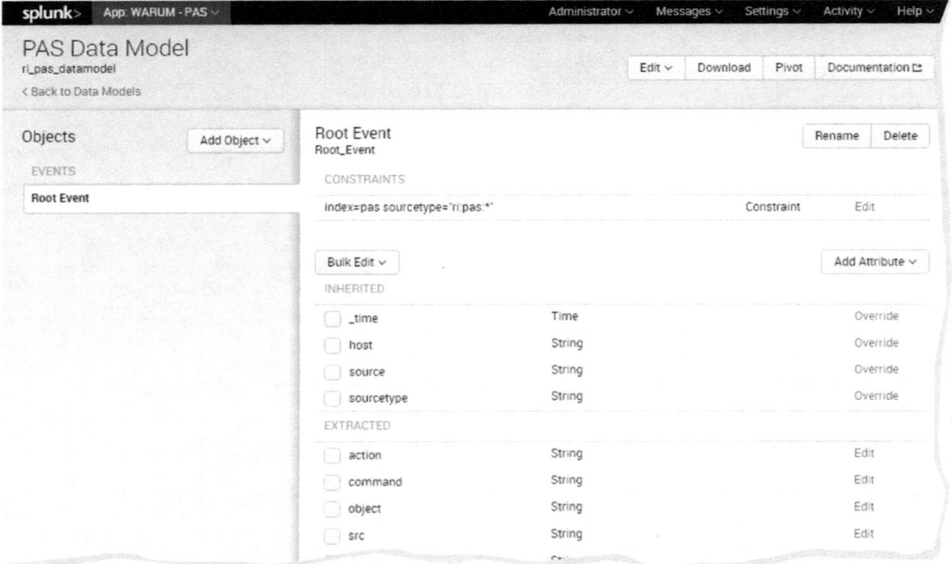

Notice how the constraint uses our tags to specify which events are included in the model.

ARCH

Mapping our data to a CIM or to a custom data model are both examples of normalizing multiple data sources to a single model.

Defining our mappings in separate add-on apps

To make it easy to maintain these mappings and keep them all in a fixed location, we package them as separate add-on apps. In the PAS app, we use these separate add-on apps specifically because we want to let customers extend the PAS app by adding their own data sources, which will require their own custom mappings. For information about how the main PAS app recognizes these add-on apps, see the section "Using the Splunk JavaScript SDK to interrogate other apps" in the chapter "Adding code: using JavaScript and Search Processing Language." The following code snippet shows the **props.conf** file from the **RI document TA** app:

```
[ri:pas:application]
MAX_TIMESTAMP_LOOKAHEAD = 150
NO_BINARY_CHECK = 1
pulldown_type = 1
FIELDALIAS-command = event_name AS command
FIELDALIAS-object_attrs = event_details AS object_attrs
FIELDALIAS-event_id = event_id AS event_id
FIELDALIAS-src = src_ip AS src
FIELDALIAS-user = user_id AS user
EXTRACT-file = event_target=(?<object_path>.+)\\(?<object>.*?)\s
EVAL-action = "updated"
EVAL-status = "success"
EVAL-change-type = "application"
```

The stanza name, **ri:pas:application**, identifies the **sourcetype** with which the mappings are associated.

SHIP

You can find out more about technology add-ons in the "Data Source Integration Manual."

Other apps use the custom knowledge objects such as the field aliases and extracts defined in our add-on apps; therefore, we give these objects **Global** rather than **App** scope.

> **SHIP**
>
> You can define the scope (individual, app, or global) of knowledge objects in either a local.meta or default.meta file. You should not ship an application that contains a local.meta file, so you should move any scoping definitions to the default.meta file.

A note about the props.conf file

For the PAS app, we are generating our own simulated events using the Eventgen app. Therefore, we are confident that the format of the event data is optimized for consumption by Splunk Enterprise. In practice, with real event data, you may be able to further improve the performance of Splunk Enterprise when it parses the event data by providing additional information in the `props.conf` file. Typically, you should include the following attributes: **TIME_PREFIX**, **MAX_TIMESTAMP_LOOKAHEAD**, **TIME_FORMAT**, **LINE_BREAKER**, **SHOULD_LINEMERGE**, **TRUNCATE, KV_MODE**. The following snippet shows an example of these attributes in use:

```
[sourcetypeA]
TIME_PREFIX = ^
MAX_TIMESTAMP_LOOKAHEAD = 25
TIME_FORMAT = %Y-%m-%d %H:%M:%S.%3N %z
LINE_BREAKER = ([\r\n]+)\d{4}-\d{2}-\d{2}\s\d{2}:\d{2}:\d{2}.\d{3}
SHOULD_LINEMERGE = False
TRUNCATE = 5000
KV_MODE = None
ANNOTATE_PUNCT = false
```

For more information about these attributes, see "props.conf" in the Admin manual.

Rebuilding our index after refactoring

As part of the effort to refactor our data inputs, create the data models, and package them in add-on apps, we renamed our sourcetypes part way through our journey: for example, we renamed the conducive:app sourcetype to ri:pas:application. We also renamed the app that contains our sample data. An unintended consequence of this was that Splunk Enterprise could no longer find the sample data and was no longer indexing our data. To fix this, we had to delete the content of the old index named **pas** completely by using the following procedure:

1. Add the **admin** user to the **can_delete** role in **Access controls** in Splunk Enterprise.
2. Stop Splunk Enterprise.
3. At an a operating system command prompt, run the following command:
   `bin/splunk clean eventdata -index pas`
4. Restart Splunk Enterprise.

For more information, see "Remove indexes and indexed data."

Using the data models

Earlier in this chapter, we describe our custom data model and how we map our log data to the Change Analysis CIM. After building our custom data model, we can refactor our existing dashboards to make use of the data model and use pivots in the search criteria. For example, the **Summary** dashboard includes several **pivot** searches that use the data model such as this one that is based on the **Root_Event** in our data model:

```
<search id = "base_search">
  <query>
    | pivot ri_pas_datamodel Root_Event count(Root_Event) AS Count SPLITROW _time AS _time PERIOD
auto SPLITROW user AS user
    SPLITROW command AS command SPLITROW object AS object
    FILTER command isNotNull $filter$ $exclude$ ROWSUMMARY 0 COLSUMMARY 0 NUMCOLS 0 SHOWOTHER 1
  </query>
</search>
```

The following example from the **Off-hours Document Access** dashboard is based on the **Invalid_Time_Access** (**Off-Hours Document Access**) child event:

```
<chart>
  <title>Documents Accessed Outside Working Hours</title>
    <searchString>| pivot ri_pas_datamodel Invalid_Time_Access count(Invalid_Time_Access) AS count
                  SPLITROW _time AS _time PERIOD auto SORT 0 _time ROWSUMMARY 0 COLSUMMARY 0
                  NUMCOLS 0 SHOWOTHER 1
    </searchString>
  <option name = "charting.chart">line</option>
</chart>
```

These search definitions now use the fields defined in our custom data model such as **_time**, **user**, **command**, and **object**.

For more information about the **pivot** command, see "pivot" in the Search Reference.

The following screenshot shows a search that uses the **Change_Analysis** CIM data model to show some of the sample data from the PAS add-ons (in this example the Document and File sample providers):

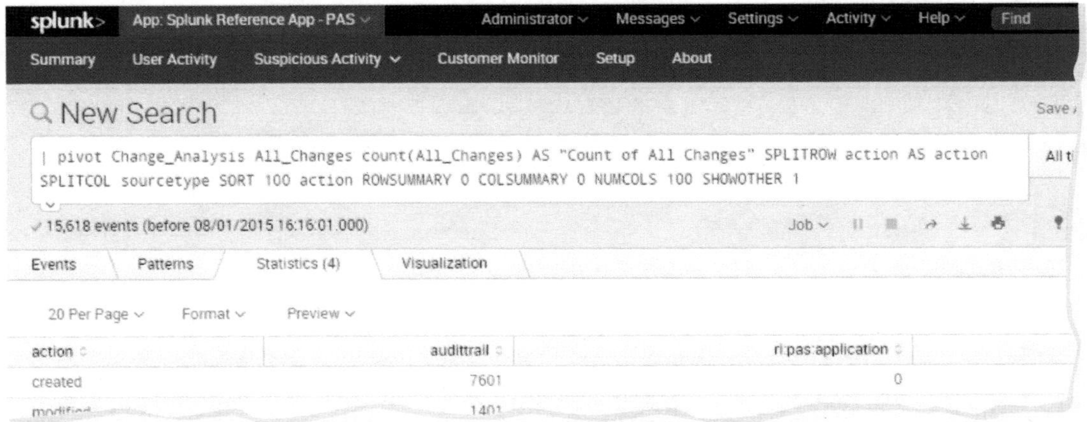

Modifying the data model to support additional queries

The following screenshot shows an example of a pivot based on the **Root Event** in our original data model that shows counts of the different commands executed by individual users. The existing dashboards in our app all use pivots similar to this one to retrieve the data they display:

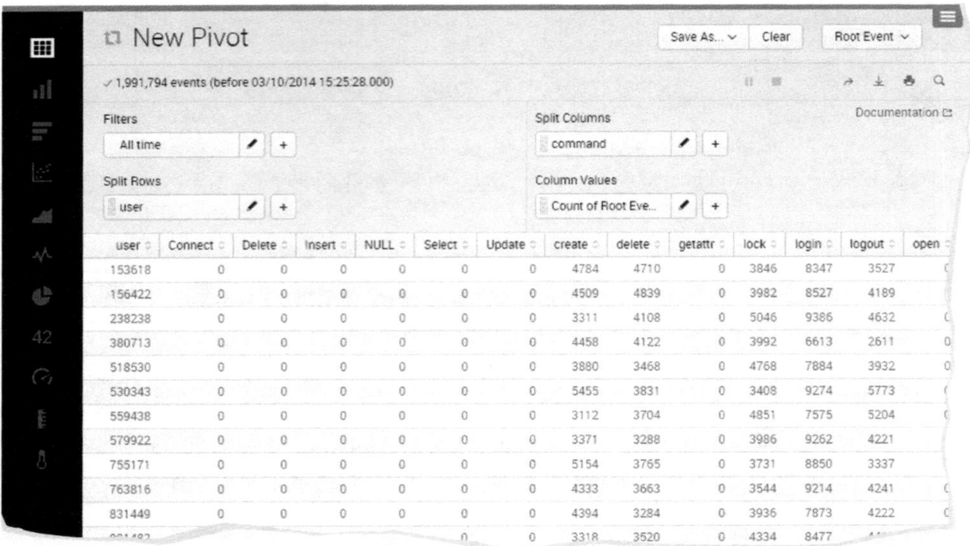

We plan to add visualizations to the summary screen that show the overall health of the system we are monitoring. These visualizations will need Key Performance Indicator (KPI) values to determine the overall health, and we need to modify our data model to enable us to query for these KPIs. Our initial set of KPIs are: a count of out of hours accesses to the system (**Invalid Time Access**), a count of accesses by terminated employees (**Terminated Access**), and a count of policy violations (**Policy Violation**).

> **DEV**
>
> The **Policy Violation** object gets removed later in our journey.

The following screenshot shows a pivot based on the **Terminated Access** event and you can see the count on each day. We can use the count of **Terminated Access** events for the last day as part of the calculation of the overall system health status:

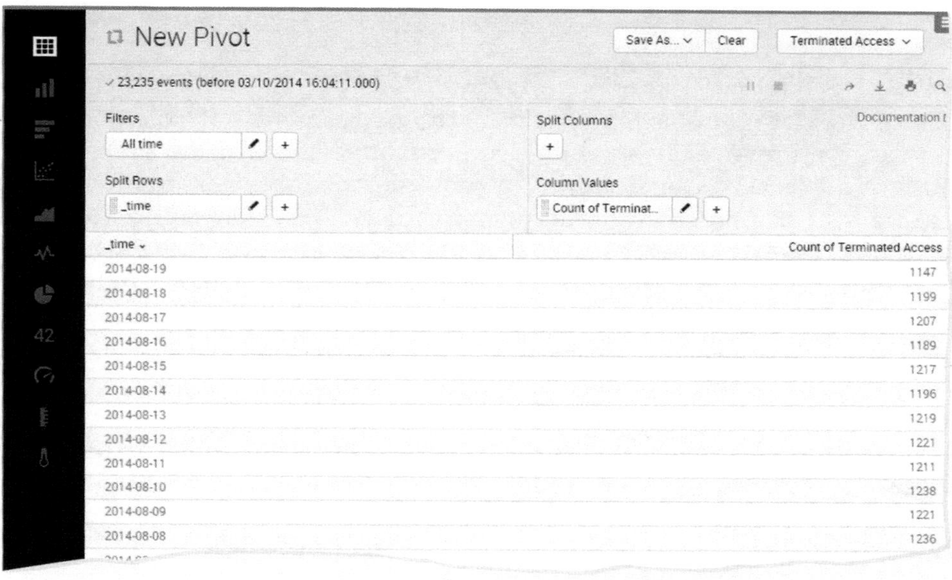

We define additional events in the **PAS Data Model**, such as **Terminated Access** events, as children of the root event. The following screenshot shows the attributes and constraint the **Terminated Access** event inherits from the root event along with the additional constraint that identifies the specific event type.

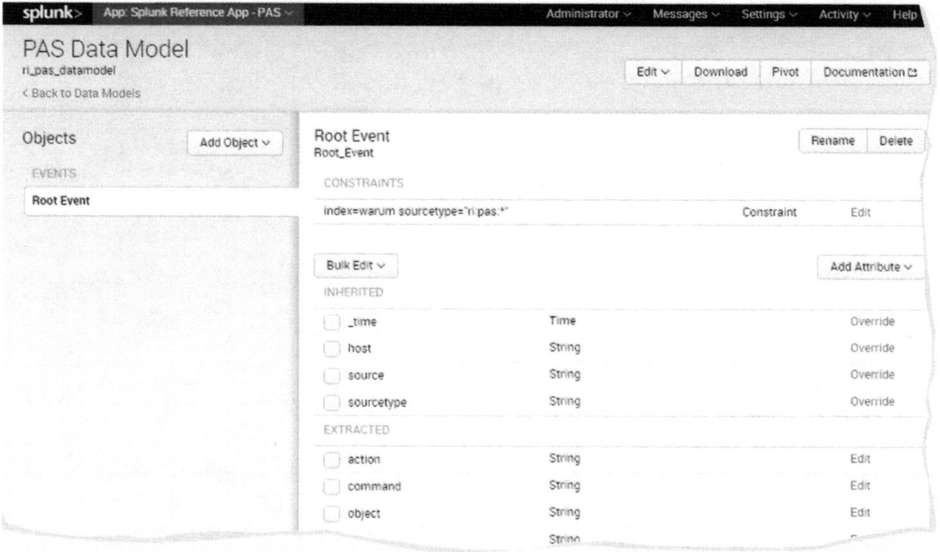

We can now use these additional event definitions in the search managers on our dashboards. For example to search for **Policy Violation** events, we use the following search definition:

```
| pivot ri_pas_datamodel Policy_Violation count(Policy_Violation)
  AS count FILTER command isNotNull $filter$ $exclude$ ROWSUMMARY 0 COLSUMMARY 0 NUMCOLS 0 SHOWOTHER 1
```

Case study: Using data models to handle large volumes of data

One reason to use data models is to optimize the performance of Splunk Enterprise when you have a large number of users who use a dashboard that runs searches across high volumes of data. For example, you have a requirement for a dashboard used by several hundred users that displays information from the last thirty days and you have multiple terabytes of new data to index every day. This is considerably more data than the PAS scenario expects, but an app such as PAS will still see performance benefits from using accelerated data models.

Using simple, inline searches on the dashboard that search for the last thirty days of data will be unusably slow in this scenario. Therefore, the first step might be to replace the inline searches with saved reports that you have accelerated for the last thirty days. While this will speed up the searches, they will typically stall at the end because Splunk Enterprise only updates the accelerated data every ten minutes. A search over the last thirty days retrieves mostly accelerated data but still has to search the raw data for the last few minutes' worth of nonaccelerated data. To work around this problem, you can modify your dashboards to report on the last thirty days of data using a time range that excludes the last ten minutes to ensure that the searches only retrieve accelerated data.

You can further improve on this approach by using scheduled reports. This lets the searches on the dashboard access cached data on the search head instead of accessing the indexers for the accelerated data. You can manually schedule the searches you need to run as reports every ten minutes, and then the searches on the dashboards can load the results of the scheduled reports from the search head using the **loadjob** command.

You can also accelerate a data model to improve the performance of pivot searches based on the data model. This provides similar performance improvements to accelerated reports, but in addition to enabling pivot searches, accelerated data models:

- Update every five minutes instead of every ten minutes.
- Let you manage the amount of disk space required to store the accelerated data because you can choose which columns to add to your data model.

PERF

It's possible to further optimize a high data volume scenario by using a custom solution instead of a data model. For example, you could run a search, with a timespan of one minute, every minute that appends data to an output lookup file, and then on the dashboard use input lookups to read this summary data.

For more information about data model acceleration, see the "Accelerate data models" section of the Knowledge Manager Manual.

For more information about using reports, see "About reports" in the Reporting Manual.

For more information about accelerated data, see "Manage report acceleration" in the Knowledge Manager Manual and "Accelerate reports" in the Reporting Manual.

For more information about scheduling reports, see "Schedule reports" in the Reporting Manual.

For more information about the **loadjob** command, see "loadjob" in Search Reference.

INTEGRATING WITH A THIRD-PARTY SYSTEM

On the **User Activity** dashboard we display information about a user that we pull from a third-party system. In the sample PAS app this third-party system is a REST endpoint we implemented using Python that simulates a directory service such as LDAP or Active Directory.

ARCH

Using a mock implementation like this let us develop the functionality in the absence of the real directory service with real user data.

The following screenshot shows how we display this information on the dashboard:

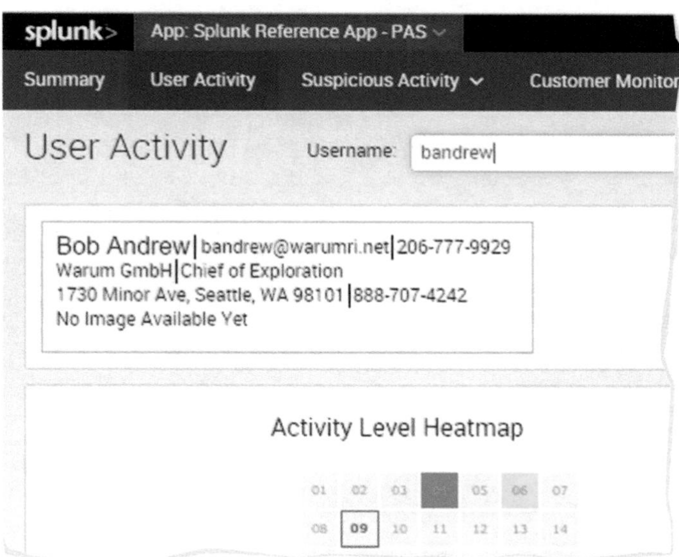

To pull the data from our simulated directory service, we use a custom search command. Splunk Enterprise lets you implement custom search commands for extending the SPL. Custom search commands are authored in Python, and are easy to do with the Splunk SDK for Python. Our custom search command is named **pasgetuserinfo** as shown in the following code snippet from the `user_activity.xml` file:

```
<search id = "user_info_search">
  <query>
    | pasgetuserinfo user=$user|s$
  </query>
</search>
```

DEV

The test repo can be found at dev.splunk.com/goto/pastestrepo

We implement this custom command in the **PAS Get User Information** add-on (you can find this sample in the test repository). The **commands.conf** file specifies the name of the custom command as shown in the following configuration snippet:

```
# [commands.conf]($SPLUNK_HOME/etc/system/README/commands.conf.spec)
[defaults]
[pasgetuserinfo]
filename = pasgetuserinfo.py
supports_getinfo = true
supports_rawargs = true
outputheader = true
```

This configuration file identifies the Python source file, **pasgetuserinfo.py**, that implements the custom event generating command. The following code sample shows the complete implementation of the **pasgetuserinfo** command:

```
import requests
import json
import sys, time
from splunklib.searchcommands import \
  dispatch, GeneratingCommand, Configuration, Option, validators
@Configuration()
class PasGetUserInfoCommand(GeneratingCommand):
  user = Option(require=True)

  def generate(self):
    url = 'http://localhost:5000/user_list/api/v1.0/users/' + self.user
    data = requests.get(url).json()
    if 'user' in data:
      # Known user.
      row = {}
      for k, v in data['user'].iteritems():
        row[str(k)] = str(v)
      yield row
    else:
      # Unknown user. Return no data.
      pass
dispatch(PasGetUserInfoCommand, sys.argv, sys.stdin, sys.stdout, __name__)
```

Notice how this code imports the **GeneratingCommand**, **Configuration**, and **Option** classes from the **splunklib.searchcommands** module in the Splunk SDK for Python. We chose a **GeneratingCommand** because we are manufacturing events. The **generate** method calls our mock REST API endpoint passing the value of the **user** option of the custom command. If the REST API recognizes the user, it returns a JSON string containing the user data. The **generate** method then returns this data as a dictionary instance. To use a real directory service, we can replace the code in the **generate** method with code to query the real service and return the data in a Python dictionary instance.

The JavaScript code behind the **User Activity** dashboard formats the data from the custom search command to display in the panel.

For more information about how to implement custom search commands in Python, see "How to create custom search commands."

USING STATEFUL CONFIGURATION DATA IN THE PAS APP

In the PAS app, the **Suspicious Activity** panel and the donut charts in the **Policy Violations** panel on the **Summary** dashboard make use of configuration data that the user creates the first time they use the app. The section "Sharing code between dashboards" in the chapter "Adding code: using JavaScript and Search Processing Language" describes how we direct the user to the **Setup** dashboard the first time they access the PAS app for providing this data. The following screenshot shows the **Setup** dashboard and the data the user must create:

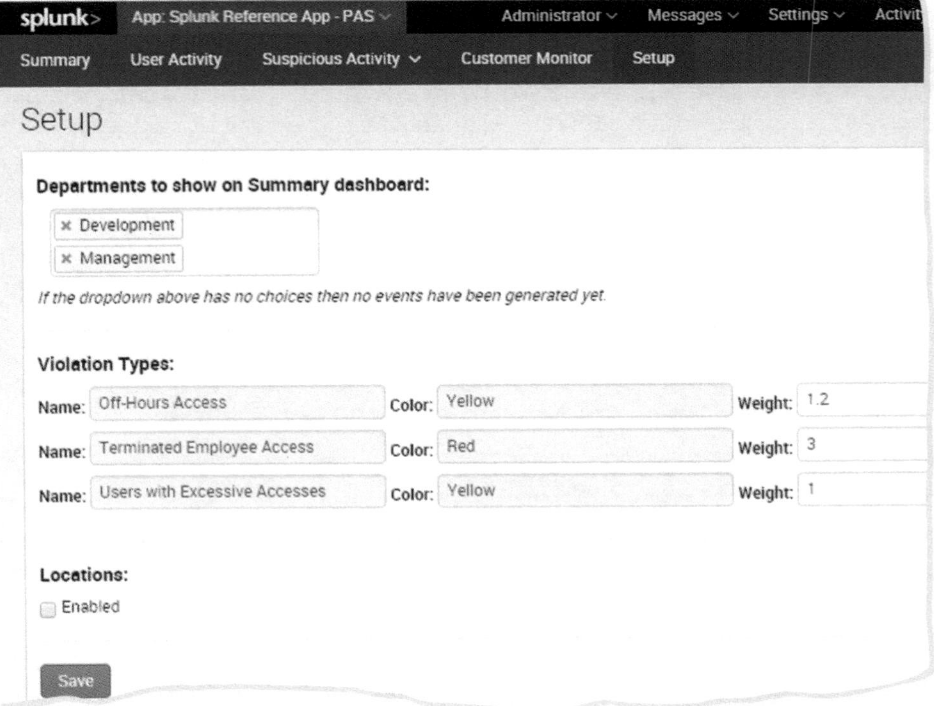

On this dashboard, the user can select the departments for which they want to see a donut chart, and provide definitions of the policy violations that should appear in the list of suspicious activities. Each policy violation type has a name, a color, and a weight that the calculations behind the visualizations use. The following screenshot from the **Summary** dashboard shows the donut charts for the **Development** and **Management** departments selected on the **Setup** dashboard and in the **Violation Types** from the **Setup** dashboard in the **Suspicious Activity** panel:

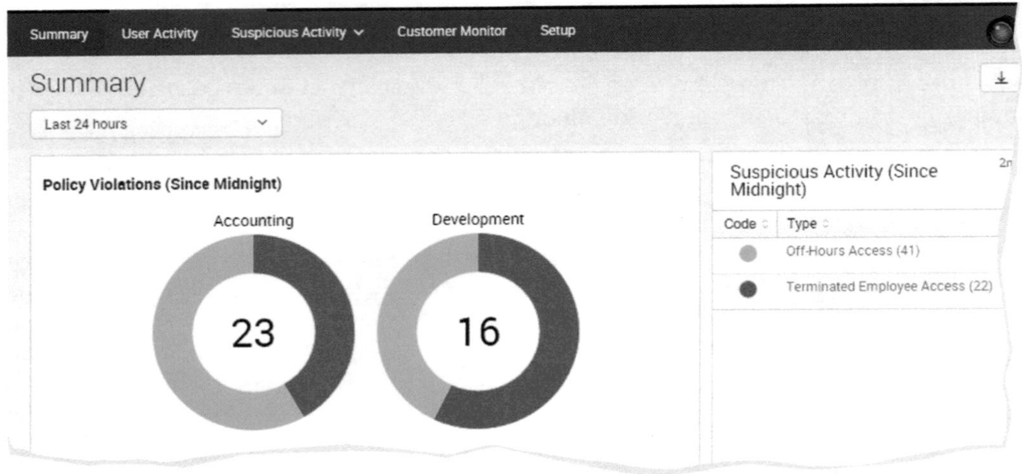

We need a mechanism to persist the configuration data the user enters on the **Setup** dashboard so it can be read by the code that renders the donuts on the **Summary** dashboard. Historically, custom REST endpoints have been the mechanism used to persist data in a scenario such as this one, and a Splunk Enterprise API is available for accessing your custom endpoint. The App KV Store is a new feature in the version of Splunk Enterprise we are using that provides a more robust and easy to use data storage management than custom REST endpoints App KV Store can even interface to a database using convenient REST operations, although, this is not one of our requirements for the PAS app. Additionally, App KV Store has built-in support for a distributed architecture of search head clusters: a considerable amount of coding is needed to add this level of functionality to a custom REST endpoint solution. All the functionality we need comes with Splunk Enterprise, therefore we decided to use App KV Store to persist our configuration data. No additional coding is needed beyond defining your data collection and invoking the App KV Store REST operations.

DEV

We use the KV Store to persist global configuration data shared by all users of the PAS app. It is possible to use the KV Store to persist per-user data.

The **Setup** dashboard uses the KV Store feature in Splunk Enterprise to persist the setup data in a collection named **ri_setup_coll** that we define in the `collections.conf` file as shown in the following configuration snippet.

```
[ri_setup_coll]
enforceTypes = true
field.departments = array
[violation_types]
enforceTypes = true
field.id = string
field.title = string
field.color = string
field.weight = number
```

We use two different collections, one for departments and one for violation types to make it easier to access this data in a search. Notice how we use arrays to store the list of departments and the policy violation types to accommodate a variable number of entries in each case. We then use a `transforms.conf` file to make the setup data in the KV store available to our searches:

```
[ri_setup]
external_type = kvstore
collection = ri_setup_coll
fields_list = departments
[violation_types]
external_type = kvstore
collection = violation_types
fields_list = id,title,color,weight
```

Now we can use the setup data in the searches behind the visualizations on the **Summary** dashboard. For example, the search **policy_violations_search** in the `summary.xml` file which extracts the data for both the donut visualizations and the **Suspicious Activity** panel includes the following **lookup** clause to use the setup data:

```
| lookup violation_types id AS ViolationType
            OUTPUTNEW title AS ViolationTypeTitle,
                      color AS ViolationColor,
                      weight AS ViolationWeight,
```

ARCH

A lookup in SPL acts like an outer join in SQL.

The **policy_violations_color_summary** search that retrieves the data for the donut visualizations uses the following **join** clause to filter the data based on the departments the user selected on the **Setup** dashboard:

```
| join type=inner department [ | inputlookup ri_setup
                               | fields departments
                               | mvexpand departments
                               | rename departments as department ]
```

The code in the **setup.js** file shows how we persist the configuration data. First we load the **kvstore** module (we have placed the library file **kvstore.js** in our components folder):

```
require([
  'splunkjs/ready!',
  'splunkjs/mvc/simplexml/ready!',
  'underscore',
  '../app/pas_ref_app/components/kvstore_backbone/kvstore',
  'splunkjs/mvc/multidropdownview'
```

Then we extend the standard **KVStore.Model** class (which is a backbone model) to include the configuration data we define in the `collections.conf` file:

```
var SetupModel = KVStore.Model.extend({
  collectionName: 'ri_setup_coll'
});
var ViolationTypeModel = KVStore.Model.extend({
  collectionName: 'violation_types'
});
var ViolationTypeCollection = KVStore.Collection.extend({
  collectionName: 'violation_types',
  model: ViolationTypeModel
});
```

Finally, we can populate a model instance and persist it using the **save** function. For example:

```
var newSetupData = {
  departments: departmentsDropdown.val()
};
...
new SetupModel()
...
newSetupModel.save(newSetupData)
```

At a later stage in the project we add a new field to the KV store to let a user toggle the display of the learning tip icons. To make this change we add a new field named **learningTipsEnabled** in the **collections.conf** file, add a new checkbox in the **setup.xml** file, and some additional code in **setup.js** to initialize and save the field value. To use the **learningTipsEnabled** configuration setting in the app, we read the value using code in the **dashboard.js** file and control the visibility of the learning tip icons using CSS. For more information about the dashboard.js and dashboard.css files, see the chapter "UI and visualizations: what the apps look like."

DEV

We also added some utility code that replaces a complete collection of data in the KV store. See the function setCollectionData in the setup.js file for more details.

For more information about how we restrict access to the KV Store, see the chapter "Packaging and deployment: reaching our destination" in this guide.

SEARCH MANAGERS THAT DON'T RETURN RESULTS

It's possible in some circumstances that the **user_info_search** on the **User Activity** dashboard does not return any results. We noticed that in this case that the **on("data", ...** callback function is not being invoked. We have modified the code in the user_info.js file to work round this problem as shown in the following code sample:

```
userInfoSearch.data("results", {
  // HACK: By default, no "data" event is fired when no results are
  //       found. Override so that it does fire in this case.
  condition: function(manager, job) {
    return (job.properties() || {}).isDone;
  }
}).on("data", function(resultsModel) {
  var rows = resultsModel.data().rows;
  if (rows.length === 0) {
    view.html("No user information found.");
  } else { ...
```

WHAT DID WE LEARN?

This section summarizes some of the key lessons learned while we were working with the data our apps use.

- You can use a modular input to pull in events from external systems.
- You can author modular inputs in several languages including JavaScript.
- You can store state in a modular input by writing to a file.
- If you are using a modular input written in JavaScript, you can instrument your code using methods such as **error** and **info** of the **ModularInputs.Logger** class. You search for these log messages in the **_internal** index in Splunk itself.
- You can store state in a modular input by writing to a file.
- You can use the CIM to provide a standard way to search against disparate sources of data. You can map existing and future sources to the CIM using aliases, extractions, event types, and tags.
- You can create your own data models to provide a richer mapping for querying your data.
- You can easily extend a data model to support additional search requirements.
- You can use the KV store to persist data that can then be referenced in searches.

- You learned how to delete an index completely and how to delete all the entries in an index. Both are useful when testing an app.
- You need to know your data to design effective apps. Different users of your app have different data and must be able to configure the app to make it work for them.

More information

To see the Auth0 app on the Splunk Apps site dev.splunk.com/goto/auth0app.

For more information about creating modular inputs using JavaScript, see "How to work with modular inputs in the Splunk SDK for JavaScript" at: dev.splunk.com/goto/modular-inputs.

For information about the **Logger** class see: dev.splunk.com/goto/loggerclass.

For information about the way intervals work in Splunk Enterprise, see "Data checkpoints" at: dev.splunk.com/goto/datacheckpoints.

For information about the Change Analysis CIM data model see: dev.splunk.com/goto/changeanalysiscim.

For more information about other Splunk CIM data models, see "Data Models" at: dev.splunk.com/goto/cimmanual.

Get the Splunk CIM add-on from: dev.splunk.com/goto/splunkcim.

To learn to accelerate data models to improve query performance see: dev.splunk.com/goto/accelerateddatamodels.

To enable data model acceleration, see: dev.splunk.com/goto/enabledatamodelacc.

To learn how to use tscollect see: dev.splunk.com/goto/tscollect.

For more information on improving the performance of Splunk Enterprise using the props.conf file see: dev.splunk.com/goto/propsconf.

For more information on rebuilding an index, see "Remove indexes and indexed data" at: dev.splunk.com/goto/removeindex.

For more information about data model acceleration, see "Accelerate data models" at: dev.splunk.com/goto/accelerateddatamodels.

For more information about using reports, see "About reports" at: dev.splunk.com/goto/aboutreports.

For more information about accelerated data, see "Manage report acceleration" and "Accelerate reports" at: dev.splunk.com/goto/managereportacceleration and dev.splunk.com/goto/acceleratereports.

For more information about scheduling reports, see "Schedule reports" at: dev.splunk.com/goto/schedulereports.

For more information about the **loadjob** command, see: dev.splunk.com/goto/loadjobref.

To learn how we use a custom search command to pull the data from our simulated directory service see: dev.splunk.com/goto/customsearchcommand.

To see the **PAS Get User Information** sample app, see the test repository at: dev.splunk.com/goto/pastestrepo.

For more information about how to implement custom search commands in Python, see "How to create custom search commands" at: dev.splunk.com/goto/createcustomsearch.

For more information on using custom REST endpoints to persist data see: dev.splunk.com/goto/customrest.

The App KV Store provides a more robust and easy to use data storage management than custom REST endpoints. To learn more see: dev.splunk.com/goto/appkvstore.

5

Adding code: using JavaScript and Search Processing Language

Practically everything in Splunk Enterprise is driven by searches behind the scenes. Searches are truly the workhorses of Splunk apps. Splunk Enterprise has its own search processing language, SPL. It includes a wide variety of useful commands: from those that correlate events and calculate statistics to those that generate, manipulate, reformat and enrich your data, build visualizations, and more.

DEV

In a nutshell, a search is a series of commands and arguments. Commands are chained together with a pipe "|" character to indicate that the output of one command feeds into the next command on the right.

Whether you are new to the Splunk search language or not the Splunk > Quick Reference Guide will be helpful. We used it as a reference frequently while creating the PAS app. In addition, Exploring Splunk offers a primer into SPL and a collection of recipes.

We chose to use the Simple XML with extensions model to build the PAS app. Therefore, we use JavaScript to add in the extension logic and behavior where necessary. This chapter also discusses some of the searches we define using the Splunk® search processing language (SPL™).

ARCH

SPL is also extensible. You can define your own search commands for custom processing, data generation, and calculations. For more information, see the "Write Custom Search Commands" section in the Search Tutorial.

CASE STUDY: BUILDING A COMPLEX QUERY WITH LOOKUPS AND TIME DATA OVERLAYS

During our journey, one of the stories we implemented involved creating a new dashboard named **Off-Hours Document Access**. The intent of this dashboard is to let a user identify possible suspicious attempts to access the document repository, such as attempts by an employee to access the repository outside of their normal working hours. This requires some information that is not included in the log files. The logs record when an employee tried to access the repository and the status of the attempt (succeeded/failed), but not the employee's work schedule. We need to look up each employee's normal work schedule and correlate it with the information in the log file. We maintain this information in a separate list of employees: for this app, we've chosen to use a CSV file as our employee database, but in a real deployment we would look up this data in an external system or store the information in the KV store and use a batch process to keep it up to date with information from the external system. To package the employee data for use in the PAS app, we created a new Splunk app called **pas_hr_info** that contains the **employee_details.csv** file and a **transforms.conf** file to define the name of the lookup:

```
[employee_details]
filename = employee_details.csv
```

For more information about defining a lookup in a static file, see Configure field lookups.

The following shows some sample records from the data in the **employee_details.csv** file:

```
date,user,shift_start,shift_end,workdays,status
08/01/2014,mbailey,17,1,"Mon,Tue,Wed,Thu,Fri",terminated
09/01/2014,kadams,17,1,"Mon,Tue,Wed,Thu,Fri",active
09/01/2014,caustin,1,9,"Mon,Tue,Wed,Thu,Fri",active
```

The **shift_start** and **shift_end** columns show the hour the employee starts and stops work. Notice how some of the shifts span midnight into the next day. The **status** column indicates the employment status. Later we will create a search and visualization to help identify attempts to access to the repository by terminated employees.

When we have our employee data, our query must relate the time the user tried to access the repository to the employee's official working hours to identify out-of-hours access.

The data model in the main PAS app now references the employee details lookup data to make it available in pivot searches. The following screenshot shows the detail of how the data model performs the lookup:

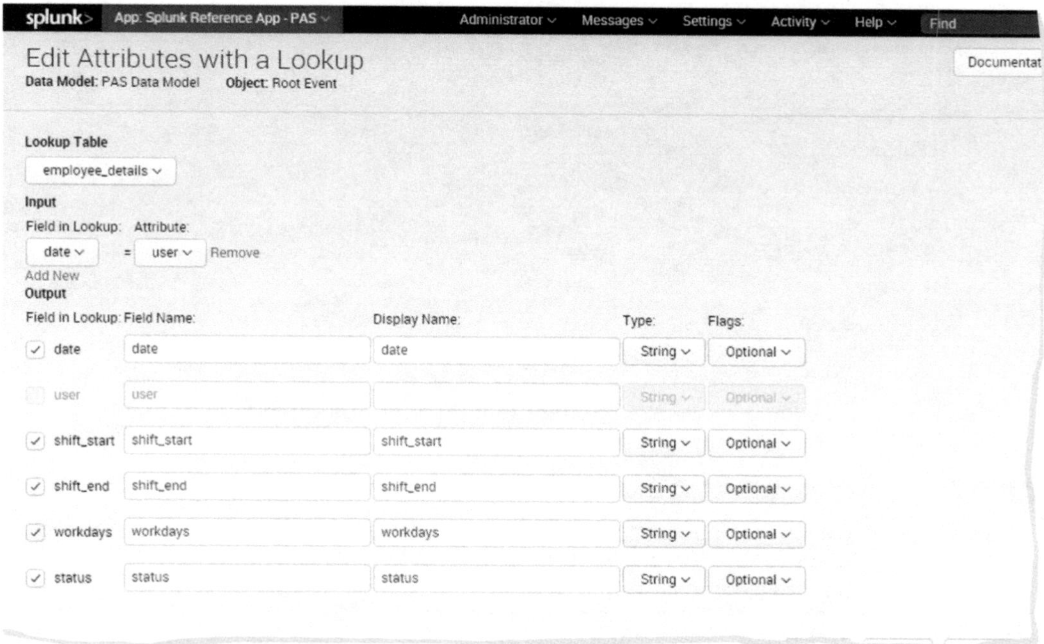

The data model also includes several eval expressions that use the lookup data to determine if a particular document access by an employee is outside of their normal working hours. Notice how some **eval expressions** refer to others:

FIELD NAME	EVAL EXPRESSION
overnight	`if(shift_start>shift_end,1,0)`
hour	`tonumber(strftime(_time,"%H"))`
valid_time	`if((overnight == 1 AND (hour > = shift_start OR hour < = shift_end)) OR (overnight == 0 AND hour> = shift_start AND hour<shift_ end),1,0)`
shift_day	`strftime(if(overnight == 1 AND hour < shift_end,relative_ time(_time,"-1d"),_time),"%a")`
workdays_mv	`split(workdays,",")`
valid_day	`mvfind(workdays_mv,shift_day)`
valid_time_access	`if(valid_time == 1 AND valid_day> = 0,1,0)`

The **Invalid_Time_Access** child event in the data model uses the calculated **valid_time_ access** attribute as the constraint to identify the events that represent out of hours access attempts:

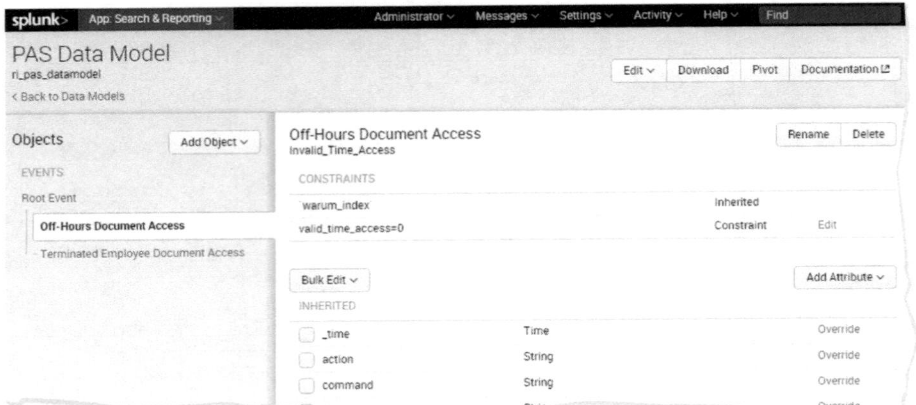

ARCH

It's better to perform any calculations in the SPL rather than in your JavaScript code. It's faster and easier to maintain.

The searches in the **Off-Hours Document Access** dashboard can now use the data model to search for out of hours access attempts, for example:

```
<chart>
  <title>Documents Accessed Outside Working Hours</title>
  <searchString>| pivot ri_pas_datamodel Invalid_Time_Access count(Invalid_Time_Access) AS count
  SPLITROW _time AS _time PERIOD auto SORT 0 _time ROWSUMMARY 0 COLSUMMARY 0 NUMCOLS 0 SHOWOTHER 1
  </searchString>
  <option name = "charting.chart">line</option>
</chart>
```

The following screenshot shows an example of the chart that snippet above renders:

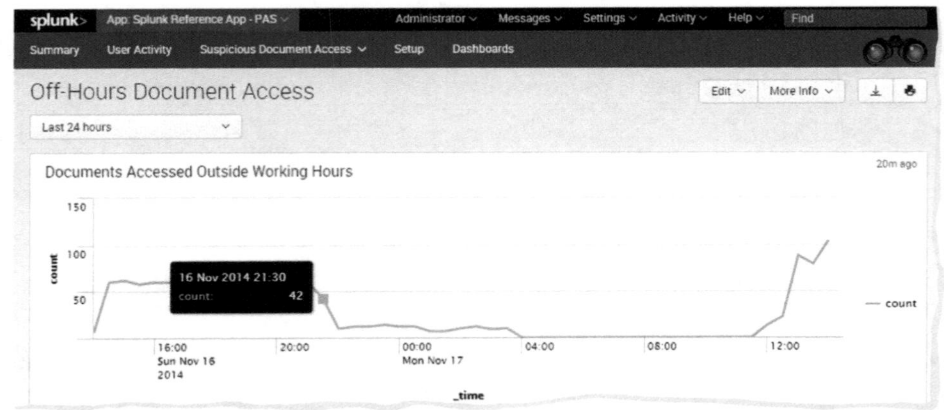

DEV

If you are testing or debugging a complex search that references app specific objects such as data models, be sure to use the **Search** dashboard in your app, rather than the generic one in the Splunk **Search & Reporting** app. In the PAS app, we can reach the **Search** dashboard at this address: http://localhost:8000/en-US/app/pas_ref_app/search. This is because the knowledge objects are saved in the app that you are using.

COMBINING PIVOTS WITH SEARCHES

During our journey we uncovered a requirement to combine the results from several **pivot** searches against our data model with several standard searches into an aggregate set of results to use in a single visualization. We identified several possible approaches: write a search string that combines the pivots and regular searches, convert the regular searches to pivots and then aggregate all the pivots, or convert the pivots to regular searches and combine all the regular searches.

Combining pivots with searches in a single search

We can combine pivots together using the following approach. Given these two pivots:

```
| pivot ri_pas_datamodel Invalid_Time_Access count(Invalid_Time_Access) AS count
  SPLITROW _time AS _time
| pivot ri_pas_datamodel Terminated_Access count(Terminated_Access) AS count SPLITROW _time AS _time
```

Then provided the data model is accelerated, we can combine them using the following technique:

```
| tstats count from datamodel = ri_pas_datamodel where nodename = Invalid_Time_Access OR nodename =
Terminate_Access groupby nodename _time span = auto | …
```

For more information on the **tsats** command, see Splunk Search Command Reference.

We could then combine this with a regular search by using **"|append []"** command to attach the regular query.

However, it is difficult to identify opportunities for optimizing this search and this approach is best used to maintain backwards compatibility within an application when developers have used different approaches (pivots and regular searches) in the past to build dashboards.

Converting everything to regular searches

We could convert our existing pivots to regular searches and then combine all the regular searches together. However, in our scenario we thought that this would result in a complex search that would be difficult to optimize manually.

Converting everything to pivots

The option we chose was to convert everything to pivots. This required some changes to our data model, but then it was easier to create the query that aggregates all the results using the technique shown previously. For the PAS app, optimizing for performance is more important than maintaining internal backwards compatibility.

Example: Combining multiple searches

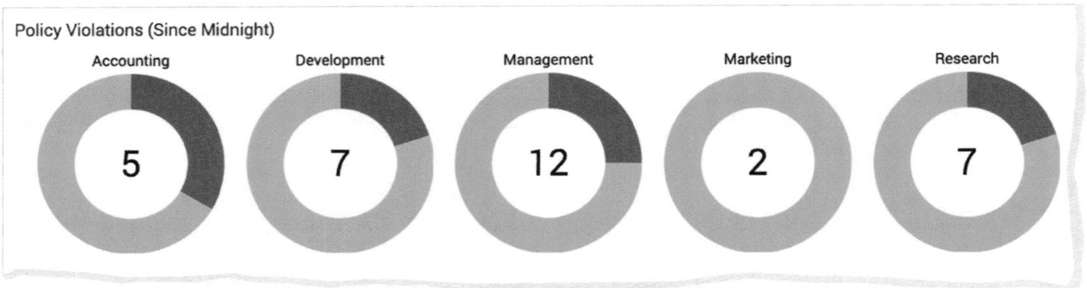

The search that drives the donut visualization on the summary screen is an example of a complex search that combines results from multiple sources. We converted the main searches to pivots before combining them together. The base search in the **`summary.xml`** file combines the results from three pivot commands by using the append command and then performs a look up for additional information about the policy violations. Each pivot searches for different policy violation types: one for out of hours access, one for access attempts by terminated employees, and one for excessive access requests by an employee.

```
<search id = "policy_violations_search">
  <query>
              | pivot ri_pas_datamodel Invalid_Time_Access SPLITROW department
                count(Invalid_Time_Access) as Invalid_Time_Access
              | eval ViolationType = "Invalid_Time_Access"
              | rename Invalid_Time_Access as ViolationCount
              | append [
                | pivot ri_pas_datamodel Terminated_Access
                  SPLITROW department count(Terminated_Access) as Terminated_Access
                | eval ViolationType = "Terminated_Access"
                | rename Terminated_Access as ViolationCount
              ]
              | append [
                | search tag = pas tag = change tag = audit
                | fields _time, user
                | bucket _time span = 1h
                | stats count as ops by _time, user
                | where ops! = 0
                | stats stdev(ops) as SD, avg(ops) as MEAN, latest(ops) as LAST_OPS by user
                | where LAST_OPS > (MEAN + SD*1.2)
                | lookup employee_details user
                | stats count as ViolationCount by department
                | eval ViolationType = "Excessive_Access"
              ]
    | lookup violation_info ViolationType
    | eval TotalViolationWeight = ViolationCount*ViolationWeight
  </query>
  <earliest>@d</earliest>
  <latest>now</latest>
</search>
```

The lookup determines the color and weight of each violation type.

DEV

Formatting the search string across multiple lines and aligning similar elements makes it much easier to read, understand, and maintain.

The second part of the query prepares the data for the visualization calculating the proportion of each color to display for each department along with the total value to display in the center of each donut:

```
<search id = "policy_violations_color_summary" base = "policy_violations_search">
  <query>
    | stats sum(TotalViolationWeight) as TotalWeight,
            sum(ViolationCount)       as ViolationCount
      by department, ViolationColor

    | eval NumYellows = if(ViolationColor = "Yellow", ViolationCount, 0)
    | eval NumReds =    if(ViolationColor = "Red",    ViolationCount, 0)
    | stats sum(NumReds)     as NumReds,
            sum(NumYellows)  as NumYellows,
            sum(TotalWeight) as TotalWeight
      by department
    | table department, NumYellows, NumReds, TotalWeight
  </query>
  <earliest>@d</earliest>
  <latest>now</latest>
</search>
```

DEV

This search uses the table command to ensure that the query returns the fields in a specific order. The visualization that depends on this query makes assumptions about the field order.

For more information about how the donut control works and how it uses the data from this query, see the section "*Using a third-party visualization library (take two, creating the donut)*" in the chapter UI and visualizations: what the apps look like.

EXAMPLE: OPTIMIZING A SEARCH

The following code snippet shows the third search in the **policy_violations_search** discussed in the previous section:

```
| search tag = pas tag = change tag = audit
  | fields _time, user
  | bucket _time span = 1h
  | stats count as ops by _time, user
  | where ops! = 0
  | stats stdev(ops) as SD, avg(ops) as MEAN, latest(ops) as LAST_OPS by user
  | where LAST_OPS > (MEAN + SD*1.2)
  | lookup employee_details user
  | stats count as ViolationCount by department
  | eval ViolationType = "Excessive_Access"
```

This illustrates several useful optimizations:

- We use the **fields** command to eliminate, as soon as possible, as many columns as we can from the search pipeline.
- We use the **fields** command, and not the **table** command, to minimize the amount of data brought over the network in a distributed deployment.
- The **stats** command reduces the number of events in the search pipeline.
- The **where ops!=0** removes any empty buckets from the pipeline.
- When we begin our calculations using the **stdev** function, we have already reduced the amount of data we are working with as much as possible.
- We have removed a number of **eval** operations from earlier iterations of the query design and inlined them.

ARCH

You can often gain insight into how Splunk Enterprise executes a search by using the job inspector. In the Splunk Web UI, visit the Jobs page from the Activity menu.

LOADING CUSTOM JAVASCRIPT CODE

The PAS app uses JavaScript extensions to the Simple XML model for building dashboards and uses several different types of JavaScript resources. These range from relatively simple JavaScript code written by us and attached to a specific dashboard, to complex, third-party libraries and components that we have integrated with our code.

Attaching JavaScript to a Simple XML dashboard

Many of our dashboards in the PAS app use JavaScript extensions to add behavior and functionality. For example, the **Summary** dashboard uses JavaScript code in the `summary.js` file. The following code snippet from `summary.xml` shows how we attach the page specific JavaScript file to this dashboard using the **script** attribute of the **form** tag:

```
<form script = "summary.js" stylesheet = "summary.css, tagmanager.css">
```

The location of the `summary.js` file is in the `appserver/static` folder. We use a naming convention (`summary.xml`, `summary.js`, and `summary.css`) to make it easy to identify which resources in the `appserver/static` folder are associated with which Simple XML dashboards in the `default/data/ui/views` folder.

In our JavaScript extension code, we typically start with code like this:

```
require([
  "splunkjs/ready!"
], function(
  …
```

DEV

RequireJS is a popular JavaScript file and module loader, optimized for in-browser use. For more information, see requirejs.org.

The purpose of this code is to ensure that the SplunkJS library is fully loaded before we execute any of our own code that may depend on the library being available. In some cases (for example in **user_activity.js**) the **require** function looks like this:

```
require([
  "splunkjs/ready!",
  "splunkjs/mvc/simplexml/ready!"
], function(
  …
```

The second **ready!** Is to ensure that the code waits for all of the panels on the Simple XML dashboard to load. This is useful if you encounter JavaScript errors when you execute code to obtain a reference to a panel such as the following:

```
var zoomSearch = mvc.Components.get("zoom_search");
```

Integrating with a third-party JavaScript component

We want to enhance the flexibility of the **Summary** screen by enabling a user to filter the data on the dashboard without any knowledge of the Splunk search syntax. For example, an investigator might want to exclude a particular heavily used document from the results because it is making it hard to see what's happening with other documents. To implement this feature, we first added a context menu to the **Top Documents** and **Top Users** panel as shown in the following screenshot:

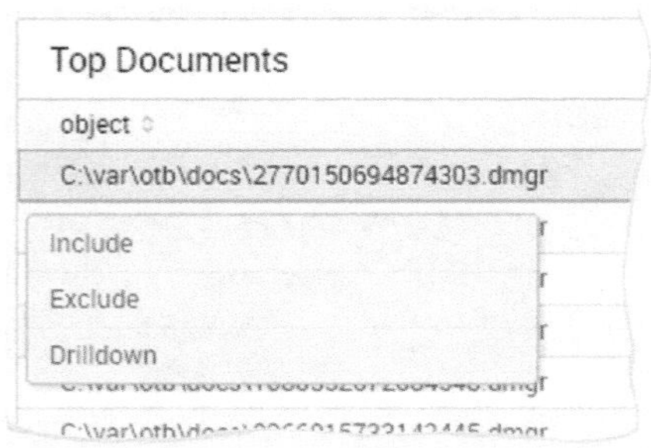

After the user clicks on the **Exclude** option, the dashboard looks like this showing the filter as a tag in the **Filter Criteria** text box:

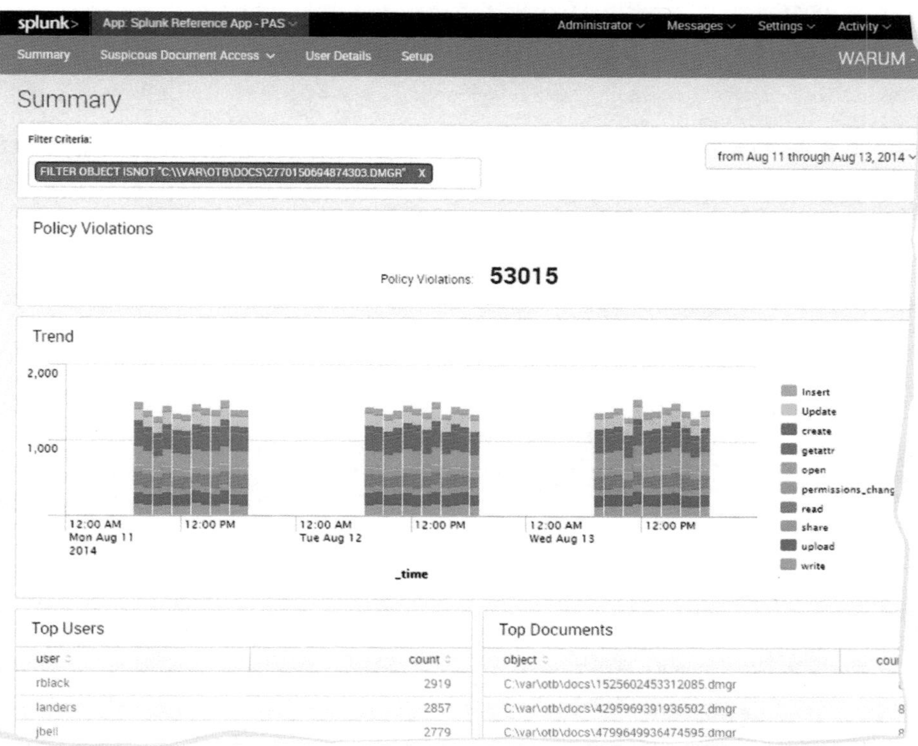

The **Filter Criteria** shows the details of the filter applied, and the search results no longer include the document. The dashboard now substitutes the filter token values (**$filter$** and **$exclude$**) in the **trend-search** search manager:

```
pivot ri_pas_datamodel Root_Event count(Root_Event) AS count SPLITROW _time AS
  _time PERIOD auto SPLITCOL command FILTER command isNotNull $filter$ $exclude$
  SORT 0 _time ROWSUMMARY 0 COLSUMMARY 0 NUMCOLS 10 SHOWOTHER 0
```

In this example, the dashboard now runs the following search to return the results:

```
pivot ri_pas_datamodel Root_Event count(Root_Event) AS count SPLITROW _time AS
  _time PERIOD auto SPLITCOL command FILTER command isNotNull
  FILTER object isNot "C:\\var\otb\docs\2770150694874303.dmgr"
  SORT 0 _time ROWSUMMARY 0 COLSUMMARY 0 NUMCOLS 10 SHOWOTHER 0
```

In the JavaScript extension, **summary.js**, we initialize and define the context menus for the bar chart and the two tables as shown in the following code snippet:

```
context.init({preventDoubleContext: false});
context.attachToChart(barchart, menuData);
context.attachToTable(user_table, menuData);
context.attachToTable(document_table, menuData);
```

The **context** object is defined in the **context.js** file we added to the app in the **static** folder (the code in **summary.js** does load this file directly: **summary.js** uses the **require** function to load **filter_component.js**, which in turn uses the **require** function to load **context.js**). You can learn more about the open source **Context.js** script at lab.jakiestfu.com/contextjs.

Loading the custom component

The extension **summary.js** also references two other JavaScript source files: **filter_component.js** and **tagmanager.js. The filter_component.js** file contains custom code written for the PAS app to manage the token values **$filter$** and **$exclude$** that appear in the search manager instances on the dashboard. The code in the **filter_component.js** file uses the Tags Manager jQuery plugin to display the filter values on the dashboard in the **Filter Criteria** text box. Tags Manager (welldonethings.com/tags/manager/v3) is an open source jQuery plugin for displaying a list of tags, letting a user edit the tag list, and that offers an API for managing the tag list programmatically.

These third-party JavaScript components make it easy to add custom behavior to the built-in visualizations. In this example, by adding a context menu to let an investigator filter the results in the screen without any knowledge of the Splunk Enterprise search syntax.

During this stage of the journey, we add a custom component to the **Summary** dashboard that provides filtering capabilities to the user. We use the following code to ensure the page loads the necessary JavaScript files and their dependencies:

```
require.config({
  paths: {
    "tagmanager": "../app/pas_ref_app/tagmanager",
  },
  shim: {
    "tagmanager": {
      deps: ["jquery"]
    }
  }
});
require([
  "splunkjs/ready!",
  "splunkjs/mvc/simplexml/ready!",
  "underscore",
  "../app/pas_ref_app/filter_component"
], function(...
```

The **require** function loads our custom filter component (along with three other modules) that is defined in the file `filter_component.js`. Notice the path we need to use (../app/pas_ref_app) to correctly load this file from the appserver/static folder. We have written our filter component module to be compatible with the **require.js** open source module loader. However, the third-party **tagmanager** module (a jQuery plugin) is not compatible with **require.js.** To work around this, we use **require.config** to define a fake compatible module, named **tagmanager,** that wraps the incompatible third-party module.

DEV

The **require.config** function is available as part of the SplunkJS Stack. It is part of the **require.js** open source module loader. You can find out more at requirejs.org.

Working with tokens in a custom component

The file **user_activity.js** illustrates how our custom component can interact with the tokens on the dashboard. In a Simple XML dashboard there are two token models: the "default" token model substitutes token values into most visualizations on the page and the "submitted" token model substitutes token values into most search expressions on the page. For our app, we would like to ignore this distinction. If we set the token **$trendTime.earliest$** to a value we want it to update everywhere, in searches and visualizations. Therefore, we define a fake token model called **tokens** that behaves like the regular default and submitted models, except that when we write to it, it updates both models. If we read from it, it reads from the default model. This enables us to simplify any code that just needs to update the tokens in both token models. The **user_activity.js** file includes the following façade definition to implement this behavior:

```
var defaultTokens = mvc.Components.get("default");
var submittedTokens = mvc.Components.get("submitted");
var tokens = {
  get: function(tokenName) {
    return defaultTokens.get(tokenName);
  },

  set: function(tokenName, tokenValue) {
    defaultTokens.set(tokenName, tokenValue);
    submittedTokens.set(tokenName, tokenValue);
  },
  on: function(eventName, callback) {
    defaultTokens.on(eventName, callback);
  }
};
```

On the **User Activity** dashboard, we then need to propagate token values to ensure that all the visualizations display correctly:

```
tokens.set({
  "trendTime.earliest": tokens.get("time.earliest"),
  "trendTime.latest": tokens.get("time.latest")
});
tokens.on("change:time.earliest change:time.latest", function(model, value) {
  tokens.set({
    "trendTime.earliest": tokens.get("time.earliest"),
    "trendTime.latest": tokens.get("time.latest")
  });
});
```

Working around a bug in a library

The JavaScript extension code for the **User Activity** dashboard contains some slightly unusual **require** related code to work around a bug in the **css!** plugin that's bundled with Splunk Enterprise. Originally, this extension loaded the **Calendar Heatmap** control using the following code, using the standard path prefix **../app/pas_ref_app:**

```
require([
  "splunkjs/ready!",
  "splunkjs/mvc/simplexml/ready!",
  "../app/pas_ref_app/components/calendarheatmap/calendarheatmap"
], function(
  mvc,
  ignored,
  CalendarHeatMap
) ...
```

However, this caused the **css!** plugin to get confused when you try to directly include a module name that contains "**..**", such as **../app/pas_ref_app/components/calendarheatmap/calendarheatmap**. Our workaround uses a path alias defined in **require.config()** so that the directly included module name, **pas_ref_app/components/calendarheatmap/calendarheatmap**, does not contain "**..**":

```
require.config({
  paths: {
    "pas_ref_app": "../app/pas_ref_app"
  }
});
require([
  "splunkjs/ready!",
  "splunkjs/mvc/simplexml/ready!",
  "pas_ref_app/components/calendarheatmap/calendarheatmap"
], function(
  mvc,
  ignored,
  CalendarHeatMap
) ...
```

Making a JavaScript file "require compatible"

Originally, the `filter_component.js` file was a simple JavaScript file that contained several function definitions such as:

- `function generateFilterComponent(mvc) { ... }`
- `function filter(tokens, field_name, field_value) { ... }`
- `function exclude(tokens, field_name, field_value) { ... }`
- `function drilldown(tokens, base_search, field_name, field_value, earliest, latest) { ... }`

The **summary.js** file used the following code to load filter_component.js and its dependencies:

```
require.config({
  paths: {
    "tagmanager": "../app/pas_ref_app/tagmanager",
    "filter_component": "../app/pas_ref_app/filter_component"
  },
  shim: {
    "filter_component": {
      deps: [
        "splunkjs/mvc/timerangeview",
        "splunkjs/mvc/radiogroupview",
        "splunkjs/mvc/textinputview",
        "../app/pas_ref_app/context",
        "tagmanager"
      ]
    },
    "tagmanager": {
      deps: ["jquery"]
    }
  }
});
require([
  "splunkjs/ready!",
  "splunkjs/mvc/simplexml/ready!",
  "underscore",
  "filter_component"
], function( ...
```

In addition to the complexity of this code, it is not good practice to load functions into the JavaScript global namespace if you can avoid it. Therefore, we have rewritten filter_component.js to be "require compatible." The **summary.js** file now uses the following, much simpler, code to load filter_component.js and its dependencies:

```
require.config({
  paths: {
    "tagmanager": "../app/pas_ref_app/tagmanager",
  },
  shim: {
    "tagmanager": {
      deps: ["jquery"]
    }
  }
});
require([
  "splunkjs/ready!",
  "splunkjs/mvc/simplexml/ready!",
  "underscore",
  "../app/pas_ref_app/filter_component"
], function( ...
```

For this to work, we made some major changes to the structure `filter_component.js` to convert it to a JavaScript module that **require.js** can load directly:

```
define(function(require, exports, module) {
  var mvc = require("splunkjs/mvc/mvc");

  var FilterComponent = {
    initialize: function() {
      ...
    },

    _filter: function(tokens, field_name, field_value) {
      ...
    },

    _exclude: function(tokens, field_name, field_value) {
      ...
    },

    _drilldown: function(tokens, base_search, field_name, field_value, earliest, latest) {
      ...
    }
  };

  return FilterComponent;
});
```

We use this structure to create an **Asynchronous Module Definition** that defines a module that **require.js** can load directly. For more information, see the "WHY AMD?" page on the requirejs.org site.

Incorporating a third-party visualization

Incorporating a third-party visualization in a dashboard is similar to incorporating a custom component. The **User Activity** dashboard includes a calendar heatmap visualization from kamisama.github.io/cal-heatmap. The resources for this visualization are in the **appserver/static/components/calendarheatmap** folder.

The panel on the dashboard is defined in the Simple XML file as shown in the following snippet:

```
<panel id = "activity_levels_panel">
  <html>
    <h3>Activity Levels</h3>
    <div id = "activity_levels"></div>
  </html>
</panel>
```

In the JavaScript extension file **user_activity.js**, the require function loads the resources:

```
require([
  "splunkjs/ready!",
  "splunkjs/mvc/simplexml/ready!",
  "pas_ref_app/components/calendarheatmap/calendarheatmap",
  "jquery",
  "splunkjs/mvc/searchmanager"
], function( ...
```

The following JavaScript code then renders the visualization:

```
new CalendarHeatMap({
  id: "activity_levels",
  managerid: "activity_levels_search",
  domain: "month",
  subDomain: "x_day",
  el: $("#activity_levels")
}).render();
```

Because this visualization was originally designed to work with Splunk Enterprise, it is easy to incorporate: for example, the **managerid** property refers to a Splunk search. However, we made a few changes to the visualization to customize its UI to our requirements by editing the **calendarheatmap.js** file.

SHARING CODE BETWEEN DASHBOARDS

It is possible to attach the same JavaScript file (for example, **setup_check.js**) to every dashboard in the app by adding it to the list of scripts as follows in each Simple XML dashboard file:

```
<form script = "setup_check.js, summary.js" stylesheet = "summary.css, tagmanager.css">
```

In this case it's simpler to add the code to the dashboard.js file that is automatically attached to every dashboard. Therefore, our **form** elements in our Simple XML dashboard files can be a little simpler:

```
<form script = "summary.js" stylesheet = "summary.css, tagmanager.css">
```

However, this did introduce a problem in the PAS app. The code in the **dashboard.js** file checks if the user has completed the app setup process. I If not it redirects the user to the **setup** dashboard. Unfortunately, this caused a loop because when the user visited the **setup** dashboard, the code determined that they had not completed the setup process and redirected them to the **setup** dashboard again. We solved this issue by adding the following code to the **dashboard.js** file to identify if the user is visiting the s**etup** dashboard.

```
var isExemptFromSetupCheck = (window.location.href.indexOf('setup') !== -1);
if (!isExemptFromSetupCheck) {
  ...
}
```

PERIODICALLY RELOADING A VISUALIZATION

We refresh the **Summary** dashboard every five minutes to force the dashboard to reexecute the searches on the page and display up-to-date data. The following code snippet from the **summary.js** file shows how we do this:

```
window.setInterval(function() {
  window.location.reload();
}, 5*60*1000); //time in ms
```

ARCH

We chose to use a scheduled search instead of a Splunk Enterprise real-time search for two reasons. We don't need real-time data (refreshing every five minutes is good enough), and we don't want the performance overhead associated with a real-time search.

USING THE SPLUNK JAVASCRIPT SDK TO INTERROGATE OTHER APPS

The **User Activity** dashboard includes a panel that displays information about user activity associated with different data sources (providers). The following screenshot shows 367 events from the **Application** provider and 1101 events from the **File** provider:

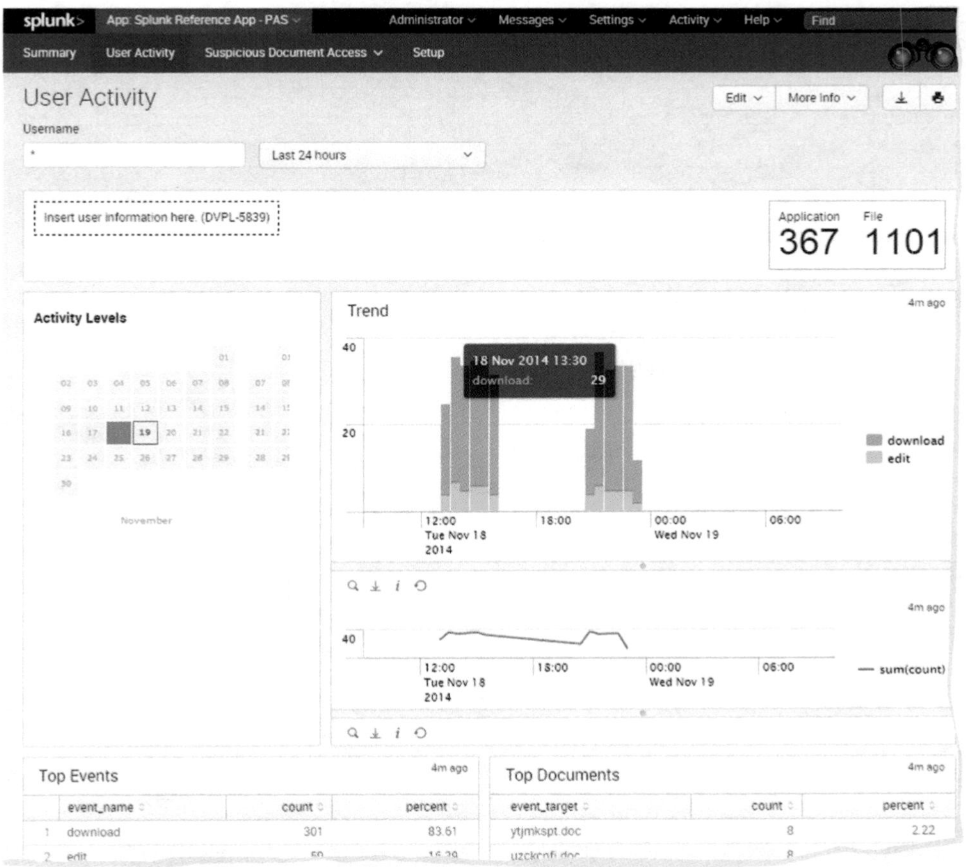

To display this information, the PAS app needs to dynamically discover which other apps are its data providers, and then add the activity count for each one to the panel. In the example shown in the screenshot, you can see information from the **Application** and **File** data provider apps. Our initial approach was to identify provider apps for the main PAS app by adding a special `pas_provider.conf` file to them. This mechanism is one way we can define a data API in Splunk Enterprise, the existence of the special `.conf` file advertises that this app can be used in a particular way by other Splunk apps. Other Splunk apps will make assumptions about the capabilities of this app because of the presence of the special `.conf` file. In the PAS app, the content of this file defines the title that the PAS app uses on the **User Activity** dashboard (**File** and **Application** in this example) and the name of the **sourcetype** provided by the app:

```
[provider]
title = File
sourcetype = ri:pas:file
```

The code in the **provider_stats.js** file performs this task using the Splunk JavaScript API inside the function **loadProviderInformation**. The following code snippets outline this process:

```
// Get access to Splunk objects via the JavaScript SDK
var service = mvc.createService();
// Look for apps that contain a pas_provider.conf file
var appsCollection = service.apps();
```

The next section of code fetches all the installed apps and iterates over the collection looking for those that contain a **pas_provider.conf** file. The parallel logic in this code is hard to follow and we plan, if time permits, to reimplement it using a JavaScript async library:

```
appsCollection.fetch(function(err) {
  ...

  var providerTitleForSourcetype = {};

  var apps = appsCollection.list();
  var numAppsLeft = apps.length;
  _.each(apps, function(app) {
    if (app.properties().disabled) {
      // Avoid querying information about disabled apps because
      // it causes JS errors.
      finishedCheckingApp();
      return;
    }
    var configFileCollection = service.configurations({
      owner: "nobody",
      app: app.name,
      sharing: "app"
    });
    configFileCollection.fetch(function(err) {
      if (err) {
        finishedCheckingApp();
      } else {
        var configFile = configFileCollection.item("pas_provider");
        if (!configFile) {
          // Assume config file is missing, meaning that this app
          // does not represent a PAS provider
          finishedCheckingApp();
```

Here it reads the contents of the pas_provider.conf file and reads the **title** and **sourcetype** values from the **provider** stanza.

```
        } else {
          configFile.fetch(function(err, config) {
            var providerStanza = configFile.item("provider");
            var stanzaContent = providerStanza.properties();

            providerTitleForSourcetype[stanzaContent.sourcetype] = stanzaContent.title;
            finishedCheckingApp();
          });
        }
      }
    });
  });
```

This last function checks if we have processed all the apps.

```
  function finishedCheckingApp() {
    numAppsLeft--;
    if (numAppsLeft === 0) {
      callback(providerTitleForSourcetype);
    }
  }
});
```

This approach lets us add new provider apps, and have our PAS app automatically recognize them and incorporate their data into the **User Activity** dashboard.

Issues with this approach

A security review of our app highlighted some concerns over the approach we implemented using the special **.conf** files to manifest that this app can be used in a particular way by other Splunk apps. The specific issue is that using JavaScript code to cross application boundaries is not a security best practice. Therefore, we had to investigate other solutions and choose an alternative approach to discovering our provider apps from the main PAS app. Furthermore, our original approach relied on the main PAS app running with administrator rights to be able to access other apps' data.

SEC

It's possible for a security administrator to further lock down the behavior of an app. For example, by restricting an app to being allowed to onlyread specific indexes.

Our solution is to use the **sourcetype** in a search result to identify which provider add-on specific events come from:

```
var providerStatsSearch = mvc.Components.get("provider_stats_search");
providerStatsSearch.data("results", {
  condition: function(manager, job) {
    return (job.properties() || {}).isDone;
  }
}).on("data", function(resultsModel) {
  var rows = resultsModel.data().rows;
  if (rows.length === 0) {
    view.html("No data providers found.");
  } else {
    view.html("");
    _.each(rows, function(row) {
      var sourcetype = row[0];
      var count = row[1];

      view.append($(PROVIDER_STAT_BOX_TEMPLATE({
        provider_title: sourcetype,
        event_count: count
      })));
    });
  }
});
```

This approach means that we can delete all the **provider.conf** files from our provider add-on apps.

We also need to change the **provider_stats_search** in the **user_activity.xml** Simple XML file that retrieves all the events for the specified user from the **pas** index to format the data correctly:

```
<search id = "provider_stats_search">
  <query>
    tag = pas tag = change tag = audit user = $user|s$ | stats count by sourcetype
    | replace "ri:pas:file" with "File" in sourcetype
    | replace "ri:pas:database" with "Database" in sourcetype
    | replace "ri:pas:application" with "Application" in sourcetype
    | replace "google:drive:activity" with "Google Drive" in sourcetype
    | table sourcetype, count
  </query>
  <earliest>$time.earliest$</earliest>
  <latest>$time.latest$</latest>
</search>
```

Notice how we use the **replace** command to pretty-print the names of the sourcetypes on the dashboard.

ARCH

This approach to displaying the sourcetype names is not ideal because it hardcodes the original names. If we change a name or add a new provider app, we will need to edit this search.

EXAMPLE: ADDING A NEW PROVIDER ADD-ON APP

At a later stage in the journey, we add a new provider app to our sample. This new provider app pulls information about document access from a Google Drive account. We don't need to make any changes to the main PAS app in order to use it because:

- The main PAS app automatically discovers the new Google Drive app because it is adding entries to the **pas** index. These events have a source type set to **google:drive:activity**.
- The Google Drive app uses mappings to convert its data into the structure that our data model defines.
- The Google Drive app defines a modular input to retrieve data from the Google Drive Activity Stream.

The following snippet shows how we map the data from Google Drive to our data model in the `props.conf` file:

```
[google:drive:activity]
MAX_TIMESTAMP_LOOKAHEAD = 150
NO_BINARY_CHECK = 1
pulldown_type = 1
FIELDALIAS-command = event AS command
FIELDALIAS-object = doc_title AS object
EVAL-action = "updated"
EVAL-status = "success"
EVAL-change-type = "google_drive"
EXTRACT-user = email = (?<user>\w+)
```

The **googledrive_addon** defines a modular input to enable Splunk Enterprise to read log data from Google Drive. We implement this in Python and use the Google Drive Python API to connect to Google Drive and access the log data from the Google Drive activity stream. We define the modular input in the **`googledrive.py`** file. There is some additional custom code in the configure_oauth.py file to support the OAuth authentication scheme that Google Drive uses. The following screenshot shows the modular input configuration page for the app in Splunk Enterprise where the user adds their OAuth credential information:

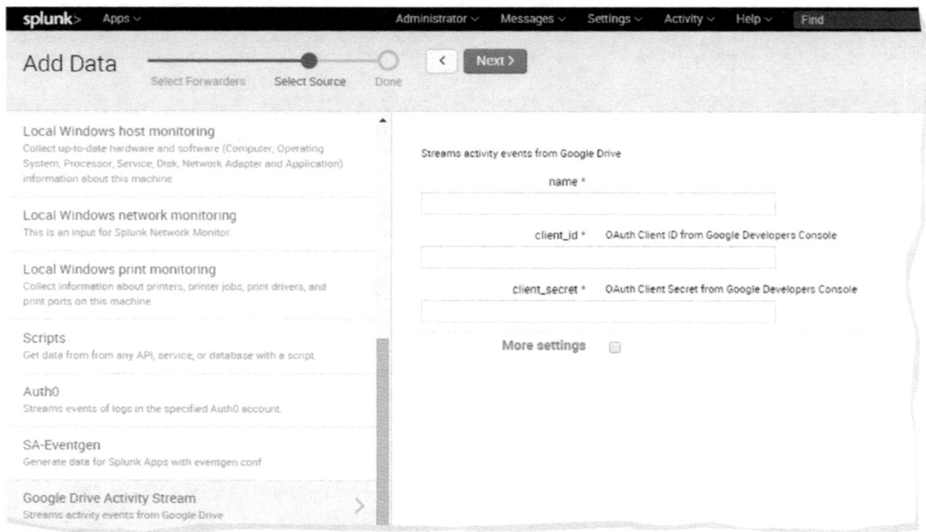

HOW WE WORK #2: PAIRING BETWEEN STAKEHOLDERS

One of the stories we began to implement during this stage of our journey was anomaly detection, where the PAS app identifies and flags anomalous behavior on a dashboard such as an unusual number of accesses to the document repository by an employee. The implementation of this story began with an architect evaluating several approaches to detecting anomalous behavior. His decision was to try out a statistical approach as "the simplest thing that could possibly work" rather than trying to implement a sophisticated machine learning based solution. This statistical approach is based on a calculation for each employee of the mean and standard deviation (SD) of the historic daily number of document accesses in the repository, and then applies a multiplier to the SD to calculate a threshold value. If, on the most recent day in the period under analysis, the number of document accesses for the employee exceeds the threshold value for that particular employee, the PAS app flags an anomaly for further investigation in case the anomaly represents a security violation.

The architect next validated his approach with the business user and this raised a number of questions and issues related to this statistical method.

First, the business user was interested to know if the approach could indicate the degree of anomaly instead of just flagging it. The code snippet below shows a column definition **TIMES_OVER_NORM** that calculates a measure of this by comparing the variation with the mean. This enables the app to display anomalies using traffic light visualizations: highlighting large anomalies in red and less significant ones in orange. The business user suggested the following as an initial way to categorize the anomalies.

SIZE OF ANOMALY	SEVERITY
> 2 * SD	High (red)
1.5 * SD to 2 *SD	Moderate (orange)
< 1.5 * SD	Low (green)

Second, the business user pointed out that this statistical approach may not work well with certain patterns of access. For example, if the search calculates the mean and SD over the previous month with the data shown in the following chart, the spike at the end of July is detected as an anomaly:

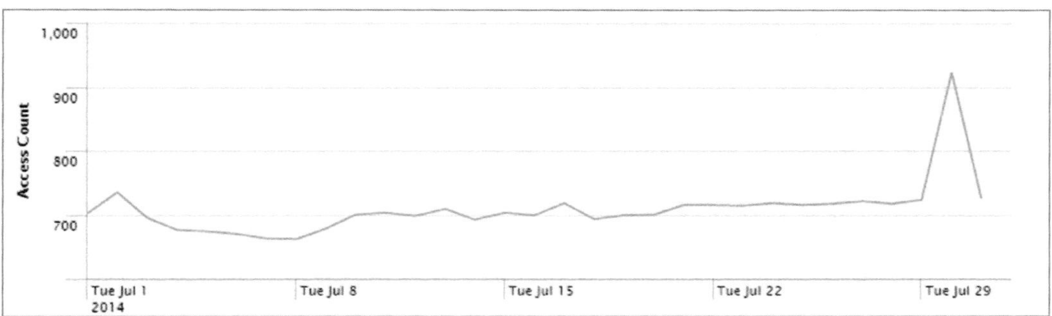

If the search calculates the mean and SD over the previous three months, the spike at the end of September may not be detected as an anomaly:

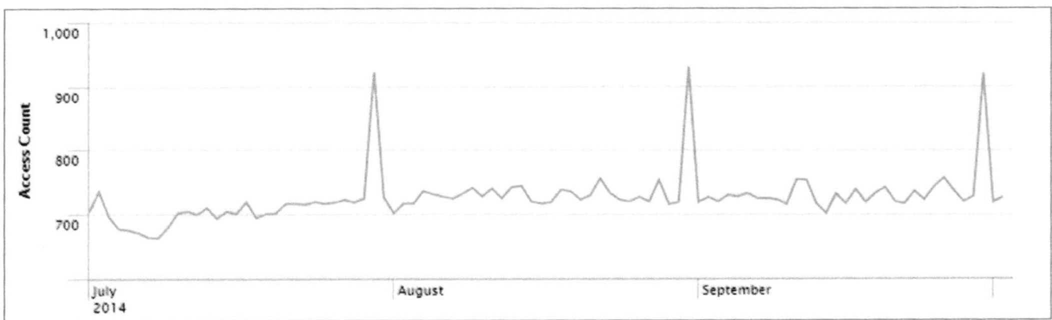

Furthermore, if we expect a spike at the end the end of each month, then this statistical approach does not spot the anomaly that the spike is missing at the end of September:

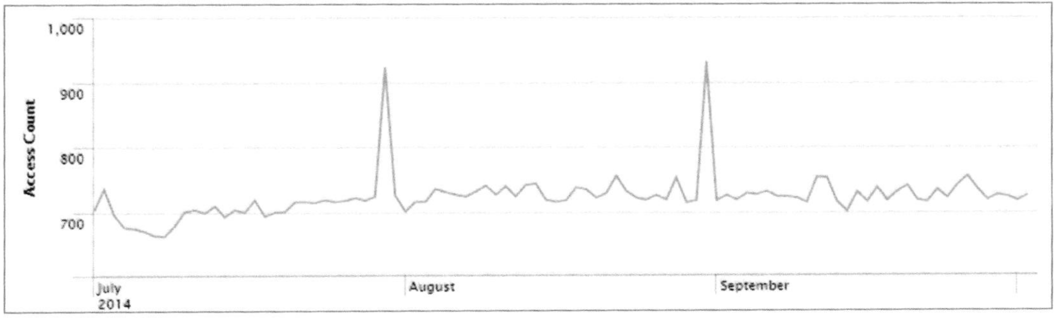

The architect and business user agreed that for the PAS app, using the simple statistical approach is acceptable if the user can specify the time range over which the app calculates the mean and SD. However, in other scenarios a more sophisticated, pattern-aware approach using more sophisticated machine learning algorithms may be necessary.

ARCH

You need to understand your data before you can use it effectively.

The architect tested his algorithm out with his own data set before bringing it to one of the developers to develop further in a pairing session. The first step for the developer was to understand the search and then modify it to work with the sample data we use with the PAS app. This revealed a problem with our sample data in that there is currently very little variation over time in the number of times each sample employee accesses the repository each day. We had to use a very low multiplier value before we saw any anomalies. Therefore, as a separate task, we need to modify our sample data generator to add more variation into the access patterns. Once the search was working with our sample data, the developer incorporated the search into a dashboard.

The architect then suggested that the search should be parameterized. As part of the application setup, a user should be able to specify the multiplier value for the threshold calculation and the time range over which the app calculates the mean and SD. The following code snippet shows the final search definition that includes the **$multiplier$** token:

```
tag = pas tag = change tag = audit
| bucket _time span = 1d
| stats count as ops by _time user
| stats stdev(ops) as SD,
  avg(ops) as MEAN,
  sparkline,
  latest(ops) as LAST_OPS by user
| eval sig_mult = SD * $multiplier$
| eval threshold = sig_mult+MEAN
| table user MEAN SD threshold LAST_OPS sparkline
| eval DELTA = LAST_OPS-threshold
| eval TIMES_OVER_NORM = round(DELTA/MEAN,0)
| eval ANOMALY = if(LAST_OPS>threshold,"true","false")
| sort -ANOMALY
```

One important thing to notice about this search is that it does not currently use our data model, but queries the index directly. The issue here lies with the **$multiplier$** token because it's not possible to perform calculations in a data model based on a token value or any other type of parameter. We will investigate further to see if there is any way we can use our data model and the **PIVOT** command in this search manager. The dashboard currently sets the time range for the calculation in code:

```
var timepicker = new TimeRangeView({
  id: "timepicker",
  managerid: "anomalous_manager",
  preset: "Last 24 hours",
  el: $("#timepicker")
}).render();
```

We implement the final version of this dashboard in the PAS app using Simple XML with no JavaScript, and reformat the query to make it more legible:

```
<form>
  <label>Anomalous Activity</label>
  <fieldset autoRun = "true" submitButton = "false">
    <input type = "time" searchWhenChanged = "true">
      <default>
        <earliestTime>-24h</earliestTime>
        <latestTime>now</latestTime>
      </default>
    </input>
  </fieldset>
  <row>
    <table>
      <searchString>
        <![CDATA[
          tag = pas tag = change tag = audit
          | bucket _time span = 1d
          | stats count as ops by _time user
          | where ops! = 0
          | stats stdev(ops) as SD,
            avg(ops) as MEAN,
            sparkline,
            latest(ops) as LAST_OPS by user
          | eval sig_mult = SD*1
          | eval threshold = sig_mult+MEAN
          | table user MEAN SD threshold LAST_OPS sparkline
          | eval DELTA=LAST_OPS-threshold
          | eval TIMES_OVER_NORM = round(DELTA/MEAN,0)
          | eval ANOMALY = if(LAST_OPS>threshold,"true","false")
          | sort -ANOMALY
        ]]>
      </searchString>
    </table>
  </row>
</form>
```

Note: Splunk KV Store JS library (with Backbone classes) ships out-of-band. We've included it in our codebase under the pas_ref_app/appserver/static/components/kvstore_backbone folder.

HOW WE WORK #3: EXPLORATORY PROGRAMMING

Splunk Enterprise 6.2 introduces a feature, the app key value store. We decided to do a spike using this new feature to see if we can use it to persist our application configuration settings from the setup screens.

We installed the KV Store Backbone app during a pairing session and discovered that the app includes a comprehensive JavaScript test suite that uses the **Mocha** unit test framework. This test suite proved invaluable in learning how to use the key value store from JavaScript. The following screenshot shows the test dashboard:

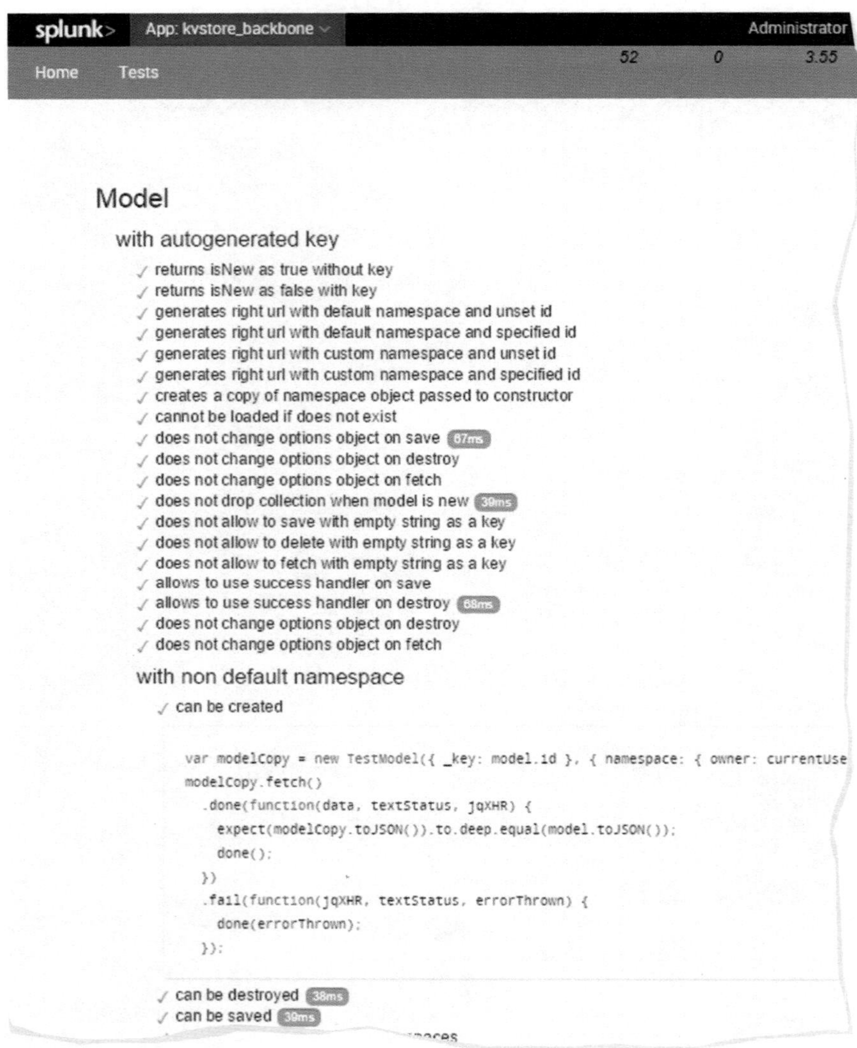

This page displays the JavaScript code that the test executes (in this example, it is retrieving an item previously uploaded to the KV store) making it easy to see how to complete a particular task. However, this page does not show all the code associated with the tests. To see how to upload an item to the KV store, we had to look at the source file that contains the test and locate the code that performs the setup for this **"can be created"** test in the `model-tests.js` file. The following code snippet shows the relevant function definition from this file:

```
// Insert one model before each test
beforeEach(function(done) {
  cleanCurrentUserCollectionAsync(function() {
    model = new TestModel({name: 'test'}, { namespace: { owner: currentUser } });
    model.save()
      .done(function(data, textStatus, jqXHR) {
        expect(model.id).to.be.a('string');
        expect(model.id).to.be.not.empty;
        expect(model.isNew()).to.be.false;
        done();
      })
      .fail(function(jqXHR, textStatus, errorThrown) {
        done(errorThrown);
      });
  });
});
```

DEV

Unit tests are a great resource for helping you to learn how to use an API. Don't forget that you can help other developers understand your code base by proving your unit tests.

You can find a useful introduction to unit testing JavaScript code with Mocha in this blog post: "Using Mocha JS, Chai JS and Sinon JS to Test your Frontend JavaScript Code."

SOME TIPS AND TRICKS

This section includes some useful tips, tricks, and recommended practices we use in our code.

This and that

Occasionally in our code you will see something similar to this snippet from the **summary.js** file that uses the variables **this** and **that**:

```
_start: function() {
  var that = this;

  // Perform initial rendering
  this._renderDonutSeriesPanel();

  // Rerender whenever the page resizes
  window.addEventListener("resize", function() {
    that._renderDonutSeriesPanel();
  }, false);
}
```

The trick of assigning **this** to **that** is very common in JavaScript. **this** is a built-in variable that refers to the current context or object, so in the **_start** function it refers to the object that this function is attached to. The **addEventListener** function has a different context, so **this** inside its function would refer to a different object than **this** in the **_start** function. In this code snippet we make sure that we use the object that **this** refers to in the **_start** function inside the function used by the **addEventListener** function.

Search escape

The user_activity.xml file in the PAS application includes the following search definition:

```
<search id = "base_search">
  <query>
    tag = pas tag = change tag = audit  user = $user|s$
    | bucket span = 5m _time
    | stats count by _time event_name event_target
  </query>
  <earliest>$time.earliest$</earliest>
  <latest>$time.latest$</latest>
</search>
```

In this search we append the search escape filter **|s** to the **user** token in case the user token contains any unusual characters that might mess up our search string.

WHAT DID WE LEARN?

This section summarizes some of the key lessons learned while we were developing our JavaScript code and Splunk searches.

- A data model can contain complex search expressions that perform lookups and calculations.
- If you need to combine results from a pivot and a regular search, it's best to either convert everything to pivots or everything to regular searches.
- We can import complex third-party JavaScript code and visualization libraries into our app.
- It's a good idea to make any custom JavaScript components you create "require compatible."
- You can share code between dashboards by placing it in the **dashboard.js** file.
- You can use the JavaScript SDK to interrogate other apps.

More information

Download the Splunk > Quick Reference Guide at: dev.splunk.com/goto/splunkrefpdf.

For a primer into SPL and a collection of recipes, see "Exploring Splunk" at: dev.splunk.com/goto/exploringsplunkpdf.

For information on creating custom search commands, see: "Write Custom Search Commands" at: dev.splunk.com/goto/aboutcustomsearchcommands.

For more information about defining a lookup in a static file, see "Configure field lookups" at: dev.splunk.com/goto/Addfieldsfromexternaldatasources.

For information about using **eval expressions**, see: dev.splunk.com/goto/evalref.

For more information on the `tsats` command, see the "Splunk Search Command Reference" at: dev.splunk.com/goto/tstats.

For more information on RequireJS, see: requirejs.org.

You can learn more about the open source **Context.js** script at lab.jakiestfu.com/contextjs.

For more information on Tags Manager, an open source jQuery plugin for displaying a list of tags, letting a user edit the tag list, and that offers an API for managing the tag list programmatically, see: welldonethings.com/tags/manager/v3.

For more information on the **Asynchronous Module Definition**, see "WHY AMD?" at: requirejs.org/docs/whyamd.html.

For information about calendar heatmap visualization, see: kamisama.github.io/cal-heatmap.

For information about the app key value store feature, see: dev.splunk.com/goto/appkvstore.

You can find a useful introduction to unit testing JavaScript code with Mocha in this blog post: "Using Mocha JS, Chai JS and Sinon JS to Test your Frontend JavaScript Code" at: blog.codeship.io/2014/01/22/testing-frontend-javascript-code-using-mocha-chai-and-sinon.html.

6

Packaging and deployment: reaching our destination

PACKAGING AND DEPLOYING THE PAS APP

Installing an app and its dependencies on a single node is pretty straightforward. The following screenshots show the result of the deployment process for a user in Splunk® Enterprise. The first screenshot shows the home page in Splunk Enterprise with the main **Splunk Reference App - PAS** in the list of installed apps. The second screenshot shows the details of all the installed apps, which includes the main **Splunk Reference App** and the various add-ons (**Splunk Reference App - HR info**, **Splunk Reference App - Application Add-on**, **Splunk Reference App - Database Add-on**, **Splunk Reference App - Files Add-on**, and **Google Drive Data Provider Add-on**). Notice how the add-ons are invisible and that not all the PAS apps share the same version number.

During this stage of our journey, we explore the options for packaging and deploying the PAS apps. We investigate how we can package the multiple apps that make up our solution in a way that makes it easy for a customer to deploy them in their own environment, and how to facilitate updates to the apps after the customer has deployed them.

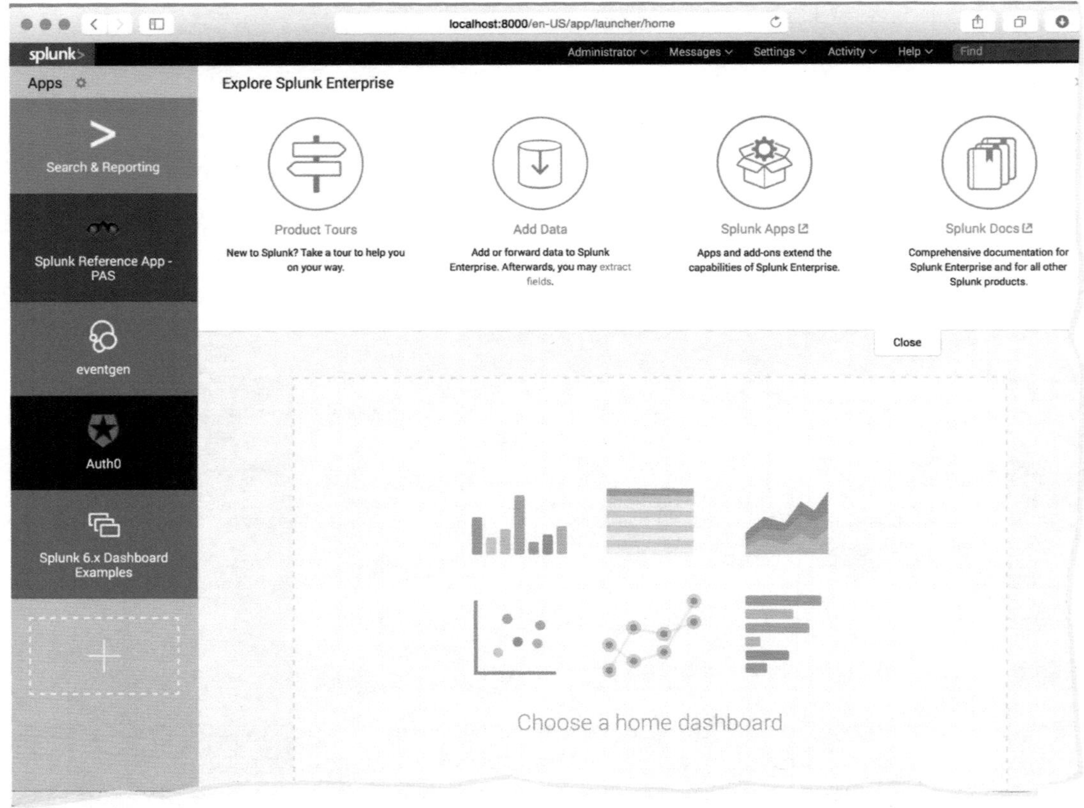

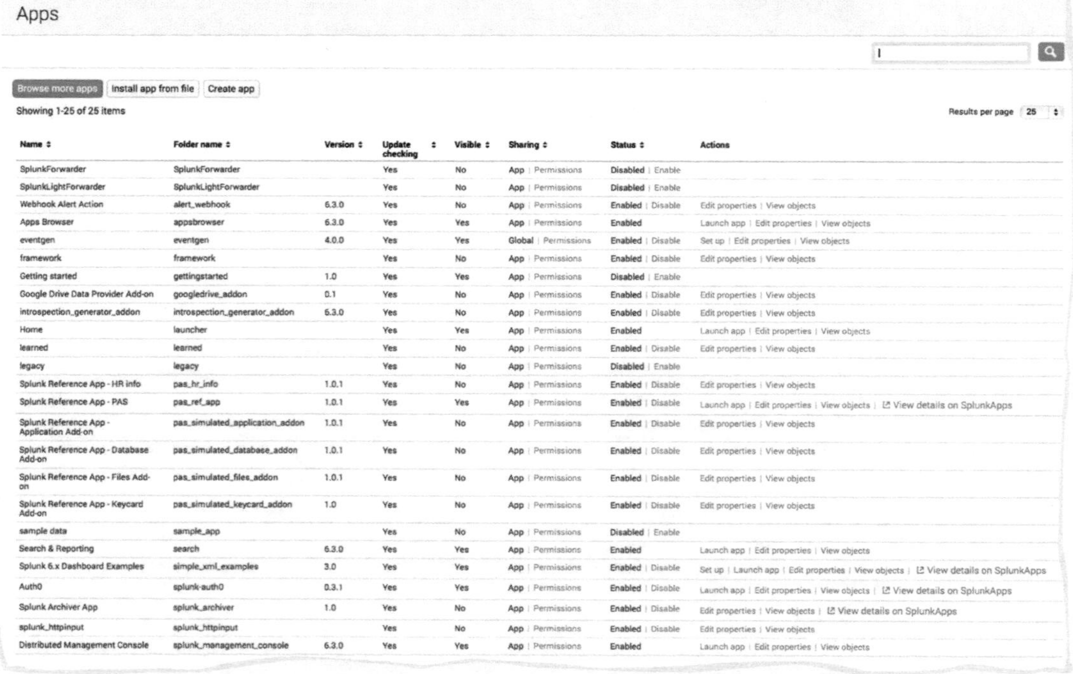

Name	Folder name	Version	Update checking	Visible	Sharing	Status	Actions
SplunkForwarder	SplunkForwarder		Yes	No	App | Permissions	Disabled | Enable	
SplunkLightForwarder	SplunkLightForwarder		Yes	No	App | Permissions	Disabled | Enable	
Webhook Alert Action	alert_webhook	6.3.0	Yes	No	App | Permissions	Enabled | Disable	Edit properties | View objects
Apps Browser	appsbrowser	6.3.0	Yes	Yes	App | Permissions	Enabled	Launch app | Edit properties | View objects
eventgen	eventgen	4.0.0	Yes	Yes	Global | Permissions	Enabled | Disable	Set up | Edit properties | View objects
framework	framework		Yes	No	App | Permissions	Enabled | Disable	Edit properties | View objects
Getting started	gettingstarted	1.0	Yes	Yes	App | Permissions	Disabled | Enable	
Google Drive Data Provider Add-on	googledrive_addon	0.1	Yes	No	App | Permissions	Enabled | Disable	Edit properties | View objects
introspection_generator_addon	introspection_generator_addon	6.3.0	Yes	No	App | Permissions	Enabled | Disable	Edit properties | View objects
Home	launcher		Yes	Yes	App | Permissions	Enabled	Launch app | Edit properties | View objects
learned	learned		Yes	No	App | Permissions	Enabled | Disable	Edit properties | View objects
legacy	legacy		Yes	No	App | Permissions	Disabled | Enable	
Splunk Reference App - HR info	pas_hr_info	1.0.1	Yes	No	App | Permissions	Enabled | Disable	Edit properties | View objects
Splunk Reference App - PAS	pas_ref_app	1.0.1	Yes	Yes	App | Permissions	Enabled | Disable	Launch app | Edit properties | View objects | View details on SplunkApps
Splunk Reference App - Application Add-on	pas_simulated_application_addon	1.0.1	Yes	No	App | Permissions	Enabled | Disable	Edit properties | View objects
Splunk Reference App - Database Add-on	pas_simulated_database_addon	1.0.1	Yes	No	App | Permissions	Enabled | Disable	Edit properties | View objects
Splunk Reference App - Files Add-on	pas_simulated_files_addon	1.0.1	Yes	No	App | Permissions	Enabled | Disable	Edit properties | View objects
Splunk Reference App - Keycard Add-on	pas_simulated_keycard_addon	1.0	Yes	No	App | Permissions	Enabled | Disable	Edit properties | View objects
sample data	sample_app		Yes	No	App | Permissions	Disabled | Enable	
Search & Reporting	search	6.3.0	Yes	Yes	App | Permissions	Enabled	Launch app | Edit properties | View objects
Splunk 6.x Dashboard Examples	simple_xml_examples	3.0	Yes	Yes	App | Permissions	Enabled | Disable	Set up | Launch app | Edit properties | View objects | View details on SplunkApps
Auth0	splunk-auth0	0.3.1	Yes	Yes	App | Permissions	Enabled | Disable	Launch app | Edit properties | View objects | View details on SplunkApps
Splunk Archiver App	splunk_archiver	1.0	Yes	No	App | Permissions	Enabled | Disable	Edit properties | View objects | View details on SplunkApps
splunk_httpinput	splunk_httpinput		Yes	No	App | Permissions	Enabled | Disable	Edit properties | View objects
Distributed Management Console	splunk_management_console	6.3.0	Yes	Yes	App | Permissions	Enabled	Launch app | Edit properties | View objects

ARCH

Distributed app deployment is more challenging, especially if the installation is not uniform across various Splunk Enterprise roles, for example: when an app has certain dependencies that need to be deployed to search heads vs. indexers vs. forwarders. Currently, the administrator would need to manually copy dependencies to the right place or use custom scripts and/or configuration management tools like Chef or Puppet to handle such complex deployments.

The remainder of this chapter describes how we packaged the apps to achieve this result.

ALTERNATIVES

The most complex part of packaging the apps was deciding how to handle the multiple Splunk apps that make up the PAS solution. Typically, a Splunk app is packaged into an `.spl` file that a customer can download and install manually or discover on the Splunkbase web site. From Splunkbase, Splunk Enterprise downloads and installs it automatically. Unfortunately, a single `.spl` file only enables installing a single Splunk app, and the PAS solution is made up of multiple Splunk apps.

We considered the following options:

SHIP

An `.spl` file is a zipped tar archive that contains all the required files for the app.

- **Creating an installer inside a Splunk app**
  Taking this approach, we could package all the dependencies inside the main app and include logic that installs them as and when they are required. The Splunk App for VMware plans to use this approach in the future.

  A variation on this approach is to have a dedicated installer app that sets up the main app and all of its dependencies, and then redirects requests to the main app it installed. The Splunk App for Enterprise Security uses this approach.
- **Using an external installer**
  Using this approach, we could create a script that automatically installs an app and its dependencies. Alternatively, we could use a third-party installer tool to build the installation scripts.
- **Ask the customer to install the app and its dependencies manually from a single ZIP file**
  Taking this approach, we could package the main app and all the add-on apps in a single ZIP archive. We would then ask the customer to unpack the archive into the etc/apps/ folder. The Splunk App for VMware currently uses this approach.
- **Ask the customer to install the main app and each dependent add-on individually**
  Taking this approach, we would add detailed installation instructions to the documentation explaining how the customer should obtain and install each of the apps individually. Optionally, we could add logic to the main app that detects missing dependencies and then prompts the customer to install them. The Splunk App for Microsoft Exchange uses this approach.

The following chart plots each of these options showing how ease of implementation maps onto ease of use for the customer.

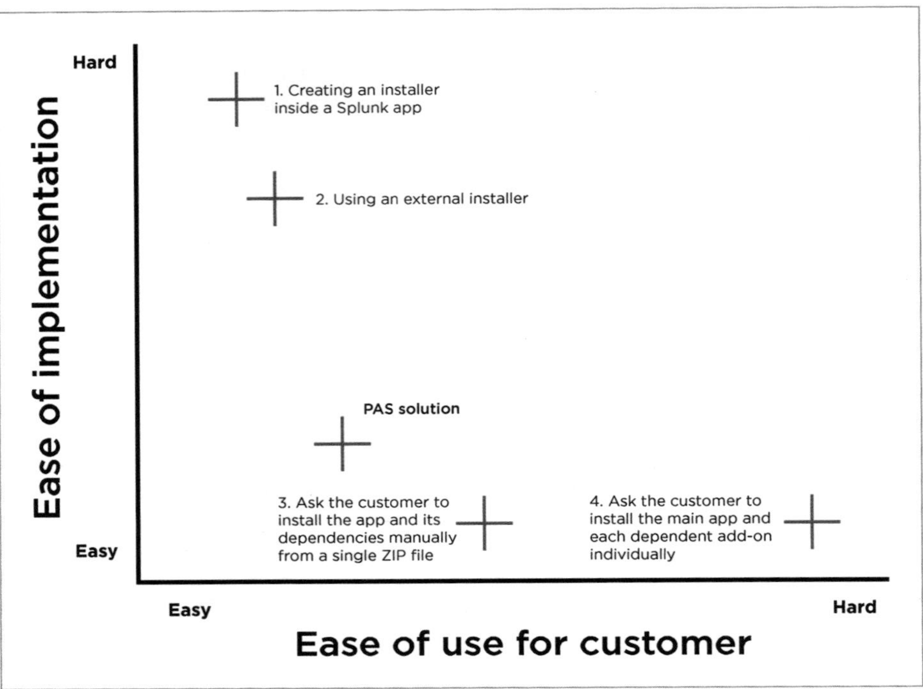

While it may be possible to check programmatically for missing dependencies in the same Splunk Enterprise instance, it is more difficult to check for missing dependencies when you expect that dependency to be installed on another machine such as a Splunk Enterprise forwarder. In this scenario, you can programmatically run some searches in your main app that look for data that the dependency provides. If you don't find the data, the main app can then prompt the customer to install and configure the missing dependency. The Splunk App for Microsoft Exchange uses this approach.

OVERVIEW OF THE SOLUTION

The approach we decided on for the PAS app is a hybrid approach. We package the main app as a standard Splunk app in an **.spl** file. In the **splunk_pas_ref_app.spl** file, we also include the other add-on apps in a subfolder along with a set of scripts that the customer runs to install them. The advantages of this approach for us are:

- It is relatively simple for us to build the **.spl** file and the installation scripts.
- We can deploy the **.spl** file to Splunkbase where customers can find it and then install it in their own environments.
- After the customer has installed the main app, it is relatively simple to run the install script to configure the add-on apps.

The disadvantages of this approach are:

- Installation is a two-step process. First, install the main PAS app in the standard way from Splunkbase. Then run the appropriate script to install the add-on apps in the local Splunk Enterprise environment.
- The scripts assume that you are deploying all the apps on the same Splunk Enterprise instance. The user must edit the scripts or install the add-on apps manually in more complex environments that have multiple Splunk instances (such as forwarders) on multiple machines.

DETAILS OF THE PACKAGING SOLUTION

This section describes the important details of how we package and deploy the PAS app. The high-level steps are:

- Make sure that you organize all the correct files into the correct folder structure.
- Create an `.spl` file.
- Upload the `.spl` file to Splunk Apps.

After you have uploaded the `.spl` file to Splunk Apps, customers can discover your app and install it in their own environments. The following screenshot shows the PAS app ready for a customer to install from the Splunkbase web site:

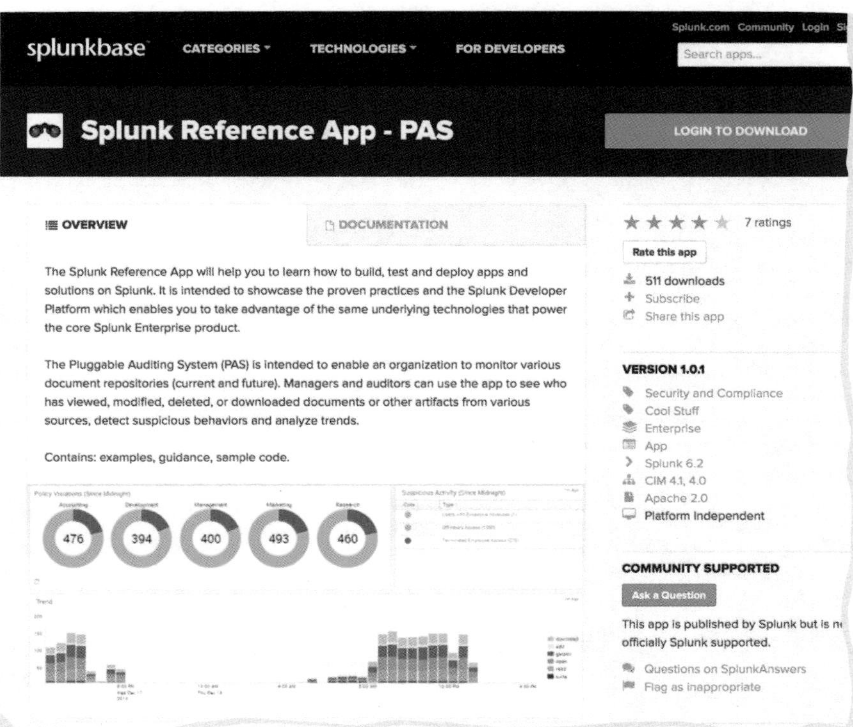

Including the add-on apps and scripts

The main PAS app has the standard folder structure of a Splunk app. For example, it contains these folders: **bin**, **default**, **metadata**, and **static**. Therefore, the customer can deploy the main PAS app in their environment in the same way as any other Splunk app. We also include all of our add-on apps in the subfolder **appserver/addons/** as shown in the following partial directory listing.

```
├──appserver
| ├──addons
| | ├──eventgen
| | | └──...
| | ├──splunk-add-on-google-drive
| | | └──...
| | ├──splunk-add-on-jira-alerts
| | | └──...
| | ├──pas_hr_info
| | | └──...
| | ├──pas_simulated_application_addon
| | | └──...
| | ├──pas_simulated_database_addon
| | | └──...
| | ├──pas_simulated_files_addon
| | | └──...
| | └──pas_simulated_keycard_addon
| | | └──...
| └──static
|   └──components
|     ├──calendarheatmap
|     | └──...
|     ├──d3
|     | └──...
|     ├──dendrogram
|     | └──...
|     └──kvstore_backbone
|       └──...
|
├──...
```

Splunk Enterprise does not locate and configure these add-on apps in this location. Therefore, in the **bin** folder in the main PAS app we include two scripts that create symbolic links in the etc/apps folder that point to these subfolders containing the add-on apps. The following **install-addons.sh** script creates the symbolic links in OS X, Linux, or *nix operating systems.

```
echo ===
echo Creating symbolic links to Splunk Reference Solution add-ons in $SPLUNK_HOME
echo ===

cd ../appserver/addons
ln -sv $PWD/* $SPLUNK_HOME/etc/apps
```

ADM

Ensure the SPLUNK_HOME environment variable is properly set.

TEST

If testing an app on different versions of Splunk Enterprise on the same box, install each version in a dedicated folder (perhaps, adding a suffix for the version, for example, splunk_630). Then, it's easy to switch between different versions by resetting SPLUNK_HOME.

The following **install-addons.ps1** PowerShell script performs the same task in Windows:

```
function createSymLinks ($source, $destination)
{
 Write-Host "Creating symbolic links to Splunk Reference Solution add-ons in" $env:SPLUNK_HOME
            "\etc\apps" - foregroundcolor black - backgroundcolor white
     $children = Get-ChildItem $source
     for ($i = 0; $i - lt $children.Count; $i++) {
      $dest = $destination + "\" + $children[$i]
      cmd /c mklink /d  $dest $children[$i].FullName
     }
}

cd ..\appserver
createSymLinks -source addons -destination $env:SPLUNK_HOME\etc\apps
```

SEC

We signed this PowerShell script to make it easier for the customer to run the script securely without weakening the execution policies.

The following screenshot shows the details of the symbolic links the script creates from a Terminal window in OS X:

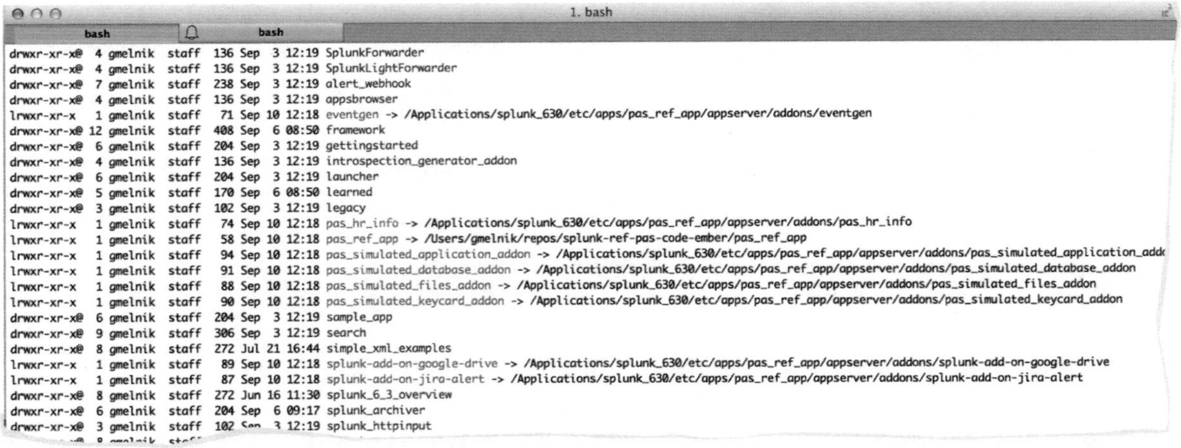

```
1. bash
bash        bash
drwxr-xr-x@  4 gmelnik  staff  136 Sep  3 12:19 SplunkForwarder
drwxr-xr-x@  4 gmelnik  staff  136 Sep  3 12:19 SplunkLightForwarder
drwxr-xr-x@  7 gmelnik  staff  238 Sep  3 12:19 alert_webhook
drwxr-xr-x@  4 gmelnik  staff  136 Sep  3 12:19 appsbrowser
lrwxr-xr-x   1 gmelnik  staff   71 Sep 10 12:18 eventgen -> /Applications/splunk_630/etc/apps/pas_ref_app/appserver/addons/eventgen
drwxr-xr-x@ 12 gmelnik  staff  408 Sep  6 08:50 framework
drwxr-xr-x@  6 gmelnik  staff  204 Sep  3 12:19 gettingstarted
drwxr-xr-x@  4 gmelnik  staff  136 Sep  3 12:19 introspection_generator_addon
drwxr-xr-x@  6 gmelnik  staff  204 Sep  3 12:19 launcher
drwxr-xr-x@  5 gmelnik  staff  170 Sep  6 08:50 learned
drwxr-xr-x@  3 gmelnik  staff  102 Sep  3 12:19 legacy
lrwxr-xr-x   1 gmelnik  staff   74 Sep 10 12:18 pas_hr_info -> /Applications/splunk_630/etc/apps/pas_ref_app/appserver/addons/pas_hr_info
lrwxr-xr-x   1 gmelnik  staff   58 Sep 10 12:18 pas_ref_app -> /Users/gmelnik/repos/splunk-ref-pas-code-ember/pas_ref_app
lrwxr-xr-x   1 gmelnik  staff   94 Sep 10 12:18 pas_simulated_application_addon -> /Applications/splunk_630/etc/apps/pas_ref_app/appserver/addons/pas_simulated_application_addc
lrwxr-xr-x   1 gmelnik  staff   91 Sep 10 12:18 pas_simulated_database_addon -> /Applications/splunk_630/etc/apps/pas_ref_app/appserver/addons/pas_simulated_database_addon
lrwxr-xr-x   1 gmelnik  staff   88 Sep 10 12:18 pas_simulated_files_addon -> /Applications/splunk_630/etc/apps/pas_ref_app/appserver/addons/pas_simulated_files_addon
lrwxr-xr-x   1 gmelnik  staff   90 Sep 10 12:18 pas_simulated_keycard_addon -> /Applications/splunk_630/etc/apps/pas_ref_app/appserver/addons/pas_simulated_keycard_addon
drwxr-xr-x@  6 gmelnik  staff  204 Sep  3 12:19 sample_app
drwxr-xr-x@  9 gmelnik  staff  306 Sep  3 12:19 search
drwxr-xr-x@  8 gmelnik  staff  272 Jul 21 16:44 simple_xml_examples
lrwxr-xr-x   1 gmelnik  staff   89 Sep 10 12:18 splunk-add-on-google-drive -> /Applications/splunk_630/etc/apps/pas_ref_app/appserver/addons/splunk-add-on-google-drive
lrwxr-xr-x   1 gmelnik  staff   87 Sep 10 12:18 splunk-add-on-jira-alert -> /Applications/splunk_630/etc/apps/pas_ref_app/appserver/addons/splunk-add-on-jira-alert
drwxr-xr-x@  8 gmelnik  staff  272 Jun 16 11:30 splunk_6_3_overview
drwxr-xr-x@  6 gmelnik  staff  204 Sep  6 09:17 splunk_archiver
drwxr-xr-x@  3 gmelnik  staff  102 Sep  3 12:19 splunk_httpinput
```

Both scripts fail gracefully if you attempt to run them a second time. They will not override existing apps or symbolic links.

Promoting add-ons to their own packages

The JIRA alert and Google Drive add-ons that we have built in support of the PAS app v1.5 have utility outside of this project. We would like to highlight them and share them with the community, while still using them in their original context within the PAS app. To this end, we have split them out into their own repositories and have linked them into the main PAS repository by use of Git submodules. In this way we can still include the apps in the main PAS package for easy deployment with our script, but we don't need to duplicate any code. We can work on that functionality with a greater focus and remain confident that we are always packaging the latest version of that code. Since our script only creates links if they don't already exist, our users can also install either of the new standalone modules before installing the PAS app with no ill effects.

We also publish these two add-ons as standalone packages on Splunkbase

Versions and other metadata

To enable updating the apps at some future time, it's important to add version numbers to both the main PAS app and the add-ons. We do this in the app.conf files for each app. The following example is from the main PAS app:

```
[install]
is_configured = 0

[package]
check_for_updates = 1
id = pas_ref_app
```

```
[ui]
is_visible = True
label = Splunk Reference App - PAS

[launcher]
author = Splunk Dev (gmelnik)
description = Splunk Reference App - PAS, including the main app and the underlying add-ons.
version = 0.90
```

SHIP

The version number can also include text. For example, **0.81 beta**.

The **package** stanza contains metadata related to app upgrades, and the **launcher** stanza determines how the Laucher page in Splunk Enterprise and the Splunkbase web site display information about the app. For more information about the contents of the **app.conf** file, see "app.conf" in the Admin Manual.

Tips and useful resources

The page "Step 8: Package your app or add-on" in the "Developing Views and Apps for Splunk Web" manual contains lots of useful resources related to packaging an app including:

- What should be in the **app.conf** file.
- How to add an icon and screenshots on Splunkbase or in the Launcher. These files must have particular resolutions and you must place them in a particular location.
- How to tar and zip your app on different platforms. Note that you must manually install the **gnutar** tool referenced on this page on OS X.

SHIP

There are also Splunk CLI commands that can be used for packaging. The latter will ignore all auxiliary git-related files:

- splunk package app appname
- git archive

SHIP

When you are creating the `.spl` file, it's a good idea to check out a clean copy of your app from your source control system and use that. This removes the risk of accidently including any temporary file or files created by Splunk Enterprise at runtime. However, you should be sure not to include files related to your source control system such as .git and .gitignore in the `.spl` package file.

When you tar and zip your app, you must add the folder that contains all your app resources as the root folder in the package.

For the PAS app, we have chosen to include in the `.spl` file the `indexes.conf` file that specifies the location of the **pas** index files. This is a convenience to let a customer downloading and installing the PAS app on a single machine get started quickly with minimal manual configuration steps. In a distributed production environment, an administrator typically needs to configure the indexes on specific machines.

DEV

If you tag your releases (`git tag -a`), GitHub will automatically package your app and create a tar zip for every associated release.

When you upload your `.spl` file to the Splunkbase web site, it validates the app folder structure and `app.conf` file. However, the Splunkbase team must approve the app before it becomes visible to Splunkbase, this usually takes about 24 hours to complete.

SHIP

When publishing your apps/add-ons on Splunkbase, follow these naming conventions: dev.splunk.com/goto/namingguide.

During the submission process you must provide various pieces of metadata. These include the app name, a short description, license details, and contact details. For more information about the submission process including naming guidelines and approval criteria, see "About submitting content" in the Working with Splunkbase Manual.

MANAGING AUTHORIZATION AND PERMISSIONS

We include two roles in the PAS app to let an administrator manage access to the functionality on the **Setup** dashboard. Any users that an administrator adds to the **pasadmin** role will be able to save the PAS configuration values on the **Setup** dashboard. Any users that an administrator adds to the **pasuser** role will only have permissions to read the configuration data created by a member of **pasadmin** role. For more information about how the **Setup** dashboard uses the App Key Value Store (KV Store) to persist global configuration settings for the PAS app, see the chapter "Working with data: where it comes from and how we manage it" in this guide.

You can view the capabilities we assign to these two roles on the **Access Controls** settings page in Splunk Enterprise. However these pages are large, so here we show just the content of the `authorize.conf` file where the settings are saved:

```
[role_admin]
srchIndexesDefault = main;pas

[role_pasuser]
importRoles = user
srchIndexesAllowed = *
srchIndexesDefault = main;pas

[role_pasadmin]
accelerate_datamodel = enabled
edit_user = enabled
importRoles = pasuser
srchIndexesAllowed = *
srchIndexesDefault = main;pas
```

In this file, you can see that we add the **pas** index to the list of indexes searched by default by members of the built-in **admin** role. The custom **pasuser** role inherits from the built-in **user** role and also searches the **pas** index by default. The custom **pasadmin** role inherits from the custom **pasuser** role and also searches the **pas** index by default. The **pasadmin** role is also authorized to accelerate data models and edit user settings.

ADM

The administrator can add any existing indexes to the pasuser and pasadmin roles. Events from customer indexes will show up in the PAS app provided they are tagged correctly.

ADM

When you define a new role, you should always inherit from an existing role and then add the required capabilities.

To restrict access to the PAS configuration settings, we set the permissions on the KV Store collections (**ri_setup** and **ri-setup-coll**) that contain the configuration settings. The following screenshot shows the permissions for the **ri-setup-coll** KV Store collection, where you can see that we give the **pasadmin** role **read** and **write** permissions, and the **pasuser** role **read** permissions only:

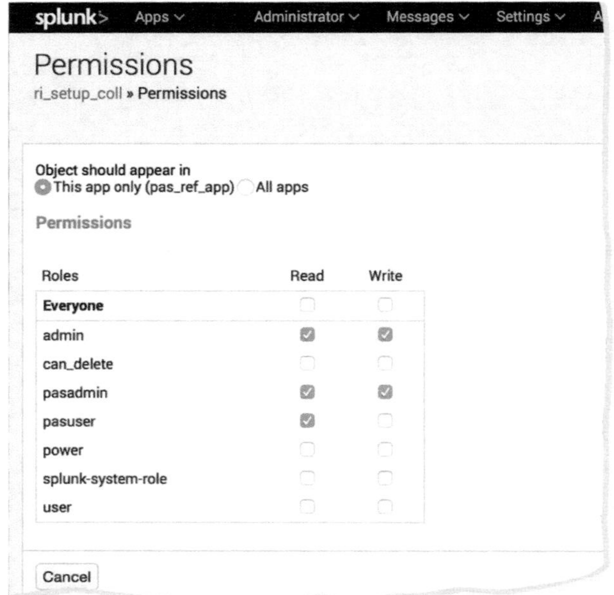

Preparing the roles and permissions for packaging

When we defined our custom roles and permissions, we used the **Settings** pages in Splunk Web UI. To include these settings it's important to copy them from the location where the Splunk Web UI saves them, to the correct files that we include in the `.spl` package.

When we create a new role from the **Settings** page, Splunk Enterprise saves the configuration in the file `etc/system/local/authorize.conf`. We copy the PAS app roles to the file `authorize.conf` in the `default` folder in the PAS app. We also remove some unused attributes (such as **cumulativeRTSrchJobsQuota** and **cumulativeSrchJobsQuota**) from the role definitions to keep them tidy (see the content of `authorize.conf` shown above).

When we change the permissions settings through the **Settings** page, Splunk Enterprise saves the configuration in the file `local.meta` in the `metadata` folder in the PAS app. This file is not included when we package the app. We must copy these permissions settings into the `default.meta` file in the `metadata` folder that is included when we package the app in the `.spl` archive file. We modify the contents of this file as shown in the following snippet from the `default.meta` file:

```
# Modify access permissions for specific kvstore collections if that level of granularity is needed
[collections/ri_setup_coll]
version = 6.2.0

[collections/violation_types]
version = 6.2.0

# Specified write permissions to admin and pasadmin roles only
[]
access = read : [pasuser,admin,pasadmin], write : [ admin, pasadmin ]
export = none
version = 6.2.0
```

Here we are using the **[ ]** stanza notation to apply the permissions to all knowledge objects in the PAS app. It's possible to set more granular permissions by overriding the permissions in a stanza that relates to a specific knowledge object.

PROGRAMMATICALLY ENABLING AND DISABLING AN ADD-ON APP

The PAS app has an optional dependency on the Eventgen app that can generate sample data for the searches in the app. We are planning to deploy a version of the PAS app to a cloud-hosted sandbox environment to let customers explore the app without installing it in a local Splunk instance. However, to avoid consuming unnecessary processing resources in the cloud we want to disable the Eventgen app by default, but let a customer enable it if they want to view pseudo-live data in the PAS app. To achieve the goal we considered four options:

- Programmatically enabling/disabling the Eventgen app using the JavaScript SDK
  When we investigated this option, we discovered that the JavaScript SDK does not support enabling and disabling apps from client-side code running in the browser. We would need to run this code server-side, and this would require a major change to the PAS app.
- Programmatically enabling/disabling the Eventgen app via REST API call
  Due to time constraints, we decided not to investigate this option any further. However, it's possible that this option is not viable using client-side code because it may be prevented by design for security reasons.
- Programmatically enabling/disabling the underlying modular input of the Eventgen app
  Again, due to time constraints, we decided not to investigate this option any further and opted for the simplest approach possible.
- Programmatically detect the status of the app and inform the user
  This is the simplest approach and is the one we chose. The next section describes this approach in more detail.

Programmatically detect the status of an app and inform the user

This approach, which is the simplest, is the approach we take in the PAS app. We detect the state of the Eventgen app using the code in the following snippet, and display an appropriate message to the user on the **Setup** page based on the current state of the Eventgen app. The code retrieves all the installed apps using **mvc** class, checks that the Eventgen app is installed, and then checks the status of the Eventgen app.

```
var service = mvc.createService();
service.apps()
  .fetch(function(err, apps) {
    if (err) {
      console.error(err);
      return;
    }

    var eventgenApp = apps.item('eventgen')
    if (eventgenApp) {
      eventgenApp.fetch(function(err, eventgenApp) {
        if (err) {
          console.error(err);
          return;
        }

        $('#eventgen-loading').addClass('hide');

        if (eventgenApp.state().content.disabled) {
          $('#eventgen-disabled’).removeClass('hide');
        } else if (!eventgenApp.state().content.disabled) {
          $('#eventgen-success’).removeClass('hide');
        }
      });
    } else {
      $('#eventgen-loading').addClass('hide');
      $('#eventgen-notinstalled').removeClass('hide');
    }
  });
```

If we detect that the Eventgen app is not installed, we show the customer a link to download and install it. If we detect that the Eventgen app is installed but disabled, we show the customer a link to the **Manage apps** page in Splunk Enterprise where the customer can manually enable the app.

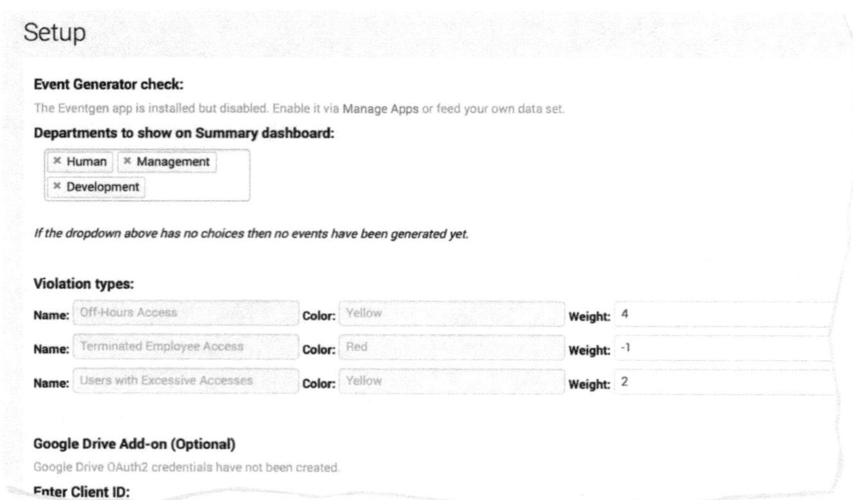

MANAGING APP UPGRADES

We plan to ship enhanced versions of the PAS app in the future and customers should be able to install the new version over the top of the current version. When we package the PAS app, we include two important pieces of information in the **app.conf** file: a version number such as 1.0.1 and the **check_for_updates** configuration value. These enable Splunk Enterprise to detect when a new version of the app is available on the Splunkbase web site and then notify the customer.

SHIP

When we upload a new version of the PAS app package to Splunkbase, the web site checks that we are uploading a later version. The site also gives us the option of keeping the new version hidden while we complete our testing. When the tests are complete, we can mark the new version as the default version for customers to install.

Note that from the perspective of the Splunkbase web site, the package containing the PAS main app and add-ons only contains a single app (the add-ons are installed by the customer) and therefore instances of Splunk Enterprise will only detect when the version of the main app is incremented. If we want to distribute new versions of the add-on apps independently of the main app, then we need to package each add-on as a separate `.spl` to upload to the Splunkbase web site. For example, we created a separate `.spl` file for our Google Drive add-on app and uploaded it to Splunkbase to let customers upgrade it independently.

APP CERTIFICATION

When submitting an app to Splunkbase, you can request an optional app certification by Splunk. Certified apps recognition constitutes high quality, including a security review, sufficient documentation, and user support. Certified apps will receive special visibility and promotion across Splunkbase to reach more users worldwide.

You can find the list of app certification criteria at dev.splunk.com/goto/appcert.

WHAT DID WE LEARN?

This section summarizes some of the key lessons learned when we were packaging and deploying our apps:

- You package an app into an `.spl` file. This file is an archive that contains all the resources your app needs to run.
- If your solution contains multiple apps (a main app and add-on apps) you must choose how you plan to deploy all these apps together.
- You can upload your `.spl` file to the Splunkbase website where customers can discover and install it.

- Apps uploaded to the Splunkbase website are validated by Splunk before they become available to customers.
- You can detect whether or not required dependencies (add-on apps) are available by including custom code in your main app.
- The Splunkbase website can notify customers when you make a new version of your app available.

MORE INFORMATION

To search for existing apps or find out more information about Splunkbase, see: splunkbase.splunk.com.

To see how other apps handled the installation of a solution containing multiple Splunk apps, see:

- The Splunk App for VMware (dev.splunk.com/goto/vmwareapp)
- The Splunk App for Enterprise Security (dev.splunk.com/goto/entsecapp)
- The Splunk App for Microsoft Exchange (dev.splunk.com/goto/exchangeapp)

For more information about the contents of the **app.conf** file, see: dev.splunk.com/goto/appconfig.

For useful resources related to packaging an app, see "Step 8: Package your app or add-on" at: dev.splunk.com/goto/packageapp.

For more information about the submission process including naming guidelines and approval criteria, see "About submitting content" at: dev.splunk.com/goto/aboutsubmittingcontent.

7

The journey continues: updating our equipment & dealing with OAuth

It's time for the next leg of our journey: We're exploring the latest release of Splunk Enterprise and updating the tools we have available for building apps. Those of you who were with us during the first leg know that we didn't get to everything we originally planned. As with many software projects, the commissioning of a new release (labeled v1.5 in the code repo) allowed us to once again consider some of the use cases we had to leave behind.

Like our previous journey we'll focus on how we can use the enhanced features of the platform to extend the functionality of our sample app. Along the way we'll explain the paths we explored, the decisions we made, and the options we rejected. Much of the team remains the same, although you may detect a slightly different tone going forward. Our previous narrator wasn't able to join us this time, but we're sure you'll find our new one just as engaging. We also had an additional developer join the team; because the PAS app was architected to be modular in nature, he was able to quickly hit the ground running.

WHAT'S NEW?

In this chapter we'll explore integrating Google Drive more closely with the PAS app. Later chapters will discuss how to use alerting to trigger various actions and HTTP Event Collector to send high volumes of data directly to Splunk Enterprise.

> **Is the journey ever really over? That's what we asked ourselves after successfully completing our first adventure and prioritizing what to achieve next. There was plenty more functionality we could add to the first version of the Splunk Reference app.**

DEALING WITH OAUTH

For the first step on our new journey, we decided to revisit the Google Drive add-on that serves as a custom data provider. We weren't entirely satisfied with the current user workflow that required the user to have shell access in order to execute a Python shell script during the OAuth 2.0 refresh token pairing and access management setup process. Users may not be comfortable or familiar with the shell or executing Python scripts, and shell access is something currently not available to Splunk Cloud users.

DEV

The OAuth protocol provides client apps with secure delegated access to server resources on behalf of a resource owner. In our case, the Google Drive REST API is the resource and our add-on is a client. For more information about OAuth 2.0, see this simplified intro. **For more information about authenticating with the Google Drive REST API, see** "Authorizing Your App with Google Drive."

BUS

It is common for consumer facing ISVs to use OAuth to protect the APIs they offer their customers and partners. It is also gaining traction among enterprises.

ORIGINAL WORKFLOW

The original user interaction workflow is summarized here. This corresponds to a "three-legged OAuth" scenario—where the add-on calls Google APIs on behalf of the user, requiring the user's consent. For more information about using OAuth 2.0 to access Google APIs, see the Google Identity Platform docs for OAuth 2.0. "Using OAuth 2.0 to Access Google APIs."

Legs 1 and 2 (Creating the Google Drive Client ID and Client secret):

1. The user creates a new Google project within the Google Developers Console.
2. Within the new project, the user enables Google Drive API access.
3. The user creates a new Client ID for native applications, and then jots down the Client ID and Client secret for later use.

Leg 3 (Getting the authentication token):

1. The user installs the Google Drive add-on from the PAS package.
2. The user goes to the command line and executes the `configure_oauth.py` script in the Google Drive add-on's **bin** directory.
3. When prompted by the script, the user enters the saved Client ID and Client secret values.

4. The user is then presented with a URL that the user copies into their computer's Clipboard. The script presents a prompt asking for a validation code, which is an alphanumeric string.
5. In a local browser window (but keeping the terminal window open), the user pastes the URL from the command-line output into the address bar, and then presses Enter/Return to go to the URL.
6. A dialog box appears, requesting access to the user's Google Drive data, which the user grants.
7. An alphanumeric validation code string appears and the user copies and pastes it into the waiting prompt in the Python shell script.

The script then exchanges the validation code for OAuth 2.0 refresh tokens. The user can use the refresh tokens to access the necessary data indefinitely, or until the user revokes access.

POSSIBLE ALTERNATIVES

To avoid our existing "three-legged OAuth" scenario, we came up with two possible alternatives. The first was ultimately rejected, and involved the "two-legged OAuth" solution, or authorization using a service account. The second involved integrating the OAuth 2.0 setup into the PAS app Setup dashboard, and removing the need for users to implement the Python setup script manually.

Method 1: Auth using a service account

A service account is an account that belongs to an app rather than to an individual user. The service account must be modified to impersonate a user, and would need domain-wide access to do so. This is a valid way of doing things with OAuth 2.0, because otherwise the add-on would have to impersonate a user by storing and using the user's actual account and credentials.

SEC

Using service accounts undermines OAuth 2.0 security and is not an acceptable solution for publicly-released code.

Using a service account can impact performance if the account owns numerous shared items in the same domain. In fact, Google strongly recommends against using service accounts as the common owner for domain-wide files. Also, only users that have a paid Google Apps domain account can use this approach. Ultimately, this is what killed this possibility.

Method 2: Integrate OAuth 2.0 setup into PAS app Setup dashboard

The second possible solution that was ultimately accepted and implemented, involved integrating the OAuth 2.0 setup with the PAS app's **Setup** dashboard. That is, we modified the PAS reference app's Setup dashboard to include Google Drive module logic. Then, the app would simply ask the user for a Client ID, and then open a new browser window from which the user could obtain a validation code to copy and paste back into the app's Setup dashboard. This approach follows a similar flow to what was already in place, but removes the need for the user to touch the command line. Plus, it allowed us to continue accurately describing the add-on as an OAuth 2.0 "native application" client.

The new workflow is summarized here:

1. The user creates a new Google project within the Google Developers Console.

2. Within the new project, the user enables Google Drive API access and the Google Admin SDK by going to **APIs & auth > APIs**, and then clicking **Enable API** for each one.

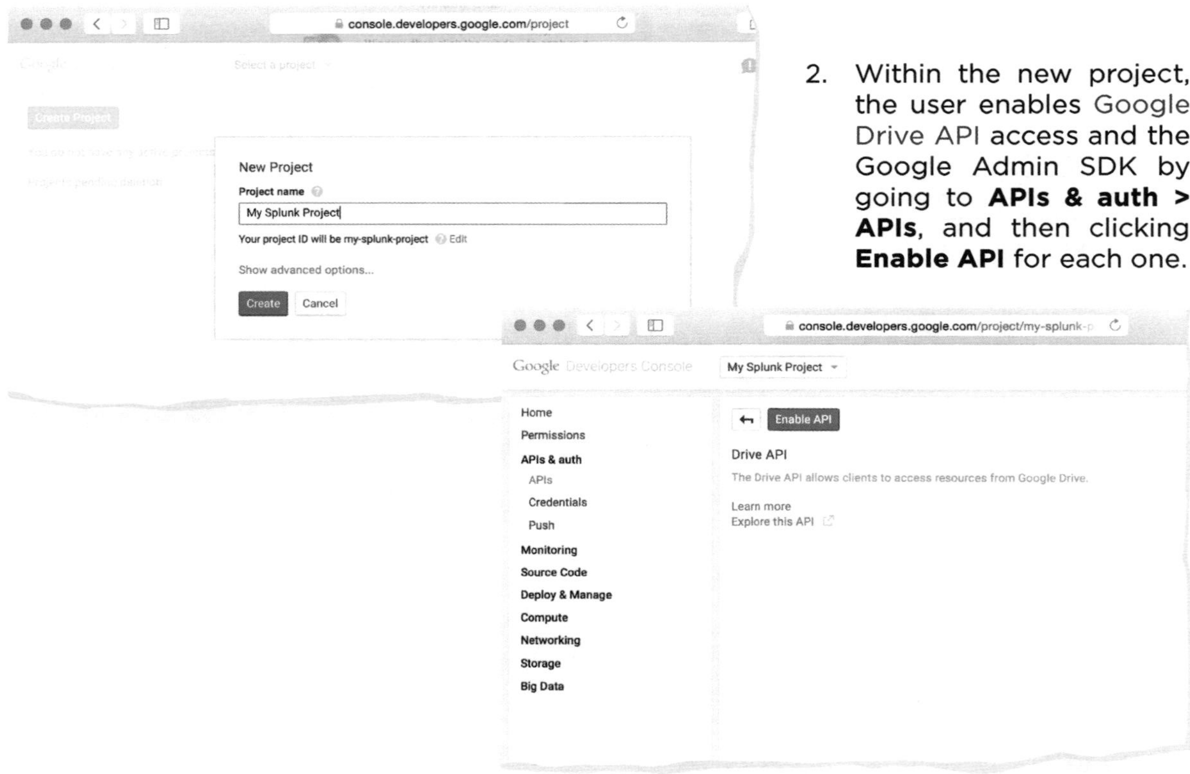

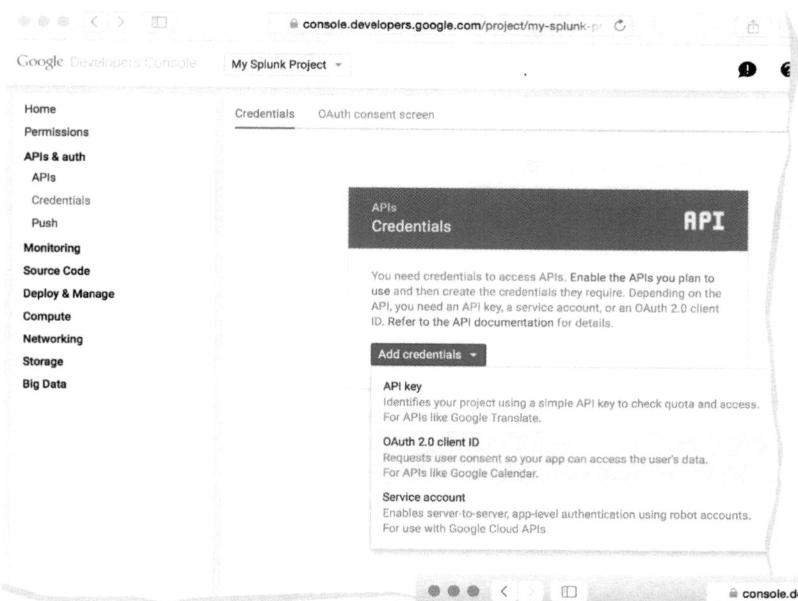

3. The user creates a new Client ID for native applications by going to **APIs & auth > Credentials**: First, the user creates an OAuth consent screen (if one doesn't already exist) by clicking **OAuth consent screen** on this page and following the instructions. Then, the user clicks **Credentials** and chooses **OAuth 2.0 client ID** from the **Add credentials** menu.

On the Create client ID page, the user chooses an application type of **Other**, fills out the requested URL information, and then clicks **Create**.

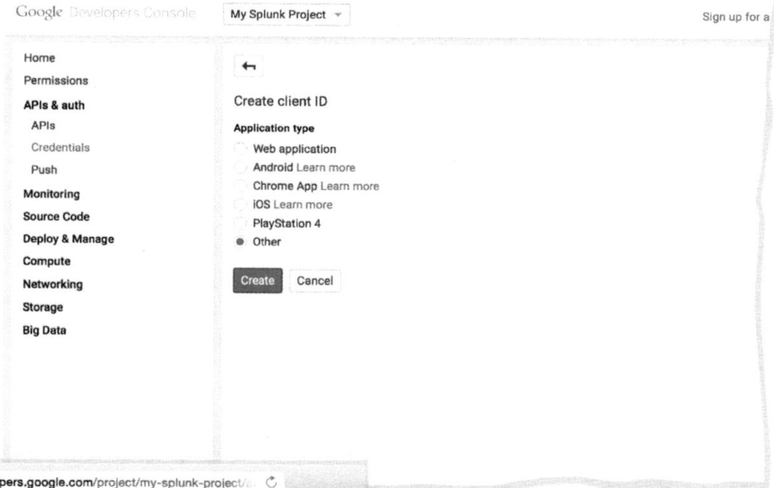

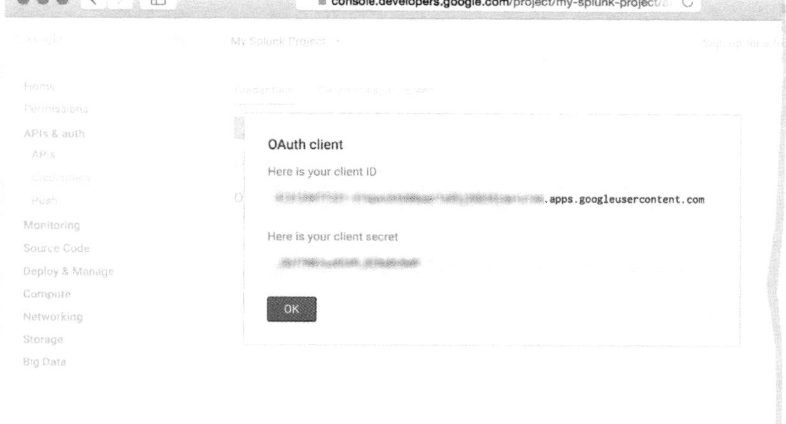

The console then displays the Client ID and Client secret. The Client ID and Client secret are always available from the Credentials page of the developers console, but the user should jot them down or copy and paste them in a safe place for quick access later in this process.

4. On the PAS **Setup** dashboard, the app prompts the user to enter a Client ID and Client secret.

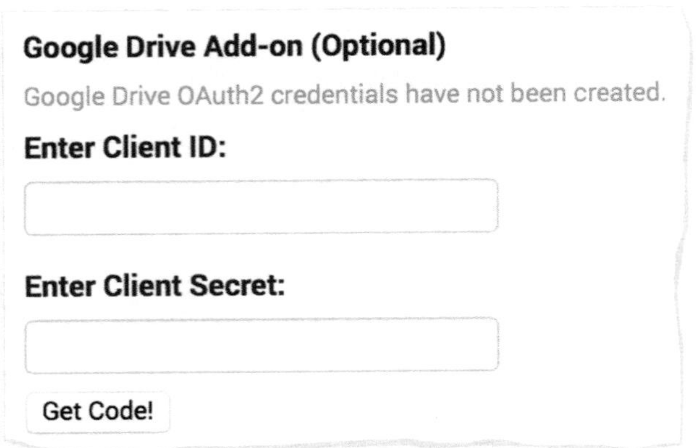

5. The user then clicks the **Get Code!** button to get a validation code.

6. A new browser window appears, and asks the user to allow or deny access to the user's Google Drive data.

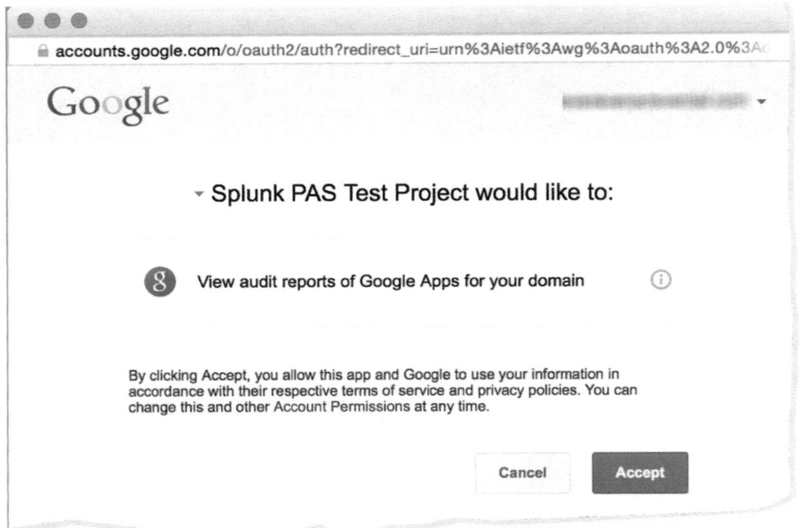

DEV

For this to work, a redirect URI is baked into the endpoint that's called when the user attempts to authenticate the app on Google's site. This prevents open redirect attacks and is typically enforced by OAuth2 providers. This is outlined at developers.google.com/identity/protocols/OAuth2InstalledApp and the value is set at "`urn:ietf:wg:oauth:2.0:oob`".

7. When the user accepts, an alphanumeric validation code string appears along with instructions to copy it back into the PAS app.

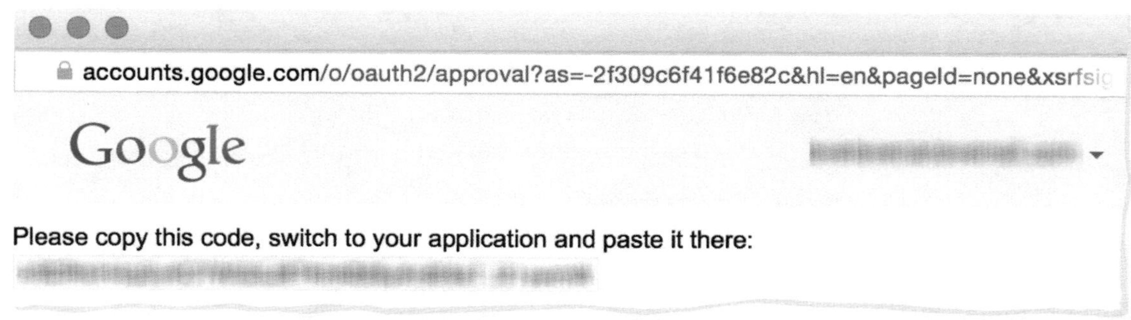

8. The user copies and pastes the validation code into the field under **Enter Authorization Code:** on the PAS **Setup** dashboard, and then clicks **Save Code!** to save the configuration.

Google Drive Add-on (Optional)

Google Drive OAuth2 credentials have not been created.

Enter Client ID:

Enter Client Secret:

Get Code!

Enter Authorization Code:

Save Code!

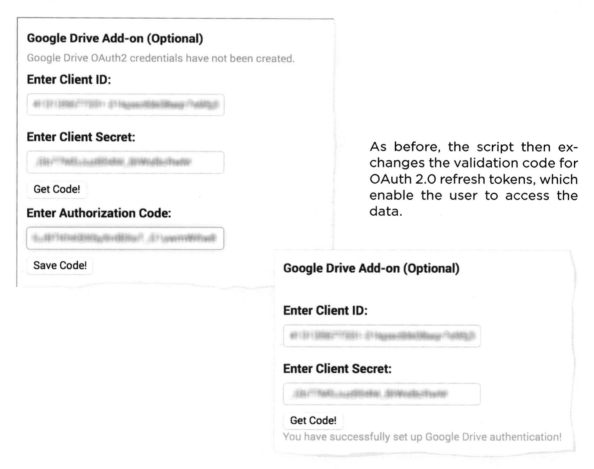

As before, the script then exchanges the validation code for OAuth 2.0 refresh tokens, which enable the user to access the data.

Google Drive Add-on (Optional)

Enter Client ID:

Enter Client Secret:

Get Code!

You have successfully set up Google Drive authentication!

To implement the changes, we made modifications to the following files within the PAS app and Google Drive add-on:

- **pas_ref_app/appserver/static/setup.js** This JavaScript file is responsible for the PAS app's setup logic. We added new UI control logic to determine when to show or hide elements during the user interaction flow. We also added new UI control logic to let users set up their Google Drive credentials right from the Setup dashboard. The dashboard now also shows whether the validation code has been generated or not.

  The relevant portion of the **setup.js** file is shown here. This code validates the user entries for the Client ID and the Client secret, and then opens an auth window if they are both present:

```
// Google Drive OAuth2 Checks
$("#getAuth").click(function() {
    var clientId = $("#clientId").val();
    var clientSecret = $("#clientSecret").val();
    if(clientId.length == 0) {
        sendUxLog("User didn't enter a Client ID");
        $("#clientIdError").removeClass('hide');
    } else {
        // hiding error prompt since input value is present
        $("#clientIdError").addClass('hide');
    }
    if(clientSecret.length == 0) {
        sendUxLog("User didn't enter a Client Secret");
        $("#clientSecretError").removeClass('hide');
    } else {
        // hiding error prompt since input value is present
        $("#clientSecretError").addClass('hide');
    }
    if(clientId.length > 0 && clientSecret.length > 0) {
        sendUxLog("Opening Google Authentication window for user to obtain Auth Code.");
        window.open(GOOGLE_SIGN_IN_BASE_URL + clientId, "popupWindow",
                    "width=600,height=600,scrollbars=yes");
        $("#codeEntry").removeClass('hide');
        $("#clientIdError").addClass('hide');
        $("#clientSecretError").addClass('hide');
    }
});
```

- **pas_ref_app/default/data/ui/views/setup.xml** This XML file is where the new static UI elements were added, including user input elements that take advantage of existing CSS styling.
- **googledrive_addon/bin/configure_oauth.py** This is the Python script that users previously had to invoke through the shell. To this file we added more robust logging, including logging to a dedicated log file at **$SPLUNK_HOME/var/splunk/log**.

- **googledrive_addon/bin/googledrive.py** This is the modular input script—the script that actually does the work of streaming Google Drive activity events back to Splunk Enterprise. To this Python script we also added more robust logging to the dedicated log file at **$SPLUNK_HOME/var/splunk/log**.

ONE FINAL CHALLENGE: EXCHANGING THE VALIDATION CODE FOR THE REFRESH TOKEN

The validation code that the user enters must be stored so that it is accessible to the existing script, so how do we get the string exchanged for a refresh token from the client side? We came up with two options: obtain the refresh token through JavaScript calls on the client side or create a new custom REST endpoint entry to call once the user enters the obtained string.

Method 1: JavaScript calls

The first possibility was quickly scuttled: Obtain the OAuth 2.0 refresh token through JavaScript calls on the client side. This was determined to be inadvisable from a best practices standpoint, as it would have required sensitive information to be stored directly on the client. Though this method might be acceptable for a quick fix in a sandboxed environment, it's not a good idea to implement it in code that is released publicly.

Method 2: New custom REST endpoint

The second possibility was the one we ultimately implemented: In the restmap.conf file, we created a new custom REST endpoint entry that the add-on calls once the user enters the validation code. That then executes the **configure_oauth.py** script that does the server-side refresh token exchange.

The relevant portion of the Google Drive add-on's **restmap.conf** file (which is located in **googledrive_addon/default**), is shown here:

```
[script:configure_oauth]
match=/configure_oauth
handlertype = python
handler = configure_oauth.oauth_exchange
```

This stanza creates the new endpoint **configure_oauth**.

Note that we used the **[script:<uniquename>]** form for the stanzas rather than the **[admin:<uniqueName>]** form. This was settled upon after some experimentation, where we observed that the more direct **[script:<uniquename>]** method resulted in more reliable script execution.

The relevant portion of the **setup.js** file is shown here. This code attempts to post to the custom REST endpoint (**/services/configure_oauth**), and exchanges the validation code for the refresh token:

```
$("#saveAuth").click(function() {
    var client_id = $("#clientId").val()
    var client_secret = $("#clientSecret").val()
    var auth_code = $("#authCode").val()
    if(auth_code.length > 0) {
        // Creating OAuth2 object for key exchange
        var oauth2_record = {
            "auth_code": auth_code,
            "client_id" : client_id,
            "client_secret" : client_secret
        }

        // Attempting to exchange auth code for refresh token via call to
        // custom RESTful endpoint.
        // Details are located in restmap.conf
        var service = mvc.createService();
        service.post("/services/configure_oauth", oauth2_record,
            function(err, response) {
                if(null!=response) {
                    $("#codeEntry").addClass('hide');
                    $("#gAuthSuccess").removeClass('hide');
                    $("#gAuthError").addClass('hide');
                } else {
                    sendDevLog("Token exchange error: " + err.status + ". Message: "
                               + err.error);
                    $("#gAuthError").removeClass('hide');
                    $("#gAuthSuccess").addClass('hide');
                }
            });
        $("#authEntryError").addClass('hide');
    } else {
        $("#authEntryError").removeClass('hide');
        $("#gAuthSuccess").addClass('hide');
    }
});
```

In addition to the **configure_oauth** endpoint, in the same **restmap.conf** file, we created the new endpoint **configure_oauth/status**:

```
[script:configure_oauth_status]
 match=/configure_oauth/status
 handlertype = python
 handler = configure_oauth.oauth_status
```

This endpoint was created so that we could build a status indicator for the PAS app's **Setup** dashboard that indicated whether the Google Drive OAuth 2.0 credentials had been successfully generated. This portion of the **setup.js** file is the code that posts to that endpoint:

```
// Determines whether or not the Google Drive OAuth2
// credentials have been generated and shows UI element
// indicating credential status
function isOauthConfigured() {
    function(err, response) {
    service.get('/services/configure_oauth/status?check=configured', "",
                function(err, response) {
            if(JSON.parse(response.data).configured==true) {
                $('#gAuthNotConfigured').addClass('hide');
                $('#gAuthConfigured').removeClass('hide');
            } else {
                $('#gAuthConfigured').addClass('hide');
                $('#gAuthNotConfigured').removeClass('hide');
            }
        });
}
```

WHAT DID WE LEARN?

Here are the key lessons we learned while creating alerts and building custom alert actions:

- A new version of Splunk Enterprise means a brand new journey: extending the functionality of our sample app with the enhanced features of the platform.
- Thinking ahead by making the app modular meant that the transition to our new main developer went smoothly.
- We decided to rework the Google Drive add-on's setup process, as the previous workflow put the burden on the user to run a Python script from the command line.
- To improve the add-on's setup process, we considered recommending using a service account, modified to impersonate a user. However, we decided against this because it undermines OAuth 2.0 security and is discouraged by Google.
- Instead, we decided to modify the PAS reference app's **Setup** dashboard to include Google Drive module logic.
- Requesting access to the user's Google Drive data, obtaining a validation code, and exchanging the validation code for OAuth 2.0 refresh tokens are now all done in the PAS app's **Setup** dashboard.
- We were able to do the bulk of the code work in the app's **setup.js** page, with minimal tweaks to the app's **setup.xml** file and two Python scripts.
- The final challenge in getting this new workflow operational was making the user-entered validation code accessible to the existing Python script so that it could be exchanged for a refresh token from the client side.
- The first possibility was quickly determined a no-go: obtaining the OAuth 2.0 refresh token through JavaScript calls on the client side would have required sensitive information to be stored on the client.

- Instead, we created a new custom REST endpoint that the add-on calls once the user enters the validation code. Calling the endpoint runs the script that does the server-side refresh token exchange.

MORE INFORMATION

For information on the three legged OAuth scenario, see "The OAuth Bible" at: oauthbible.com/#oauth-2-three-legged.

For more info on OAuth2, see "OAuth2 Simplified" at: aaronparecki.com/articles/2012/07/29/1/oauth2-simplified.

For more information on authenticating with the Google Drive REST API, see "Authorizing Your App with Google Drive" at developers.google.com/drive/web/about-auth.

To learn how Google Drive exchanges a validation code for OAuth 2.0 tokens, see "Using OAuth 2.0 for Web Server Applications" at: developers.google.com/identity/protocols/OAuth2WebServer.

To learn about authorization through a service account, see "Using OAuth 2.0 for Server to Server Applications" at: developers.google.com/api-client-library/ruby/auth/service-accounts.

For information about why Google doesn't recommend using service accounts as the common owner for domain-wide files, see: "Perform Google Apps Domain-Wide Delegation of Authority" at: developers.google.com/drive/web/delegation.

For more about authenticating an app on the Google site using OAuth, see: developers.google.com/identity/protocols/OAuth2InstalledApp.

To learn how to create a modular input script: dev.splunk.com/goto/modinputscript.

To learn how to custom REST endpoint entry: dev.splunk.com/goto/restmapconf.

8

New adventures require new tools: alerting

While deciding which use cases to focus on it became clear that a prime candidate was alerting: the ability to trigger notifications or custom actions based on search results. And with fine-tuned control over what happens when alerts are triggered, we discovered that our possibilities for where to go next were almost endless.

The final key element from Chapter 1, "Planning a journey," was:

> *A workflow solution with capabilities such as triggering incidents for review, categorizing them by type, assigning tasks to the relevant personnel, capturing details relevant to the investigation in an unalterable manner, and escalating incidents.*

Unfortunately, as we also mentioned in Chapter 1, we were not able to implement all of the goals we set forth originally. By implementing the concept of alerts in Splunk Enterprise it would seem that we have the start to this solution.

CONSIDERING ALERTS

An alert is an action that a search triggers based on the results of the search. When creating an alert, you specify a condition, such as a threshold or trend setting, that triggers the alert and the actions to take when the alert triggers. You can also create scheduled alerts, where you specify a scheduled search that will trigger an alert when it generates results.

This chapter shows how using Splunk alerting can help you automatically trigger various actions based on real-time metrics and/or schedules. It will also walk you through building a custom alert action.

So far so good, but what kind of alert actions do we have to choose from? Historically, Splunk Enterprise alert actions have included listing triggered alerts in a Triggered Alerts list (accessible from the **Activity** menu), sending e-mails, and running a script. As you know, the PAS app's end users are typically non-technical business users who prefer a friendly UI over entering complex search strings or scripts. Therefore, while an e-mail or an RSS feed would certainly be acceptable to our users, we can't expect them to write a script.

ADM

Scripted alerts require manual setup and offer limited configuration. Previously, the end user would have to directly edit script or .conf files to include connection-level credentials or custom configurations.

What's more, we want to build some flexibility into our alerts. Back at the start of the journey, we said:

> *In addition to the end users, there is a technical role for configuring the app with rules for triggering alerts specific to the organization and its requirements. Some organizations may configure these rules once when they deploy the app, others may have the requirement to be able to update these rules in response to changes in the business environment or to emerging threats. This may require some basic technical knowledge of Splunk Enterprise.*

Fair enough, but what if we could create alert actions that admins or non-technical users could configure and change on their own, without needing much technical Splunk Enterprise knowledge?

Enter the **custom alert action framework** in Splunk Enterprise 6.3 that enables packaged integration with both popular third-party systems and your internal enterprise systems to automate workflows and improve efficiency.

PERF

You can troubleshoot alert action performance or diagnose errors with ease: alert actions are logged and indexed by Splunk Enterprise. Specifically, messages printed to stderr are logged to **splunkd.log**. You can access alert action logs directly from the Alert Actions management page (at **Settings > Alert actions**): in the log column for the action you want to diagnose, click **View log events**. Or just enter the following search query, where `<action_name>` indicates the name of the alert action: `index=_internal sourcetype=splunkd component=sendmodalert action="<action_name>"`.

OUR ALERTING SCENARIOS FROM A BUSINESS PERSPECTIVE

During meetings with SMEs and our business partners, we discussed a number of options for alerts, but for our purposes, we decided to create solutions for the following two user scenarios:

- **Manager/compliance officer:** When an excessive usage policy is violated by a user, send an e-mail to the manager or compliance officer, and lock the user's account. (In the case of our reference app, we accomplished this by setting the user's `status` to `locked` in the **pas_simulated_users_addon**.)
- **Network administrator:** When a terminated employee modifies a file on the network, automatically respond by creating an Atlassian JIRA issue to investigate the matter, and by locking the terminated user's account.

BUS

JIRA is an issue tracking and project planning system that many companies use to track work items. We wanted to choose something that was relatively easy to hook into, and that would be familiar to developers.

BUS

It is also possible to use an alert as a means to perform scheduled exports of data from Splunk Enterprise.

Implementation-wise, we realized that the first scenario would require two alert actions that are already built into Splunk Enterprise. We'll tackle them first, and then concentrate on the JIRA scenario.

EXCESSIVE USAGE POLICY VIOLATION ALERT

The Excessive Usage Policy Violation alert is triggered when a user violates the excessive usage policy. Excessive usage of network assets can indicate that the user's account has been compromised or that the user is engaged in illicit behavior. When the Excessive Usage Policy Violation alert is triggered, we want Splunk Enterprise to send an e-mail to the user's manager or to a compliance officer, and we want the user's account to be locked.

Built-in e-mail alert action workflow

When the alert is triggered, the first thing we want Splunk Enterprise to do is to send an e-mail to the user's manager or to a compliance officer.

ADM

Before you can send e-mail notifications of alerts, you need to configure the e-mail notification settings in Splunk Enterprise. We don't cover that here, so see "Configure email notification settings" **for all the details.**

E-mail notification alert actions are easy and quick to set up. First, create the search that you plan to use to identify the trigger scenario. There are several possible ways to do this, but let's simplify things and say that we want to be notified when a user logs on more than five times in an hour. Therefore, we'd start with a search that shows successful login attempts, sorted by user. We'll set the trigger conditions a bit later, but here's an example search:

```
index=_audit action="login attempt" info=succeeded | stats count by user | where count > 5
```

From the search app, click **Save As** in the upper-right corner, and then click **Alert**. Give the alert a title and a description, and then, next to **Permissions**, choose whether it should be private or shared with other users. Next, choose **Real-time** as the alert's type, because you want Splunk Enterprise to send the alert as soon as the trigger condition occurs, not on a periodic basis.

Under **Trigger Conditions**, you choose when you want the alert to trigger. Since we're looking for the e-mail to be sent as soon as five successful login attempts occur, we choose the second option, **Number of Results**, and then fill out the rest of the window as shown here:

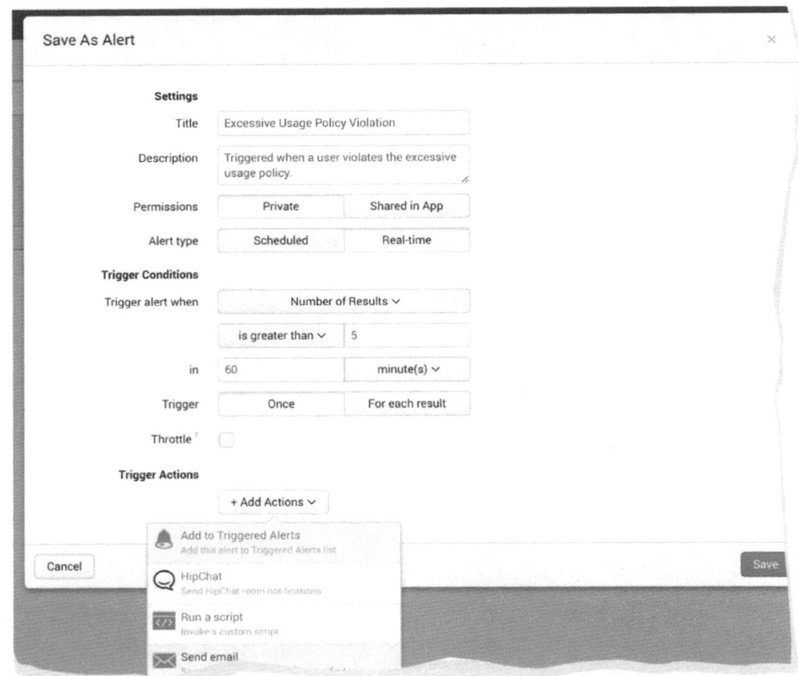

A few settings to pay special attention to are the **Trigger** toggle and the **Throttle** checkbox. Next to **Trigger**, choose **Once** to have a single e-mail sent with all of the users who have met the alert conditions, or choose **For each result** to receive an e-mail for each user that meets the alert conditions. When you select the **Throttle** checkbox, you indicate that alert notifications should be suppressed for the indicated period of time and (if you've chosen to trigger for each result) any specified field values. The default time period is 60 seconds, but you can change that to be any length of time you want. Both of these settings will help keep your e-mail inbox from being overwhelmed with alert notification e-mails.

Now it's time to specify the e-mail to send. Under **Trigger Actions**, we click **Add Actions**, and then **Send email**.

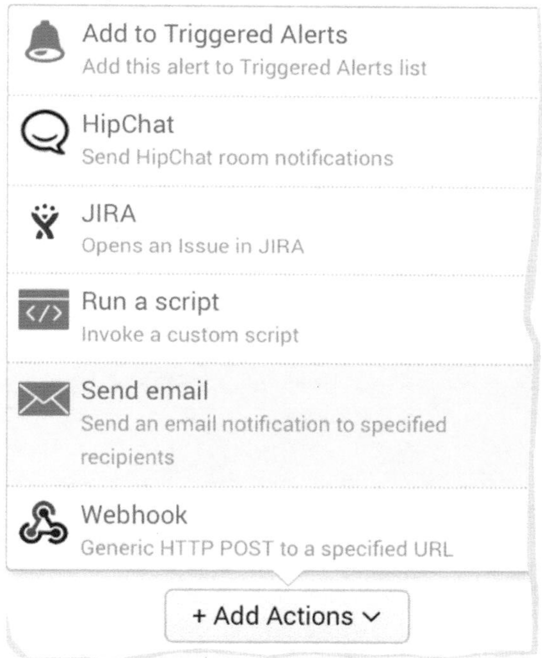

The fields in this section are self-explanatory, but note that we can use tokens in the e-mail subject and body to add specificity to the alert. For example, the subject and body fields are prefilled with text that uses the **`$name$`** token, which will be replaced by the name of the search when the alert is sent.

You can even include information from the trigger search results themselves by using the `$result.`*`fieldname`*`$` token and replacing *fieldname* with the name of the field to include—for instance, the field name that contains the user name of the user who violated the excessive use policy. This way, the information is available at a glance to the e-mail recipient, even if that person is not a Splunk Enterprise user. Keep in mind, though, that the token retrieves information from only the first search result. This can lead to problems if multiple users violate the policy, only the first user would be reported. Set the **Trigger** option discussed previously to **For each result** to ensure you get notifications for all violating users.

Here is our complete alert:

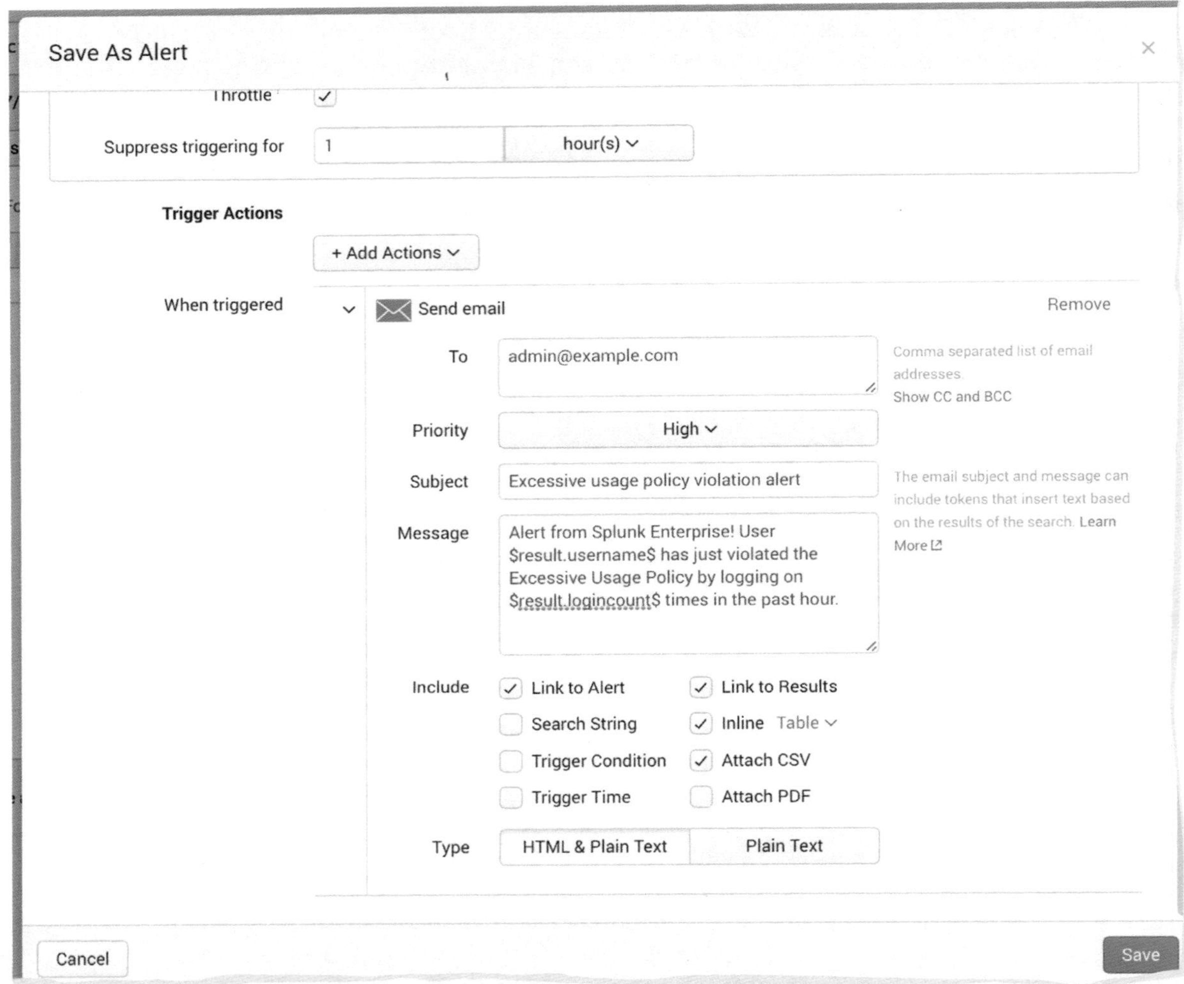

Note that, based on the settings we've chosen next to **Include**, not only will a link to the alert and to the search results be included in the e-mail, it will also include the search results themselves inline and in an attached .CSV file.

Built-in webhook alert action workflow

After the e-mail is sent, notifying the user's manager or a compliance officer of the violation, the second thing we want to do is automatically lock the user's account. Using built-in support for webhooks in Splunk Enterprise 6.3, we can send an HTTP POST request to a REST endpoint to cause it to lock a given user's account.

The webhook alert action mechanism is simple: When an alert is triggered, the webhook will make an HTTP POST request on the URL. The webhook passes JSON-formatted information about the alert in the body of the POST request.

When should you consider using the Splunk Enterprise built-in webhook alert action? There are a few situations where it's ideal:

- When the target application is flexible enough to take a defined JSON payload and transform it in a way that's useful to you. We talk more about the format of the JSON payload later in this section.
- When you have full control over the target application and can modify it to accept this predefined payload. In our case, since we developed the PAS app and all its supplemental apps, we could modify them as needed to accept the JSON payload and take the appropriate action.
- When the action does not require any user configurable parameters. At this time, the JSON payload format can't be changed.

BUS

You can perform a different action upon triggering the alert, such as sending an SMS text message, making an alert message appear in a chat room, or posting a notification to a webpage. For maximum customizability, we recommend you build or reuse a custom alert action packaged as an add-on that is specific to the API of the service on which you want the alert action triggered.

Of course, whether you use a webhook or create a custom alert action is up to you. If you already subscribe to a webhook-enabled service such as Zapier **or** Twilio**, or you're already running an internal webhook-compatible app, it's probably simplest to take advantage of the built-in webhook functionality in Splunk Enterprise rather than creating a custom alert action. Unlike an e-mail alert, before you can use the webhook alert action, you must configure the app or service that will be the recipient of the alert to accept a JSON-formatted data packet. If you're using a service like Zapier or Twilio, you're guided through the process of setting up a webhook input, and then given a URL to enter when you set up your webhook alert action. If you're configuring a service manually, you'll need to know the contents and structure of the JSON sent with each alert.**

Webhooks are great as a quick solution for a service you already use, but building your own custom alert action gives you the most customization options and is the more flexible alternative.

For the PAS app, we first added two new endpoints to **pas_simulated_users_addon** to simulate the account lock and unlock states. To `pas_simulated_users_addon/user-api/app.py`, we added the following:

```
@app.route('/user_list/api/v1.0/users/lock/<string:user_name>', methods=['POST'])
def lock_user_account(user_name):
    try:
        user = filter(lambda t: t['UserName'] == user_name, users)
        user[0]["AccountStatus"] = 'Account Locked'
        if len(user) == 0:
            abort(404)
        return jsonify({'user': user[0]["AccountStatus"]})
    except Exception, e:
        print >> sys.stderr, "ERROR Error sending message: %s" % e
        return jsonify({'Error': "Account lock attempt failed!"})
@app.route('/user_list/api/v1.0/users/unlock/<string:user_name>', methods=['POST'])
def unlock_user_account(user_name):
    try:
        user = filter(lambda t: t['UserName'] == user_name, users)
        user[0]["AccountStatus"] = 'Account Unlocked'
        if len(user) == 0:
            abort(404)
        return jsonify({'user': user[0]["AccountStatus"]})
    except Exception, e:
        print >> sys.stderr, "ERROR Error sending message: %s" % e
        return jsonify({'Error': "Account lock attempt failed!"})
```

This Python code defines the following endpoints, where `<username>` indicates a username in the PAS simulated user database:

- Locks the user's account:
  http://localhost:5000/user_list/api/v1.0/users/lock/<username>
- Unlocks the user's account:
  http://localhost:5000/user_list/api/v1.0/users/unlock/<username>

If the action is successful, the endpoint returns the following JSON: `{"user": "Account Locked"}` or `{"user": "Account Unlocked"}`, respectively. If the specified user does not exist, the following JSON is returned: `{"error": "Not found"}`.

For a webhook, the POST request's JSON data payload includes the search ID (SID) for the search that triggered the alert, the search owner and app, and the first results row from the search that triggered the alert. Here's an example JSON data packet:


```
{
    "result": {
        "user": "nick",
        "client_ip": "10.4.0.28",
        "status": "failure",
        "reason": "user-initiated"
    },
    "sid": "scheduler__admin__search__W2_at_1427942640_178",
    "results_link": "http:// splunk.local:8000/app/search/@go?sid=scheduler__admin__search__W2_
                     at_1427942640_178",
    "search_name": Failed_Login_Attempts,
    "owner": "admin",
    "app": "search"
}
```

Be aware that the contents of the `"result"` key will always vary, depending on the search that is triggering the alert action. However, the `"result"` key will always be followed by the `"sid"`, `"results_link"`, `"search_name"`, `"owner"`, and `"app"` keys, in that order. In the case of the PAS simulated users add-on, the only thing crucial for our purposes is the username included in the endpoint. The content of the JSON packet is ignored.

Once we've set up the receiver of the alert data, the process for creating a webhook alert action is similar to that for an e-mail alert. In fact, we can simply add the webhook alert action to the e-mail alert action we just created. Go to the search app within Splunk Enterprise, click the **Alerts** button in the top navigation bar, find the alert we created, and click **Edit > Edit Actions**. You'll see the existing e-mail alert action. Now, from the **Add Actions** menu, choose **Webhook**.

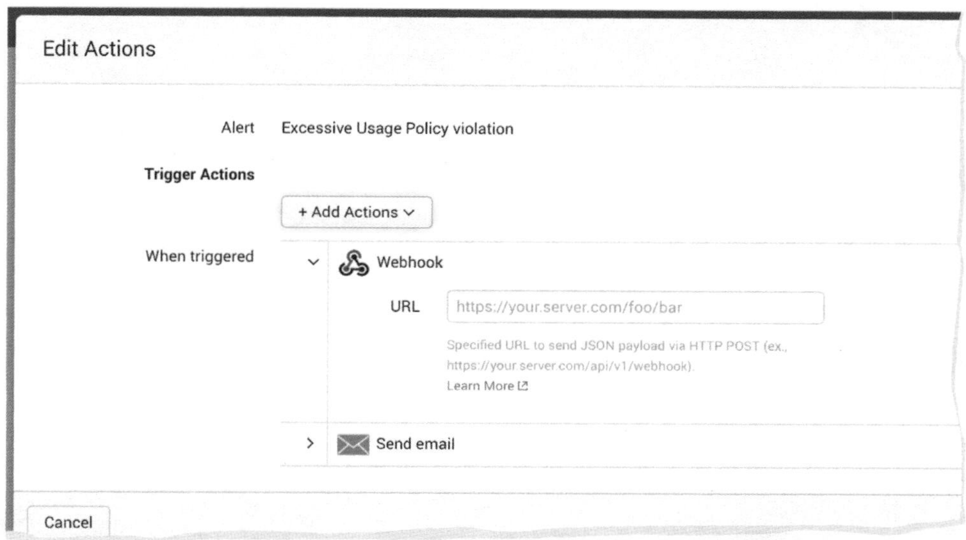

Enter the URL of the web resource that will be receiving the alert data. Recall from the e-mail alert action setup that we used tokens to indicate where to insert incident-specific data. They work here, too, so for the PAS app, we entered the following endpoint URL into this field: http://localhost:5000/user_list/api/v1.0/users/lock/$result.user_id$. When the alert is triggered, the $result.user_id$ token will be replaced with the appropriate username, sending an HTTP POST request to the lock endpoint for that user.

Each time a webhook alert is triggered, Splunk Enterprise makes an HTTP POST request to the URL you entered. The POST request carries the data payload to deliver to the URL. For more information about using webhook alert actions, see "Use a webhook alert action" in the Splunk documentation, "Alerting Manual".

DEV

The webhook functionality is built into Splunk Enterprise as an app, and is located here: `$SPLUNK_HOME/etc/apps/alert_webhook`. If you are so inclined, you can clone it, and then modify it however you want. For example, you might choose to do this if your application accepts a specific payload that does not match to the Splunk Enterprise default.

SEC

When setting up webhook alert actions, keep in mind that the built-in webhook functionality only supports plain, no-auth HTTP communications.

CUSTOM ALERT ACTION AUTHORING WORKFLOW

The next logical step in alerting was also introduced in Splunk Enterprise 6.3: custom alert actions, made possible by a new custom alert action framework. Custom alert actions are seamlessly integrated into the alert workflow. When creating an alert, users simply choose a custom alert action from the **Add actions** menu. As a developer, you specify what input parameters users can configure. You may choose to do this if your application accepts a specific payload that does not match the Splunk default.

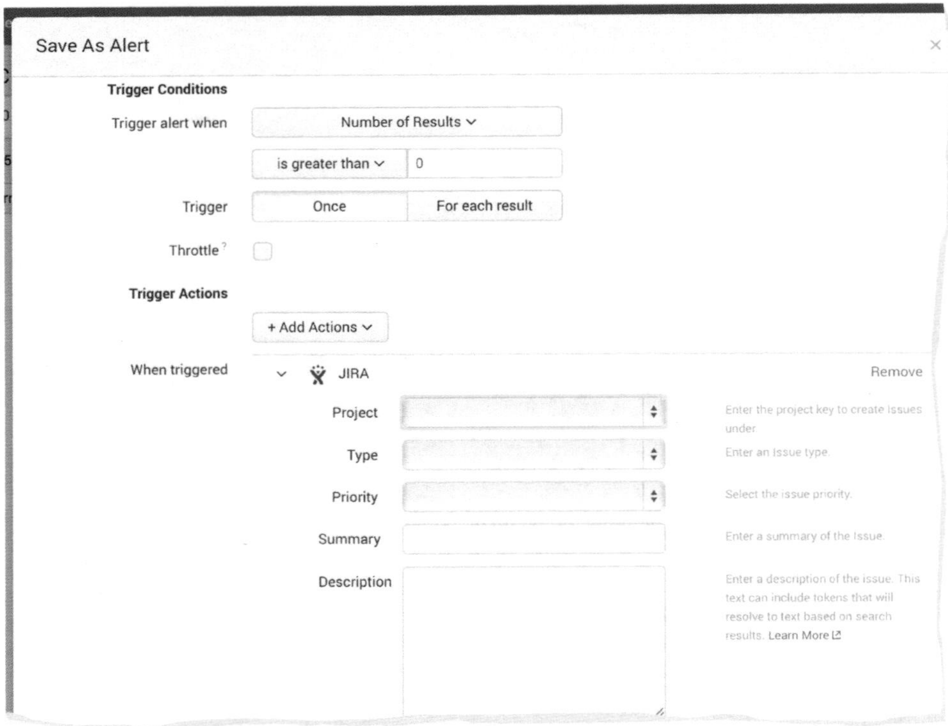

Custom alert actions, like alerts, can be access control list (ACL)-controlled, packaged, and distributed within apps, but they are fully modular. That is, they can be reused by other apps, or even invoked on demand when performing searches. To demonstrate this, the custom alert action we develop in this chapter is completely separate from the PAS app. Once installed, it is available to the PAS app on a user's Splunk Enterprise instance—and, in fact, to all apps to which a user has permissions—but they require a separate, additional install.

DEV

For an example of the kinds of alert actions that you can create, check out the ones built into Splunk Enterprise. In Splunk Enterprise 6.3 or later, go to **Settings > Alert actions.**

The Terminated Employee Access JIRA alert action is triggered when a terminated employee accesses a file on the network. At that instant, we want to create a new JIRA issue and assign it to a manager or compliance officer, and also lock the terminated user's account.

> **Note:** Since we've already covered how we went about locking the user's account in the previous section, we won't cover it again here.

SHIP

If you want to use the JIRA alert action in your Splunk app, we've made it available independently from the main PAS reference app. Find it on Splunkbase.

The Splunk documentation contains detailed instructions for creating a new custom alert action in the "Developing Views and Apps for Splunk Web Manual", starting with the topic "Custom alert actions overview." We won't go into quite as much detail here, but we'll talk about our experience with the process, and cover a few gotchas we discovered along the way.

DEV

We've made it easy to create a new custom alert action by including an alert action template with the PAS app download package. In the **spikes** folder, open the alertaction_app_template folder and you'll see all of the files we talk about in this section, with the correct file structure already in place. All you have to do is fill in the blanks.

The custom alert actions documentation lists the following basic steps for creating a new custom alert action. As mentioned in the docs, you can follow them in any order, but we proceeded pretty much as listed:

- **Create configuration files.** These are the **.conf** (and **.conf.spec**) files that define the configuration of the custom alert action and the app that implements it. The **.conf** files are where attributes and settings are stored. The **.conf.spec** files are where the settings are documented, and they also serve as a template against which the **.conf** files are validated upon startup. In addition, the metadata file **default.meta** defines permissions and scope.

- **Create a script.** The **.py** script executes the custom alert action, which in our case is to connect to JIRA and create a new issue using the settings defined in the **.conf** files. The script follows a workflow that gets information about the triggered alert and then runs the alert action.
- Define a user **interface.** This is an HTML fragment that defines the appearance of the alert action's input controls. The controls are contained in Bootstrap control groups.
- **Add optional components.** These can include **.spec** files that describe custom parameters in your **.conf** files, an app setup file (**setup.xml**) that populates global configuration settings, a **.conf** file with validation rules (**restmap.conf**), an endpoint for confidential information storage (**storage/passwords**), and an icon file. Of these, our JIRA custom alert action only has a **setup.xml** file. We explain why later, in "Define a user interface" and "Storing user passwords securely."

Create configuration files

Recall that the JIRA alert action's **.conf** (and **.conf.spec**) files define the attributes and settings of the alert action. We need to figure out what those fields are, but first let's take a look at the file structure of the "**jira_alerts**" add-on. As we start talking about different files and their locations, you'll want to refer back to the following to help orient yourself:

```
[jira_alerts]
├── appserver
| └── static
| | ├── appIcon.png
| | └── jira_alert_action.png
├── bin
| └── generate_jira_dialog.py
| └── jira_alerts_install_endpoint.py
| └── jira_helpers.py
| └── jira.py
├── default
| ├── alert_actions.conf
| ├── app.conf
| ├── data
| | └── ui
| | | └── alerts
| | | | └── jira.html
├── metadata
| └── default.meta
├── README
| ├── alert_actions.conf.spec
| └── savedsearches.conf.spec
```

In addition to the directories listed here, the local directory will be created at the same level as the **default** directory when users add their first JIRA alert action to an alert.

alert_actions.conf

By inspecting the Atlassian API that lets you remotely trigger issue creation in JIRA, we identified several attributes that we'll need from the user (and some that are optional) before we can automatically create a new JIRA issue. First, we identified the following three JIRA database-specific parameters:

- The address of the JIRA server.
- The JIRA username under which to file issues.
- The JIRA user's password.

These three custom parameters, because they represent global values but can still be changed by the user, are specified in a stanza corresponding to the alert action within the **alert_actions.conf.spec** file (in the **README** directory) and created and stored in the alert_actions.conf file (in the **local** directory) as alert actions are added by users . (The only exception, in our case, was passwords, which our developers stored hashed in **passwords.conf** using a custom Python script and the method discussed in "Storing user passwords securely.") Custom parameters are named using the form **param.[param_name]**. Our JIRA alert action's **alert_actions.conf.spec** file appears as follows:

```
[jira]
param.jira_url = <string>
param.jira_username = <string>
param.jira_password = <string>
```

The parameters are assigned to a data type in the **alert_actions.conf.spec** file. When Splunk Enterprise starts, it validates **local/alert_actions.conf** against **alert_actions.conf.spec** to ensure the correct value types have been specified.

If we'd wanted to, we could have entered values for any of these parameters inside a corresponding stanza in **alert_actions.conf** to preset the fields for users since these values are typically assigned on a per-database basis. Admins will want to do this if users will always be using the same JIRA URL, username, and password to create new issues using the alert action.

All custom alert actions are required to have several parameters defined. These values are specified and stored in the **alert_actions.conf** file within the **default** directory. Our JIRA alert action's **alert_actions.conf** file looks like this:

```
[jira]
is_custom = 1
disabled = 0
label = JIRA
description = Opens an Issue in JIRA
icon_path = jira_alert_action.png
payload_format = json
```

These parameters are all optional, except for the **is_custom** parameter. However, we recommend you include all of them in the **default** directory's **alert_actions.conf** file. Notice that there are no parameters that start with **param.** because none of them are custom parameters.

savedsearches.conf

In addition to the three custom parameters that are specific to a JIRA database (stored in `local/alert_actions.conf`) and the parameters common to all alert actions (stored in `default/alert_actions.conf`), we'll also need the following per-alert action information:

- The JIRA project key (short name of the JIRA project) under which to create issues.
- A summary (title) for each new issue created.
- A description of each new issue created.
- The JIRA issue type (Task, Bug, Documentation, and so on) to assign to each new issue.
- An assignee for each new issue.

Because these values are going to be different every time a user creates a new JIRA alert action, they're stored as custom attributes in the savedsearches.conf file in the **local** directory of the app where you'll be using the alert actions—the search app, more than likely. The `savedsearches.conf` file is compared to the `savedsearches.conf.spec` file in the **README** directory upon startup to check its syntax. Our JIRA alert action's `savedsearches.conf.spec` file appears as follows. The first setting (`action.jira`) is a Boolean value that indicates whether the alert action is enabled:

```
# JIRA alert settings
action.jira = [0|1]
action.jira.param.project_key = <string>
action.jira.param.summary = <string>
action.jira.param.description = <string>
action.jira.param.issue_type = <string>
action.jira.param.assignee = <string>
```

Note that the custom attributes are named using the form `action.[stanza_name].param.[param_name]`, where `[stanza_name]` represents the name of the stanza in `alert_actions.conf`, and `[param_name]` represents the name of the parameter in `alert_actions.conf`. This is the standard format for these parameters, is specified in the Splunk documentation.

If you, or an admin, want to set any custom parameters to default values that will be preset every time a user creates a new alert, assign them in the `alert_actions.conf` file rather than `savedsearches.conf`, and place the file in the **local** directory.

When a user uses an alert action for the first time, a **local** directory is created at the same level as **default**, and a new copy of `savedsearches.conf` is generated if they don't already exist. Within the `savedsearches.conf` file, a new stanza is created using the name the user gave the alert action. All of the fields described above, plus several more that are necessary for an alert action, are stored within the stanza. Every time a user creates a new alert using the alert action, its settings are stored in a new stanza.

The following stanza was created within **savedsearches.conf** when we attached the JIRA alert action to an alert:

```
[Terminated Employee Access]
action.email.pdf.footer_enabled = 1
action.email.pdf.header_enabled = 1
action.email.pdf.html_image_rendering = 1
action.email.reportServerEnabled = 0
action.email.useNSSubject = 1
action.jira = 1
action.jira.param.description = A terminated employee with username $result.user_id$ accessed
internal files $result.count$ times in the last hour.
action.jira.param.issue_type = Incident
action.jira.param.password = dfdskl
action.jira.param.priority = Critical
action.jira.param.project_key = SUP
action.jira.param.summary = Terminated Employee Access: $result.user_id$
action.jira.param.username = user123
alert.suppress = 0
alert.track = 0
counttype = number of events
cron_schedule = 0 6 * * 1
dispatch.earliest_time = -1w
dispatch.latest_time = now
enableSched = 1
quantity = 1
relation = greater than
request.ui_dispatch_app = search
request.ui_dispatch_view = search
search = | data model ri_pas_datamodel Terminated_Access search | stats count by user_id
```

Notice that the search trigger is listed at the very end of the stanza. Be aware that attributes in **savedsearches.conf** take precedence over global settings in **alert_actions.conf** on a per instance basis.

app.conf

The app.conf file maintains the state of an app in Splunk Enterprise, plus it enables customization of aspects of an app, such as custom alert actions. When creating a modular alert action like ours—an alert action that is effectively stand-alone, and that exists in its own add-on bucket—the **app.conf** contents are minimal. Here is the entire contents of the JIRA alert action's **app.conf** file:

SEC

The credential line in the app.conf file was added later in the development process, and has to do with encrypting user credentials (in this case, JIRA passwords). For more information, see "Storing user passwords securely."

```
#
# Splunk app configuration file
#
[install]
is_configured = 0
[ui]
is_visible = false
label = JIRA Ticket Creation
[launcher]
author =
description =
version = 1.0
[credential::jira_password:]

[package]
id = jira_alerts
```

The **alert_actions.conf** and **app.conf** files are the only ones required when you create a new alert action. The **.spec** files are not required, but we highly recommend that developers include them. To find out about the other, optional configuration files, see the Create custom alert configuration files topic in Splunk documentation.

default.meta

The default.meta file contains ownership information, read and write controls, and export settings for alert actions. Each app or add-on has its own **default.meta** file, which is stored in the **metadata** directory.

The contents of the JIRA alert action's **default.meta** file are:

```
[]
access = read : [ * ], write : [ admin ]

[alert_actions/jira]
export = system

[alerts]
export = system

[restmap]
export = system
```

The first pair of lines sets the access controls. Setting **read** to * allows all users to read the alert action's contents. Setting **write** to **admin** allows only Splunk Enterprise administrators to share objects into the alert action.

The other pairs of lines define settings for exporting the alert action to other apps and add-ons. Setting **export** to **system** for each of the contexts inside the brackets makes them each available in all apps.

For all the details about assembling the **default.meta** file, see the fifth step in the building apps documentation, "Set permissions."

Create a script

The next step was to create a Python script to execute the custom alert action. We want the script to connect to JIRA and create a new issue using the settings stored in the **savedsearches.conf** file. Custom alert action scripts follow a workflow that gets information about the triggered alert and then runs the alert action.

Our JIRA alert action script (**jira.py** in the **bin** directory, the other scripts in that directory are discussed in the next section) follows the typical script workflow, as described in the "Create a custom alert action script" topic in the Splunk documentation:

- **Check the execution mode, based on command line arguments.** Specifically, when the alert action is triggered, it runs the script with the **--execute** argument, which indicates to our script that it should do its thing.
- **Read configuration payload from stdin.** In our case, the payload is a data packet in JSON format with properly formatted attribute-value pairs. Within the payload, the **"configuration"** attribute is set to a value that contains the appropriate JIRA values. That is, it contains the values that we specified in **savedsearches.conf** and any the user entered when setting up the alert action, with tokens replaced by actual values. To illustrate what we mean, here's a sample JSON payload. Compare the contents of the **"configuration"** attribute to the stanza from **savedsearches.conf** from the previous section.


```
{
  "app": "pas_ref_app",
  "owner": "admin",
  "results_file": "C:\\Program Files\\SplunkBeta\\var\\run\\splunk\\dispatch\\
                   scheduler__admin_cGFzX3JlZl9hcHA__RMD5de437274897e69c9_at_1436395080_45
                   \\per_result_alert\\tmp_2.csv.gz",
  "results_link": "http:\/\/localhost:8000\/app\/pas_ref_app\/search?
                   q=%7Cloadjob%20scheduler__admin_cGFzX3JlZl9hcHA__RMD5de437274897e69c9_at_1436395080_
                   45%20%7C%20head%203%20%7C%20tail%201&earliest=0&latest=now",
  "server_host": "SPLUNKPC",
  "server_uri": "https:\/\/127.0.0.1:8089",
  "session_key": "Ls2dhEfbOVo3j52MPF4v82bglhpT7QUnFERZhcfB6NHYj6m^4Rzpr6VXln2ZTlnFSXpMxburc_n42T\
                  VWxZ5NHvAi3D_q12a_iZbhZNfJmlcK^0x^4qSzfM1nFGcIt07j2y1z4KRRKo",
  "sid": "scheduler__admin_cGFzX3JlZl9hcHA__RMD5de437274897e69c9_at_1436395080_45",
  "search_name": "Terminated Employee Access",
  "configuration": {
    "description": "The user rblack has accessed files 7 times in the past hour.",
    "issue_type": "3",
    "jira_url": "http:\/\/myjiraserver:8080",
    "jira_username": "theuser",
    "project_key": "SIM",
    "summary": "Terminated User Access: rblack"
  },
  "result": {
    "count": "7",
    "user_id": "rblack"
  }
}
```

- **Run the alert action.** Our script then gets the value of that **"configuration"** attribute, and parses it. First, it gets the URL of the JIRA server (**'jira_url'**), and then tacks on the appropriate RESTful endpoint (to create a new issue in JIRA, it's **"rest/api/latest/issue"**). Now it knows where to send the data. Then, the script assembles a JSON data packet in the appropriate format for JIRA. Finally, the script creates an outbound request object and sends it to the JIRA endpoint.
- **Terminate.** It's a good idea to account for any anomalies that might occur before terminating. For example, our script accounts for an incorrect command line argument, receiving an HTTP status code of 200, and generating an exception by printing an error message. The script then terminates using **exit()**.

You place the script in your app's **bin** directory.

DEV

One of our developers ran into some issues with the Python script during development and wasn't immediately sure how to troubleshoot them. He discovered a solution made possible by the fact that custom alert action executions are logged (at both a splunkd process level and a script level) to the internal index. He first added some exception handling in the form of print statements to stderr, such as the following, inside a try-catch statement:

```
# create outbound request object
try:
    headers = {"Content-Type": "application/json"}
    result = requests.post(url=jira_url, data=body, headers=headers, auth=(username, password))
    print >>sys.stderr, "INFO Jira server HTTP status= %s" % result.text
    print >>sys.stderr, "INFO Jira server response: %s" % result.text
except Exception, e:
    print >> sys.stderr, "ERROR Error sending message: %s" % e
    return False
```

Here's the query he used to check the status of his previous alert action executions, where **<alert_action_name>** indicates the name of the custom alert action:

```
index=_internal sourcetype=splunkd component=sendmodalert action="<alert_action_name>"
```

Define a user interface

The final main step is to create a user interface. This is the interface that users will see when they choose the JIRA custom alert action from the available alert actions menu. In our case, it also included a setup interface that users must complete before using the alert action.

This step went through a major iteration before the final version due to the requirement that the interface be written in HTML. At first, our developers had hoped to use the classic web development combination of HTML and JavaScript to create an interface that could dynamically change according to the options users choose. For example, though there are default JIRA issue types, it's most common for JIRA administrators and project managers to create their own issue types. Plus, issue types can vary depending on the project in which a new issue is created.

With JavaScript out of the picture for this phase of the alert action development, our developers came up with a configuration pane that looked like this:

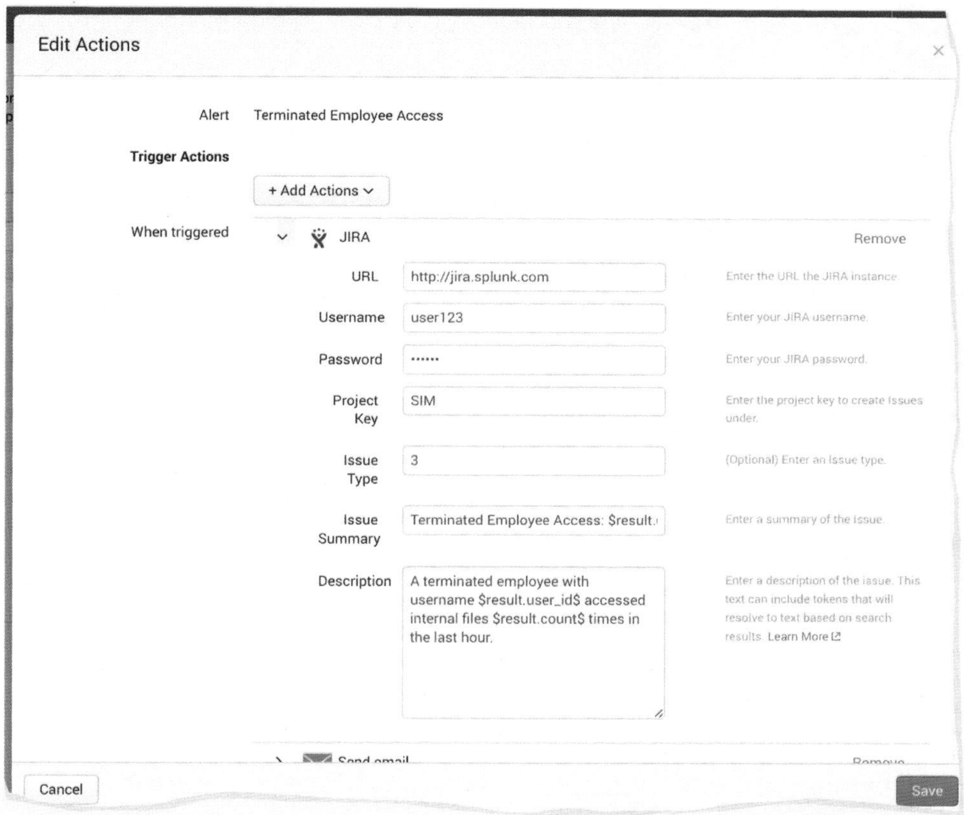

Note that, to specify values for project and issue type, users would have to enter the exact values or be faced with error messages and unpredictable behavior. We could have also used pop-up menus for the values, but, again, they would have had to be hard-coded.

That's all fine for values that will be different with each alert, such as the issue summary and description, but we were still not satisfied with the limitation of hard-coded HTML for the UI. That's when our developers realized that, though JavaScript was out of the question, Python scripting was clearly something that is supported in this context.

So, we refactored this portion of the JIRA alert action setup and configuration workflow. We moved the JIRA server, username, and password entry to a new setup page for enabling the JIRA alert action, and then updated the UI portion of the custom alert action workflow to invoke a new Python script that imports values from the JIRA server using the user-supplied credentials.

To be able to choose existing project, issue type, and priority values when creating a new JIRA alert, users must first invoke the setup page. To do this, go to **Settings > Alert Actions**. Then click **Setup JIRA Ticket Creation**.

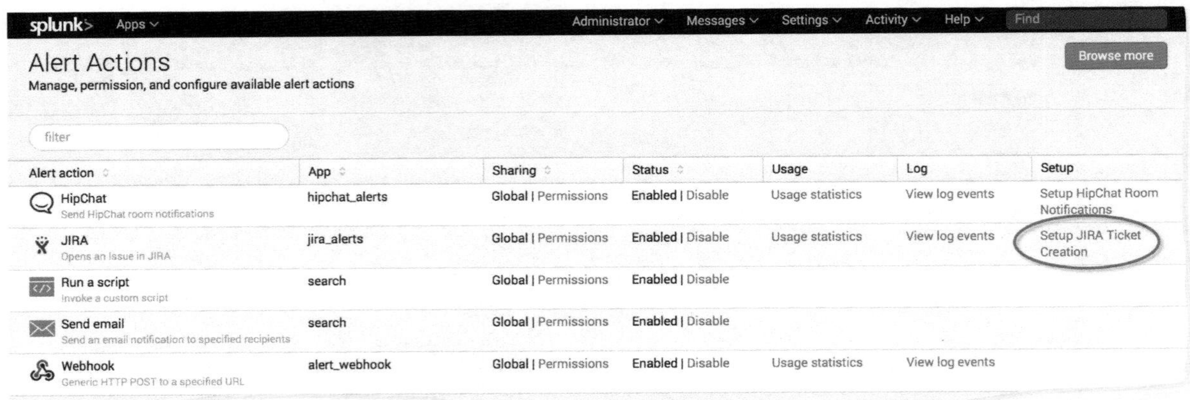

The new setup page is shown here. It's defined in the `setup.xml` file in the **default** directory.

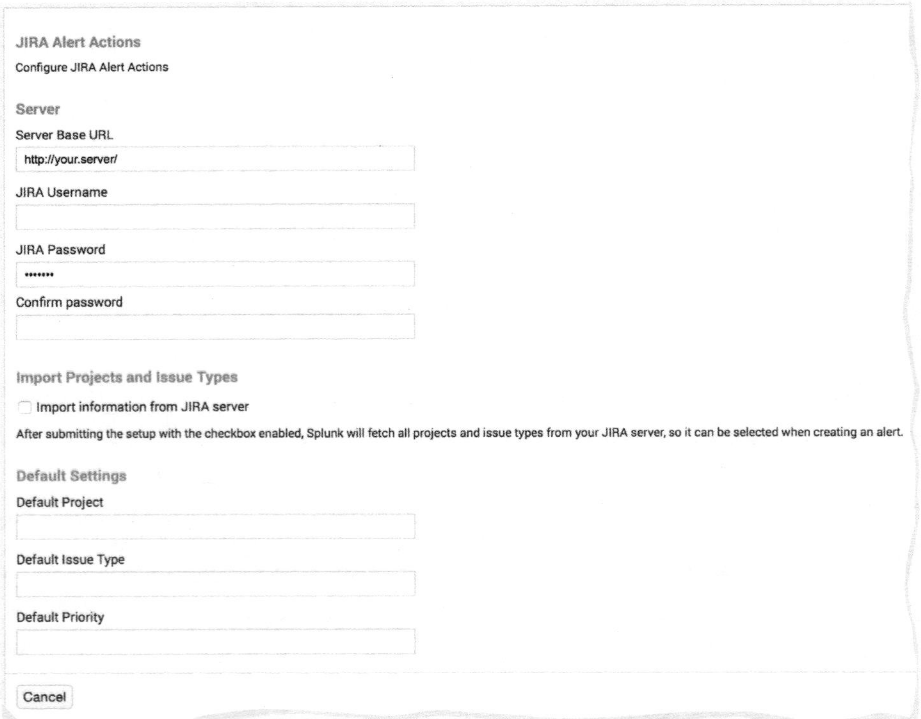

Notice that the page has three sections:

- The **Server** section is where users enter the JIRA server's URL, their username, and their password. The password is stored securely using the method described in the section "Storing user passwords securely," later in this chapter.
- The **Import Projects and Issue Types** section is where users can choose whether to have Splunk Enterprise contact the JIRA server and fill in projects and issue types dynamically when setting the alert action. This option is off by default.
- The **Default Settings** section is where users can set the default project, issue type, and priority for new JIRA alerts. When creating new alerts, users can always change the values from the defaults.

Once they've filled in their JIRA credentials on the setup page, users have the option to import project names and issue types from the JIRA server. If they choose this option, the Python script `generate_jira_dialog.py` (along with the script `jira_helpers.py`) generates a static HTML page using a template and the values it retrieves from the JIRA server using the user-provided credentials.

The following is the new configuration pane for adding trigger actions. In this case, the alert action has already been set up with a valid JIRA server, username, and password, so the **Project**, **Type**, and **Priority** settings are now pop-up menus that are prefilled with values from the server.

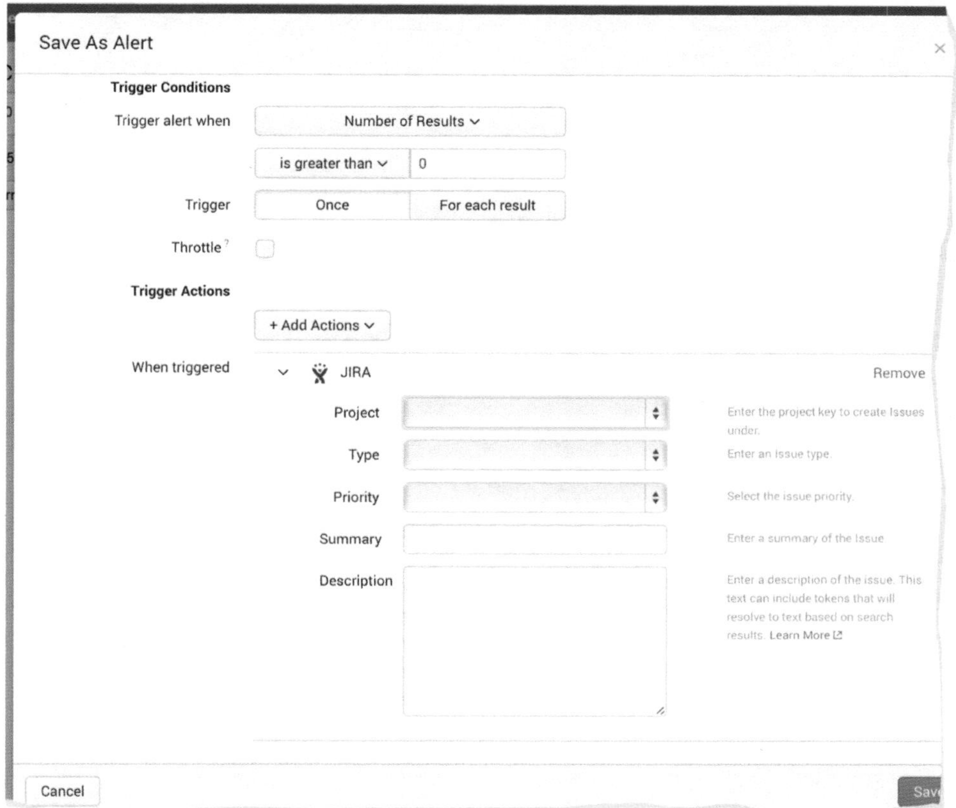

Be aware that the markup you use must be consistent with Bootstrap version 2.3.2 (just like the rest of the Splunk Enterprise UI). You add controls within Bootstrap control groups. Match the **name** attribute for each **<input>** tag with the parameters defined in the **savedsearches.conf.spec** file. The value that the user enters into the text input (or chooses from a pop-up menu) ends up in **savedsearches.conf** when the user saves the alert action. For example, this control group contains the control where users enter their JIRA username:

```
<div class="control-group">
<label class="control-label" for="username">Username</label>

    <div class="controls">
        <input type="text" name="action.jira.param.username" id="username" />
        <span class="help-block">Enter your JIRA username.</span>
    </div>
<div>
```

DEV

Don't forget to validate user input! Use the validation stanzas in restmap.conf. For example, the following stanza verifies whether a URL is valid, and displays a message if it's not:

```
[validation:savedsearch]
action.webhook.param.url = validate( match('action.webhook.param.url', "^https?://[^\s]+$"),
"Webhook URL is invalid")
```

For more information, search for "Validation stanzas" on the restmap.conf reference page.

The script builds the HTML file, gives it the same name as the main script file (**jira.py**), appends it with ".html" (**jira.html**), and then places it within the app's directory as follows: **/local/data/ui/alert_actions/**

In case users opt out of retrieving project, type, and priority values from the JIRA server, we also created an alternate, static HTML page that allows them to enter values manually. The file, just like the one our script creates, is named **jira.html**, and is located at **/default/data/ui/alert_actions/**.

Testing

Throughout the alert action development process, we engaged in rigorous unit testing, which we wholeheartedly recommend before releasing even something as seemingly simple as an e-mail, webhook, or custom alert action into the wild. This included:

- **Observe real-time notification:** In our case, it's relatively easy to test out these alerts. Simply perform the actions that we know should trigger the alerts. For example, do what you've intended to invoke the JIRA alert, and then check the database you specified to be sure that a new issue has been created. We were able to do this relatively easily since Atlassian provides JIRA on a trial basis. We installed it in our sandbox environment and tested it out with relatively little added effort. The drawback here is that this is appropriate for exploratory testing, not automated testing.
- **On-demand invocation:** Invoke alerts using the search language. You can do this using the `sendalert` command. Its syntax is as follows, where `<alert_action>` indicates the alert action to test, `<action_specific_params>` indicates any alert action-specific parameters that must be set, and `<value>` indicates the parameter's value:

```
sendalert <alert_action> param.<action_specific_params>="<value>"
```

For example, here's an example search query that invokes the JIRA alert action we created previously in this chapter.

```
| sendalert jira param.description="TEST RUN" param.issue_type="3" param.project_key="SIM"
param.summary="TESTING ONLY"
```

- **Subcutaneous testing:** This type of testing is ideal for automated testing. It indicates a type of testing that doesn't rely on visually verifying in the user interface that things are working correctly. For example, consider the alert actions that involve locking user accounts. Regardless of the type of system that is administering your accounts, there are likely many more ways to verify whether an account has been locked than by logging in using the UI to visually confirm it. For example, can you automate the process of querying an LDAP or Active Directory server? On the Splunk Enterprise side, if the alert action results in data generation or changes the state of a Splunk index or some other internal file, you can execute a Splunk query or call to the REST API to confirm whether something significant comes back.
- **Manual invocation:** Shift test focus to the alert script by taking the alert trigger out of the equation. For example, try creating a fake payload, and then piping it directly to the alert script with a Python command such as the following:

  ```
  $ cat fakepayload.json | splunk cmd python myalertscript.py
  ```

In addition to unit testing, we have enriched our set of acceptance tests to test the alerting scenarios end-to-end using Selenium test automation.

TEST

For more, be sure to check out our JIRA alert action testing README file: `jira_alerts/bin/TEST_README.txt`.

Problems encountered

One of our developer encountered two significant problems, both stemming from being limited to static HTML when crafting the user interface. He also had some advice for setting up his testing environment.

No JavaScript support when creating custom alert action UI

When creating JIRA issues, input elements such as "issue type" are meant to be loaded in dynamically because JIRA users are able to create custom issue types at will.

At first, the lack of JavaScript support in the custom alert action UI made us think that we would have to be content with default JIRA issue types, which are built into all JIRA instances. However, doing so would have meant the app became more brittle and could easily have broken if Atlassian decided to modify the structure of the default issue types. Developers would have to use the "swivel chair" approach and manually reproduce any custom issue types in the action alert static HTML.

Our developer then realized that, even though JavaScript wasn't a possibility, Python scripting is clearly something that is supported in this context. So he refactored the UI portion of the custom alert action workflow to include the Python scripts mentioned above.

DEV

You may have to get creative to work around the lack of JavaScript support in the custom alert action UI.

Storing user passwords securely

Being limited to static HTML also means that we are limited to using HTTP basic access authentication. Something like OAuth2 would be preferable, but that would require the use of custom JavaScript, which is currently not supported. A consequence of using HTTP basic auth is that we must ask the user for a username and password. The password is masked in the UI, but Splunk Enterprise saves the input value as cleartext in `alert_actions.conf`. This is not good, for fairly obvious reasons. Thankfully, a workaround was crafted using Python scripting, the setup.xml file, and the Splunk Enterprise password endpoint to handle encryption of the user's password. In the custom alert action Python script, a GET request can be made to the following endpoint to retrieve the unencrypted password:

```
<SPLUNK_BASE_URL>/servicesNS/nobody/jira_alerts/storage/passwords/%3Ajira_password%3A?
output_mode=json
```

The `"jira_password"` parameter name is defined in the `app.conf` file. Most of the heavy lifting of obscuring user passwords is accomplished in the `jira_alerts_install_endpoint.py` script. It handles running the user-entered password through the Splunk Enterprise internal hash mechanism, and then writing the result to the `passwords.conf` file. When the time comes to decode the hashed password, the **get_jira_password()** method within the main `jira.py` script takes care of it.

DEV

Be aware that because the hashed password is stored in app.conf, you can only use this method for global-level settings. You can't securely store credentials on a per-alert basis.

The GET call also needs an authorization header with a session key value that can be obtained directly from the JSON payload.

SEC

Use `setup.xml` and the `storage/passwords` endpoint to encrypt any passwords that you'll be requesting from users.

Setup advice

Our developer set up his testing environment by installing JIRA on his Windows machine. He had a few caveats to share:

- Be sure to manually turn on **Accept remote API calls** in the system config.
- Create a project of the type that you want to add issues to.
- Create a non-admin test user in User Management.
- Assign that user to the project you created.

To test that the JIRA REST endpoint (which, as we mentioned previously, is http://your_jira_server:8080/rest/api/latest/issue) worked as expected using basic authentication, our developer used Chrome's Postman application. It did!

WHAT DID WE LEARN?

Here are the key lessons we have learned while creating alerts and building custom alert actions:

- Alerts are actions that a search triggers based on the results of the search.
- You can easily create a new alert just by saving your search as one.
- You have a number of alert actions available to you–both built-in and custom-made.
- You can attach e-mail and script actions to your alerts, or cause an alert notification to be added to the Triggered Alerts list in Splunk Enterprise.
- You can use a webhook alert action to define a custom callback on a particular web resource.
- A webhook alert action simply sends an HTTP POST request containing a JSON data packet to an endpoint URL that you specify.
- You can attach multiple actions to an alert.

- It is possible to set the throttling controls to suppress an alert to a longer time window to avoid alert flooding.
- You can create your own alert actions using the Custom Alert Action Framework.
- You create custom alert actions by creating and assembling the appropriate files, defining the right parameters, writing alert logic in Python, and defining a user interface.
- Unit testing custom alert actions is essential, and is made easier by using the **sendalert** search command.
- You can also test custom alert actions by observing a real-time notification you initiate through automated subcutaneous testing, or by manually sending a fake payload through your Python script.
- You can package your custom alert actions as Splunk add-ons and distribute them through Splunkbase to a wider community.

MORE INFORMATION

To learn more about alerts, see "About alerts" at: dev.splunk.com/goto/aboutalerts.

To try JIRA for free, download it from the Atlassian web site: atlassian.com/jira.

For more information about JIRA, see: en.wikipedia.org/wiki/JIRA.

To learn how to configure email notification settings, see "Configure email notification settings" at: dev.splunk.com/goto/configureemail.

For more information about webhooks, see: en.wikipedia.org/wiki/Webhook.

For information on webhook-enabled services such as Zapier or Twilio, see:

- zapier.com
- twilio.com

For more information about using webhook alert actions, see "Use a webhook alert action" at: dev.splunk.com/goto/webhookalert.

For more information on creating custom alerts see "About custom alert actions" at: dev.splunk.com/goto/createcustomalerts.

Download the JIRA Alert add on from Splunkbase at: dev.splunk.com/goto/jiraalertaddon

For detailed instructions on creating a new custom alert action see the "Developing Views and Apps for Splunk Web Manual," starting with the topic "Custom alert actions overview" at: dev.splunk.com/goto/modalertsintro.

Download the Alert Action app template from GitHub at: dev.splunk.com/goto/alertactiontemplate.

The custom alert actions documentation lists the following basic steps for creating a new custom alert action, see "About building apps with custom alert actions" at: dev.splunk.com/goto/modalertscreate.

To download Bootstrap go to: getbootstrap.com.

For information on creating and storing information in the **alert_actions.conf** file, see: dev.splunk.com/goto/alertactionsconf.

For instructions on defining parameters in custom alert actions, see "Set up the alert actions configuration file" at: dev.splunk.com/goto/setupalertconfig.

For more information on the savedsearches.conf file, see: dev.splunk.com/goto/savedsearchesconf.

For instructions on defining parameters in the savedsearches.conf file, see "Set up the saved searches configuration file" at: dev.splunk.com/goto/customsavedsearchesconf.

For more information on the app.conf file, see: dev.splunk.com/goto/appconf.

To find out about the other, optional configuration files, see "Create custom alert configuration files" topic at: dev.splunk.com/goto/customalertconfig.

For more information of the alert action settings contained in the `default.meta` file see: dev.splunk.com/goto/defaultmetaconf.

For all the details about assembling the `default.meta` file, see the fifth step in the building apps documentation, "Set permissions" at: dev.splunk.com/goto/setpermissions.

To learn more about the typical script workflow, see "Create a custom alert action script" at: dev.splunk.com/goto/customalertscript.

For information about the final main step creating a user interface, see "Define a custom alert action user interface" at: dev.splunk.com/goto/customalertui.

For more information on "Validation stanzas" see the `restmap.conf` reference page at: dev.splunk.com/goto/restmapconf.

To learn more about using Selenium test automation, see: seleniumhq.org.

To learn how to use JIRA to create custom Issue types, see "Defining Issue Type Field Values" at: confluence.atlassian.com/display/JIRA/Defining+Issue+Type+Field+Values.

For information on default JIRA issue types see "What is an Issue" at: confluence.atlassian.com/display/JIRA/What+is+an+Issue#WhatisanIssue-IssueType.

For information on custom alerts using Python scripting and the setup.xml file, see: dev.splunk.com/goto/customalertoptionalitems.

9

Building in telemetry with high-performance data collection

Consider the two scenarios that our business stakeholders brought to us. Each is very different from the other, but each ended up being a perfect candidate for us to explore.

Scenario 1 (the "keycard scenario"): Our business partners wanted a way to track when and where their employees and contractors were accessing company resources and real estate. Both employees and contractors already have to use their company-issued keycards to gain access. How could the company get a high volume of those access events per minute into Splunk Enterprise, preferably without having to set up a Splunk forwarder, and then view that data in a useful and insightful way, such as on a map?

Scenario 2 (the "telemetry scenario"): Our business stakeholders were developing a web-based app and wanted to use Splunk Enterprise to collect and organize both debug and usage data for the app. Because the data could be coming from anyone, anywhere in the world, they didn't want it to contain any Splunk-specific information, and certainly didn't want it to include any Splunk Enterprise credential information.

Both of these scenarios are prime candidates for a new feature in Splunk Enterprise 6.3: a developer-focused way of getting data in called "HTTP Event Collector." Let's first examine the feature in more detail, and then look at the different ways in which it came in handy in the PAS app.

This chapter demonstrates a powerful and efficient new way to get data directly into Splunk Enterprise from network sources—the HTTP Event Collector. In addition, it touches on a brand-new visualization scheme: geographic visualizations with choropleth maps.

ALL ABOUT HTTP EVENT COLLECTOR

HTTP Event Collector (or *"**EC**"*) is a new way to send data to Splunk Enterprise. With EC, the data source (or sources) send data packaged within JSON-formatted data packets through HTTP or HTTPS directly to Splunk Enterprise. No extra software is required on the client side, though there are logging libraries available for several programming languages—including Java, C#, and JavaScript—to help automate the process of properly formatting the data. EC uses specialized tokens, so you don't need to hard-code your Splunk Enterprise credentials in your app or supporting files. It's also scalable. Use Deployment Server to deploy your tokens and configuration files to other Splunk Enterprise instances, and then use a load balancer to distribute incoming HTTP Event Collector data evenly to indexers.

Getting data into Splunk Enterprise using HTTP Event Collector is different from the other data input methods:

- First, you have to turn on the feature. Doing so opens up the EC port (8088 by default, though you can change that) and causes Splunk Enterprise to start listening on it for incoming requests.
- Then, generate an HTTP Event Collector authentication token ("*EC token*"). EC tokens are sent in the headers of incoming data packets to authenticate them with Splunk Enterprise. You generate a new token on your Splunk Enterprise instance, and then give it to the sender of the data.
- Next, send the data, placing the token in the authorization header of every JSON data packet that is sent. If there is a problem, Splunk Enterprise doesn't accept the data, and sends back a 401 (Unauthorized) status code to the sender.
- If a data packet has a valid, active token in its auth header, Splunk Enterprise accepts the data packet, sends back a 200 (OK) status code to the sender, and indexes the packet's event data.

DEV

Problems that you can encounter when sending data include: an invalid or missing token in the auth header, incorrectly formatted JSON, JSON that doesn't conform to the EC event protocol, an invalid timestamp, an invalid or disallowed index, and so on.

You can send any kind of data to Splunk Enterprise through HTTP Event Collector , but it must be contained within a JSON payload envelope. Here's a sample event in JSON format, created according to the EC event protocol:

```
{
    "event": { "hello": "world" }
}
```

This is the simplest kind of event—one that contains just event data. You can also specify values such as a timestamp, a hostname, source and sourcetype values, and a preferred index, but doing so through the event data itself is uncommon and not recommended.

You can also batch events. That is, you are not limited to one event per data packet; you can send multiple events in a single request and Splunk Enterprise will index each event individually.

For all the details about the EC's JSON event format, see "About the JSON event protocol in HTTP Event Collector."

USING HTTP EVENT COLLECTOR

Trying out HTTP Event Collector is easy, and only requires a brief detour from our journey. In this section we'll enable EC, create a new HTTP Event Collector token, and then send some data. You don't even need to have the PAS reference app installed.

First, turn on EC. Unless you've already used it, EC is disabled by default. To enable it, go to **Settings > Data inputs > HTTP Event Collector**. Then click the **Global Settings** button in the upper-right corner. This will bring up the following configuration screen for EC:

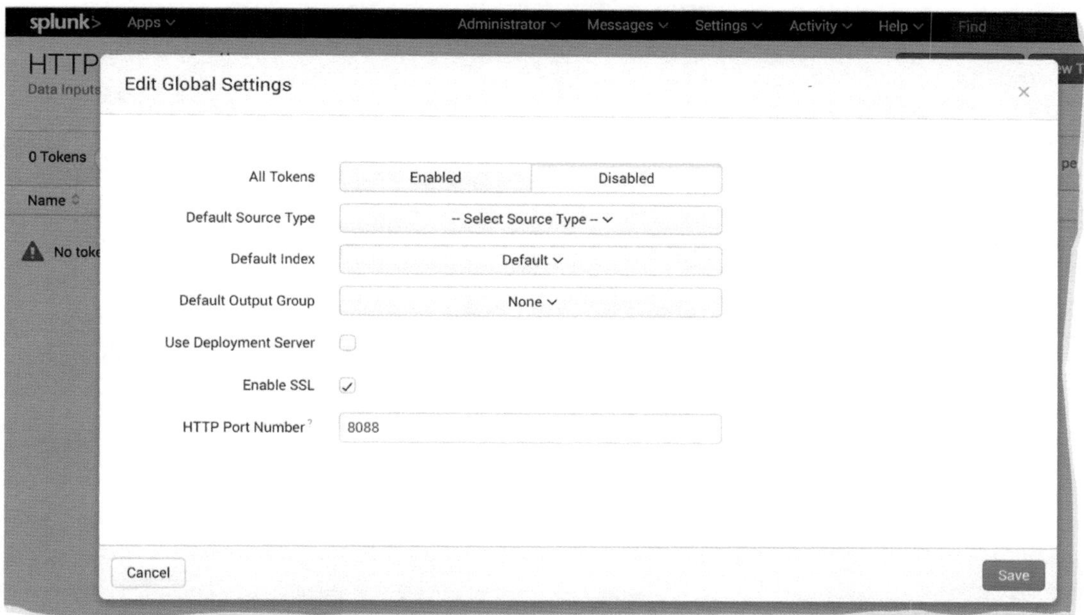

Click the **Enable** button, and then click **Save**. You've just turned on HTTP Event Collector.

Now that EC is turned on, let's create a new HTTP Event Collector token. From the **HTTP Event Collector** page, click the **New Token** button.

The **Select Source** screen of the **Add Data** workflow appears. This is where you name and describe the EC input, specify (if you want) a **source** field name to give to all data accepted with this input's token, and optionally specify an output group (a named group of Splunk indexers).

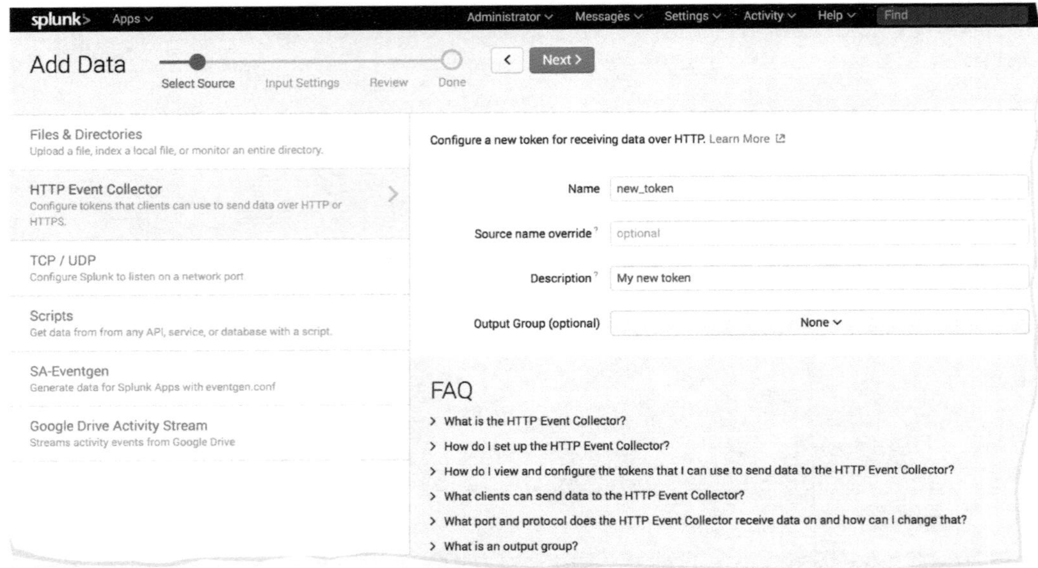

Enter at least a name for the input, and then click **Next**.

The **Input Settings** screen appears. On this screen, you determine how to assign a **sourcetype** field value to incoming data (either automatically, by specifying an existing one, or by creating a new one) and what indexes are allowed to index the data accepted with this input's token. You also specify the default index to use to index data bearing this input's token.

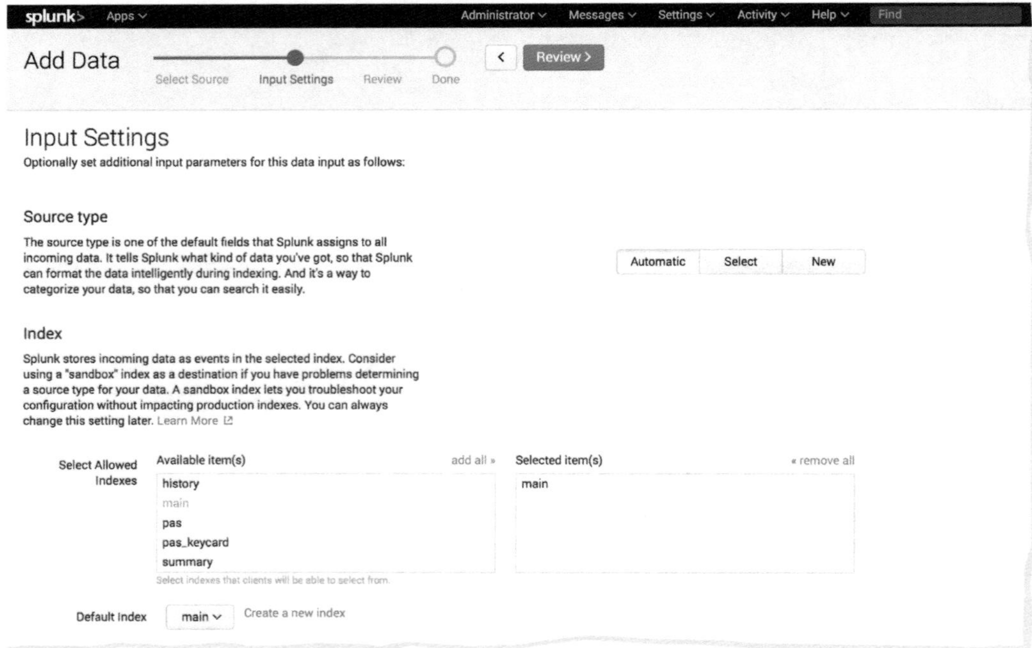

On the **Input Settings** page, leave the **Source type** as **Automatic**, and then choose at least one index that is not used for production, or real-world, purposes. Then, click **Review**. The **Review** page appears.

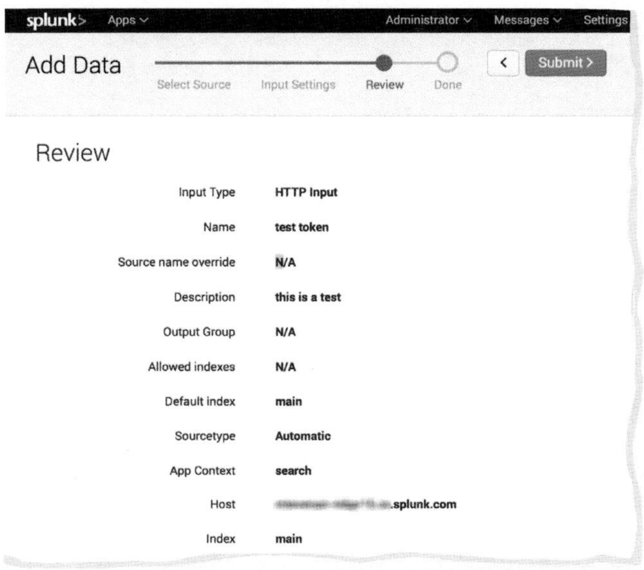

Review your input settings, and then click **Submit**. You'll see a message that says, "Token input has been created successfully." A token value is simply a globally-unique identifier (GUID) that Splunk Enterprise has generated to identify data intended for this EC input. You can click the token value from this screen and copy it to your Clipboard for later use, or go back to **Settings > Data inputs > HTTP Event Collector**, and you'll see that your new input is listed along with its token value and all its other pertinent information.

Select the entire token value, and then copy it to the Clipboard. Now we'll use it to send some data.

Open a command prompt window or terminal. Type the following cURL statement to test out your token. Be sure to replace *<host>* with your Splunk Enterprise server's hostname, and *<token>* with the token you just copied to the Clipboard:

```
curl -k https://<host>:8088/services/collector -H 'Authorization: Splunk <token>' -d
'{"event":"Hello, World!"}'
```

DEV

Because of the way Windows handles single and double quotes, this cURL command will not work on Windows. To get it to work on Windows, you can either replace the single quotation marks (') with double quotation marks (") and then escape the inner double quotation marks, or you can use an app like Postman for Google Chrome to send the request instead. In fact, because of Postman's powerful feature set and its ability to run cross-platform, we highly recommend it. www.getpostman.com

If everything is working correctly, you will see the following response:

```
{"text":"Success","code":0}
```

This means that Splunk Enterprise has received the data. Let's check it out within the search app.

Back in Splunk Enterprise, on the **Apps** menu, click **Search & Reporting**. In the search box, type the following, making sure to replace *<input_name>* with the name you gave your input:

```
source="http:<input_name>"
```

That's it! Press **Return** or **Enter**, and you'll see that Splunk Enterprise has found one event that corresponds to your input's name.

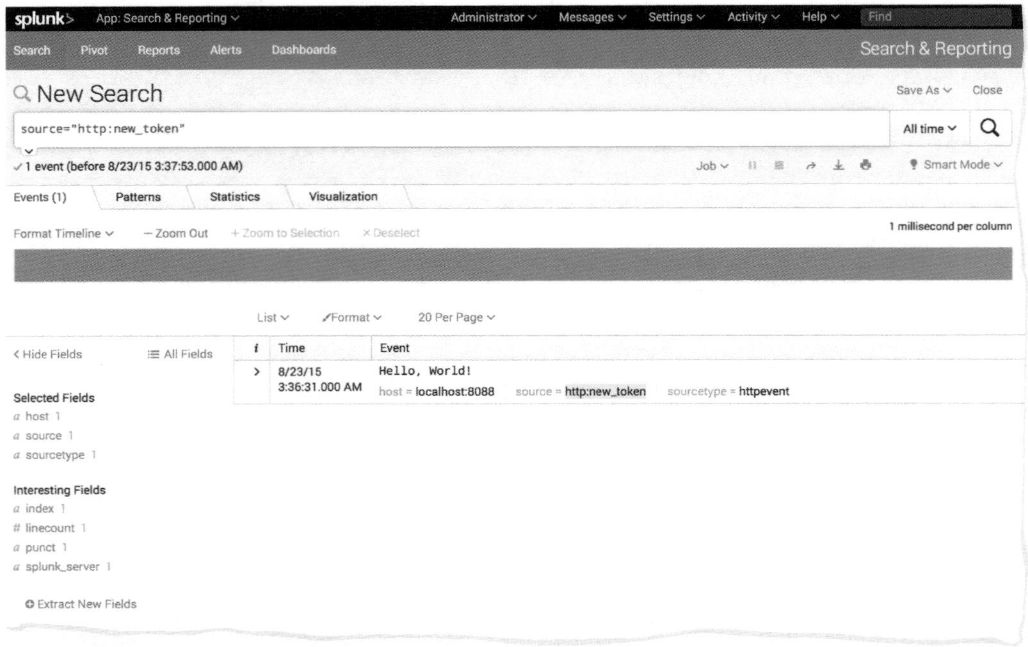

THE KEYCARD SCENARIO

Recall from earlier in this chapter our keycard scenario:

> *Our business partners wanted a way to track when and where their employees and contractors were accessing company resources and real estate. Both employees and contractors already have to use their company-issued keycards to gain access. How could the company get a high volume of those access events per minute into Splunk Enterprise, preferably without having to set up a Splunk forwarder, and then view that data in a useful and insightful way, such as on a map?*

Sending one event is fine and good, but how do we expand this very basic introductory scenario so that we can leverage HTTP Event Collector for our keycard scenario? What if we wanted to multiply the number of events received by thousands or even tens of thousands? Also, how do we test it to an extent where our business stakeholders will be reasonably confident that it will work as described in the wild? And given that location is a key component to our data, how can we best summarize and display it? These questions were to constitute the next leg in our journey.

BUS

HTTP Event Collector is capable of dealing with tens or even hundreds of thousands of events per minute. In our scenario, we didn't need to reach this capacity, but in product testing, the EC has hit very impressive performance testing goals.

Ultimately, this scenario involved not much coding or setup on the Splunk Enterprise side. Most of our time was spent finding an adequate solution to simulate sending as much dynamic event data as we needed. The following is a discussion of what we did and didn't do, and how we could have done things differently.

Hardware and architecture

We decided to start small: a single Splunk Enterprise instance with no load balancers or external indexers. We knew this was feasible because this was a dedicated machine for testing purposes, and based on past experience we were confident that HTTP Event Collector could handle what we would throw at it.

ARCH

In a production environment, depending on the number of access points that would be sending data to EC, we would likely need to scale up our Splunk Enterprise infrastructure to include a load balancer and an output group containing several additional indexers. Luckily, EC supports load balancing, and can adapt to fit any size implementation.

Choosing an index

We decided that the index that we had been using for PAS-specific testing operations would suffice as the default index for storing our keycard event data as well. You can set the default index per token when creating a new HTTP Event Collector input.

ADM

In our sandbox, the PAS index sufficed as the default index for keycard event data, as it was able to consume what amounted to hundreds of events per minute. However, depending again on the size of your potential data set, you might want to create an index that is dedicated to this type of data. Having EC data living in its own index is the fastest possible way to query it. While the default index may have been fine for this use case, in a production system where data comes in from multiple places, separate indexes allow faster retrieval. Beyond that, there is also the benefit of being able to easily archive separate indexes.

SEC

Another reason to create a keycard event data-specific index is security. Consider sending keycard or other similarly sensitive data to its own index. If your keycard data has a separate security policy, this will ensure it doesn't blend with other PAS data. Also, you can't lock down only certain data within an index. Data is locked down at the index level, so it's all or nothing. That is, you can assign a Splunk Enterprise role access to an index (and assign a Splunk Enterprise user that role), but you can't give a role the ability to only search on specific categories of events within an index.

Creating the token

As you saw when we ran through the basic steps to send an event to HTTP Event Collector, creating a token is easy. For our testing purposes, we called our EC input **"pas_keycard."** We assigned the **"pas_keycard"** index as the input's default, and decided to assign events a custom source type that we called **"ri:pas:keycard."** We didn't specify a source to assign to events.

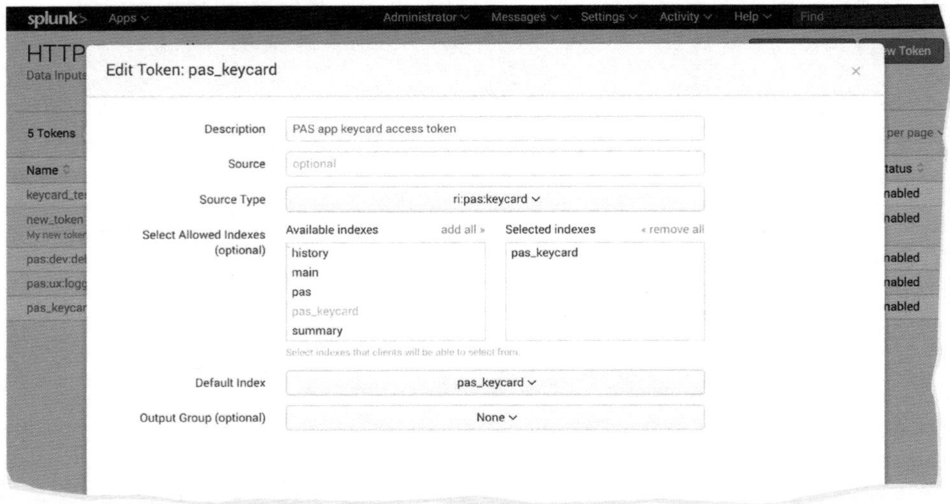

Why should you care what we called these input attributes? Because thinking strategically about what you call the input's attributes can make it easier to interpret the data later. For example, leaving the **Source** field empty was probably a good call, since we'll likely be receiving data from a number of different places. We could name the source values as events come in and base them on a building name, a server name, and so on. However, we may not need to do this if the data senders' hostnames are descriptive enough. Keep in mind that if the source is empty and the client does not send one, then the source will be *http:<token_name>*, where *<token_name>* is the name you gave the EC input when you created it.

DEV

Token strategy is worth spending some time thinking over. For example, some developers choose to use different tokens for each different app, operating system, or device form factor from which they receive data. Since tokens can easily be bound to different indexes, you can automatically partition the data for faster retrieval. This kind of thinking is an essential part of planning an EC rollout.

Sending the data

The actual packaging and sending of data is done on the data source. Recall from before that HTTP Event Collector doesn't care what's doing the packaging and sending of data, or what the data consists of, as long as the data is packaged inside of the EC JSON-formatted data packet. Packaging and sending event data can be done in a number of ways:

- A Splunk logging library (such as Splunk logging for Java, .NET, or JavaScript).
- A JavaScript request library.
- The Java Apache HTTP client.
- Some other client, as long as the data is packaged in JSON according to the event protocol specification.

Our priority was spinning up a way to simulate hundreds of keycard events per minute being generated and sent to EC.

Based on conversations with the Splunk test team, a few possibilities were considered: ApacheBench, Siege, and Apache JMeter. Our developers found that they've all got some strengths and weaknesses:

- ApacheBench (or ab) is a command-line program that is used to test servers with HTTP. It must be run using a cron-style scheduler, and delegated by a shell script that handles creation and post-execution cleanup of a data set. A shell script would need to be created that generated keycard events based on a range of values kept in a flat file that ApacheBench would consume. The flat file would need to change after every execution of ApacheBench.
- Joe Dog Software's Siege is a utility that is used to do HTTP load testing and benchmarking. It was considered because of its apparent support for payload templates. That would have allowed our developer to skip the payload generation and deletion steps.

- Apache JMeter is a Java-based load-testing tool that is used to measure performance for many different types of servers, including HTTP. Though our developers found it to be somewhat unwieldy and not very user friendly, it did allow for the creation of a dynamic payload without the need to write and maintain a separate codebase. Basically, we could configure the tool, run it, and be done. In fact, JMeter allows users to easily run a test indefinitely, rather than a one-and-done script execution cycle.

Ultimately, we went with Apache JMeter. Its ability to dynamically generate event payloads was the deciding factor.

> **TEST**
>
> We have included Apache JMeter in the PAS app's test repo in the **pas_http_input_keycard_simulator** directory. Be sure you have Java installed before installing it. See the README file for more information. When you run JMeter, note that the configuration options are in the left navigation tree. It's been set up to run with the PAS app. The only thing that you will need to change are the hostname and token values. For our testing, we used the values that are in the following four files: **HTTPInputTest.jmx, building_names.csv, location.csv, usernames.csv.** Of course, you should feel free to adjust values and change the files as you see fit.

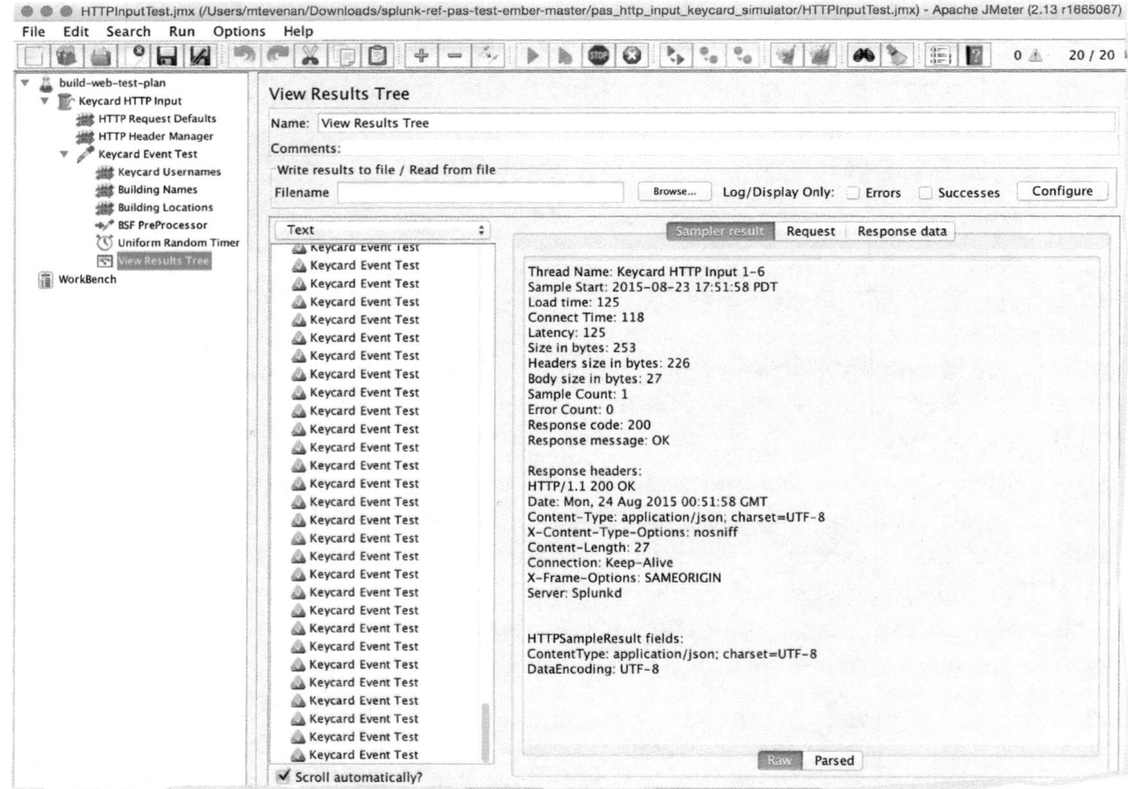

Using JMeter, we generated hundreds of events per minute, getting random values for building name, location (latitude and longitude), and more. JMeter was able to spin up as many threads as we wanted (within reason given hardware constraints).

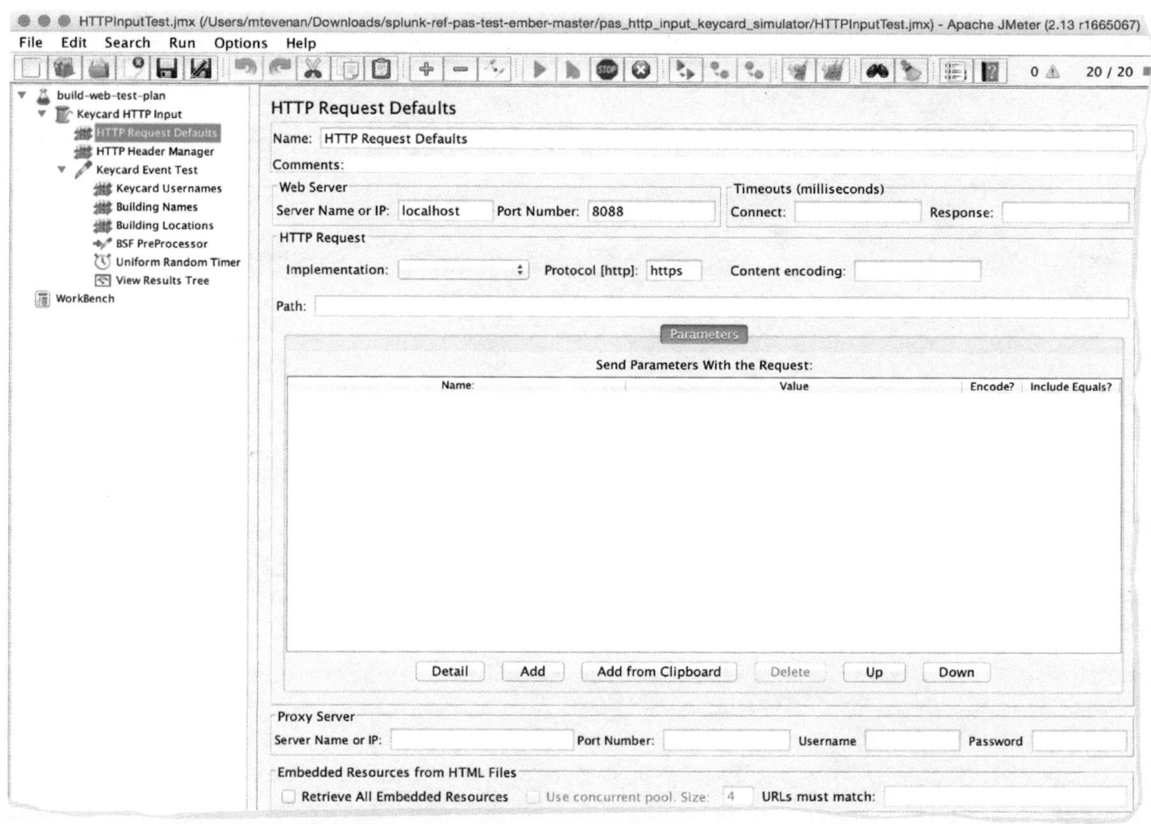

The format of the events that JMeter generated was as follows:

```
{
    "user": "<username>",
    "lat": "<latitude>",
    "long": "<longitude>",
    "timestamp": "<unix epoch timestamp>",
    "type": "<cabinet | door>",
    "security_level": [0-3],
    "building_name": "<building_name>",
    "floor": [0-9]
}
```

Here's a sample event, viewed in Splunk Enterprise search:

i	Time	Event
>	8/23/15 6:25:44.000 PM	{ [-] building_name: Building 2 floor: 5 lat: 37.7875 long: -122.3998041895141 status: closed timestamp: 1440379534609 username: jstewart } Show as raw text host = localhost:8088 source = http:new_token sourcetype = httpevent

Visualizing the data

HTTP Event Collector came through, accepting and indexing the data exactly as it should have. But now that we had the data, what was the best way to transform it? Given how integral location was to our data (Where did the keycard access occur?), how could we best summarize and display it?

Another new feature in Splunk Enterprise 6.3, geographic visualizations using choropleth maps, was ideal for this requirement. In particular, the ability to display data on a map using proportional shading could help enormously in visually tracking keycard access over time, spikes in access events, and so on.

In addition to choropleth maps, available geographic visualizations in Splunk Enterprise now include map visualizations that represent data as points of different sizes on a map to show relative event volumes, plus non-map geographic visualizations such as bar charts that show comparative metrics by city or country.

If your data contains location information for each event, you can create a geographic visualization. Since our data contained latitude and longitude values, we were able to relatively easily create a map visualization.

The options for geographic visualizations are numerous, so we'll refer you to the step-by-step Splunk documentation on how to build a geographic query for the details. To see the dashboard we built into the PAS app, click **Keycard Activity** in the navigation bar at the top:

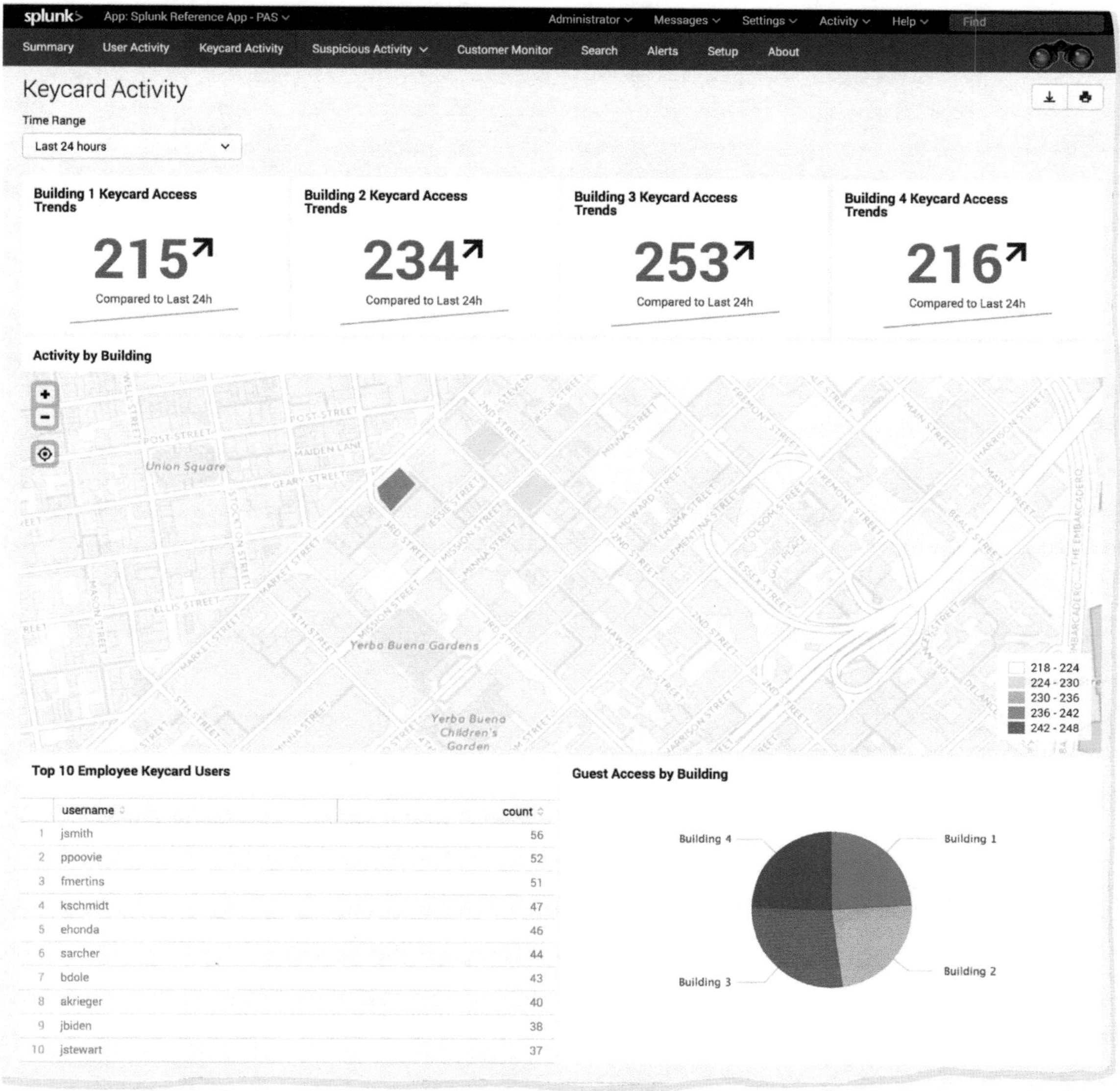

Inspect each dashboard panel to see the exact search commands we used. In particular, pay attention to how we used the geom search command, which is the piece that actually generates the map.

THE TELEMETRY SCENARIO

Recall from earlier in this chapter our telemetry scenario:

> *Our business stakeholders were developing a web browser-based app and wanted to use Splunk Enterprise to collect and organize both debug and usage data for the app. Because the data could be coming from anyone, anywhere in the world, they didn't want it to contain any Splunk-specific information, and certainly didn't want it to include any Splunk Enterprise credential information.*

To summarize, our requirements for this scenario were twofold:

- Implement browser-based debug logging to Splunk Enterprise. Consider a developer who has created a web app that generates logging statements to the JavaScript console. How can we send these messages with HTTP to a Splunk Enterprise instance?
- Implement browser-based user interaction telemetry to Splunk Enterprise. Consider a developer who wants to know what a user is doing once he or she logs in to a web app with their browser. What does the user click on first? In what order do users choose options and complete tasks? And so on…

To demonstrate how this can be done, we considered creating a dummy web app that just logs debug statements and user activity and then sends it to HTTP Event Collector. But then we realized that we've already got a prime candidate for this type of feature: the PAS app itself.

Wiring up events

The first thing to do was to ensure that the PAS app's debugging and user interaction events were sufficiently wired to log the data we needed. The bulk of the work was done in the **setup.js** file that you can find at **pas_ref_app/appserver/static/setup.js**.

When you take a look at the file, you'll see quite a few calls to either the **sendDevLog** or **sendUxLog** JavaScript functions. Let's take a look at the method definitions in code.

The **sendDevLog** function is attached to events that would be of interest to a developer trying to debug the app. For example, the following code snippet is executed when the setup page's check for the Eventgen tool returns an error. In that case, the app calls **sendDevLog** with the error message as its parameter:

```
...
        var eventgenApp = apps.item('eventgen')
        if (eventgenApp) {
            eventgenApp.fetch(function(err, eventgenApp) {
                if (err) {
                    sendDevLog(err);
                    console.error(err);
                    return;
                }
...
```

We also wired pertinent status messages to be logged using the **sendDevLog** function, such as the following status message for the Google Drive add-in:

```
...
        // Show the Google Drive app configuration section if the app is present and enabled
        var googleDriveApp = apps.item('googledrive_addon');
        if (googleDriveApp && !googleDriveApp.state().content.disabled) {
            sendDevLog( "Enabling Google Drive Add-on in Setup interface.")
            $('#googleDriveModule').removeClass('hide');
        }
...
```

The **sendUxLog** function is attached to events that occur in response to user actions—both status messages and error messages. This includes entering values into fields, choosing values from pop-up menus, opening windows such as the Google authentication window, entering invalid or missing values, and so on. For example, the following code snippet sends a status message when a user enters a weight value in the **Violation types** section of the **Setup** page:

```
...
    sendUxLog("Saving " + viol_title + ": user selected weight: " + viol_weight);
...
```

The following snippet shows **sendUxLog** executing if, after the user clicks **Save**, the app isn't able to save its configuration successfully. Note that, because this is purely UX logging, the function just sends a message that indicates what the user was trying to do and that the operation was unsuccessful. It does not include any debugging information.

```
...
    sendUxLog("Unable to save changes!");
...
```

Sending the data

Now let's take a look at how we wrote these functions. As you can see, both the **sendDevLog** and **sendUxLog** functions end up calling the same logging function, **sendLog**. The difference is that **sendDevLog** calls it using the developer logging-specific token (dev_debug_key), while **sendUxLog** calls it using the UX logging-specific token (ux_logging_key):

```
function sendUxLog(message) {
    if(dev_debug_key.length>0) {
        sendLog(message, ux_logging_key);
    } else {
        console.log("UX Logging - No HTTP Input Key has been set! Event logging disabled.");
    }
}

function sendDevLog(message) {
    if(dev_debug_key.length>0) {
        sendLog(message, dev_debug_key);
    } else {
        console.log("Dev Debug - No HTTP Input Key has been set! Event logging disabled.");
    }
}
```

Here's the definition of the **sendLog** function from the code:

```
function sendLog(message, authCode) {
    var http_request = new XMLHttpRequest();
    var http_input_url = "http://mysplunkserver:8088/services/collector";
    // Using lower-level call to XMLHttpRequest due to issues with how
    // JQuery handles CORS requests
    var xhr = createCORSRequest('POST', http_input_url);
    xhr.setRequestHeader('Content-Type', 'text/plain');
    xhr.setRequestHeader('Authorization', 'Splunk ' + authCode);

    var log_message = {
        "event":
            {
                "username": currentUser,
                "message": message
            }
        };

        xhr.send(JSON.stringify(log_message));
}
```

This code is pretty straightforward. First, it specifies the HTTP Event Collector URL (**<hostname>:<port>/services/collector**). Then, it calls the **createCORSRequest** function to create a new XMLHttpRequest (XHR) object. The **createCORSRequest** function was necessary (as opposed to just creating an XHR object by calling XMLHttpRequest directly) because of cross-site scripting issues that we discuss in "Problems encountered," later in this chapter. The function then assembles the event by creating the authorization header and then forming the JSON-format message. It then sends the message.

Viewing the data

Let's get interactive with the last portion of this section and try out HTTP Event Collector logging from the PAS app right now. This procedure assumes that you've installed the PAS app on your local Splunk Enterprise instance, and that you've turned on EC as described earlier in this chapter.

1. Create two new tokens and name them according to the type of data we'll be receiving. For instance, we named ours "pas:dev:debug" and "pas:ux:logging." Choose the "pas" index as the default index, and choose a source type that accurately describes the data. We chose the existing "**ri:pas:application**" source type.
2. Open the **setup.js** file (at **pas_ref_app/appserver/static/setup.js**) using a text editor. At the top of the file, paste the corresponding token values between the quotation marks next to the following variable declarations:

   ```
   var dev_debug_key = "";
   var ux_logging_key = "";
   ```

3. Within the **sendLog** function near the bottom of the file, replace the value within the quotation marks next to the `http_input_url` variable with your server's HTTP Event Collector endpoint (*<hostname>:<port>*`/services/collector`).
4. Save the file, and then restart Splunk Enterprise. Alternatively, you can call the **`debug/refresh`** endpoint and then clear your browser's cache or force-refresh the page so that your browser retrieves the updated script.
5. Open the PAS app and then click **Setup** in the top navigation bar. Then log some events. That is, enter some in-range or out-of-range values in fields, choose options from pop-up menus, and so on. Finally, click **Save**.

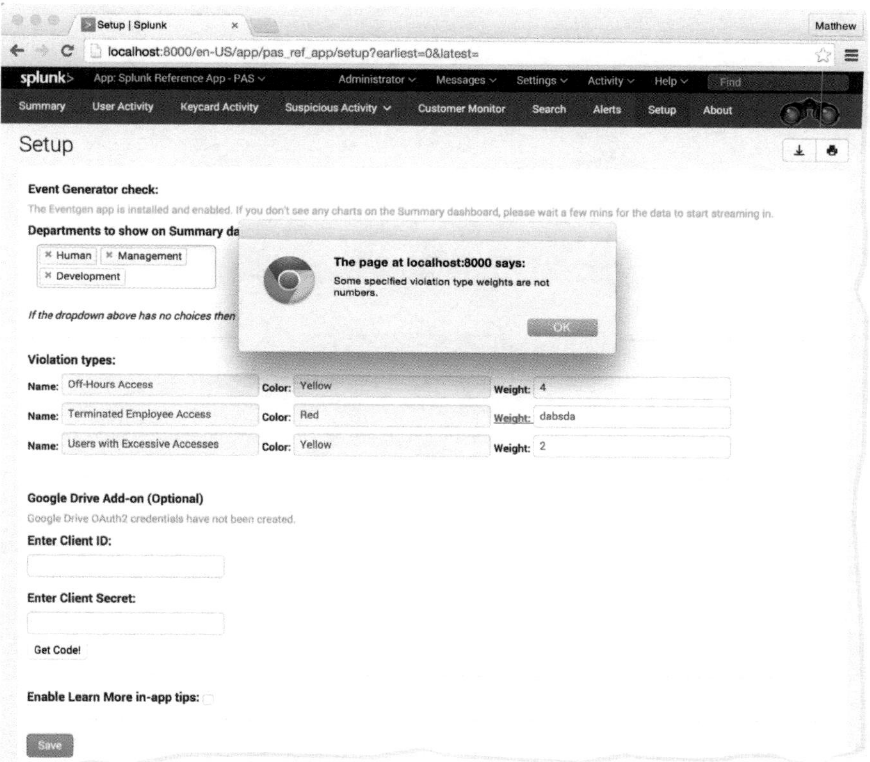

6. Click the **Search** button from the top nav bar, and enter a search that will find this specific data. For instance, since we assigned the logging data a source type of "ri:pas:application," we used the following query:

```
index=pas sourcetype="ri:pas:application"
```

The search results you see should look something like the following.

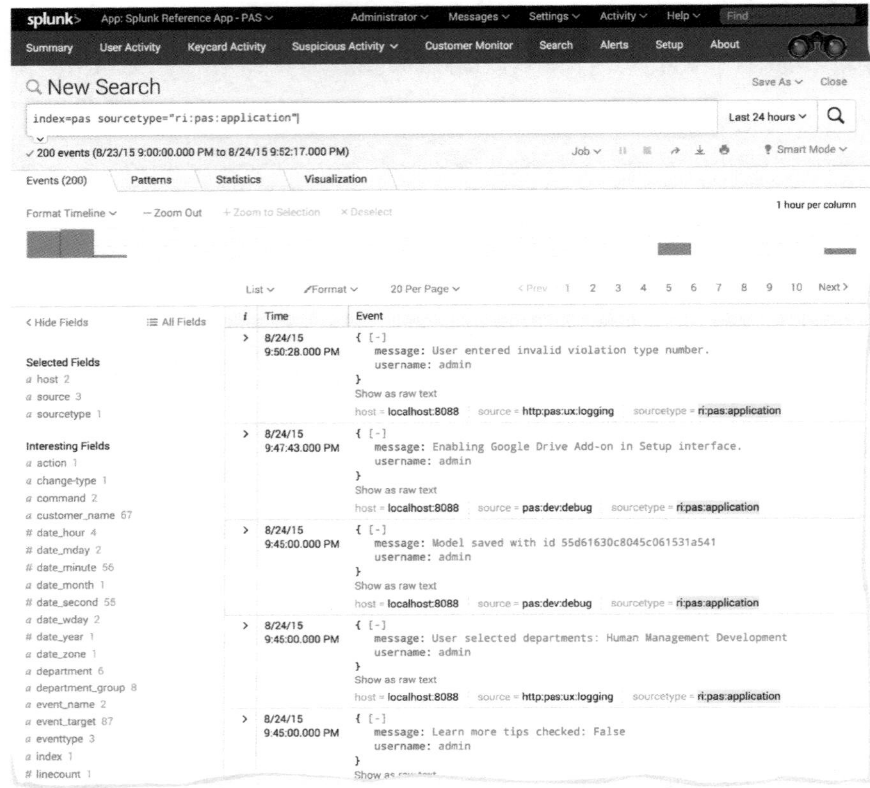

In these results you see somewhat of a play-by-play of what you just did on the **Setup** page.

> **Note:** If you don't see anything when you perform the search, read ahead to the "Problems encountered" section and make the .conf file additions described there. You are probably running up against cross-site scripting (XSS) restrictions.

Keep in mind that, even though we added this capability to the PAS app, which is a Splunk Enterprise app, you are in no way limited to doing this with just Splunk Enterprise apps. You can add the capability to log data to HTTP Event Collector to any browser-based app.

> **ADM**
>
> **If you are familiar with Splunk Enterprise forwarders, you might be asking why you should bother with EC when a forwarder will do the same thing. While a forwarder could certainly be used to forward JavaScript console debug data to Splunk Enterprise, the UX component of this scenario is something that simply can't be accomplished using a forwarder. A forwarder can't capture this type of granular data. Even if you were running a forwarder on the backend to monitor web logs, you wouldn't get this level of detail, because you would only get the requests that users made, not a record of everything the user did in the browser.**

PROBLEMS ENCOUNTERED

Getting HTTP Event Collector up and running and logging meaningful data was pleasantly quick and easy, but one issue did present some significant challenges we had to overcome: **cross-site scripting (XSS)** restrictions.

Our developers immediately encountered XSS issues when trying to send data with JavaScript to EC. A domain is the combination of a URI and a port number. The JavaScript that was served by the PAS app through Splunk Enterprise came from port 8000 by default. The default EC port is 8088.

ADM

The EC port is 8088 by default. You can change it by editing its global settings, but be aware of other services that might already be using whatever port number you change it to. For example, it cannot be the same as Splunk Web (8000) or the Splunk Enterprise REST API (8089).

This means that a POST to EC is interpreted as an entirely different domain. You could use a self-signed certificate to authenticate, but while that will work in browsers such as Firefox or Safari, it won't work in Chrome, which requires a valid certificate authority (CA)-signed certificate. To avoid the need to recommend one browser over another, not to mention the hassle and expense of purchasing a signed certificate, we searched for alternatives.

We could have turned off SSL encryption and sent data through HTTP versus HTTPS, but we didn't want to do anything security-related in our reference app that we wouldn't recommend doing in a production environment. We definitely do not recommend sending data to EC without encryption.

The next option was to leverage support built into Splunk Enterprise for cross-origin resource sharing (CORS). To enable support for CORS, we first had to make adjustments in the Splunk Enterprise `server.conf` and `web.conf` files:

- We added a `server.conf` file to `$SPLUNK_HOME/etc/apps/pas_ref_app/local/`, and pasted the following two lines into it:
  ```
  [httpServer]
  crossOriginSharingPolicy = *
  ```
- We added a `web.conf` file to `$SPLUNK_HOME/etc/apps/pas_ref_app/local/`, and pasted the following two lines into it:
  ```
  [settings]
  crossOriginSharingPolicy = *
  ```

However, even with CORS functionality enabled in Splunk Enterprise, we ran into issues when attempting to use jQuery to send a JSON payload to EC. It turns out that Splunk Enterprise uses custom JavaScript code that modifies the HTTP headers we were attempting to send and that effectively ruined any attempt to communicate using jQuery.

Because the jQuery library is simply a wrapper around the XMLHttpRequest object, building our own request from scratch was the next obvious step. This is how the **createCORSRequest** function that we mentioned in the "Sending the data" subsection of the telemetry scenario came about:

```
// Create the XHR object.
function createCORSRequest(method, url) {
      var xhr = new XMLHttpRequest();
      if ("withCredentials" in xhr) {
            // XHR for Chrome/Firefox/Opera/Safari.
            xhr.open(method, url, true);
      } else if (typeof XDomainRequest != "undefined") {
            // XDomainRequest for IE.
            xhr = new XDomainRequest();
            xhr.open(method, url);
      } else {
            // CORS not supported.
            xhr = null;
      }
      return xhr;
}
```

For more information about the `server.conf` file's format, see dev.splunk.com/goto/serverconf. For more information about the `web.conf` file's format, see dev.splunk.com/goto/webconf.

SEC

Overcoming XSS issues is essential to be able to use EC effectively. Hopefully our experiences will help make yours easier.

WHAT HAVE WE LEARNED?

Here are the key lessons we have learned while working with HTTP Event Collector:

- HTTP Event Collector (or EC) is a great new way to get data directly into Splunk Enterprise from network sources.
- EC sends data in JSON format through HTTP or HTTPS to port 8088 on a Splunk Enterprise server.
- You can also use a load balancer to distribute high volumes of EC data evenly to indexers.
- EC is disabled by default, but can be enabled in the Data inputs section of Splunk Enterprise.
- A unique token contained in the auth header of your data is what tells EC on Splunk Enterprise that the data is valid.

- You can assign field values (such as **source**, **sourcetype**, **index**, and so on) to data based on the token the data contains in its header.
- EC is great for sending high volumes of data to Splunk Enterprise, such as usage telemetry data.
- You can also use EC to send debugging and user interaction data about your app directly to Splunk Enterprise.
- Sending data to EC on Splunk Enterprise opens you up to cross-site scripting (XSS) restrictions.
- Splunk Enterprise has built-in support for cross-origin resource sharing (CORS), which we leveraged to overcome the XSS restrictions we encountered.

MORE INFORMATION

For information on using Deployment Server to deploy your tokens and configuration files to other Splunk Enterprise instances, see "Deployment server architecture" at: dev.splunk.com/goto/deploymentserverarch.

For information about the EC's JSON event format, see "About the JSON event protocol in HTTP Event Collector" at: dev.splunk.com/goto/jsonformat.

To take advantage of Postman's powerful feature set and its ability to run cross-platform, download from: getpostman.com.

For tools to simulate events, check out:

- ApacheBench (httpd.apache.org/docs/2.2/en/programs/ab)
- Siege (joedog.org/siege-home)
- Apache JMeter (jmeter.apache.org)

For the step-by-step instructions on how to build a geographic query see "Mapping data" at: dev.splunk.com/goto/mappingdata.

For information about generating maps using the **geom** search command: dev.splunk.com/goto/geomcommand.

For information about creating a new XMLHttpRequest (XHR) object, see developer.mozilla.org/docs/Web/API/XMLHttpRequest.

For information on cross-site scripting (XSS) restrictions, see: en.wikipedia.org/wiki/Cross-site_scripting.

For information on cross-origin resource sharing (CORS), see: developer.mozilla.org/docs/Web/HTTP/Access_control_CORS.

For information on server.conf, see: dev.splunk.com/goto/serverconf.

For information on web.conf files, see: dev.splunk.com/goto/webconf.

Part II
ESSENTIALS

Welcome to the *Essentials*! Here we describe the fundamental patterns and practices that have been found to be the most useful in developing Splunk® apps.

The content of the first part of the Splunk Developer Guide, the *Journey*, is rooted in the development of two concrete reference apps (PAS and Auth0) and two reference add-ons (Google Drive data provider and Atlassian JIRA custom alert action). Here we've generalized the lessons learned. We still cover the full spectrum of application development from getting data into Splunk Enterprise to packaging and distributing your app. Topics are arranged in the order one might typically follow in designing and implementing an app. Each topic combines design and implementation guidelines in a way that supports an iterative development process.

Because app complexity can range from the very simple to the very complex, with complex apps requiring in-depth understanding of Splunk Enterprise programming, operational concepts, and features, we provide a generalized description of the patterns and approaches with references to specialized examples, where appropriate.

ARCH

Many of these patterns and techniques will be familiar to web developers.

While the *Essentials* part might not cover all situations, it does cover most common cases and sets you off in the right direction.

You can find complete developer documentation on the main Splunk>dev web site. You might also find many of the discussions on the Splunk>answers web site to be applicable to your programming questions, particularly, under the developer, development, and webframework tags.

Also, because design problems are usually domain-specific, we provide enough guidance to get you started on an approach that has generally been found to be the most effective, while illuminating the advantages and disadvantages of alternative solutions.

These guidelines cover not only Splunk Enterprise operational and programming concepts that the application deals with directly, but also consider performance, quality, and maintenance issues in recommending particular approaches.

The topics are grouped into the following main categories:

- **Getting data in:** Given your domain-specific data set, how do you get the data into a Splunk app?
- **Searching the data:** Once you have your data in a Splunk app, how to you find the information important to you?
- **Visualizing data:** How do you process, analyze, manifest, and interact with the data so that it is meaningful?
- **Acting on data:** How do you instruct Splunk Enterprise to trigger notifications and/or custom actions so that you don't have to monitor your data constantly?
- **Packaging and deploying:** What's needed to distribute, publish, deploy, and configure your application?

By designing and implementing your app with the guidelines presented in the *Essentials* in mind, we hope your app will not only meet the functional objectives for acquiring, processing, and visualizing your data but will also be robust, maintainable, extensible, and meeting predictable performance requirements.

10

Splunk apps and add-ons: what & why?

HIGH-LEVEL PERSPECTIVE

A Splunk *app* is a prebuilt collection of additional capabilities packaged for a specific technology, or use cases, which allows a more effective usage of Splunk Enterprise. You can use Splunk apps to gain the specific insights you need from your machine data.

Depending on the type and complexity of those use cases, and also whether the developer wants certain app parts to be configured or distributed separately (potentially by a third party), an app may rely on various *add-ons.*

An add-on is a technical component that can be re-used across a number of different use cases and packaged with one or more Splunk apps. Add-ons may contain one or more *knowledge objects*, which encapsulate a specific functionality focused on a single concern and its configuration. Using an add-on should help to reduce the technical risk and cost of building an app.

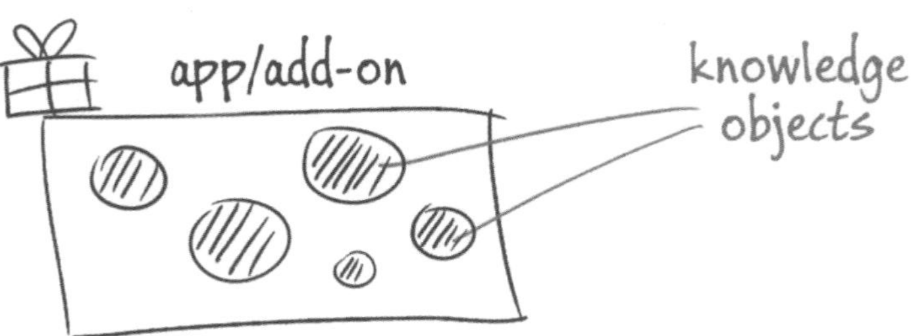

Splunk apps allow developers to extend data ingestion and processing capabilities of Splunk Enterprise for your specific needs. Apps facilitate more efficient completion of domain-specific tasks by the end user.

Many *add-ons provide* data ingestion capabilities, in other words, they feed the data into Splunk Enterprise.

ARCH

Feeding data via a data provider isn't always required, because many data sources are easily captured with a file or network input, or through another app like DB Connect.

If preparsing is required, such as for large XML files, or a modular input is needed, such as for API derived data, the add-on is the place for that work. All such add-ons should also provide the field extractions, lookups, and event types needed to map data to the Common Information Model (CIM). This allows customers to easily use the new data source in data models, pivots, and CIM-based apps like Enterprise Security.

Other types of add-ons are used to extend the Splunk Enterprise platform across the board. They could consist of custom search commands, macros, custom REST endpoints, custom alert actions, or reusable JavaScript or Python libraries.

Apps and add-ons can be combined into a comprehensive *solution*.

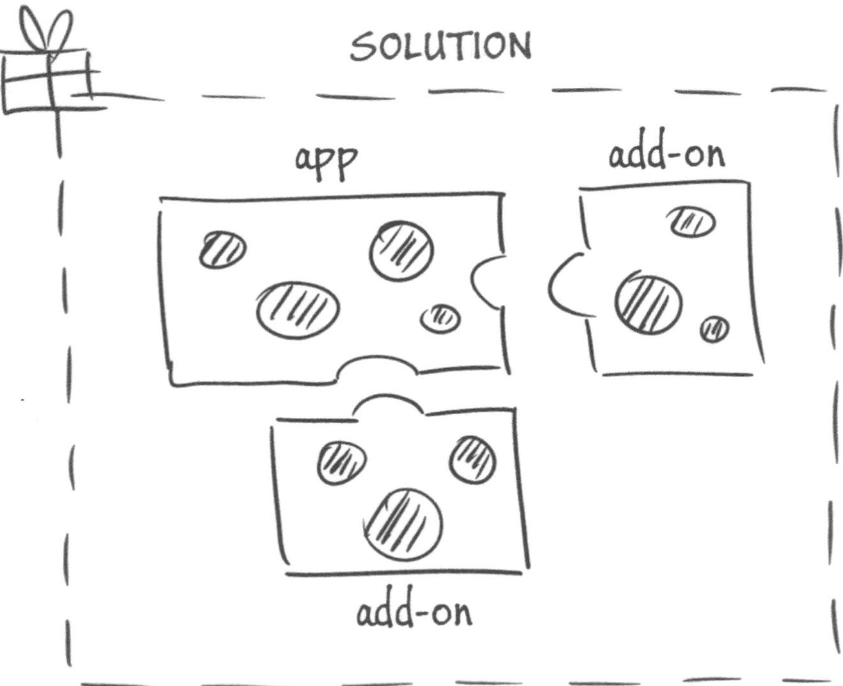

You can also apply user/role-based permissions and access controls to Splunk apps and add-ons, thus providing a level of control when you are deploying and sharing apps across your organization.

The apps and add-ons, that Splunk partners provide, enrich the overall Splunk Enterprise platform.

As a solution evolves and supports an ever larger set of capabilities, it can itself become a chassis that supports the building of new apps. An example of such a chassis is Splunk Enterprise Security.

LOW-LEVEL TECHNICAL PERSPECTIVE

When you want to extend Splunk Enterprise with new functionality, such as new types of data visualizations or support for consuming new types of data sources, you configure Splunk Enterprise with these new extensions by adding *knowledge objects*. Knowledge objects are collected and packaged together in modular units called *apps*. For simple extensions of Splunk Enterprise, it is sufficient to put all objects into the same app. However, it is sometimes convenient or necessary to partition the knowledge objects to reside in multiple apps.

For example, if you have a distributed Splunk Enterprise deployment, the knowledge objects related to data ingestion need to be deployed on Splunk Enterprise instances in the forwarder role. The knowledge objects related to dashboards need to be deployed on the Splunk Enterprise instances in the search head role. Therefore, it is convenient to package the objects into two apps, one for the forwarder and one for the search head.

Another example of why you would want to decompose your knowledge objects into separate apps is if you want to enable the use of plugin-like functionality. Consider an app that displays flight traffic information from multiple flight traffic systems. A primary app could be written to look for other subordinate apps that each provides support for a specific flight traffic system.

When partitioning knowledge objects into various apps in the preceding fashion, you end up with several different apps, as shown in the figure above. The primary app is often just called the app by customers because it is the one most visible to them, and the others apps are sometimes called add-ons because they are not generally visible. In this sense an app can serve the role of an app or an add-on when talking to customers.

Physically, knowledge objects are declared and configured in .conf files that reside in the file system. These .conf files are organized into a particular directory layout that forms an app. These app directories are deployed to an individual Splunk Enterprise instance in the `$SPLUNK_HOME/etc/apps` directory.

Because Splunk Enterprise is a data platform, a very common type of add-on is one that provides access to new data sources.

> **ARCH**
>
> **In the PAS Reference app (see *Journey*) we call this type of add-ons *data providers*.**

These must specify an API to communicate with other apps. This API takes a different form than in many other kinds of development, in that the API is not comprised of classes and functions. Instead, the API is exposed in the form of the code that ingests data in a well-defined format that can be queried by searches in other apps. This kind of API is sometimes called a *data API*.

DEV

APIs always have to be well-defined in order to work, but they should be ideally documented as well.

WHY BUILD SPLUNK APPS?

Building Splunk apps, add-ons, and solutions and contributing to the larger community of Splunk partners and developers has a number benefits, including:

Driving your business

Listing apps and add-ons on Splunkbase exposes your business to thousands of Splunk Enterprise customers worldwide. Even though there are hundreds of apps available now, there are countless technologies, data sources, use cases, and industry verticals still to address.

You can offer your Splunk app with a freemium model, upselling customers on features and functionality for direct revenue opportunities. Offering Splunk apps and add-ons can generate license revenue or service revenue if you are a Splunk reseller/partner.

Contributing to a large, growing community

Become part of the growing Splunk ecosystem and interact with developers around the world who are working with the power of the Splunk Enterprise platform to build new, innovative data solutions. Connect with other Splunk Enterprise developers online at Splunk > Answers and the Splunk IRC channel (#splunk channel on EFNET) and catch up with Splunk Enterprise developers in person at local meetups, developer conferences and our flagship conference—the .conf.

Building valuable skills

Learning to build Splunk apps and add-ons exposes you to a rich landscape of software development and IT concepts that will add to your development skill set. Working with the Splunk Enterprise platform involves web development, backend development, APIs, networking concepts, Big Data concepts, OS skills, statistics, math, and more.

PERSPECTIVE OF A SYSTEM INTEGRATOR, CONDUCIVE CONSULTING

Building a Splunk app is a great way to:

- Engage business users in the process of designing and building a solution that is user friendly and not dependent on the IT team after it is deployed.
- Demonstrate the power of Splunk Enterprise as a platform and flexible framework for creating specific solutions within in any industry.
- Better understand the flexibility that Splunk Enterprise offers to convert raw data from disparate sources into valuable business information and operational intelligence.
- Integrate and extend the power of Splunk Enterprise beyond IT Operations department into virtually any area of the business.
- Showcase the ability of the Splunk Enterprise to communicate complex data in a visually intuitive manner, making the information valuable and usable to the business user.
- Leverage the Splunk Enterprise framework and app ecosystem to reduce costs as compared to building a stand-alone application.

APP CERTFICIATION

Splunk offers optional free certification for apps and add-ons created by developers in our community. During certification Splunk performs a review of your source code for security vulnerabilities and examines it to ensure it conforms to Splunk development recommended practices. This gives your users the additional confidence of knowing that Splunk has reviewed your code.

BUS

Certified apps not only get special recognition on Splunkbase, your team could receive access to pre-release builds of Splunk Enterprise (contingent on having an NDA in place).

Refer to the App certification criteria for details on requirements for certification.

More information

Review the topic "What is Splunk Enterprise knowledge?" In the Knowledge Manager Manual at: dev.splunk.com/goto/knowledgemgr.

List your apps and add-ons on Splunkbase: apps.splunk.com.

Connect with other developers building Splunk apps online at Splunk > Answers: answers.splunk.com.

Catch up with other developers building Splunk apps in person at the .conf: conf.splunk.com.

For details on the certifying your app see "App certification criteria" at: dev.splunk.com/goto/appcert.

11

Parts of an app

APP ARCHITECTURE

The easiest way to introduce Splunk app architecture is to think about a typical 3-tier web application:

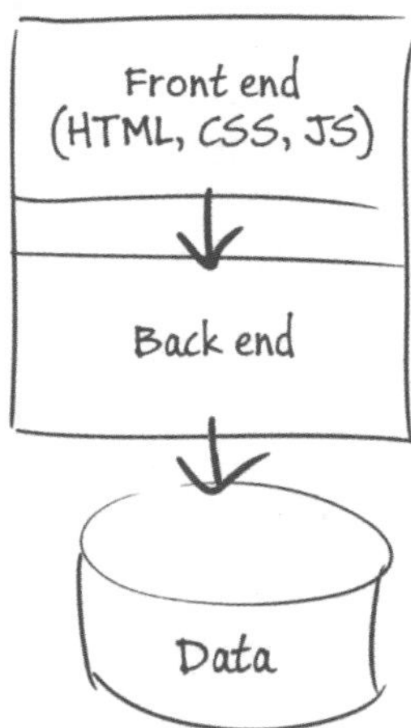

The fundamental purpose of a Splunk® app is to get data into Splunk, extract the parts of the data that are meaningful to the app, and render the data in a form that facilitates easy interpretation of the data. This chapter gives you an overview of a Splunk app architecture, draws parallels to the more traditional web app architecture, and introduces the key Splunk technologies.

In the Splunk app, the front end corresponds to **splunkweb** and the back end corresponds to **splunkd**. The data tier is fused with **splunkd**. The diagram below depicts a typical Splunk app architecture.

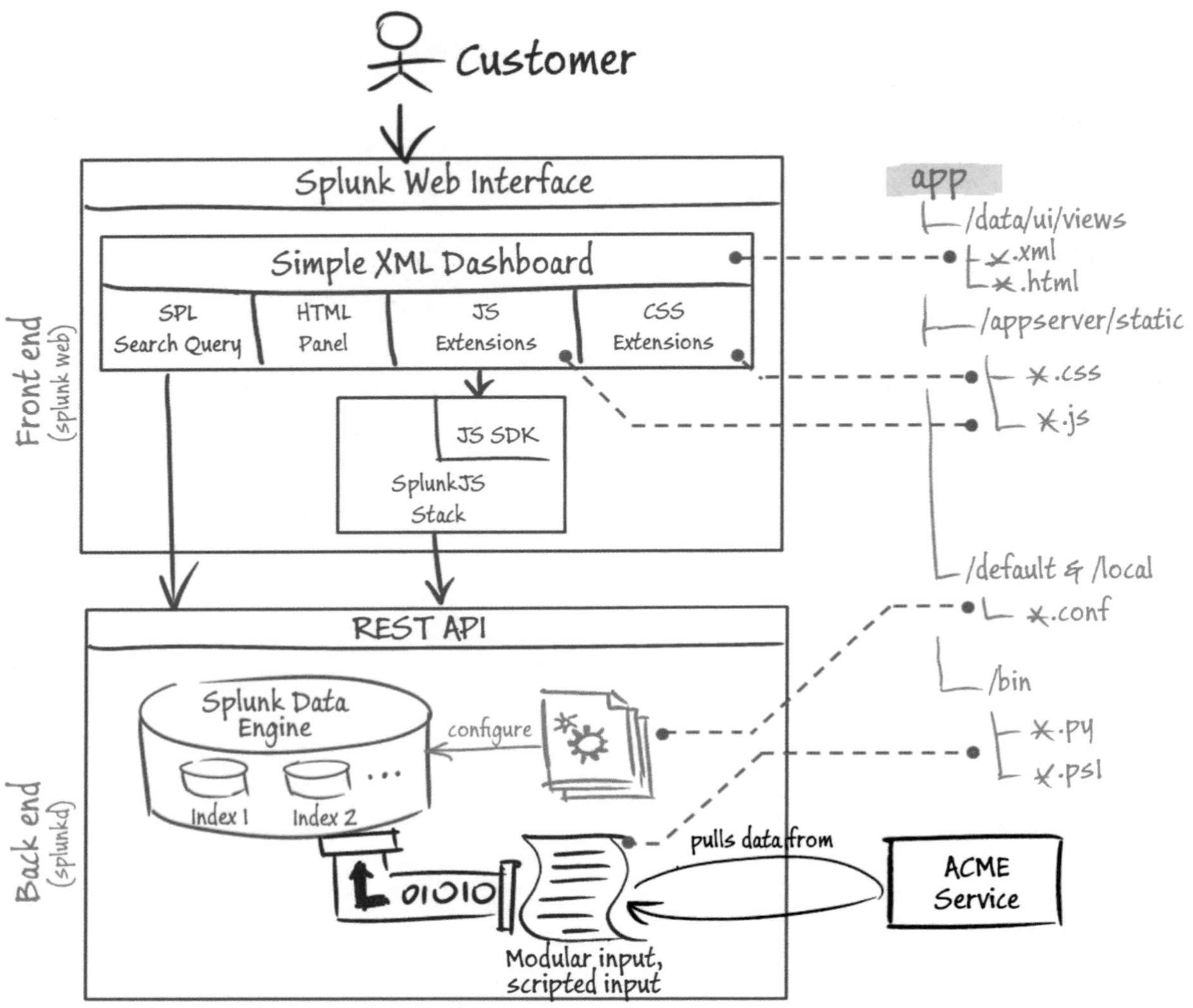

The dotted lines (●- - -●) link files in the Splunk app directory structure to the conceptual piece that they define.

On the traditional front end, you have HTML, CSS, and JavaScript to compose your web pages. Similarly, in splunkweb you have **dashboards** composed of **HTML panels**, **CSS extensions**, and **JS extensions**.

- Libraries for Splunk Enterprise views and search managers for working with searches and interacting with Splunk data.
- Backbone.js provides an MVC framework as a structure for your code.
- RequireJS is a JavaScript module loader that manages dependencies.
- jQuery helps manage the HTML DOM.

DEV

The SplunkJS stack includes a number of tools for web developers.

ARCH

For apps that require more specialized capabilities not provided by splunkweb and Simple XML, developers can implement standalone HTML, CSS, and JavaScript together with the SplunkJS Stack. This means the app would run on a web server of your choice, not splunkweb. This gives you additional flexibility in terms of both implementation and deployment.

The back end is a thin layer on top of the Splunk Enterprise data engine responsible for ingesting and storing data. For now just treat it as a black box.

In a Splunk app the various pieces comprising the app are represented as files in the file system that are installed on the Splunk server. For example:

- A **dashboard** is stored in $SPLUNK_HOME/etc/apps/$APP_NAME/data/ui/views/$DASHBOARD_NAME.xml.
- A **JS extension** is stored in $SPLUNK_HOME/etc/apps/$APP_NAME/appserver/static/$DASHBOARD_NAME.js.
- A **modular input**, which is script that pulls data from a data source (depicted as ACME Service on the diagram), is stored in $SPLUNK_HOME/etc/apps/$APP_NAME/bin/$INPUT_NAME.py.

ARCH

Some apps only introduce data ingestion facilities but no UI/front end.

The Splunk data engine is configured by a large number of .conf files, each of which has different effects. See Appendix C for the details.

SPLUNK REST API AND SDKS

The REST API provides a well-defined, programmatic interface to server resources, such as configuration files, processing states, and core Splunk Enterprise functionality. You can interact with a Splunk Enterprise instance and do most of the same things that you can using **splunkweb** — including authentication, creating and running searches, managing search jobs, creating and managing indexes and inputs, and configuring Splunk Enterprise.

DEV

The REST API is extremely flexible with over 170 endpoints. It's fully documented and supported. See the REST API Reference Manual: dev.splunk.com/goto/restapi.

As a convenience, Splunk SDKs provide you with broad coverage of the REST API in a language-specific fashion to ease your access to the Splunk engine. Currently, there are six SDKs available, for Python, Java, C#, JavaScript, PHP, and Ruby.

DEV

Splunk encourages and accepts community contributions to its SDKs. For more details see dev.splunk.com/goto/opensource.

These SDKs are mainly wrappers around the REST API that do a lot of the work for you, such as:

- *Handling HTTP access.*
- *Authenticating*: When you log in using a username and password, Splunk returns a session key. The SDKs automatically remember and append this session key to subsequent requests.
- Parsing the XML responses from REST API requests.
- *Managing namespaces*: A namespace is the user/app context for accessing a resource, which is specified by a Splunk username, a Splunk app (such as the default Search app), and a sharing mode. The SDKs send requests based on the namespace that was used for logging in, or you can specify a namespace to access a specific resource. For example, you can list all apps, or only the apps that a specific user has access to.
- *Simplifying access to REST endpoints*: The SDKs provide access to the REST API in the native style of different programming languages.

- *Building the correct URL for an endpoint*: The SDKs build out the complete REST URLs in the correct format, with the namespace and any additional parameters you specify.
- *Displaying simplified output for searches*: The REST API returns search results (events) in XML, JSON, or CSV, but in a raw format. The SDKs provide results readers (helper classes for Python and Java, a code example for JavaScript) that parse these events and return them in a simplified structure with clear key-value pairs.

SDKs also offer support for extensibility, for example, modular input support for Java, Python, C#, and JavaScript as well as custom search commands for Python.

DEV

Keep in mind, SDKs do not necessarily offer full feature-parity with the REST API.

APP DIRECTORY STRUCTURE

All of the packaged components for a given app must reside in a directory under **$SPLUNK_HOME/etc/apps** (as shown in the diagram below)

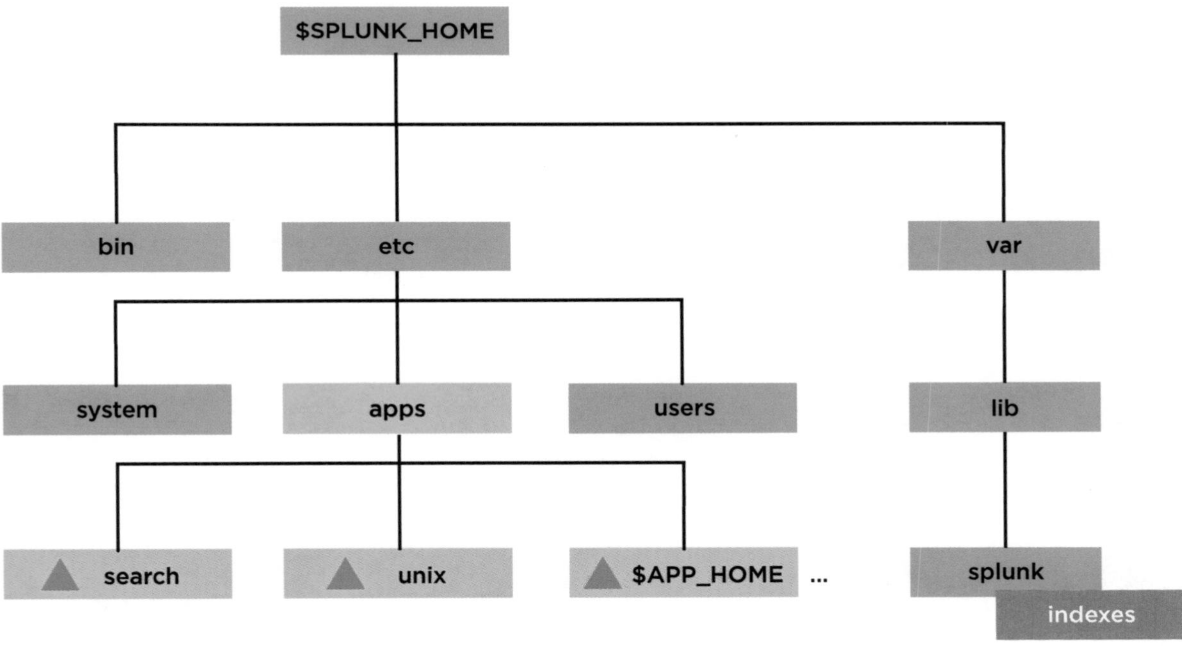

Each app is further structured as follows:

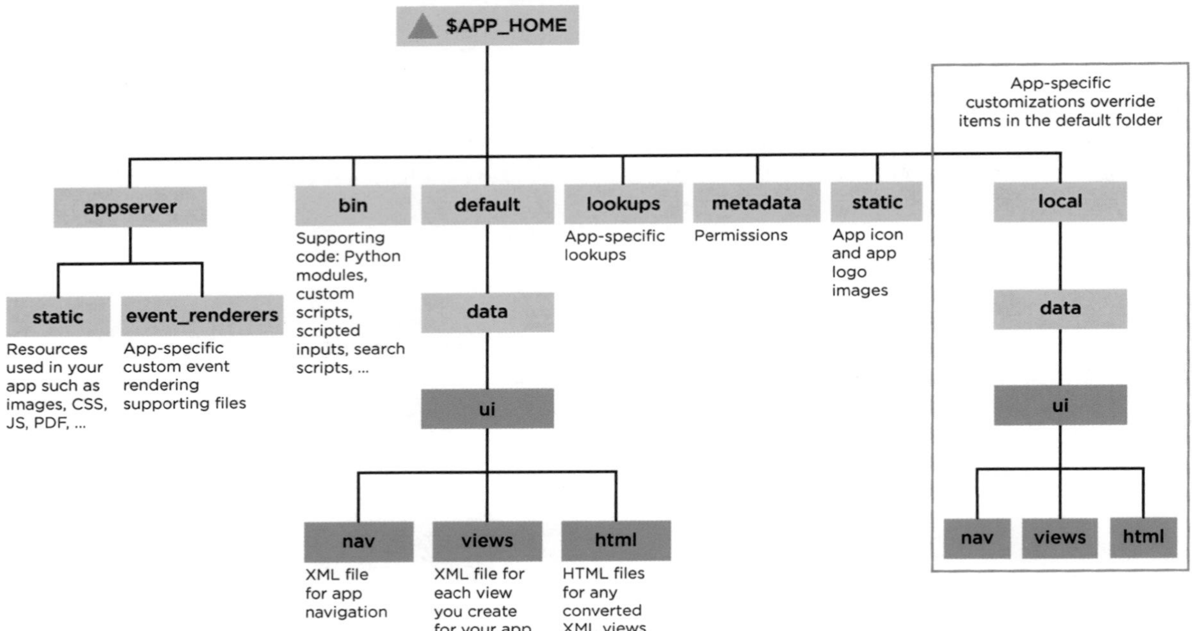

APP CONFIGURATION

Splunk Enterprise uses configuration files to control almost all data processing. Appendix C provides a cheat sheet of various configuration files, including their meaning and usage.

Splunk Enterprise decides how to evaluate a configuration file and other artifacts (for example, dashboard XML files) based on the various contexts that the file operates within. As an app developer, you really only need to worry about the **local** vs. **default** distinction. The configuration in **local** is considered modified by the user, and the **default** is the one shipped with the app.

DEV

When a user modifies a configuration setting in **splunkweb** (through the UI), it changes a copy of the configuration file in **$APP_HOME/local**. The value of the default attribute of the configuration file is left unchanged in **$APP_HOME/default.**

When you develop or modify an app using the Splunk Web interface (edit source), you are actually editing the **local** file. It's ok to do for a quick test. You should move the configuration to **default** to make it final. When developing in an IDE or standalone text editor, you should directly modify the configuration in **default**.

DEV

Changes to your dashboards (in **local**) through the web interface take effect immediately. Changes in **default** require you to hit the Splunk Refresh View endpoint. Some changes still require a Splunk Enterprise restart.

SHIP

Never ship your app with files in the **$APP_HOME/local** directory. Otherwise, it could clobber configurations that a customer made to their copy of the app. Besides, during an app upgrade the **default** configuration will be overridden while the **local** is preserved.

SPLUNK EXTENSIBILITY SURFACE

The extensibility surface area of Splunk Enterprise is vast. It includes the following types of knowledge objects grouped by different phases of Splunk processing pipeline:

Data ingestion & indexing

Input

- Scripted inputs
- Modular inputs
- Custom (trained) source types
- Custom sources

Data ingestion pipeline

- Field extractions
- Field transformations

Indexing

- Custom indexes

Searching

Search authoring

- Custom search commands
- Macros (basic, parametrized)
- Saved searches

Data classification

- Event types
- Transactions

Data enrichment

- Lookups
- KV store collections
- Workflow actions

Data normalization

- Tags
- Aliases

Data mining

- `cluster & dedup`
- `anomalousvalue`
- `kmeans`
- `shape`
- `predict commands...`

Processing & reporting

Search-time mapping

- Data models

CIM extensions

Custom UI/visualizations

- Pages, views & dashboards
- JS Extensions
- CSS Extensions
- Custom setup screens

Scheduled processing

- Scheduled reports

Alerting

- Scripted alerts
- Custom alerts

Branding & navigation

- Custom app navigation & branding

Manageability

- Custom splunkweb controllers
- Custom splunkd endpoints

Concepts are bold, artifacts are not.

ARCH

In the design of your app, you might consider partitioning your app into parts that are likely to be reusable by other apps and parts that might be candidates for extension at some future date. Add-ons facilitate reuse by multiple apps. Reuse is considerably enhanced if your app is Common Information Model (CIM)-compliant and new add-ons map to the CIM definition.

The following topics summarize the areas that need to be considered by almost all Splunk Enterprise apps. Each of these are covered in more detail in the remainder of the *Essentials* chapters.

Get your data into your app

Before your app can do anything related to data, you first need to get the data into your app. This is the first topic we address because understanding the structure and content of your data is usually the first step in designing your app. Understanding the source, quantity, performance, fields, and overall structure of your data influences how you decide to acquire the data and how to construct your search commands in the next step. Practically, you might consider the search commands you'll need and even how the data maps to the user interface in parallel with developing your data acquisition strategy.

In the data onboarding topics, we discuss what kind of data is significant to the way Splunk Enterprise handles data, propose optimum data structures (where that option is available to you), recommend programming mechanisms and ways to make your data reusable, and how to simulate your data input during early app development phases.

Efficiently search your data

The goal of search is to find the exact information you need in what's likely a huge amount of data. It's often the proverbial "searching for a needle in a haystack." Splunk Enterprise provides sophisticated search capabilities for finding the needle, supported by a powerful search language, and it's the function of your app to render the data in a useful and meaningful way, usually as a visualization.

In the search topics, we propose a processing model that favors efficient searches and introduce you to fundamental search patterns that apply to most search problems. We go into some detail on things you can do with your data in transforming it from the raw format to meaningful information. More advanced topics present ways to make your searches more efficient. Finally, we suggest guidelines to help troubleshoot your search implementation.

Understand your data

The ultimate objective of your app is to provide meaningful information about your data set. This almost always involves rendering a transformation of the raw data to a visualization. If you look at the app architecture diagram above, this is the front end programming of your app, and Splunk Enterprise provides a number of web programming tools and utilities to facilitate data visualization. In Visualizing data, we'll enumerate the various mechanisms available, like Simple XML, HTML, CSS, and JavaScript combinations, and illuminate the tradeoffs for different use cases.

In designing your app, this might be the place you start if you know a priori what information you want to display and have some flexibility in specifying the format of the incoming data. Usually, however, this is not the case and you'll need to do some level of concurrent design, considering what data are rendered along with the raw data format and search optimization.

Act on data

Splunk Enterprise is always monitoring your data, and it gives you numerous different ways to observe trends and visualize your data at any time. But you don't have to monitor your data constantly to be able to identify when you need to act on it. With alerting, you can tell Splunk Enterprise when to inform the appropriate stakeholders to take action, or even tell Splunk Enterprise to initiate those actions itself. In Acting on data, we describe the types of alerts available and how to manage them as well as how to create a custom alert action.

Package your app

Once your app is installed on a site, you'll most likely need the flexibility of being able to parameterize it for the environment and capabilities of a particular installation. These include tasks like setting remote IP addresses, user roles and credentials, and many other domain- and use case-specific properties.

In the packaging section and topics we describe the Splunk Enterprise mechanisms and conventions for setting up your app and how to package your app for distribution and installation on a Splunk Enterprise instance.

More information

The SplunkJS stack includes a number of tools for web developers:

- Backbone.js (backbonejs.org) provides an MVC framework as a structure for your code.
- RequireJS (requirejs.org) manages dependencies.
- jQuery (jquery.com) helps manage HTML DOM.

See the REST API Reference Manual at: dev.splunk.com/goto/restapi.

The Splunk SDKs provide you with broad coverage of the REST API in a language-specific fashion to ease your access to the Splunk engine. Currently, there are six SDKs available:

- Python (dev.splunk.com/python)
- Java (dev.splunk.com/java)
- C# (dev.splunk.com/csharp)
- JavaScript (dev.splunk.com/javascript)
- PHP (dev.splunk.com/php)
- Ruby (dev.splunk.com/ruby)

Splunk encourages and accepts community contributions to its SDKs. For more details see dev.splunk.com/goto/opensource.

12

Getting data in

Getting data into your Splunk Enterprise app is the essential first step toward understanding your data. The app infrastructure provides a number of mechanisms for ingesting data—from reading simple, well-known log file formats like Apache logs, to invoking programs to handle custom data formats. We provide suggestions for how to acquire the data for particular app scenarios, and for how to normalize your data to make it available to other apps, ensuring your data is robust and flexible. Deciding how you're going to get the data into your app often occurs in parallel with understanding how you're going to search your data. You might even need to augment your data at index time to make your data more meaningful.

CONFIGURING INPUT SOURCES

To realize the full potential of Splunk Enterprise, you first have to give it data. When you give Splunk Enterprise data, it *indexes* the data by transforming it into a series of *events* that contain searchable *fields*. To feed a new set of data to Splunk Enterprise, you configure a *data input* by pointing Splunk Enterprise to the source of the data and then describing it.

Splunk Enterprise can index many different kinds of data, as illustrated by the following diagram.

This chapter will help you decide the best method for getting data into your Splunk app, as well as provide tips on how to work with your data.

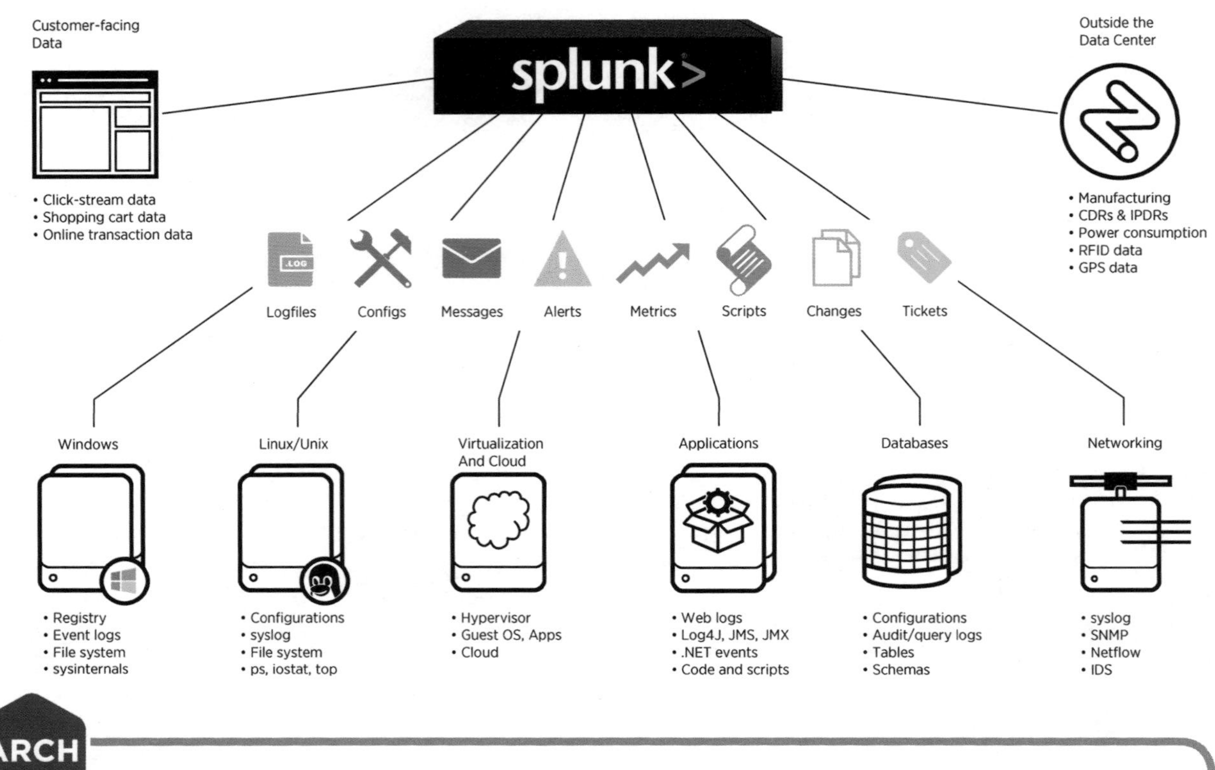

ARCH

Splunk Enterprise works best with time-series data (data with timestamps)

Specifying your input source

Here are some of the ways you can specify your input source.

Add-ons. Splunk Enterprise has a large and growing number of technical add-ons that support preconfigured inputs for particular types of data sources.

BUS

Splunk Enterprise is an extensible platform. In addition to a number of preconfigured inputs, the developer community makes it easy to get your data into Splunk Enterprise by building and sharing add-ons and tools for you to reuse. Check out splunkbase.splunk.com **to see what's available.**

For information about using apps and add-ons to input data to Splunk Enterprise, see "Use apps to get data in" in the "Getting Data In Manual."

Splunk Web. You can use a GUI-based approach to add and configure most inputs. To add data in Splunk Web, click **Add data** from either Splunk Home or the **Settings** menu. To configure existing data inputs, go to **Settings > Data inputs**.

For more information about how to add data using Splunk Web, see "How do you want to add data?" in the "Getting Data In Manual."

Command line interface (CLI). You can use the CLI to add and configure most input types. To add a data input, navigate to `$SPLUNK_HOME/bin/` and use the `./splunk add` command, followed by the `monitor` object and the path you want Splunk Enterprise to monitor. For example, the following adds `/var/log/` as a data input:

```
./splunk add monitor /var/log/
```

To learn more about CLI syntax, see "Administrative CLI commands" in the "Admin Manual."

The inputs.conf file. Input sources are not automatically discovered. You need to specify your inputs in the `inputs.conf` file. You can use Splunk Web or the CLI to declare and configure your input as a stanza in the `inputs.conf` file that you can then edit directly. You configure your data input by adding attribute/value pairs to your `inputs.conf` data input stanza. You can specify multiple attribute/value pairs. When not specified, a default value is assigned for the attribute.

Here's a simple example of adding a network input:

```
[tcp://:9995]
connection_host = dns
sourcetype = log4j
source = tcp:9995
```

ARCH

All data indexed into Splunk Enterprise is assigned a source type that helps identify the data format of the event and where it came from.

This input configuration stanza listens on TCP port 9995 for raw data from any remote server. The data source host is defined as the DNS name of the remote server and all data is assigned the "log4j" source type and "tcp:9995" source identifier.

For a complete list of input types and attributes, see the inputs.conf spec file documentation. Additionally, if you use forwarders to send data from remote servers, you can specify some inputs during forwarder installation.

DEV

Include both Windows and Unix style slashes in stanzas for portability.

ARCH

Be aware that compressed data sent by a forwarder is automatically unzipped by the receiving indexer.

Input type classification

Splunk Enterprise supports the input types described below.

Files and directories

Much of the data you might be interested in comes directly from files and directories; practically every system produces a log file. For the most part, you can use file and directory monitoring input processors to get data from files and directories. File and directory monitoring simply involves setting up your `inputs.conf` file. No coding is involved. We recommend using time-based log files whenever possible.

ADM

A good alternative for file-based inputs is to use *forwarders*. The advantages of using those on production servers include: load balancing and buffering, better scalability and performance, and stronger security. Optionally, you can encrypt or compress the data. For more information, see the "Forwarding Data Manual."

DEV

When monitoring a directory, Splunk Enterprise allows you to *whitelist* files that you want to index and/or *blacklist* files that you don't want to index. Check out the inputs.conf specification for other configuration options.

For more information about monitoring files and directories, see "Get data from files and directories" in the "Getting Data In Manual."

Network events

Splunk Enterprise can index data received from a network port, including SNMP events and alert notifications from remote servers. For example, you can index remote data from syslog-ng or any other app that transmits data using TCP. You can also receive and index UDP data, but we recommend using TCP when possible for greater reliability.

ARCH

Sending log data with syslog is still the primary method to capture network device data from firewalls, routers, switches, and so on.

ADM

A good alternative for network inputs is to use an agent. In this case you send data to an output file and let an agent (a *forwarder*) send data to an indexer. This provides load balancing, greater resiliency, and better scalability.

For more information about capturing data from network sources, see "Get network events" in the "Getting Data In Manual."

Windows sources

Splunk Enterprise includes a wide range of Windows-specific inputs. It also provides pages in **Settings** for defining the following Windows-specific input types:

- Windows event log, registry, perfmon and WMI data
- Active Directory data
- Performance monitoring data

ADM

Important: You can index and search Windows data using an instance of Splunk Enterprise that is not running on Windows, but you must first use an instance running on Windows to acquire the data. You can do this using an agent (a Splunk forwarder) running on Windows. Configure the forwarder to gather Windows inputs then forward the data to your non-Windows instance.

For more information about acquiring and indexing Windows data with Splunk Enterprise, see "Get Windows data" in the "Getting Data In Manual."

Other input sources

Splunk Enterprise also provides support for scripted and modular inputs for getting data from APIs and other remote data interfaces. These kinds of inputs typically involve programming, and we discuss the capabilities and tradeoffs later in this chapter.

ADM

Scripted and modular inputs are bundled as Splunk add-ons, and once installed, contain all the necessary code and configuration to add themselves to the Data inputs section of Splunk Enterprise for further customization and management.

For more information about all the other ways to get data into Splunk Enterprise, see "Other ways to get stuff in" in the "Getting Data In Manual."

LOGGING—PROVEN OPERATIONAL PRACTICES

When it comes to data collection, remember:

- Log events from everything, everywhere. This includes apps, web servers, databases, networks, configuration logs, and external system communications, as well as performance data.
- Monitor at the source type level.
- Use Splunk Enterprise forwarders.
- Use rotation and retention policies.
- Use smaller log files. It's better to use the size of the log as opposed to the time markers to implement your rolling strategy.
- Keep the latest two logs in text format before you compress; otherwise you may be missing delayed events.
- Use a blacklist to eliminate compressed files from file monitor inputs and to avoid event duplication.

SEC

The NIST Guide to Computer Security Log Management **contains many useful recommendations on log generation, storage, and effectively balancing a limited quantity of log management resources with a continuous, ever growing supply of log data.**

USE TIMESTAMPS

One of the most powerful Splunk Enterprise features is the ability to extract fields from events when you search, creating structure out of unstructured data. An accurate timestamp is critical to understanding the proper sequence of events, to aid in debugging and analysis, and for deriving transactions. Splunk Enterprise automatically timestamps events that don't include timestamps. However, when you have the option to define the format of your data, be sure to include timestamps. Some timestamp-related tips for adding value to your data include:

- Use the most verbose time granularity possible, preferably with an event resolution granularity of microseconds.
- Put the timestamp at the beginning of the line. The further you place a timestamp from the beginning of the event, the more difficult it is to distinguish the timestamp from other data.
- Include a four-digit year and time zone, preferably a GMT/UTC offset.
- Ideally, use epoch time—which is already normalized to UTC so no parsing is needed—for easy ingestion by Splunk Enterprise. But remember that this 10-digit string can also be mistaken for data.

The typical format of time-stamped data is a key-value pair. (JSON-formatted data is becoming more common, although time extraction is more difficult for JSON data.) Splunk Enterprise classifies source data by source type, such as "**syslog**," "**access_combined**," or "**apache_error**," and extracts timestamps, dividing the data into individual events, which can be a single- or multiple-line events. Each timed event is then written to the index for later retrieval using a search command.

FORMAT LOG DATA EFFICIENTLY

When you define your data format, there are a number of policies and configuration settings that can improve the performance and reliable attribute/value pair extraction of your input data.

Employ the following policies to ensure that events and fields can be easily parsed:

- Begin the log line event with a timestamp.
- Use clear key-value pairs.
- Use the Common Information Model (discussed later in this chapter) when using key-value pairs.
- Create human readable events in text format, including JSON.
- Use unique identifiers.
- Use developer-friendly formats.
- Log more than debugging events.
- Use categories.
- Identify the source.
- Minimize multi-line events.

As a minimum, set the following **props.conf** file attributes to improve event breaking and timestamp recognition performance:

- **TIME_PREFIX**: Provides the exact location to start looking for a timestamp pattern. The more precise this is, the faster timestamp processing is.
- **MAX_TIMESTAMP_LOOKAHEAD**: Indicates how far after **TIME_PREFIX** the timestamp pattern extends. **MAX_TIMESTAMP_LOOKAHEAD** has to include the length of the timestamp itself.
- **TIME_FORMAT**: Indicates the exact timestamp format. **TIME_FORMAT** uses **strptime** rules.
- **LINE_BREAKER**: Indicates how to break the stream into events. This setting requires a capture group followed immediately by the breaking point. Capture group content is discarded. By defining **LINE_BREAKER** you're specifying a break on a definite pattern.
- **SHOULD_LINEMERGE**: Indicates not to engage line merging (breaking on newlines and merging on timestamps), which is known to consume resources, especially for multiline events.

- **TRUNCATE:** The maximum line/event length, in bytes. The default is 10KB. It's prudent to have a non-default value depending on expected event length.
- KV_MODE: If you do not have input events as KV pairs, or any other similarly structured format, disable KV_MODE. It is helpful to indicate exactly what should be looked for.
- ANNOTATE_PUNCT: Unless you expect punctuation to be used in your searches, disable its extraction.

SEC

Punctuation is useful in security use cases, especially when classifying and grouping similar events and looking for anomalous events. For more information, see the "Classify and group similar events" **section of the Knowledge Manager Manual.**

Following those simple guidelines can significantly improve your data ingestion experience.

CHOOSE MODULAR INPUTS OVER SCRIPTED INPUTS

For input data that cannot be loaded using standard Splunk Enterprise inputs, you need to acquire your data using custom data ingestion techniques. This usually involves writing code that pulls data using an API, makes network requests, reads from multiple files, or does custom filtering.

Splunk Enterprise offers two mechanisms for defining and handling custom input through custom programming: scripted inputs and modular inputs. Scripted inputs are a legacy Splunk Enterprise mechanism that have generally been superseded by modular inputs, which offer greater flexibility and capability. Both have SDK support for popular languages. If your programming language is not supported by the SDK, you might need to write a low-level modular input. Modular inputs support custom input types, each with its own parameters and a graphical UI for validation. A scripted input is a single script that has no parameterization capability unless you've created a custom UI, and it must be shell-executable with specific STDIN and STDOUT formats. Scripted inputs tend to be more restrictive than modular inputs but are not without their unique capabilities as the following table shows.

FEATURE	SCRIPTED INPUTS	MODULAR INPUTS
Configuration	Inline arguments Separate, non-Splunk configuration	Parameters defined in `inputs.conf` Splunk Web fields treated as native inputs in Settings Validation support
Specify event boundaries	Yes But with additional complexity in your script	Yes XML streaming simplifies specifying event boundaries
Single instance mode	Yes Requires manual implementation	Yes
Multi-platform support	No	Yes You can package your script to include versions for separate platforms
Checkpointing	Yes Requires manual implementation	Yes
Run as Splunk Enterprise user	Yes You can specify which Splunk Enterprise user can run the script	No All modular input scripts are run as Splunk Enterprise system user
Custom REST endpoints	No	Yes Modular inputs can be accessed using REST
Endpoint permissions	N/A	Access implemented using Splunk Enterprise capabilities

Modular inputs can be used almost anywhere a scripted input is used. However, while scripted input might offer a quick and easy implementation when compared with the development effort of a modular input, a scripted input might not be as easy to use as a modular input.

UX

Scripted inputs are quick and easy, but may not be the easiest for an end user. Modular inputs require more upfront work, but are easier for end user interaction.

Working with modular inputs

SDKs are available, including developer documentation, for working with modular inputs in the Python, JavaScript, Java, and C# languages. You might also find the Implement modular inputs section of the developer documentation useful for detailed information about how to create a modular input. For other languages, you would need to write a low-level modular input through the Splunk REST API, which requires more effort.

> **DEV**
>
> **Splunk provides additional tooling for building modular inputs: the** Eclipse Plug-in **and the** Visual Studio Extension.

Your custom input requires that you provide an input handling function and, as with other input mechanisms, register the input source through the `inputs.conf` file. Your input function parses events in your data and sends them to your app using the `write_event()` method. Review the Auth0 app to see how we used modular inputs with Node.js to add validation to the continuation token implementation. To summarize the main features of a modular input:

> **ARCH**
>
> **It is also possible to create custom UI setup pages for adding and editing your modular input configurations.**

To summarize the main features of a modular input:

- Each instance you create is separately configurable, and supported by a configuration UI.
- It runs custom code that you write.
- Parameters are automatically validated and you are alerted in the UI of a parameter violation.
- It offers a rich programming model using the SDKs, which removes a lot of error-prone and redundant plumbing code.

Working with scripted inputs

If you are new to scripted inputs, it might be helpful to read the Splunk documentation:

- Scripted inputs overview
- Getting Data In

Like modular inputs, you register your scripted input in the **inputs.conf** file. Any script that the operating system can run can be used for scripted input. And any output from the script, to STDOUT by default, also ends up in your index.

> **ARCH**
>
> **Scripted inputs are often much easier to implement than modular inputs if all you are doing is retrieving data from a source and adding it to Splunk Enterprise.**

> **DEV**
>
> **A session key will be passed to the script if** `passAuth=true`**, so you can interact with the** Splunk REST API.

Additionally, there are some guidelines that can make developing and debugging scripted input easier.

Do not hard code paths in scripts

When referencing file paths in the Splunk Enterprise folder, use the **$SPLUNK_HOME** environment variable. This environment variable will be automatically expanded to the correct path based on the operating system Splunk Enterprise is running on.

Use the Splunk Enterprise Entity class or position files as a placeholder

Often, you may be calling an API with a scripted or modular input. In order to only query a specific range of values, use either the Splunk Enterprise **Entity** class or a position file to keep track of where the last run left off so the next run will pick up at that position. Where your input runs will dictate whether you should use the **Entity** class or a position file. For position files, avoid using files that start with a dot, as operating systems usually treat these types of files as special files. For example, instead of **.pos**, use **acme.pos**.

Use error trapping and logging

The following example demonstrates how to use the Python logging facility:

```
import logging
try:
    # Some code that may fail like opening a file
except IOError, err:
logging.error('%s - ERROR - File may not exist %s\n' % (time.strftime("%Y-%m-%d %H:%M:%S"),
              str(err)))
pass
```

Information logged with **logging.error()** will be written to **splunkd.log** as well as a special "**_internal**" index that can used for troubleshooting. Anything written to **STDERR** is also written to **splunkd.log** so you could use the following statement in place of **logging.error()**, above:

```
sys.stderr.write('%s - ERROR - File may not exist %s\n' % (time.strftime("%Y-%m-%d %H:%M:%S"),
                 str(err)))
```

DEV

It's best to use a separate/dedicated file other than splunkd.log to log modular input errors or events of interest.

Test scripts using Splunk Enterprise CMD

To see the output of a script as if it was run by the Splunk Enterprise system, use the following:

On *nix, Linux, or OS X use:

```
/Applications/Splunk/bin/splunk cmd python /Applications/Splunk/etc/apps/<your app>/bin/<your
script>
```

On Windows, use:

```
C:\Program Files\Splunk\bin\splunk.exe cmd C:\Program Files\Splunk\etc\apps\<your app>\bin\<your
script>
```

Use configuration files to store user preferences

Configuration files store specific settings that will vary for different environments. Examples include REST endpoints, API levels, or any specific setting. Configuration files are stored in either of the following locations and cascade:

```
$SPLUNK_HOME/etc/apps/<your_app>/default
$SPLUNK_HOME/etc/apps/<your_app>/local
```

DEV

A developer should not be thinking about the local directory.

For example, if there is a configuration file called **acme.conf** in both the default and local directories, settings from the local folder will override settings in the default directory.

Use Splunk Enterprise methods to read cascaded settings

The Splunk Enterprise **cli_common** library contains methods for reading combined settings from configuration files. The following Python example shows how to use **cli_common** functions:

```
import splunk.clilib.cli_common
def __init__(self,obj):
    self.object = obj
    self.settings = splunk.clilib.cli_common.getConfStanza("acme", "default")
```

SHIP

Never package/ship your app or add-ons with the local **directory.**

Use script methods to construct file paths

Here is a Python example:

```
abs_file_path = os.path.join(script_dir, rel_path)
Example (PowerShell):
$positionFile = Join-Path $positionFilePath $positionFileName
```

Managing initial data collection

Production servers often have large volumes of historical data that may not be worth collecting. When deploying your app, before starting to index, consider archiving, then deleting old data that should not be indexed and placing historical data in a separate location.

ADM

To avoid causing license violations, it may also be prudent to batch uploads of historical data and spread it over time.

Distributed deployment considerations

Many Splunk Enterprise apps can be deployed in a variety of environments—from a standalone, single-instance server to a distributed environment with multiple servers. The Deployment topologies web page describes the different levels of distributed deployment. Choosing a topology depends on an organization's requirements. When developing a Splunk Enterprise app, it's necessary to understand the implications of a distributed architecture on app design, setup, management, and performance.

An app is a unit of modularization and, as such, inherently supports distributed deployment. Like server functionality, which can be all-in-one or distributed, an app can also include all the functionality or have its knowledge objects divided into different sets, to be deployed on different Splunk Enterprise instances. Because you might not know ahead of time the context your app will need to run in, it's a good idea to keep a few considerations in mind when designing your app:

- **Plan for a distributed architecture.** You need to understand the distributed topologies and the roles of each server instance. Typically, this means that data input needs to be one of the roles, on a particular instance, and separate from other types of knowledge objects that can reside on other instances.
- **Consider the scale of deployment.** There is likely a part of your app, such as the UI, that resides only on the search head and a part of your app that needs to reside on the entire indexing tier.
- **Consider the rate of data growth.** Expect that the amount of data your app needs to process will be significantly greater in the future than it is today.

A logical app decomposition strategy is to separate your app into those parts that run on the search head and those parts that run on the indexing tier. The parts that go on the indexers let you ingest the data. The parts that go on the search head let you view the data. Dividing your app among dedicated nodes also lets other apps benefit from your implementation if they need to handle the same interface or implement the same logic. Partitioned apps can share things like a generally useful search string or a parser that correctly ingests data from a particular source.

The main issue in handling large amounts of data is running out of disk space. When an indexer runs out of space, it stops indexing, possibly resulting in data loss. When a search head runs out of space, it stops searching. There are a few strategies and mechanisms you can keep employ in your design to take advantage of the Splunk Enterprise distributed architecture and mitigate against data loss.

ADM

You can view detailed performance information about your Splunk Enterprise deployment and configure platform alerts using the Distributed Management Console (DMC)**.**

You can use data model acceleration, which moves the TSIDX idea to the indexing tier so disk space is not taken up on the search head. An advantage of data model acceleration over other acceleration methods is that if new data arrives that has not yet been summarized, it will be summarized automatically.

Use the same `props.conf` and `transforms.conf` files on each node to provide the field extraction and index time rules. This ensures uniformity of configuration across a large environment. An indexer will only read the part of the file related to indexing and a forwarder will only read the part of the file related to forwarding. In short, make distributed apps easier to create and manage by avoiding duplication.

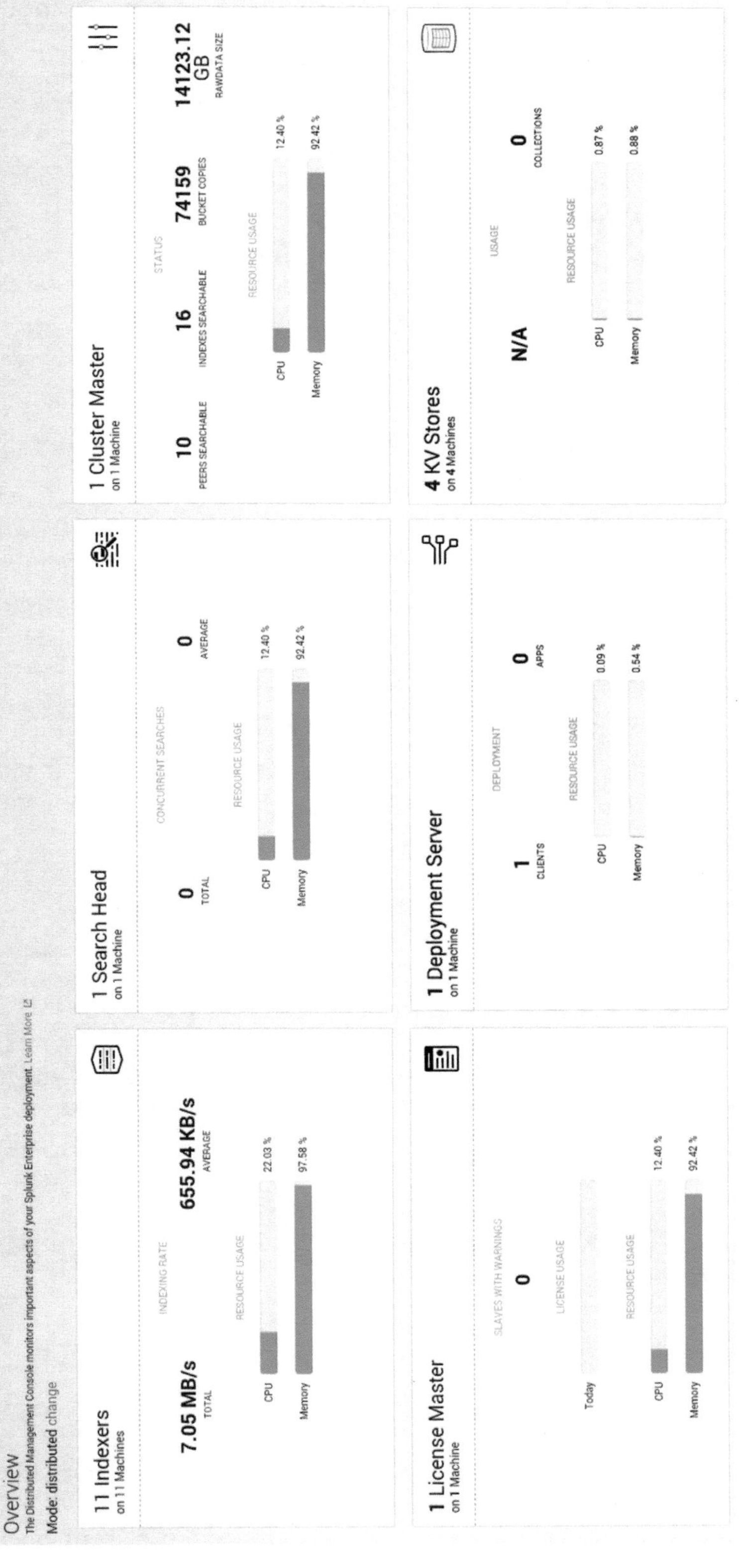
Overview
The Distributed Management Console monitors important aspects of your Splunk Enterprise deployment. Learn More
Mode: distributed change
11 Indexers
on 11 Machines
INDEXING RATE
7.05 MB/s
TOTAL
655.94 KB/s
AVERAGE
RESOURCE USAGE
CPU
22.03 %
Memory
97.58 %
1 Search Head
on 1 Machine
CONCURRENT SEARCHES
0
TOTAL
0
AVERAGE
RESOURCE USAGE
CPU
12.40 %
Memory
92.42 %
1 Cluster Master
on 1 Machine
STATUS
10
PEERS SEARCHABLE
16
INDEXES SEARCHABLE
74159
BUCKET COPIES
14123.12 GB
RAWDATA SIZE
RESOURCE USAGE
CPU
12.40 %
Memory
92.42 %
1 License Master
on 1 Machine
SLAVES WITH WARNINGS
0
LICENSE USAGE
Today
RESOURCE USAGE
CPU
12.40 %
Memory
92.42 %
1 Deployment Server
on 1 Machine
DEPLOYMENT
1
CLIENTS
0
APPS
RESOURCE USAGE
CPU
0.09 %
Memory
0.54 %
4 KV Stores
on 4 Machines
USAGE
N/A
0
COLLECTIONS
RESOURCE USAGE
CPU
0.87 %
Memory
0.88 %

As units of modularization, create small apps targeted for specific functionality:

- **Indexing rules.** Anything search-time related and that uses the `props.conf` and `transforms.conf` configuration files for field extraction.
- **Data collection.** The code that ingests data from a particular source.
- **Dashboards.** Saved searches that populate dashboards and the dashboards, themselves, along with supporting JavaScript and CSS code.

By designing and implementing your app for a distributed architecture from the beginning, you are likely to produce a more useful and maintainable app. Some additional things to keep in mind:

- Put all basic configuration in the `indexes.conf` file.
- Be agnostic about the configuration management system for deploying and managing your app, which might be Deployment Server, a third-party tool like Chef or Puppet, or others.
- On the search head, be deliberate about search optimization. In particular, delete as many columns and rows as possible before search pinch points (reports and the `stats` command).
- On the indexer, use a focused index but use a macro to make it configurable so the index destination only needs to be changed in one place.

CHOOSE THE SDK OVER UDP/TCP OR REST

While other input mechanisms are inherently a pull interface, SDK, UDP/TCP, and REST input mechanisms can both pull and push. In case of a pull, a Splunk Enterprise instance requests (pulls) the data. In case of a push, the data transfer is initiated by the external system and not by Splunk Enterprise. The discussion of both approaches and implementation details of the Auth0 reference application is included in the *Journey*.

ARCH

Favor pulling data using an SDK over pushing.

While a push-style interface can be responsive to the time-sensitive requirements of the application, it is also possible that the external system providing the data can be blocked if the data rate is too high and there is insufficient buffering. In terms of performance, UDP/TCP transfer ranks as the highest performing method, followed by using the SDK, and a basic REST interface as the lowest performing method.

Another disadvantage of these protocols is that authentication and authorization are needed for the data to reach the server but Splunk Enterprise does not currently support third-party authentication providers.

USE CIM TO NORMALIZE LOG DATA

One task you might want your app to perform is to consider conceptually-related data that comes from different sources, or from the same source but whose representation has changed over time. While the data might look different, it is the same kind of data and you want to analyze and report on the data as if it were from a single source. The obvious way to solve this problem is to write a separate search for each different data representation.

However, that approach is limited, especially when the number of sources or different representations is large.

For example, say you are monitoring antivirus program results produced by a number of different antivirus program vendors. Instead of searching the results produced by each vendor and then somehow associating those results, you prefer to normalize those results, where similar notifications and alarms map to the same event at the conceptual level, before handing the results to your app. Or, suppose the format or representation of the data changes so you have older data in one form and newer data in another form, but both old and new data contain essentially the same information. It would be helpful to have a mechanism that normalizes the results before they get to your app.

The Splunk Enterprise Common Information Model (CIM) is intended as an easy way to provide data normalization, and includes supported data models for common application domains. CIM is implemented as an add-on that normalizes your data and presents the data as knowledge objects for your app to process. See the "Knowledge Manager Manual" for an introduction to CIM and the "Common Information Model Add-on Manual" for a list of data models and more detailed information about how to use CIM. This document shows the tags you need for the model, how they're mapped, what each field and its data type are, and whether the field is required. You will also need to use the Pivot Editor, so read the "Data Model and Pivot Tutorial" to learn how to use the tool with data models. For an example of our experience with CIM in the *Journey*, review "Working with data: where it comes from and how we manage it."

CIM simplifies the work you and your app need to do by presenting the data at a conceptual level instead of needing to use all the data available to represent an entity. Some of that data might not be important to your app. CIM lets you ask simple, generalized questions about your data and generalizes your query across all data sources. It is easier to write a search against the generalization than against separate but similar data items. However, your data can often align with more than one model, so one of the first things you'll need to do is analyze your data and see which model is the best fit. This manual process requires you to inspect the data coming into your app.

An important fact about CIM is that the conceptual model you define for your data is applied at search time, not index time. So you can always go back to your raw data, if needed. You can still choose to accelerate your data model to get improved performance, trading off indexer load for fast access to search results.

A disadvantage of the CIM implementation is that the models are not structurally related entities, so you can't ingest the results of one data model into another data model. The models are separate entities populated at search time. Also, data is mapped to the least common denominator across all your data sources. CIM does not attempt to resolve all of the disparate data but, because associations are made at search time, the raw events are still available to your application.

> **DEV**
> Appendix C provides a cheat sheet with the configuration file name associations to their functions.

A number of .conf files and search language constructs are involved in using CIM to define your data sources, tags, and data transformations. Your raw data sources are defined in the `inputs.conf` file. You perform extractions, lookups, define regular expressions, and apply tags to your data items using the `props.conf`, `transforms.conf`, `eventtypes.conf`, and `tags.`

conf files. The next step is to use the **models.conf** file to apply a model schema, optionally using acceleration to improve performance, and using constraints to select data and add meaning to your data. Define your searches in the **savedsearches.conf** file.

DEV

Data model configuration is stored in `datamodels.conf` **using a JSON structure. However, it's easier to manage this configuration in the UI.**

Common steps for creating a CIM-compliant app include using the UI to:

1. Create your new app. Be sure to make app configurations globally accessible. Also, it is easier to create CIM mapping for your app if you have the Splunk CIM add-on installed.
2. Edit your **transforms.conf** file and map existing field names to applicable model field names. Optionally, provide regex definitions to extract fields. Choose the supported model that best matches your application. Alternatively, you can extract fields using the interactive field extractor or the **props.conf** file. A time-saving step is to verify your definitions using the Search app.
3. Tag events by creating an **eventtype** and defining a **tag** for it. You might need to create field aliases for your data to match what the model requires.
4. In the UI, click **Data Models**, and then **Pivot** to view results. If the results were not what you expected, click **Missing Extractions** to help diagnose the problem. You might have a missing tag that is required for the model.

In summary, CIM is a good choice if you want to design your app for interoperability. Benefits are that you can do searches by calling one macro using tags instead of doing separate searches for all the commands. CIM permits different vendors and data sources to interoperate and creates relevant data that works with apps dedicated to solving specific problems.

USE HTTP EVENT COLLECTOR

A new feature in Splunk Enterprise 6.3, HTTP Event Collector lets you send data directly to Splunk Enterprise over HTTP. HTTP Event Collector can accept data from anywhere, as long as it's sent over HTTP and enclosed in a series of correctly formatted JSON data packets. You don't need to run any extra software on the client side. Though Splunk logging libraries that automate the data transmission process are available for Java, C#, and JavaScript, the client does not require any Splunk software to send data to HTTP Event Collector (or "EC") on Splunk Enterprise. EC uses specialized tokens, so you don't need to hard code your Splunk Enterprise credentials in your client app or supporting files. You can also scale out EC by using a load balancer to distribute incoming EC data evenly to indexers.

The basics of HTTP Event Collector on Splunk Enterprise are relatively simple:

1. Turn on EC in Splunk Enterprise by enabling the HTTP Event Collector endpoint. It is not enabled by default.
2. From the Splunk Enterprise instance, generate an EC token.

3. On the machine that will log data to Splunk Enterprise, create a POST request, and set its authentication header to include the EC token.
4. POST data in JSON format to the EC token receiver.

HTTP Event Collector is great for data input scenarios like the following:

- **Logging application diagnostics during development**: Build logging into Java or C# apps that send debug data directly to EC running on Splunk Enterprise.
- **Logging in a distributed indexer configuration**: Index huge amounts of EC data by taking advantage of built-in Splunk Enterprise load balancing capabilities.
- **Logging in a secure network**: No external or cloud-based services are required to collect data.
- **Logging data from the browser**: Build logging into webpages using JavaScript that sends usage data directly to EC running on Splunk Enterprise.
- **Logging data from automation scripts**: Add logging to different stages of automated IT processes.
- **Sending data with specific source type**: Assign incoming data a source type based on data source, token, and so on, and then define search time extractions and event types based on the source type.

For more information about HTTP Event Collector, see "Building in telemetry with high-performance data collection" or see "Introduction to Splunk HTTP Event Collector" on the Splunk Developer Portal.

TESTING AND STAGING DATA INPUTS

Inputs are distinctive and some can be quite idiosyncratic. Therefore, you should designate a part of your Splunk Enterprise deployment to testing and staging. Use the sandbox for testing all new inputs (custom built or obtained from Splunk or other providers) before putting them into the production environment.

If you are unable to procure a sandbox Splunk Enterprise deployment, at least use a staging index for testing to avoid polluting your main indexes. The staging index can be deleted when tests have completed.

> **TEST**
> Make sure that your sample data set is large enough and robust enough to detect edge cases.

SIMULATE YOUR EVENT STREAM

You usually want to begin testing the input handling part of your app early in the development cycle and for that, you need data to be available. But, for some reason, a live feed isn't available, the data is not immediately available in the format or volume you need, or the data is available but to limit your testing time you only want the data from a certain time interval or with specific values. In such cases, you can simulate your data. Splunk provides Eventgen, an event generation tool, for you to use. The tool can replay events in a file or series of files, or randomly extract entries from a file and generate events at random intervals and change particular fields or values according to your specification. You can use the Eventgen tool to not only generate known and random events for your app, but to configure the tool to generate events that reflect natural usage patterns.

For your sample data, it's often convenient to start with an existing log file and use the **eventgen.conf** specification to do token replacement. You can also create a file of tokens and let the **eventgen.conf** replacement settings generate data the way you want it to look.

> **DEV**
>
> **Eventgen is included with the PAS reference app download and install script. We preconfigured it to generate events for the Off-Hours Access and Terminated Employee Access scenarios. Run the** `install_addons.sh` **script (or** `install_addons.ps1` **script for Windows PowerShell) at** `$SPLUNK_HOME/etc/apps/pas_ref_app/bin/` **to install the PAS app, and it will install and configure Eventgen at the same time. The script creates a symbolic link in the** `$SPLUNK_HOME/etc/apps/` **folder to the** `$SPLUNK_HOME/etc/apps/pas_ref_app/appserver/addons/eventgen` **folder. When you restart Splunk Enterprise, Eventgen starts and immediately begins creating events according to the PAS settings.**

Here are the basic steps you'll need to follow to install and set up Eventgen using your own custom settings:

1. Download Eventgen from GitHub.
2. Install the app by extracting the downloaded **eventgen-dev.zip** file to your **$SPLUNK_HOME/etc/apps/** folder, and then rename the decompressed folder to **eventgen**.
3. Create a **samples** folder in the folder for the app that will use the Eventgen data: **$SPLUNK_HOME/etc/apps/$MYAPP/samples** (where **$MYAPP** represents your app folder).
4. Set permissions for your app so it is accessible by all other apps.
5. Put your sample data in the **/samples** folder you just created. This is the data that Eventgen uses to replicate data as input to your app.
6. In the **$SPLUNK_HOME/etc/apps/$MYAPP/local** folder, create the **eventgen.conf** file. You can also copy and modify the **$SPLUNK_HOME/etc/apps/eventgen/README/eventgen.conf.example** file you downloaded earlier.
7. Edit the first stanza of the **eventgen.conf** file to reference the sample data file in the **samples** folder.
8. Restart your Splunk Enterprise instance.

> **SHIP**
>
> **If you intend to ship Eventgen configuration with your app, include it in the** `default` **folder, not** `local`**.**

The Eventgen tool can be run as an add-on, or as a scripted or modular input inside your app. See the **$SPLUNK_HOME/etc/apps/eventgen/README/eventgen.conf.spec** file for a complete description of the options available to you for generating sample data. You can also view the eventgen.conf.spec file on GitHub.

In addition to the preconfigured Eventgen install provided by the PAS reference app as a part of the *Journey*, see a good, example-based description in the Eventgen tutorial on GitHub. Eventgen can also be run as a standalone utility, using **eventgen.py** in the **$SPLUNK_HOME/etc/apps/eventgen/bin** folder. The tutorial provides descriptions of the proper settings for the various modes of operation and for getting the data in the **samples** folder into your app.

See how we used Eventgen in the "Test and sample data" section in the "Platform and tools: a kitbag for our Journey" chapter of the *Journey*. You can find other interesting examples in the Splunk Blog's Tips & Tricks category with a basic introduction to Eventgen, how to create random data in events, and how to sample events randomly from the data set.

Appendix B contains tips for troubleshooting Eventgen.

MORE INFORMATION

Check out splunkbase.splunk.com to see what Splunk apps are available.

For information about using apps and add-ons to input data to Splunk Enterprise, see "Use apps to get data in" in the "Getting Data In Manual" at: dev.splunk.com/gotot/usingapps.

For more information about how to add data using Splunk Web, see "How do you want to add data?" in the "Getting Data In Manual" at: dev.splunk.com/goto/wanttoadddata.

To learn more about CLI syntax, see "Administrative CLI commands" in the "Admin Manual" at: dev.splunk.com/goto/cliadmincommands.

For a complete list of input types and attributes, see the inputs.conf spec file documentation at: dev.splunk.com/goto/inputsconf.

For information on using forwarders, see "Forwarding Data" at: dev.splunk.com/goto/forwardingandreceivingdata.

For more information about monitoring files and directories, see "Get data from files and directories" in the "Getting Data In Manual" at: dev.splunk.com/goto/monitorfiles.

For more information about capturing data from network sources, see "Get network events" in the "Getting Data In Manual" at: dev.splunk.com/goto/monitornetworkports.

For more information about acquiring and indexing Windows data with Splunk Enterprise, see "Get Windows data" in the "Getting Data In Manual" at: dev.splunk.com/goto/aboutwindowsdata.

For more information about all the other ways to get data into Splunk Enterprise, see "Other ways to get stuff in" in the "Getting Data In Manual" at: dev.splunk.com/goto/monitorfifoqueues.

The NIST Guide to Computer Security Log Management contains many useful recommendations on log generation, storage, and other topics: csrc.nist.gov/publications/nistpubs/800-92/SP800-92.pdf.

For more information on using punctuation, see "Classify and group similar events" at: dev.splunk.com/goto/classifyandgroupsimilarevents.

SDKs are available, including developer guide documentation, for working with modular input in the following languages:

- Python (dev.splunk.com/goto/pythonsdkmodinput)
- JavaScript (dev.splunk.com/goto/modularinputs)
- Java (dev.splunk.com/goto/javasdkmodinput)
- C# (dev.splunk.com/goto/cssdkmodinput)

For detailed information about how to create a modular input, see: dev.splunk.com/goto/overviewmodinputs.

Splunk provides additional tooling for building modular inputs:

- Eclipse Plug-in (dev.splunk.com/goto/eclipseplugin)
- Visual Studio Extension (dev.splunk.com/goto/vsextension)

If you are new to scripted input, read the Splunk documentation that introduces scripted input:

- Scripted inputs overview (dev.splunk.com/goto/scriptedinputsintro)
- Getting Data In (dev.splunk.com/goto/scriptedinputsintro)

For information about using the Splunk REST API, see: dev.splunk.com/goto/inputsconfig.

For information on the different levels of distributed deployment see "Deployment topologies" at: dev.splunk.com/goto/deploymenttopologies.

You can view detailed performance information about your Splunk Enterprise deployment using the Distributed Management Console (DMC) at: dev.splunk.com/goto/configmonitorconsole.

For a discussion of push and pull requests and implementation details of the Auth0 reference application, see: dev.splunk.com/goto/datainmodular.

For an introduction to CIM, see the Knowledge Manager Manual at: dev.splunk.com/goto/understandcim.

For a list of data models and more detailed information about how to use CIM, see the Common Information Model Add-on Manual at: dev.splunk.com/goto/cimoverview.

To learn how to use the Pivot Editor with data models, see the tutorial at: dev.splunk.com/goto/pivottutorial.

For an example of our experience with CIM in the *Journey*, review "Working with data: where it comes from and how we manage it" at: dev.splunk.com/goto/jrndata.

For more information about HTTP Event Collector, see "Introduction to Splunk HTTP Event Collector" on the Splunk Developer Portal at: dev.splunk.com/goto/httpecintro.

The Splunk Eventgen tool available on GitHub at: dev.splunk.com/goto/eventgen.

You can view the eventgen.conf.spec file on GitHub at: dev.splunk.com/goto/eventgenconfspec.

For a good, example-based description of how to use Eventgen, see the tutorial on GitHub at: dev.splunk.com/goto/eventgentut.

See how we used Eventgen in the Test and sample data section in the "Platform and tools: a kitbag for our journey" at: dev.splunk.com/goto/jrntestsample.

You can find other interesting examples at Splunk Blog: Tips & Tricks:

- A basic introduction to Eventgen (dev.splunk.com/goto/easysampledata)
- How to create random data in events (dev.splunk.com/goto/easysampledata2)
- How to sample events randomly from the data set (dev.splunk.com/goto/easysampledata3)

Appendix B contains tips for troubleshooting Eventgen, see: dev.splunk.com/goto/appendixeventgen.

13

Searching the data

Search is at the heart of any app and is the fundamental tool available for extracting the knowledge you're interested in from the great amount of data available. The Splunk® Enterprise search language provides powerful constructs for sifting through your data once you have ingested and indexed the data. It provides an extensive set of commands, arguments, and functions that enable you to filter, modify, reorder, and group your search results.

Additional documentation that you might find helpful includes the Search Manual for a comprehensive description of all the things you can do using the search facilities and the Search Reference for a description of search language syntax. A particularly handy cheat sheet is the search language Quick Reference Guide.

SEARCH CONCEPTS

Here are key search terms and concepts.

Search

The *Search Processing Language (SPL)* is the language you use to specify a search of your data. Generally, a search is a series of commands and arguments, chained together with the pipe ("|") character. For example, the following retrieves indexed **access_combined** events (which correspond to the HTTP web log) that contain the term "error" and, for those events, reports the most common URI values:

```
error sourcetype=access_combined | top uri
```

This chapter introduces you to a search process model that can be applied to almost any application, and suggests some optimum search language facilities to use at each step of the process. This includes basic search operations and optimizations, advanced techniques, and basic troubleshooting guidance.

DEV

The way commands are pipe-delimited is analogous to how a Unix shell or Windows PowerShell connects line-processing programs together with pipes.

Syntactically, searches are made up of 5 basic components:

- **Search terms** – what are we looking for?
  Keywords, phrases, Booleans, and so on.
- **Commands** – what should we do with the results?
  Create a chart, compute statistics, evaluate, apply conditional logic, and format, and so on.
- **Functions** – how should we chart, compute, or evaluate?
  Get a sum, get an average, transform the values, and so on.
- **Arguments** – are there variables we should apply to this function?
  Calculate average value for a specific field, convert milliseconds to seconds, and so on.
- **Clauses** – how should we group the results?
  Get the average of values for the price field grouped by product, and so on.

The following diagram represents a search broken into its syntax components:

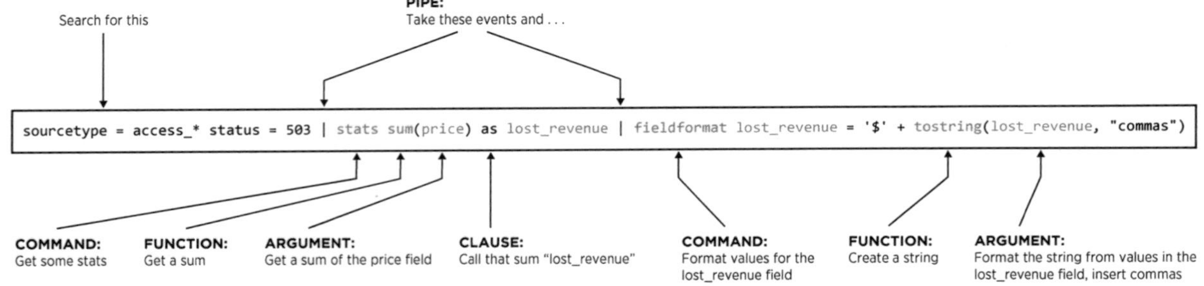

DEV

Keyword arguments to the search command are not case sensitive, but field names are.

Search command

The **search** command is the simplest and most powerful SPL command. It is invoked implicitly at the beginning of a search.

When it's not the first command in a search, the **search** command can filter a set of results from the previous search. To do this, use the search command like any other command, with a pipe character followed by an explicit command name. For example, if we augment the previous search, it will search for the Web log events that that have the term "error," find the top URIs, and filter any URIs that only occur once.

```
error sourcetype=access_combined | top uri | search count>1
```

Event

An *event* is a single data entry, or key-value pair associated with a timestamp. Specifically, an event is a set of values associated with a timestamp. For example, here is an event in a Web activity logfile:

```
173.26.34.223 - - [01/Jul/2009:12:05:27 -0700] "GET /trade/app?action=logout HTTP/1.1" 200 2953
```

While many events are short, a line or two, some can be long, for example: a full text document, a configuration file, or java stack trace. Splunk Enterprise uses line-breaking rules to determine how to delineate events for display in search results.

DEV

Splunk Enterprise is intelligent enough to handle most multiline events correctly by default. In rare cases it doesn't, see "Configure event line breaking" **for information on how to customize line breaking behavior.**

Field

Fields are searchable name/value pairs in event data. As events are processed at index time and search time, fields are automatically extracted. At index time, a small set of default fields are extracted for each event, including "`host`," "`source`," and "`sourcetype`." At search time, Splunk extracts a wider range of fields from the event data, including obvious name-value pairs, such as "`user_id=jdoe`", and user-defined patterns.

Host

A *host* is the name of the device where an event originates. A host provides an easy way to find all data originating from a particular device.

Source/Sourcetype

A *source* is the name of the file, stream, or other input from which a particular event originates. For example, "`/var/log/messages`" or "`UDP:514`." Sources are classified by sourcetype, which can either be well known, such as "`access_combined`" in HTTP Web server logs, or can be created on the fly when a source is detected with data and formatting not previously seen. Events with the same sourcetype can come from different sources. Events from the "`/var/log/messages`" file and events from a syslog input on `udp:514` can both have "`sourcetype=linux_syslog`".

Eventtype

Eventtypes are cross-referenced searches that categorize events at search time. Eventtypes are essentially dynamic tags that get attached to an event if it matches the search definition of the eventtype. For example, if you defined an eventtype called "`problem`" that has a search definition of "`error OR warn OR fatal OR fail`", any time your search result contains "`error`," "`warn`," "`fatal`," or "`fail`," the eventtype value is "`problem`".

Tag

A *tag* is a field value alias. For example, if two host names refer to the same computer, you could give both host values the same tag, such as "**hal9000**", and when you search for the "**hal9000**" tag, events for all hosts having that tag are returned.

ARCH

Tags are useful when normalizing data at search time. See "Tagging our Events" **in "Working with data: Where it comes from and how we manage it" for an example of tagging in action.**

A PROCESS MODEL FOR SEARCH

To better understand the way search works in Splunk Enterprise, consider the following figure, which represents a conceptual search process model.

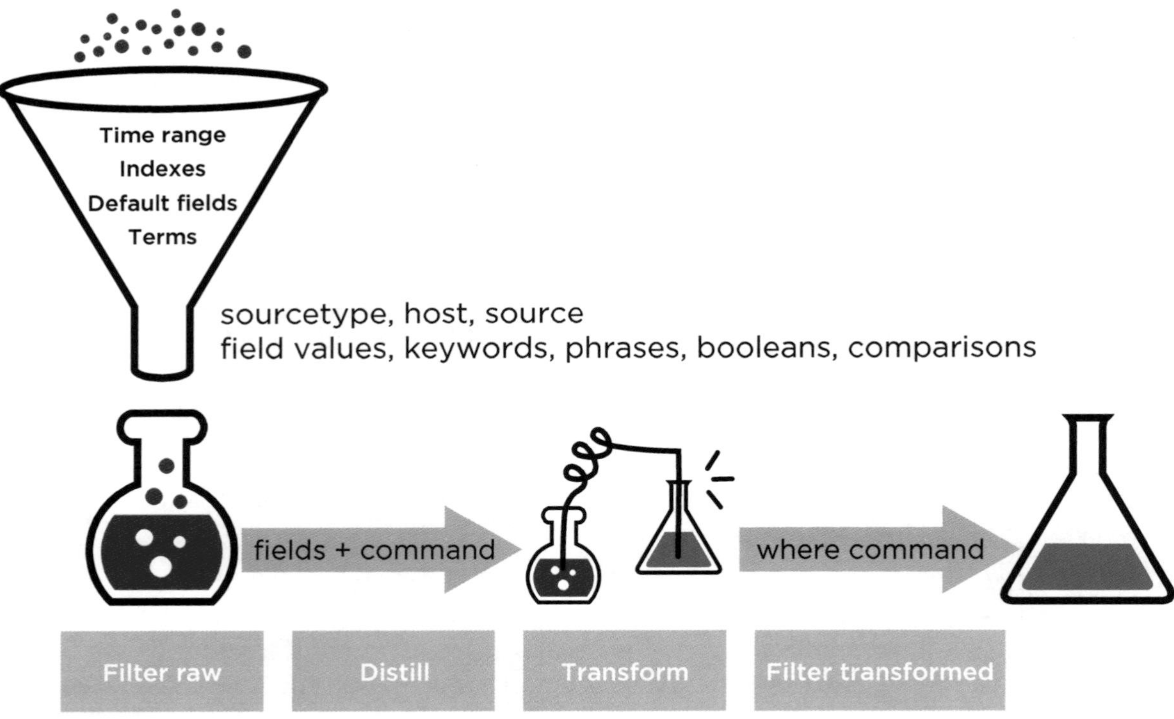

All search methodology can apply this model to some degree, depending on data complexity and the particular knowledge you want to extract from your data.

When you add raw data, Splunk Enterprise breaks the data into individual events, timestamps the events, and stores them in an index. The index can later be searched and analyzed. By default, your data is stored in the "`main`" index, but you can create and specify other indexes for different data inputs.

You want to select only the data you care about from the large amount of available data, and can use a four-stage process model to do that. The stages are displayed along the horizontal axis: Filter raw, Distill, Transform, and Filter (transformed), again, with each stage refining your search results in a way that's efficient for the particular stage. Let's consider each stage in detail.

The first Filter stage represents the most basic level of data extraction, which itself has different levels of extraction along the vertical axis. Filtering rows before filtering columns is the most efficient approach, and should be done early to reduce the number of events you have to work with. A *row* is an event and a column is a field within an event.

Time, or a time range, is usually the most effective filter. After time, select an index or a list of indices appropriate for your organization. Your organization might have data allocated to different indexes according to data sensitivity, retention periods, or some other organizational grouping. Next, filter on the default fields of timestamp, which shows when the event occurred, sourcetype, which identifies the event, and host plus source, which identifies the source location of the event. Finally, select any other desired terms of interest to you, including field values, keywords, and phrases. You can apply Boolean or comparison operations to your terms to extract data of even greater value.

Use the Distill stage to further refine your search to keep only those fields you want. You need only use the `fields` command if there is some benefit for you. For example, use `fields` to enumerate only those fields you want:

```
sourcetype=access_combined | fields clientip, action, status, categoryid, product_name
```

This only applies if your search returns a set of events. Also, remember that field names are case sensitive and must exactly match the field name in your data.

The Transform stage gives you the opportunity to transform search result data into the data structures required for visualizations or compute additional custom fields. Example transforms are:

- The `stats` and `contingency` commands.
- Data manipulation commands, like `eval`, `rename`, and others.
- Statistical visualization commands, like `timechart`, `chart` and `table`.

Optionally, the Transform stage may include a Data Enrichment substage that involves adding or cross-referencing data from an external source (for example, a .csv file) using the lookups.

Using the transformed data from the previous stage, the Filter Transformed stage will filter the data again, using the `where` command, to reduce the number of columns and get exactly the data you want and in the format you want. You could append another `search` command, but the where command is considered the more powerful option.

The following sections about searching will provide you with more detail about the facilities and language constructs available to you in each stage.

BECOME FAMILIAR WITH FUNDAMENTAL SEARCH PATTERNS

The following are some examples of constructs you will commonly use to search your data. These are only some of the most common features of the search language and it might be helpful to have the Quick Reference Guide at hand to see similar functions available to you.

Search on keywords

Everything in your data is searchable. Using nothing more than keywords and a time range, you can learn a lot about your data. The simplest search command is to simply specify one or more keywords you want to search for in your data. Search returns all events that include the keyword(s) anywhere in the raw text of the event's data.

Because a keyword-only search returns every event matching your keyword, the next obvious step is to narrow your search, unless you actually want to know the total number of occurrences. A first step in narrowing search results might be to use Boolean operators. The search language supports the following Boolean operators: `AND`, `OR`, `XOR`, and `NOT`.

The AND operator is always implied between search terms so you don't need to specify it.

DEV

For efficient searches use inclusion (`AND`, `OR`, and `XOR`) rather than exclusion (`NOT`), which is the more expensive operation.

Another simple way to narrowing your search results is to use comparison operators (such as !=, <=, >=).

PERF

Use the Search Job Inspector to see timing differences between various ways of formulating your searches and to optimize them.

Use the appropriate search mode

Splunk Enterprise supports several search modes:

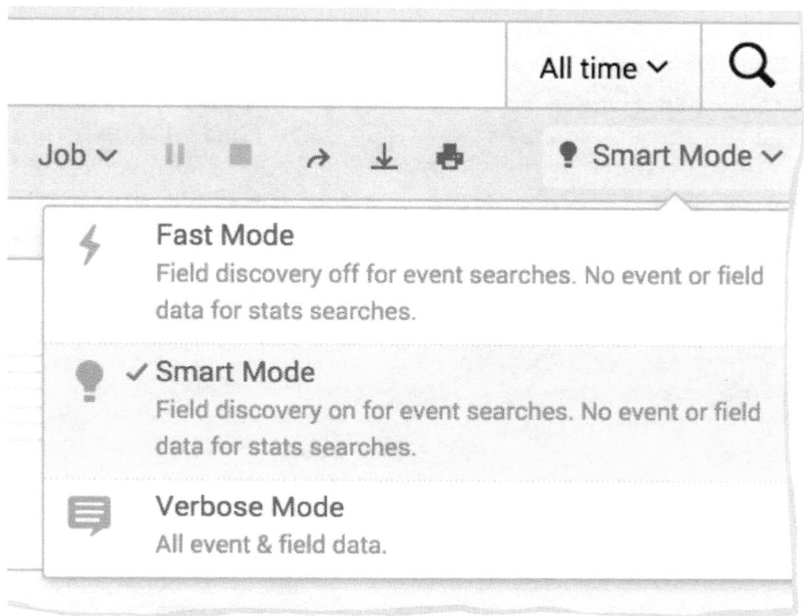

The Fast Mode gives you performance over completeness. On the converse, the Verbose Mode gives you completeness over performance. The Smart Mode (default) is a combination of Fast and Verbose modes. It is designed to give you the best results for your search with the field discovery turned on (like in the Verbose Mode) to extract all possible fields while reporting as configured in the Fast Mode.

Avoid using "All time" searches

By default the Search app uses "All time" in the time range picker. While it might be fine when exploring your data in real time, it is something you'd want to avoid in your apps (at least as a default option) as it will drastically impact the performance.

PERF

Change the default value from "All time" to a specific preset or range in your app. Consider disabling the All Time search option all together to make sure that an inexperienced user doesn't bring the whole search head to its knees (negatively impacting the experience for all other users) with a very expensive search.

Distill searches

To get an even better understanding of your data, you'll need to use fields. When you run simple searches based on arbitrary keywords, Splunk Enterprise matches the raw text of your data. Often, a field is a value at a fixed position in your event line. A field can also be a name-value pair, where there is a single value assigned to the field. A field can also be multivalued, where it occurs more than once in an event and can have a different value at each occurrence.

Fields are searchable name-value pairs that distinguish one event from another because not all events have the same fields and field values. Searches with fields are more targeted and retrieve more exact matches against your data. Some examples of fields are **`clientip`** for IP addresses accessing your Web server, **`_time`** for the timestamp of an event, and **`host`** for the domain name of a server. Splunk Enterprise extracts some default fields for each event at index time. These are the **`host`**, **`source`**, and **`sourcetype`** fields. At search time, the search extracts other fields that it identifies in your data. A familiar multivalue field example is the email address. While the From field contains a single email address value, the To and Cc fields can have multiple email address values. Field names are case sensitive but field values are not. Here's an example of a search to check for errors, which doesn't use fields:

```
error OR failed OR severe OR (sourcetype=access_* (404 OR 500 OR 503))
```

And the same search using fields:

```
error OR failed OR severe OR (sourcetype=access_* (status=404 OR status=500 OR status=503))
```

The first example is likely to return more results than the second. When you run simple searches based on arbitrary keywords, the search matches the raw text of your data. When you add fields to your search the search looks for events that have those specific field/value pairs. The second example returns only those results that have those specified values for the status field.

DEV

While Splunk Enterprise is pretty intelligent about extracting known fields, there are mechanisms for you to guide it at search time with regular expressions (see `rex` and `erex` commands). You can also use the Interactive Field Extractor (IFX), which provides a nifty UI for doing so. See "Build field extractions with the field extractor" **for more information.**

When considering performance, note that searches that only operate on fields perform faster because a full-text search is no longer needed.

DEV

Apply powerful filtering commands as early in your search as possible. Filtering to one thousand events and then ten events is faster than filtering to one million events and then narrowing to ten.

Transform searches

So far, we've only obtained search results that match keywords we've provided, and applied some simple yet powerful filtering to the results. But, if you want to get even more insight into your data and start to abstract what the data is telling you, you'll want to transform your search results using search language commands.

Two general types of transformation commands available to you are transformation by aggregation and transformation by annotation. The **stats** command is an example of transformation by aggregation. Given a number of events that you want to summarize, you can use stats functions like **avg()**, **min()**, **max()**, and **count()** to aggregate the values of a particular field found in all those events.

The **eval** command lets you create a new field based on a computation that uses other fields. Examples include **isnum()**, **isstr()**, **isnull()**, and **len()** functions. The general form is **eval <newfield>=<computed expression on existing field>**. You can even have conditional logic on a field using the **if()** conditional to reassign the value of a field based on the current value. You can also use the **eval** command to annotate a field by evaluating an expression and saving the result in a field, when you use **eval** with **stats** you need to rename the field:

```
stats count, count(eval(action="purchase")) AS Purchases
```

Enrich data with lookup tables

You can map field values in your events to field values used in external sources using *lookup* tables. This allows to enrich your event data by adding more meaningful information and searchable fields to them. For example, say you have a mapping between error codes and textual descriptions of what they mean; or you have a mapping between email addresses and Active Directory usernames and groups.

Lookups let you reference fields in an external table that match fields in your event data. A lookup table can be a static CSV file, a KV store collection, or the output of a Python script. You can also use the results of a search to populate the CSV file or KV store collection and then set that up as a lookup table. For more information about field lookups, see Configure CSV and external lookups and Configure KV store lookups. Using a script you can connect to a relational database as well (the blog post "Enriching Data with DB Lookups" explains how).

After you configure a fields lookup, you can invoke it from the Search app or with the **lookup** command. Elements of a dashboard view can also be populated with lookup data.

Use subsearches prudently

A subsearch is a search with a search pipeline as an argument. Subsearches are delineated by brackets and evaluated first. The result of the subsearch is used as an argument in the outer search. The main use cases for subsearches include finding events that:

- Have matching values for a common field in the results of a subsearch (for example, looking for the products that are selling in multiple sales regions, or looking for users who are logged into both the VPN and the corporate network).

- Do not have matching values for a common field in the results of a subsearch (for example, identifying products that are selling in one region but not another, or looking for tailgaters—those users who logged into the corporate network but didn't badge in).
- Have matching values for a field with a different name in the results of a subsearch (looking for failed login attempts on the corporate network and the web servers)

Here's a walkthrough of a scenario that uses a subsearch (depicted in purple). Here we want to find all tailgaters during the last hour:

```
sourcetype=winauthentication_security
(EventCode=540 OR EventCode=673)
NOT [
     search sourcetype="history_access"
     EventDescription=Access
     | dedup User
     | fields User
]
```

4. Perform the outer search for authenticated users who are NOT found in the subsearch

1. Perform the subsearch and find all users who badged into a building.

2. Remove the duplicates.

3. Return a list of only user names — this step is needed for performance. Without it, the outer search will match all fields.

DEV

To troubleshoot subsearches, run both searches independently to be sure events are being returned. Additionally, you can use the Search Job Inspector.

DEV

The rule of thumb is to use subsearches only as a last resort. In terms of performance, subsearches are expensive, and are limited by both time (by default, only the events found during 60 seconds are returned) and the size of the result set (up to 10,000 entries by default), which limits their use on large datasets.

Check for optimization opportunities

Here are a few things you'll want to keep in mind that are fundamental to making your searches as efficient as possible.

Filter early

Filter early in the pipeline on the fields you have before transforming to remove fields you don't want. If you compute new fields, then filter on those fields.

Eliminate rows before columns

Usually, it is faster to remove rows so remove rows before columns. When removing columns, use the `table` or `fields` commands. Note that the `fields` command performs better than the `table` command in a distributed search.

Avoid real-time searches

Real-time searches are expensive and should not be used if your needs are not real time. In performance-sensitive contexts, you can specify a periodic search with a small time interval in the dashboard, to approximate a real-time search.

Avoid expensive commands

Expensive commands include subsearches, `append`, `appendcols`, `transaction`, `fillnull`, and `join`. While these are intuitive, handy, and powerful tools they are computationally expensive. When possible, use the more efficient `eval` and `stats` commands, instead.

DEV

For a good example of how to replace `append` and `join` with more performant commands, see this post.

Favor search-time field extractions over index-time field extractions

Search-time field extractions will yield better performance than index-time field extractions.

Use the `TERM()` operator

The `TERM()` operator can give you a significant performance boost by treating the operand as a single term in the index, even if it contains characters that are usually recognized as breaks or delimiters.

Minimize scope

Scope your search as minimally, temporally, and on as few indexes as possible.

TAKE ADVANTAGE OF ADVANCED SEARCH TECHNIQUES

Some of the more advanced search capabilities that we'll discuss here can be powerful mechanisms for getting even more meaningful information from your data.

Accelerate your data

To efficiently report on large volumes of data, you need to create data summaries that are populated by the results of background runs of the search upon which the report is based. When you next run the report against data that has been summarized in this manner, it should complete significantly faster because the summaries are much smaller than the original events from which they were generated.

Splunk Enterprise provides three data summary creation methods:

- **Report acceleration.** Uses automatically-created summaries to speed up completion times for certain kinds of reports.
- **Data model acceleration.** Uses automatically-created summaries to speed up completion times for pivots.

- **Summary indexing.** Enables acceleration of searches and reports by manually creating summary indexes that exist separately from the main indexes.

The primary difference between report acceleration and data model acceleration is:

- Report acceleration and summary indexing speed up individual searches on a report-by-report basis by building collections of precomputed search result aggregates.
- Data model acceleration speeds up reporting for the specified set of attributes (fields) that you define in a data model.
- Report acceleration is good for most slow-completing reports that have 100KB or more hot bucket events that meet the qualifying conditions for report acceleration.

Report acceleration is preferable over summary indexing for the following reasons:

- Kicking off report acceleration is as easy as clicking a checkbox and selecting a time range.
- Splunk Enterprise automatically shares report acceleration summaries with similar searches.
- Report acceleration features automatic backfill.
- Report acceleration summaries are stored alongside the buckets in your indexes.

In general, however, data model acceleration is faster than report acceleration.

For a complete overview of the acceleration mechanisms, read the "Overview of summary-based search and pivot acceleration."

Report acceleration

Report acceleration is used to accelerate individual reports. It's easy to set up for any transforming search or report that runs over a large dataset.

When you accelerate a report, Splunk Enterprise runs a background process that builds a data summary based on the results returned by the report. When you next run the search, Splunk Enterprise runs it against this summary instead of the full index. Because this summary is smaller than the full index and contains pre-computed summary data relevant to the search, the search should complete much quicker than it did without report acceleration.

For a report to qualify for acceleration its search string must use a transforming command, such as `chart`, `timechart`, `stats`, and `top`. Additionally, if there are any other commands before the first transforming command they must be streamable, which means that they apply a transformation to each event returned by the search.

To learn more, read the Accelerate reports documentation.

Data model acceleration

Data model acceleration creates summaries for the specific set of fields you want to report on, accelerating the dataset represented by the collection of fields instead of the dataset represented by a full search. Data model acceleration summaries take the form of time-series index files (TSIDX), which have the `.tsidx` file extension. These summaries are optimized to accelerate a range of analytical searches involving a specific set of fields, which are the set of fields defined as attributes in the accelerated data model.

Use the `tstats` command to perform statistical queries on indexed fields in TSIDX files.

Data model acceleration makes use of High Performance Analytics Store (HPAS) technology, which is similar to report acceleration in that it builds summaries alongside the buckets in your indexes. Also, like report acceleration, persistent data model acceleration is easy to enable in the UI by selecting the data model you want to accelerate and select a summary range. Once you do this, Splunk Enterprise starts building a summary that spans the specified range. When the summary is complete, any pivot, report, or dashboard panel that uses an accelerated data model object will run against the summary instead of the full array of raw data whenever possible, and you should see a significant improvement in performance.

To learn more, read the Accelerate data models documentation.

Summary indexing

Use summary indexing on large datasets to efficiently create reports that don't qualify for report acceleration. With summary indexing, you set up a search that extracts the precise information you frequently want. It's similar to report acceleration in that it involves populating a data summary with the results of a search, but with summary indexing the data summary is actually a special summary index that is built and stored on the search head. Each time Splunk Enterprise runs this search it saves the results into a summary index that you designate. You can then run searches and reports on this significantly smaller summary index, resulting in faster reports.

Summary indexing allows the cost of a computationally expensive report to be spread over time.

To read more about summary indexing, see the Summary Indexing documentation.

Use prediction

What if you have data with missing fields or fields whose values you suspect might not be accurate, such as with human-entered data or otherwise noisy data? You would like to use a predicted value to validate an actual value or fill in a missing value. For such cases, you can train search to predict the missing or suspect fields, using the train command.

Your first step is to train search to learn what a field value is expected to be based on known fields. For example, to train search to predict the gender given a name:

```
index=_internal | fields name, gender | train name2gender from gender
```

Behind the scenes, this search builds a model, **name2gender**, which you can use in subsequent searches to predict missing or inaccurate gender from the name field. Once trained, you can use the model in subsequent searches to guess the suspect field:

```
index=_internal | guess name2gender into gender
```

SPL has basic **predict, trendline** and **x11** commands to help with your prediction and trending computations.

For an example of how to use search to predict fields, download the Predict App from Splunkbase.

Use correlation

Finding associations and correlations between data fields, and operating on multiple search results, can provide powerful insights into your data. The following commands can be used to build correlation searches:

SEARCH COMMAND	DESCRIPTION
append	Appends subsearch results to current results.
appendcols	Appends the fields of the subsearch results to current results, first results to first result, second to second, and so on.
appendpipe	Appends the result of the subpipeline applied to the current result set to results.
arules	Finds association rules between field values.
associate	Identifies correlations between fields.
contingency	Builds a contingency table for two fields.
correlate	Calculates the correlation between different fields.
diff	Returns the difference between two search results.
join	SQL-like joining of results from the main results pipeline with the results from the subpipeline.
lookup	Explicitly invokes field value lookups.
selfjoin	Joins results with itself.
set	Performs set operations (union, diff, intersect) on subsearches.
stats	Provides statistics, grouped optionally by fields. See also, functions for `stats`, `chart`, and `timechart`.
transaction	Groups search results into transactions.

Use custom search commands

You can use the Splunk SDK for Python to extend the Splunk Enterprise search language. The **`GeneratingCommand`** class lets you query any data source, such as an external API, to generate events. The custom search command is deployed as a Splunk Enterprise application and invoked by piping events from the application into search. The general search command syntax is,

```
| <customCommand> [[<parmameterName>=<parameterValue>] ...]
```

If your custom search queries an external API, you'll need credentials to access the API.

You need to implement the **`generate()`** function in your command, deriving from the **`GeneratingCommand`** class and adding logic that creates events and outputs the events to Splunk Enterprise. Be sure to install and run **`setup`** for the SDK. A template is provided with the SDK that you can use as a starting point for creating the new custom command. See the "Building custom search commands in Python part I – A simple Generating command" blog post for an example of how to create a new command starting from the template.

Like all apps, the custom search command must also reside in its own folder in the **$SPLUNK_HOME/etc/apps** folder. The yield line is where you specify your event:

```
yield {'_time': <timeValue>, 'event_no': <eventNumber>, '_raw': <eventData> }
```

The parameters are:

- **_time.** The event timestamp.
- **event_no.** An example of a generated field, which is a field that can be selected in the field picker, this is the message count of the event.
- **_raw** (optional). The event data.

Once you've implemented the custom search command, you can test it from the Python command line, passing the parameters your command expects and the data source:

```
python <customCommand>.py __EXECUTE__ <parameterName>=<parameterValue> < <dataSource>
```

TROUBLESHOOT YOUR SEARCHES

A convenient way to test and troubleshoot your search string is to use the Search app. If you have a complex search with multiple piped segments, try removing pipe segments one at a time until you find the source of the error. Divide and conquer!

TEST

A convenient data source for testing is a CSV file.

Another handy tool to use is the Search Job Inspector. It allows to:

- Examine overall statistics of the search, events processed, results returned, and processing time.
- Determine how the search was processed.
- Troubleshoot a search's performance.
- Understand the impact of specific knowledge object processing, such as tags, event types, lookups and so on, within the search.

Here's an example of the execution costs for a search:

```
index=pas | dedup customer_name
```

The search commands component of the total execution costs might look something like this:

Search job inspector

This search has completed and has returned **93** results by scanning **65,607** events in **4.387** seconds.

(SID: 1427824811.25) search.log

Execution costs

Duration (seconds)	Component	Invocations	Input count	Output count
0.04	command.dedup	24	1,773	9
0.02	command.fields	23	65,607	65,60
0.72	command.prededup	23	65,607	1,77
3.58	command.search	23	-	65,60
0.26	command.search.index	23	-	
0.10	command.search.calcfields	21	65,607	65,60
0.10	command.search.fieldalias	21	65,607	65,60
0.00	command.search.index.usec_1_8	155	-	
0.00	command.search.index.usec_8_64	4	-	
0.87	command.search.kv	21	-	
0.77	command.search.tags	21	65,607	65,60
0.71	command.search.typer	21	65,607	65,607
0.71	command.search.rawdata	21	-	
0.02	command.search.lookups	21	65,607	65,607

Note: You can inspect a search as long as it exists and has not expired even if it hasn't completed.

The **`command.search`** component and everything under it, gives you the performance impact of the **search** command portion of your search, which is everything before the pipe character. The **`command.prededup`** gives you the performance impact of processing the results of the **search** command before passing it into the **dedup** command.

PERF

To evaluate performance, don't use results count over time. A more telling metric is the scan count over time. In the example above: resultsCount/time = 93 / 4.387 = 21.20 eps (events per second; scanCount/time = 65,507 / 4.387 ≈ 15K eps.

10-20K eps is generally considered to be good performance.

MORE INFORMATION

Additional documentation that you might find helpful regarding search includes:

- Search Manual (dev.splunk.com/goto/searchmanual)
- Search Reference (dev.splunk.com/goto/searchrefmanual)
- Quick Reference Guide (dev.splunk.com/goto/searchrefcard)

For information on how to customize line breaking behavior see: "Configure event line breaking" at: dev.splunk.com/goto/indexmultilineevents.

For an example of tagging in action see "Tagging our Events" in "Working with data: Where it comes from and how we manage it" at: dev.splunk.com/goto/tagevents.

To see timing differences between various ways of formulating your searches and to optimize them, read "View search job properties with the Search Job Inspector" at: dev.splunk.com/goto/searchjobinsp.

To see how disabling the All Time search option can optimize search, see: dev.splunk.com/goto/disablealltime.

See "Build field extractions with the field extractor" for more information on using the Interactive Field Extractor (IFX): dev.splunk.com/goto/extractfields.

For more information about field lookups:

- Configure CSV and external lookups: (dev.splunk.com/goto/Addfieldsfromexternaldatasources)
- Configure KV store lookups: (dev.splunk.com/goto/configurekvstore)
- Enriching Data with DB Lookups: (dev.splunk.com/goto/enrichingdata)

To lean how elements of a dashboard view can also be populated with lookup data, see: dev.splunk.com/goto/lookupsandviews.

For a good example of how to replace append and join with more performant commands, see dev.splunk.com/goto/multifieldcompare.

For a complete overview of the acceleration mechanisms, read the "Overview of summary-based search and pivot acceleration" at: dev.splunk.com/goto/aboutsummaryindexing.

To learn more about accelerating reports, read the Accelerate reports documentation: dev.splunk.com/goto/acceleratereports.

To learn more about accelerating data models, read the Accelerate data models documentation: dev.splunk.com/goto/acceleratedatamodels.

To learn more about summary indexing, see the summary indexing documentation: dev.splunk.com/goto/usesummaryindexing.

For an example of how to use search to predict fields, download the Predict App from Splunkbase at: dev.splunk.com/goto/predictapp.

For an example of how to create a new command starting from the template, see the "Building custom search commands in Python part I – A simple Generating command" blog post: dev.splunk.com/goto/pythoncustomsearch.

14

Visualizing data

> "What is to be sought in designs for the display of information is the clear portrayal of complexity. Not the complication of the simple; rather the task of the designer is to give visual access to the subtle and the difficult - that is, the revelation of the complex."
>
> ~ Epilogue to *The Visual Display of Quantitative Information* by Edward R. Tufte

How can you leverage Splunk Enterprise to help you get insight into your data set? Even with the most carefully optimized search, you'll likely need more than tabulated search results. In this chapter, we'll explore some of the visualization options available to you as an app developer. These range from basic but powerful built-in tools for organizing and rendering your data to custom-built or third-party programs for displaying your data in the most useful way. The method you choose depends mainly on domain-specific knowledge, user interface (UI) requirements, and data representation complexity, all of which are likely the main reasons you're building a custom app.

Depending on your needs and the complexity of your app, you will need at least a working knowledge of the front-end technologies: HTML, JavaScript, and CSS. Minimally, you'll also need to know how to work with Simple XML. If you're doing more advanced programming, you should be familiar with the SplunkJS Stack and the Splunk SDK for JavaScript. For full app customization flexibility, you can use open source libraries and APIs you might already be familiar with, like jQuery, backbone.js, and D3.

Also, be aware that we make a distinction between UI and visualization throughout this chapter. A **visualization** is a representation of your data in either graphic or text form, whereas the **UI** provides the visual container in which your visualization is rendered, and might include interactive functionality if it's needed.

Now that you've gotten your data in and searched the data to extract the information most relevant to you, you want to view the results. Moreover, you want to represent and organize the results in a way that visually gives you the most insight about your data.

For example, the following is a screen shot from the Splunk Dashboard Examples app. This app includes many dashboards like this one, with a visualization (in this case, a bubble chart) at the top of the dashboard and, further down in the UI, the code that makes it work.

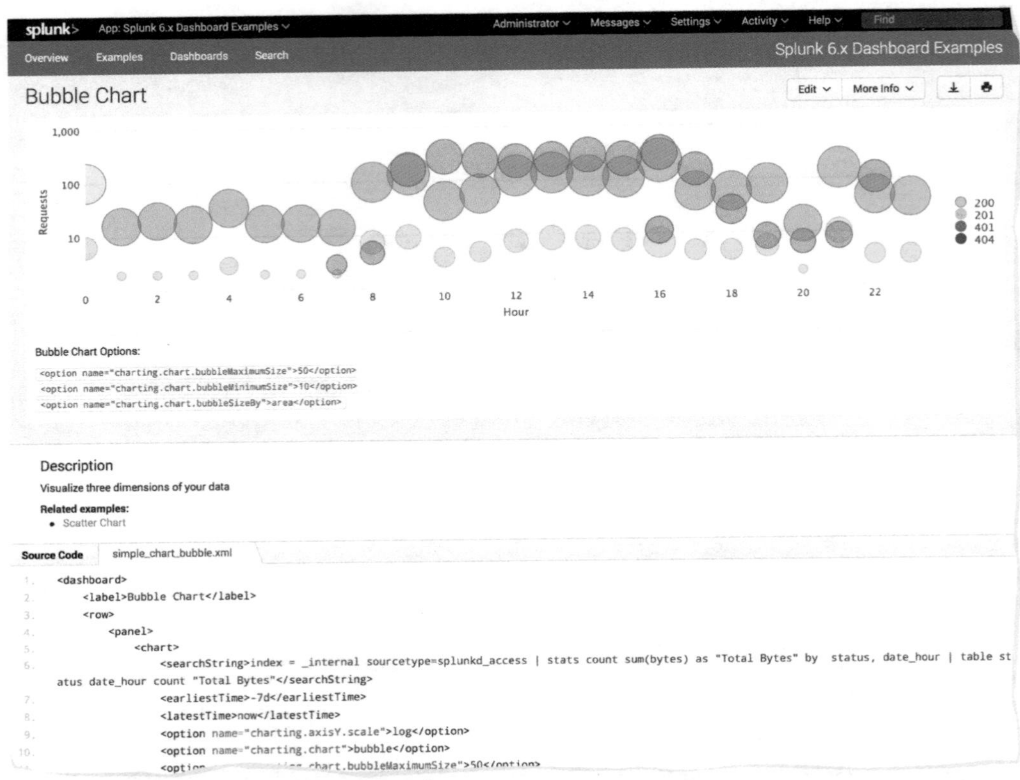

CHOOSE A UI TECHNOLOGY

The following table shows the technologies available to you as an app developer. In order of complexity, the list runs from tweaking dashboards by using an interactive editor or editing the underlying Simple XML, to full programmatic development using HTML, CSS, and JavaScript. We highlight the pros and cons of each approach.

UI TECHNOLOGY	MECHANISM	RECOMMENDATION WITH DESCRIPTION
Simple XML-based dashboards	**Simple XML** **XML file**	**Start here.** Lets you build simple dashboards. Splunk Enterprise includes interactive tools for creating and modifying dashboards, and an XML editor that you can use to edit dashboard definition markup. This approach is ideal for simple apps that require only basic customization and that do not require complex navigation between different dashboards.
Simple XML-based dashboard extensions	**Simple XML with JavaScript or CSS extensions** **XML file**	**When you reach the limits of Simple XML, add JavaScript and CSS into your arsenal.** Extends the capabilities of Simple XML by adding more layout options, visualizations, and custom behaviors. This is useful for adding additional capabilities to a Simple XML dashboard, but it adds to the complexity of the app because your app now includes custom JavaS-cript and CSS resources. JavaScript libraries can include the SplunkJS stack, third-party libraries, or your own custom JavaScript code.
HTML dashboards	**Simple XML converted to HTML with custom JavaScript** **HTML panel in XML file**	**Not recommended.** Converts a Simple XML dashboard to HTML, and then adds JavaScript. This gives you full control of the rendering of the page. You should use caution with this method due to serious maintainability concerns: The generated dashboards end up being specific to the Splunk Enterprise version on which the dashboards have been generated, and therefore will likely not be future-proof. Also, this is a one-way conversion. That is, you can't go back to Simple XML once you've converted to HTML.

You'll most likely start with Simple XML because it's the easiest way to begin, particularly for prototyping an interface. It has enough functionality and power to let you design your interface before you need to move to more advanced techniques. In fact, the UI and visualization requirements of many applications are often met using Simple XML alone. An example of an application that uses only Simple XML is the Auth0 app described in the *Journey*. The PAS reference app from the *Journey*, however, required user interaction and data representation that made it necessary for its developers to extend the Simple XML implementation with custom JavaScript and CSS.

Start with Simple XML by creating dashboards using the dashboard editor. Simple XML is the mechanism upon which dashboards are implemented. You can then modify the Simple XML for your dashboard using the Splunk Enterprise XML Source Editor. See "Build dashboards using Simple XML" in the "Dashboards and Visualizations Manual" to learn how to work with Simple XML. Refer to the Simple XML Reference in the same manual for a description of the Simple XML syntax.

You may want to take advantage of the built-in token passing and management mechanism. Searches in Simple XML dashboards use tokens as a variable to dynamically specify fields, field values, and search terms. Tokens are useful for capturing input values from forms, implementing dynamic drilldown operations, and specifying the conditional display of panels in a dashboard.

DEV

In a search, token name syntax uses $...$ delimiters.

If your application has more complex UI and visualization requirements, add JavaScript and CSS extensions to the dashboards you've created. JavaScript extensions are built using the SplunkJS stack (**splunkjs/mvc/**). The SplunkJS stack gives your app access to views and to the search manager. You can also use third-party JavaScript for even more custom functionality. For more information about using the SplunkJS stack, including reference documentation, see the Splunk Web Framework Component Reference.

Converting Simple XML to HTML to work on a dashboard directly in HTML, CSS, and JavaScript may offer you easier and more powerful customization. However, this approach is not recommended, because when you convert a Splunk dashboard to HTML, you can no longer edit it interactively within Splunk Web, nor can you generate PDFs or schedule delivery using Splunk Enterprise mechanisms. Use the conversion approach only when customization is needed that can't be achieved with either of the other mechanisms, but remember that your implementation might need to be updated with each major Splunk Enterprise release and might not be backward compatible. That is, the implementation will be specific to the Splunk Enterprise version for which it was implemented.

DEV

Be aware that you can't reverse the development steps to generate Simple XML from your custom HTML. Because of these maintenance issues, if this much customization is needed, it might be better to build your app outside of Splunk Enterprise and use Splunk simply as a data store.

BUS

It is possible to export your dashboards into PDF. Find more information in "Generate dashboard PDFs" **in the "Dashboards and Visualizations Manual."**

A dashboard typically consists of panels, with each panel providing a different view of your data. You can choose a UI technology on a per-panel basis, so a dashboard can have a mix of panels created using only Simple XML and panels created using Simple XML with JavaScript or CSS extensions. We advise that you begin with the simplest implementation—using Simple XML—and progress to more advanced implementations only as needed.

EXPLORE BUILT-IN VISUALIZATIONS

Splunk Enterprise comes with a number of built-in UI controls and visualizations defined in Simple XML. The following table lists some of the most common visualization elements and input types. All elements listed here are contained within `form` or `panel` elements within a dashboard. Simple XML also provides built-in support for enabling interaction between visualizations, such as specifying search parameters and drill-down dependencies. For an exhaustive list and detailed descriptions of all available elements, see the Simple XML Reference.

GENERAL ELEMENTS	
`label`	Header text for a dashboard or form.
`description`	Text below a dashboard, form, or panel.
INPUT TYPES	
`checkbox`	Checkbox input with option to populate labels and values with search and saved search results.
`dropdown`	Dropdown menu input with option to populate labels and values with search and saved search results.
`multiselect`	Multiple choice input with option to populate labels and values with search and saved search results.
`radio`	Radio button input with option to populate labels and values with search and saved search results.
`text`	Text input.
`time`	Time picker input.
PANEL ELEMENTS	
`chart`	Search data displayed in a chart.
`event`	Search data displayed as individual events.
`html`	Inline HTML text display.
`list`	Data list display.
`map`	Geographic coordinates mapped as interactive markers on a world map. Choropleth maps are now supported.
`single`	Single value search result display with support for at-a-glance, single-value indicators with historical context and trend indicators.
`table`	Tabulated search results.
`title`	Specifies text for the title of a panel or for visualization elements.
Sparkline options	Sparkline display formatting options.
`fields`	Comma-separated list of fields display.

DEV

For an interactive overview of various types of built-in visualizations, download and install the Splunk Dashboard Examples app.

We've included an illustration of the most popular built-in visualizations here.

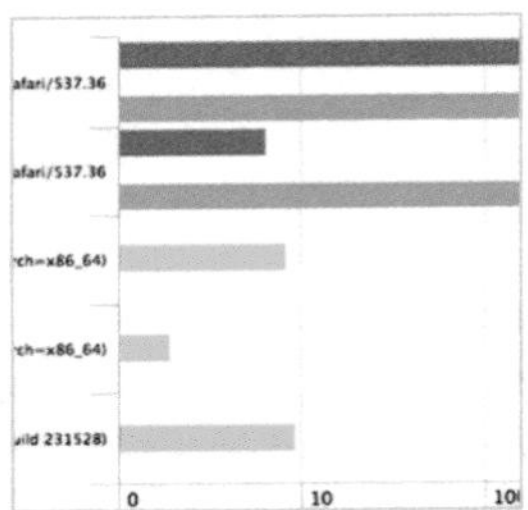

Bar Chart

Plot proportional data using a horizontal bar chart.

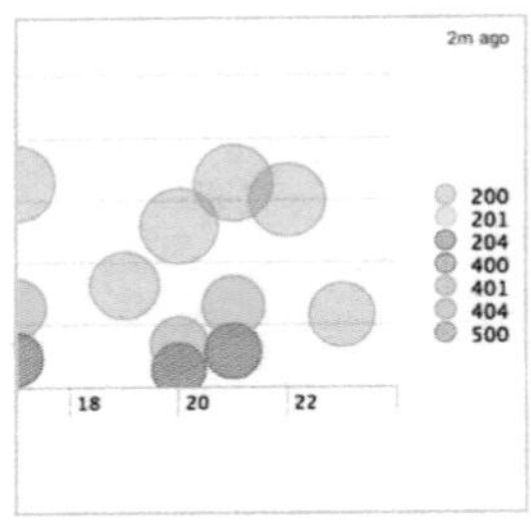

Bubble Chart

Bubble charts can help visualize data in three dimensions.

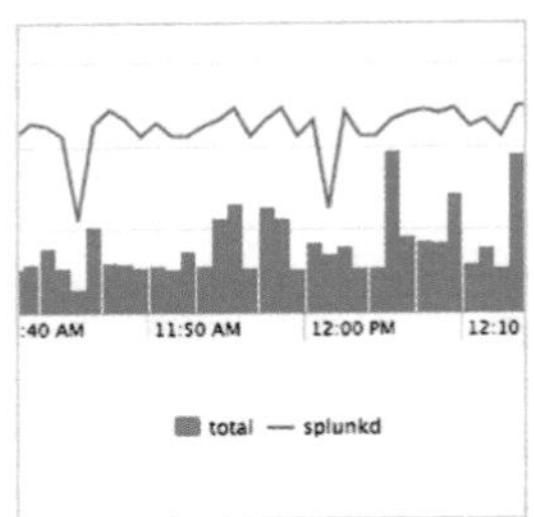

Chart Overlay

Show limits and other data on one chart.

Gauges

Visualize a single numeric value.

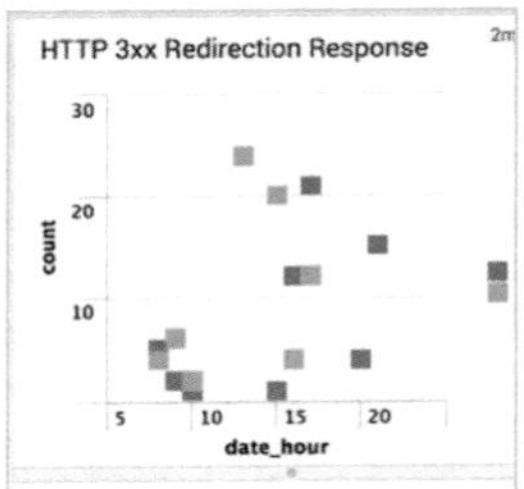

Scatter Chart

Plot a set of individual dots on a two-dimentional chart.

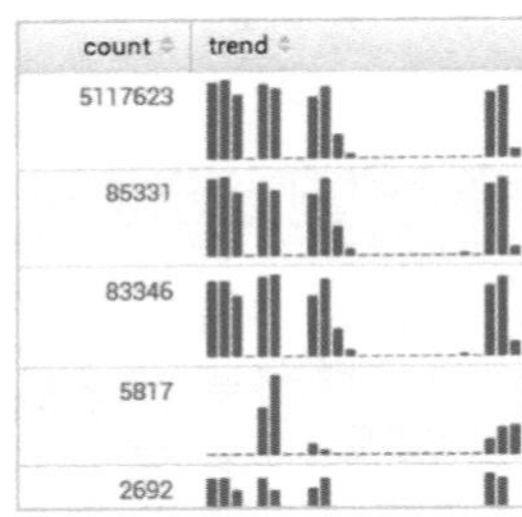

count	trend
5117623	
85331	
83346	
5817	
2692	

Table Element with Sparklines

Configure basic and advanced sparkline formatting options.

user	hist	realtime
admin	0.04	1.00
splunk-system-user	2.00	0.00
system total	0.06	1.00
admin	0.10	1.01
splunk-system-user	2.00	0.00
system total	0.14	1.01
admin	0.04	1.15
splunk-system-user	2.00	0.00
system total	0.08	1.15
admin	0.05	1.00

Table Cell Highlighting

Color table cells based on conditions having multiple field values.

count
341334
164
4989
122
226
5657
81
9927

Table Icon Set (Inline)

Add icons to table cells based on custom conditions.

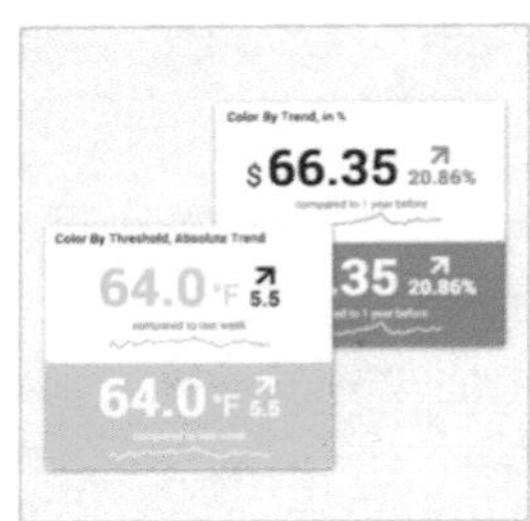

Single Value Element with Color

Display the customized annotations trend, for single value element.

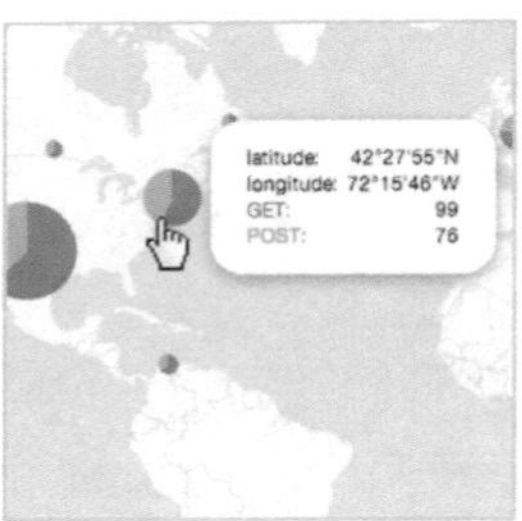

Map Element

Plot geographical data on integrated maps.

Supports drilldown.

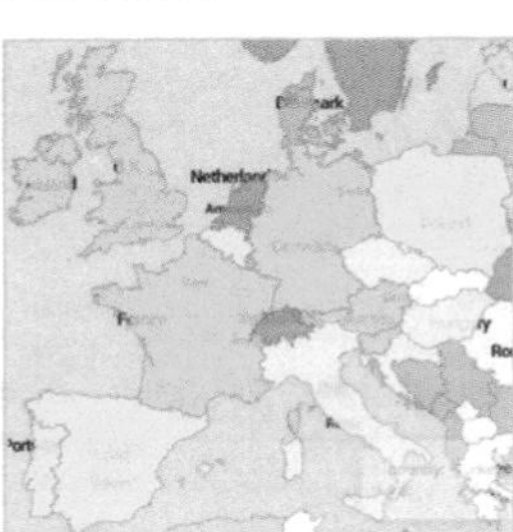

Choropleth Maps

Visualize a metric that varies across a (custom) geographic region.

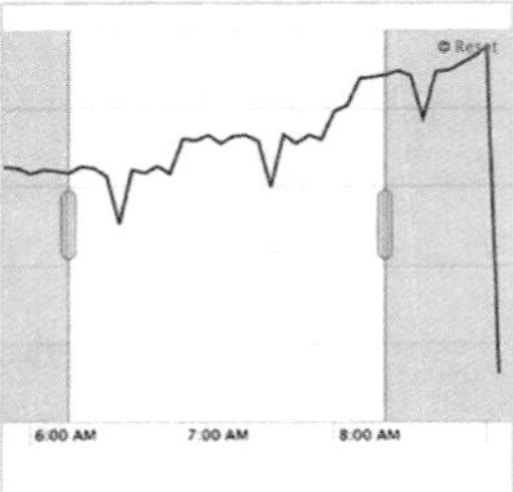

Pan and Zoom Chart Controls

Charts allow you to select a range to zoom in. Alternateively you can use that data to drilldown further into your data.

ADD CUSTOM VISUALIZATIONS TO A DASHBOARD

The built-in Splunk Enterprise data visualization capabilities might not fully meet the needs of your particular application. You might decide that your own visualization libraries, third-party libraries, or open source libraries would provide more pertinent ways to represent your data. Fortunately, Splunk Enterprise provides the ability to seamlessly integrate external JavaScript libraries with your client-side code. For example, some common third-party libraries that you might already find in use within apps on Splunkbase include D3.js and Raphaël. Illustrated here is an example dashboard with a custom Sankey diagram visualization, from the Splunk Dashboard Examples app. This visualization uses a custom Sankey plug-in that utilizes jQuery and D3.js.

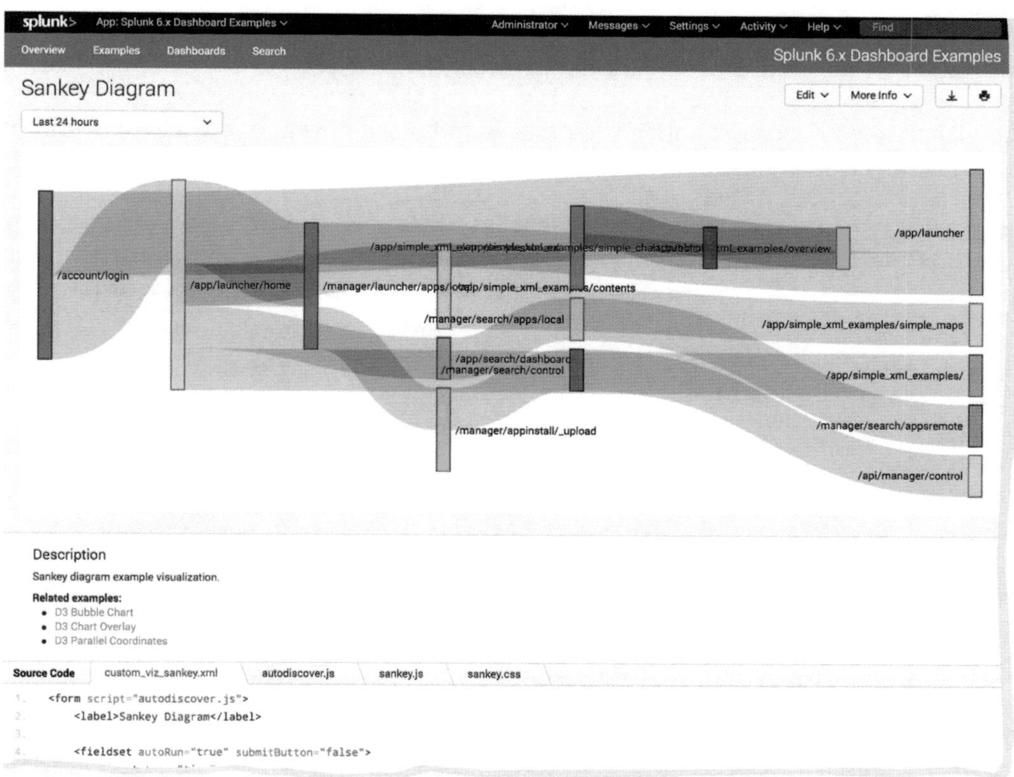

The easiest way to integrate external JavaScript libraries is to call the library from your dashboard's Simple XML markup. While the implementation details can potentially be challenging depending on the complexity of your application and of the external library, you'll need to complete a few basic steps to use the library from your dashboard:

1. As a starting point, it's helpful to use a visualization from an existing Splunk Enterprise dashboard example as a template and modify a copy of the example so that it calls the external library instead of the built-in visualization. Copy the template to **$SPLUNK_HOME/etc/appserver/static/<*myApp*>** and make the changes needed to call the external code.

2. Next, you'll need to override the `SimpleSplunkView.updateView` method and implement your new visualization. Modify the **updateView** method to load the new libraries, use the visualization data received from the **formatData** method, write data to the target element, and make any desired CSS changes.
3. Create or modify the target **<div>** or **<svg>** elements to hold the data.
4. In the **formatData** method, reformat the search results to the format expected by your external visualization library. Copy the custom visualization code into the **formatData** method and make the changes needed to format search results into the visualization format. This data gets passed to the **updateView** method.
5. Modify your CSS to make any desired styling changes to your visualization.

MAKE CUSTOM VISUALIZATIONS REUSABLE

Suppose you want to use a custom visualization to give you an interesting view of your data that is not available with out-of-the-box Splunk Enterprise charts. The obvious solution is to create a new component that does exactly what you need for your application. The problem with this approach is the tendency to hard code definitions and functionalities to meet your immediate needs, which means that your nifty new component most likely can't be used by another application or even multiple times within the same app or dashboard. By designing and implementing the component for a single application, you lose the potential benefits you and your organization might have obtained from employing a few reuse principles.

The following reuse principles promote not only flexibility as a means for achieving reuse but also ease-of-use so the effort you put into building the component is more likely to be leveraged by other app developers.

Parameterization

Parameterize your component so the value of properties that are likely to differ among applications can be set at runtime, or as late as possible. Use late binding. Some examples are names of elements on a page like titles, and cardinality like number of rows and columns.

A prime candidate for parameterization is the name of **<div>** elements. Custom Splunk Enterprise components typically insert data into an empty **<div>** element in a panel. By parameterizing the name of the **<div>** element, you can use the name expected by the application. Parameterization also permits you to populate multiple **<div>** elements in the same panel. This also applies to CSS selectors like **#viz-node_id**, or to JQuery node names, depending on how the application is implemented.

Simplicity

Use good API design practices to define a simple interface for your component. This is admittedly subjective, but in general, the simpler the interface, the easier it is to reuse the component.

Dependencies

Each component should declare its own dependencies, such as **underscore** and any other components on which the custom component depends.

Location

Put your custom components in a dedicated location so they are easy to find and reference. One recommendation is to put your components in **appserver/static/components/<*componentPackageName*>** folders. Use the Node.js **require** method, and specify the correct component pathname.

Documentation

Reuse is greatly facilitated by having adequate documentation. Document usage, parameters, return values, and error conditions for the component constructor and all methods.

Comment your code to document the method interfaces. This keeps the documentation close to the code it describes, and is more likely to keep the documentation current with code changes.

We started this chapter with a quote from Edward R. Tufte's classic book on displaying data, and we think the following quote is a fitting summary for how you should think about designing your own visualizations.

> "Excellence ... consists of complex ideas communicated with clarity, precision, and efficiency ...
>
> - show the data
> - induce the viewer to think about the substance rather than about methodology...
> - avoid distorting what the data have to say
> - present many numbers in a small space
> - make large data sets coherent
> - encourage the eye to compare different pieces of data
> - reveal the data at several levels of detail ...
> - serve a reasonably clear purpose: description, exploration, tabulation, or decoration
> - be closely integrated with the statistical and verbal descriptions of a data set."
>
> ~ *The Visual Display of Quantitative Information* by Edward R. Tufte

MORE INFORMATION

To learn how to work with Simple XML, see "About editing simple XML" at: dev.splunk.com/goto/simplifiedxmloverview.

If you're doing more advanced programming, you should be familiar with the SplunkJS Stack (dev.splunk.com/goto/splunkjsstack) and the Splunk SDK for JavaScript (dev.splunk.com/goto/javascriptsdkover).

To learn to create and edit dashboards, see "About the Dashboard Editor" at: dev.splunk.com/goto/dashboardeditor.

To learn how to work with Simple XML, see "Build dashboards using Simple XML" at: dev.splunk.com/goto/simplifiedxmloverview.

For a description of the Simple XML syntax, see the "Simple XML Reference" at: dev.splunk.com/goto/panelreference.

To learn how to take advantage of the built-in token passing and management mechanism, see "Token usage in dashboards" at: dev.splunk.com/goto/tokens.

For more information about using the SplunkJS stack, see the "Splunk Web Framework Component Reference" at: dev.splunk.com/goto/webframeref.

To export your dashboards into PDF format, see "Generate dashboard PDFs" at: dev.splunk.com/goto/dashboardpdfs.

For an interactive overview of various types of built-in visualizations, download and install the Splunk Dashboard Examples app at: dev.splunk.com/goto/dashboardexampleapp.

Some common third-party libraries that you might find in use in apps on Splunkbase include:

- jQuery (jquery.com)
- D3.js (d3js.org)
- Raphaël (raphaeljs.com)

For information about the `SimpleSplunkView.updateView` method, see: dev.splunk.com/goto/simplesplunkview.

15

Acting on data

Data is generated around the clock. Splunk Enterprise is always monitoring your data, and it gives you numerous different ways to observe trends and visualize your data at any time. But you don't have to monitor your data constantly to be able to identify when you need to act on it. With alerting, you can tell Splunk Enterprise when to inform the appropriate stakeholders to take action, or even tell Splunk Enterprise to initiate those actions itself. In this chapter, we talk about what alerts are in the context of Splunk Enterprise, the types of alerts available and how to manage them, what alert actions are and what Splunk Enterprise can do when an alert is triggered. We'll also talk a bit about creating custom alert actions and integration with the Splunk SDK for JavaScript.

DEV

If you're just interested in creating custom alert actions, which are developer-crafted, customizable actions that are initiated when an alert is triggered, you might want to go directly to the "New adventures require new tools: alerting" **chapter in the** ***Journey*****.**

You've got your data in, searched it, and transformed and viewed it. You know how Splunk Enterprise makes it easy to recognize, at a glance, when your data is telling you that something is wrong and action is needed. With *alerts*, there's no glance required: Splunk Enterprise can tell you the moment something happens—an action is logged, a value is reached, a threshold is passed, and so on—and even trigger actions based on what's happening.

ALL ABOUT ALERTS

An alert is a notification mechanism to let you know when an event of interest has occurred. You can configure Splunk Enterprise to trigger an alert whenever a search returns a result that matches a threshold or trend setting that you specify.

When getting started with alerts, consider the following:

- **Conditions:** What are the events that you want to know about?
- **Type and frequency:** How often do you want to be made aware of events?
- **Alert action:** What should happen when an alert occurs?

Consider also the different types of alerts available in Splunk Enterprise:

- A **per-result alert** is based on a real-time search, and is triggered whenever the search returns a result that you specify. For example, a per-result alert could be triggered by a failed login attempt.
- A **scheduled alert** runs a search according to a schedule that you set, and is triggered by search results that you specify. For example, you could create a scheduled alert that runs a daily search of nationwide song airplay and notifies you which ten songs were played the most.
- A **rolling-window alert** is based on a real-time search, and is triggered by conditions that occur during a window of time, both of which you specify. For example, you could create a rolling-window alert that notifies you if an employee's keycard is used to access company resources more than ten times within a one-hour period.

If you want more information about the different alert types, along with example scenarios for each, see "Alert types and scenarios" in the Alerting Manual.

ALERT SCENARIOS

You've probably already come up with a few possible uses for alerting in your Splunk Enterprise deployment. Here are a few more to get you thinking even more about how to make alerting work for you:

- When a server hits a predefined load or an extreme burst in activity occurs, have Splunk Enterprise notify you.
- When web server performance slows to below a certain average response time, have Splunk Enterprise notify you and execute a script to disable certain functionality for trial users so that your web site remains usable for paying customers.
- When the load of your application is very low, have Splunk Enterprise start an action to perform certain background processing tasks that are not time critical, but resource intensive.
- When a specific type of error occurs on any host, have Splunk Enterprise notify you.

- When CPU on a host hits above 90% for a certain period of time, have Splunk Enterprise notify you through multiple channels.
- When the usage patterns of a particular user are flagged as anomalous, have Splunk Enterprise notify you and lock the account.
- Once a day, trigger an alert that notifies you when the number of items sold that day (or some other benchmark figure) is less than a certain number.
- Once an hour or so, trigger an alert that notifies you when the number of 404 or other errors exceeds a certain threshold.
- Use a rolling window alert to trigger an alert when a user has three consecutive failed logins or unsuccessfully tries to access restricted network assets within a certain time period.
- Use a rolling window alert to trigger an alert when a host is unable to complete a repeating automated task such as an hourly file transfer to another host.
- Use a webhook to open a bug in your company's bug tracking system when a certain debugging statement is logged.
- Use a webhook to post a message to your IT department's chatroom when a server is unreachable or an unusual number of errors has been returned.

More alert action scenarios are available in topic "Alert examples" in the Alerting Manual.

CREATING A NEW ALERT

You always start the alert creation process in the same way: create a search and then save it as an alert.

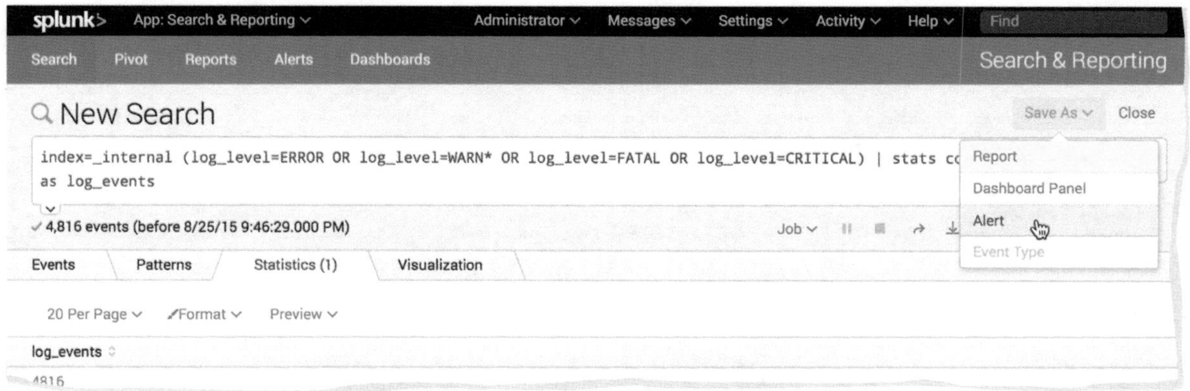

Enter a search query. In the upper-right corner, click **Save As**, and then **Alert**. The **Save As Alert** window appears.

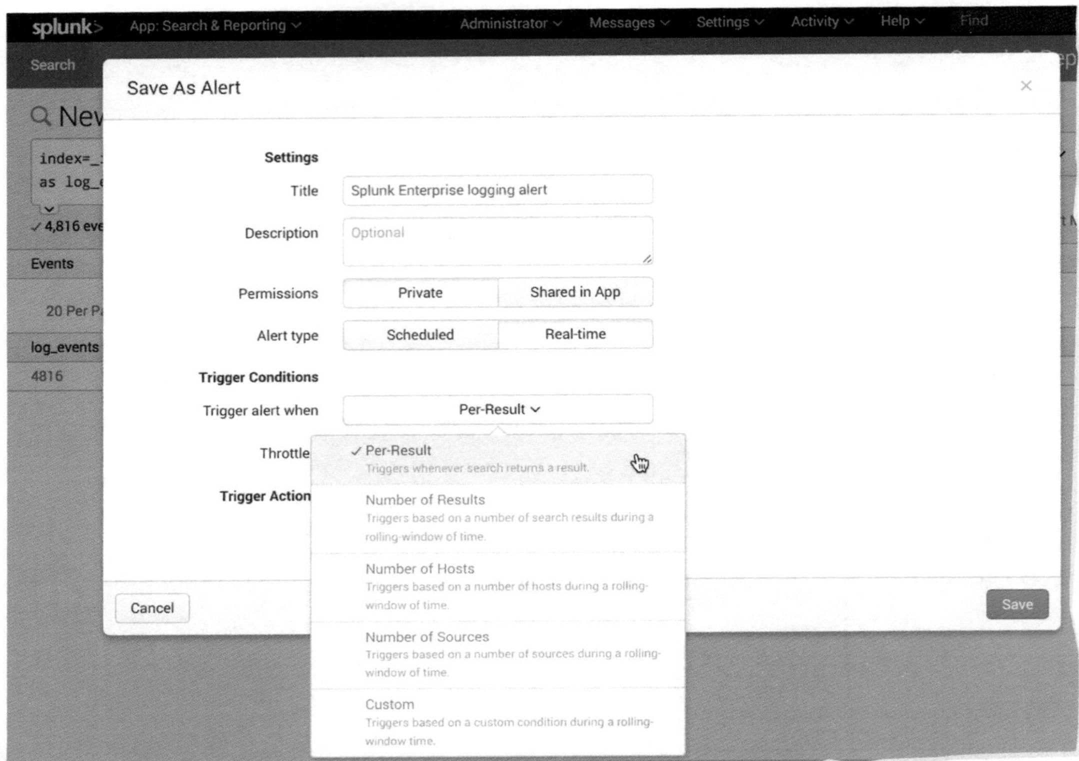

In the **Settings** section, you enter a title for the alert, an optional description, specify whether the alert is shared with others or private, and what type it is.

- For a per-result alert, choose **Real-time** next to **Alert type**, and then **Per-Result** next to **Trigger alert when**. Per-result alerts are always real-time alerts, because you want to be notified as soon as the trigger condition occurs.
- For a scheduled alert, choose **Scheduled** next to **Alert type**. Next to **Trigger alert when**, choose whether to trigger the alert based on the number of search results, hosts, or sources during a scheduled search, or choose **Custom** to enter a custom condition to evaluate against the search results at the scheduled time.
- For a rolling-window alert, choose **Real-time** next to **Alert type**. Next to **Trigger alert when**, choose whether to trigger the alert based on the number of search results, hosts, or sources during a rolling window of time, or choose **Custom** to enter a custom condition to evaluate against the search results during the window. You'll then need to enter values for the number of results and the time window.

Select the **Throttle** checkbox to suppress alert triggering for a period of time that you define. This prevents you from being overwhelmed with triggered alert actions, should your alert be triggered more frequently than you had expected.

The final step in creating an alert is specifying a trigger action, or *alert action*. We go into detail about alert actions in the next section.

ALERT ACTIONS

Alert actions are initiated when an alert is triggered. You specify an alert action in the final step of creating an alert.

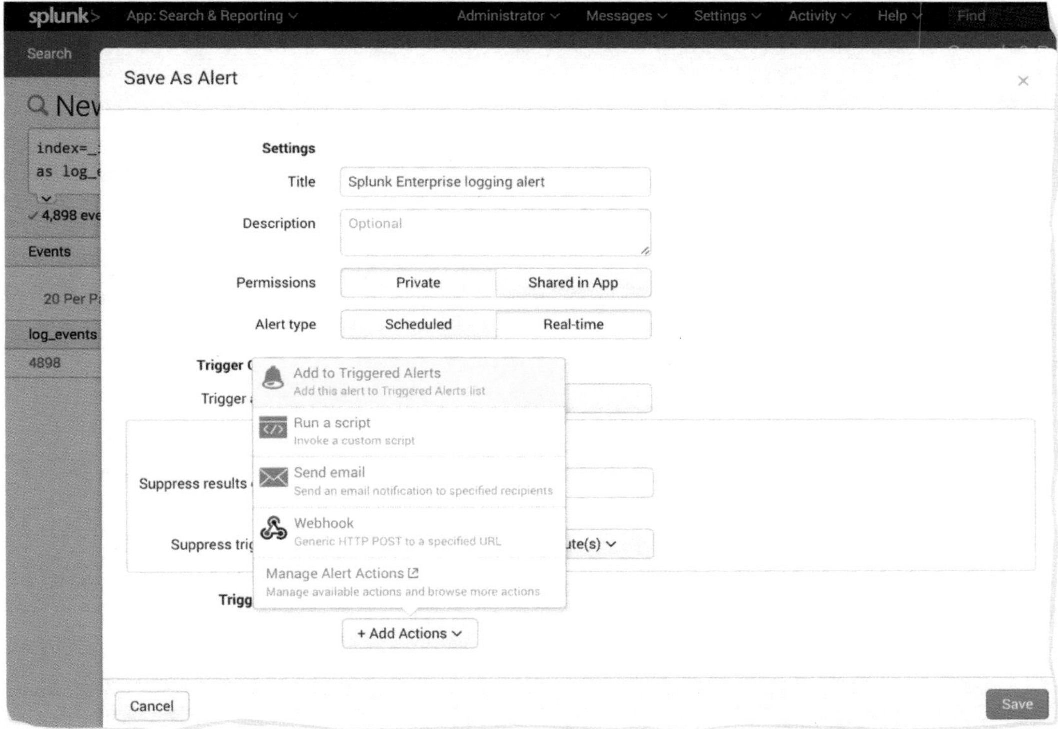

You have several options when it comes to alert actions:

- **Add to Triggered Alerts:** Great for testing out alert triggers, this action simply adds the triggered alert to the Triggered Alerts list in Splunk Enterprise. To access the Triggered Alerts list, go to **Activity > Triggered Alerts**.
- **Run a script:** This alert action invokes a custom script. Store custom scripts within `/bin/scripts` or within an app's `/bin/scripts` directory. Keep in mind, however, that running a script when an alert is triggered has been deprecated in Splunk Enterprise 6.3, and therefore is not recommended for use.

- **Send email:** By far the most common alert action, this one sends an email when an alert is triggered. For more information about this alert action, see "Email notification action" in the Alerting Manual.
- **Webhook alert action:** This alert action lets you invoke a webhook when the alert is triggered. Webhooks allow you to make HTTP POST requests on a particular web resource. These resources can include ones you create yourself or that are developed and hosted by services such as Zapier or Twilio. For more information on webhook alert actions, see "Use a webhook alert action" in the Alerting Manual. You should also check out the section on webhook alert actions in the "New adventures require new tools: alerting" chapter in the Journey.
- **Custom alert actions:** These are available if they've already been installed and configured on your Splunk Enterprise instance. Custom alert actions are enabled by the custom alert action framework. With the framework, developers can create, package, and distribute customized trigger actions based on any alert use case imaginable.

To manage or configure the installed alert actions, go to **Settings > Alert Actions**. From here, you can click **Browse more** to search for and browse custom alert actions that others have created and posted to Splunkbase.

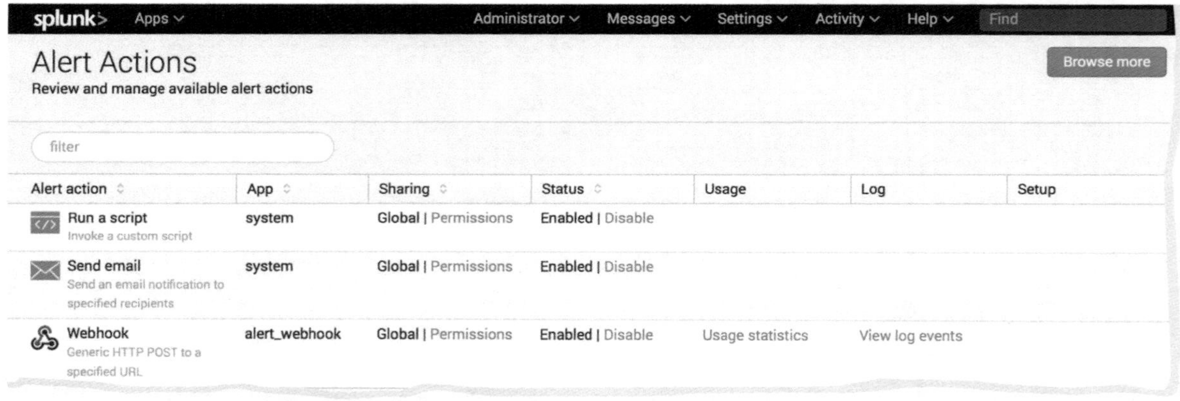

The next section describes custom alert actions in more detail and tells you where to go to learn how to create them.

CUSTOM ALERT ACTIONS

The custom alert action framework lets developers add new functionality and integration for alerts. Custom alert actions, like alerts, can be access control list (ACL)-managed, packaged, and distributed within apps, but they are fully modular, and can be reused throughout Splunk Enterprise.

DEV

A custom alert action is packaged within an app, and is made up of several files laid out in a set directory structure. A generic directory structure for a typical custom alert action appears within detailed instructions for creating a new custom alert action in "Custom alert actions overview" in the Developing Views and Apps for Splunk Web Manual. We also list the structure of our reference app's custom alert action—along with an account of our real-life experience creating a custom alert action from scratch—in the "New adventures require new tools: alerting" chapter in the *Journey*.

The process of creating a custom alert action is straightforward but multifaceted. To ease the process, we've created a custom alert action template and included it with the PAS reference app download package. In the **spikes** folder, open the alertaction_app_template folder and you'll see all of the necessary files, already placed in the correct file structure. From there, follow the four basic steps for building a custom alert action into an app:

1. Create configuration files. (We've done this step for you, but you should know what is in the configuration files and what they do before you proceed.)
2. Create a script.
3. Define a user interface.
4. Add optional components.

UX

Depending on how you engineer your custom alert action, you may need your users to set it up first. For example, our reference app's custom alert action requires users to set up their JIRA server and other configuration settings before they can assign the alert action to an alert. Be sure to add a setup step to your documentation.

SPLUNK SDK FOR JAVASCRIPT INTEGRATION

The Splunk SDK for JavaScript gives you programmatic access to your Splunk Enterprise instance's triggered (or "fired," in the SDK's lexicon) alerts. Once you integrate the SDK's alerting classes into your JavaScript app, you can retrieve fired alerts, fired alert groups, fired alert group collections, and their properties. You can also retrieve information about fired alerts of specific saved searches.

DEV

The term "app" in this context refers to an external application developed in JavaScript that interacts with your Splunk Enterprise instance. It does not refer to a Splunk app that runs on Splunk Enterprise.

For detailed information about how to use the SDK for alerting, including code examples, see "How to work with alerts using the Splunk SDK for JavaScript" in the Splunk SDK for JavaScript documentation. The Splunk SDK for JavaScript download package also contains complete code examples that you can run in your browser, in the files **examples/firedalerts.js** and **examples/firedalerts_async.js**.

MORE INFORMATION

To learn how to create per-result alerts, see the "Alerting Manual" at: dev.splunk.com/goto/perresultalerts.

If you want more information about the different alert types, along with example scenarios for each, see "Alert types and scenarios" in the Alerting Manual at: dev.splunk.com/goto/alertscenarios.

For more information about email notifications, see "Email notification action" in the Alerting Manual *at:* dev.splunk.com/goto/emailnotification.

For information on webhook-enabled services such as Zapier or Twilio, see:

- zapier.com
- twilio.com

For detailed instructions on creating a new custom alert action see the Developing Views and Apps for Splunk Web Manual, starting with the topic "Custom alert actions overview" at: dev.splunk.com/goto/modalertsintro.

For more information about using webhook alert actions, see "Use a webhook alert action" at: dev.splunk.com/goto/webhookalert.

Download and complete the alert action app template from: dev.splunk.com/goto/alertactiontemplate.

To create configuration files, see: dev.splunk.com/goto/customalertconfig.

To create a custom alert action script, see: dev.splunk.com/goto/customalertscript.

To define a user interface for an alert, see: dev.splunk.com/goto/customalertui.

To add optional components, see: dev.splunk.com/goto/customalertoptionalitems.

For detailed information about how to use the SDK for alerting, see "How to work with alerts using the Splunk SDK for JavaScript" at: dev.splunk.com/goto/workwithalerts.

16

Packaging and publishing

PACKAGING YOUR APP

One of the last tasks you'll need to do before publishing your app is to define the Splunk Web navigation scheme. This includes ordering all the panels you've implemented and specifying menu options. After you've built views for your app, specify how to arrange them in the navigation bar in Splunk Web. You can customize this navigation to work however you want, using the instructions below. Specify the order to display your views and which menu you want to display them in. The details of how to do this are described in "Step 6: Build navigation for your app" in the Splunk app building tutorial.

As the tutorial mentions, app navigation is defined in the `$SPLUNK_HOME/etc/apps/<app_name>/default/data/ui/nav/default.xml` file. A RelaxNG schema is defined for the navigation XML that you can view by selecting the nav **RelaxNG** link on the **Deployment Services** page for your Splunk Enterprise instance, at `http://<host>:8000/info`.

Now that you've designed, implemented, and tested the main part of your app and have a good understanding of what your app needs to run, you're ready to perform some final setup activities before your app can be distributed to the general public. These include providing a setup UI for configuring the elements of your app that aren't known until runtime, making sure your app has a look-and-feel consistent with other Splunk Enterprise apps, and preparing your app for distribution.

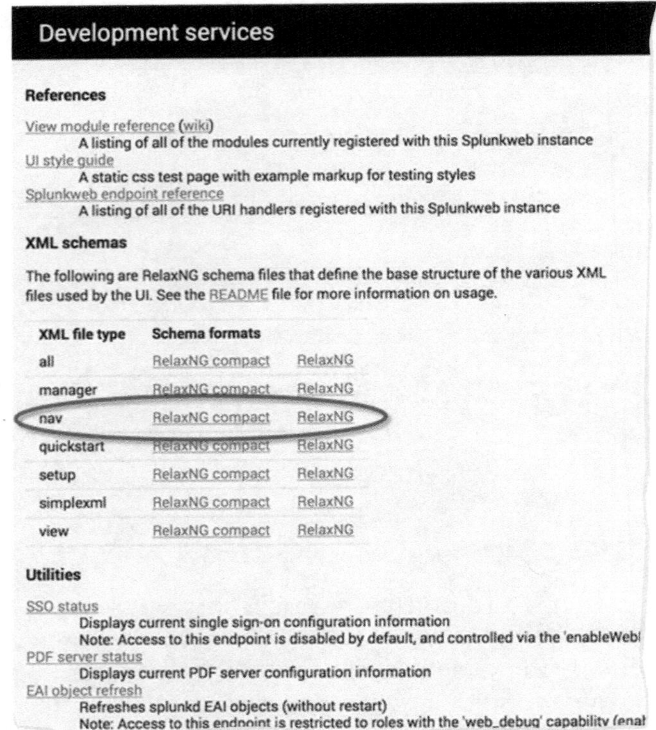

Choose an installation method

You'll need to consider the possible options for installing your app's different components. Consider that the different parts might run on different hardware and that all components might not be installed at the same time, such as when only a single component of your app needs to be upgraded. The following table lists the options for installing Splunk Enterprise app components, including an estimation of the degree of difficulty of a particular approach. The approach you choose depends on your particular environment, your app complexity, and your requirements for reuse and extensibility.

TYPE OF INSTALLER	CHARACTERISTICS	EASE OF DEVELOPMENT	EASE OF INSTALLATION
Internal installer			
	The main app contains information about all dependencies and installs components the first time the app is run, if they are not already installed.	Intermediate	Trivial
	A standalone installer app installs all app components and redirects to the main app when installation is complete.	Difficult	Trivial
External installer			
	An external installer installs the app components, such as a script.	Intermediate/ Difficult	Easy
Manual bulk installer			
	A compressed file (.zip) containing all components extracts all of the components into the /etc directory of all targets.	Trivial	Intermediate
Manual per-dependency installer			
	The documentation describes how to get each app component and how to install the component on a particular target.	Easy	Difficult
	The main app detects if dependent apps have been installed correctly and prompts you to manually install each dependent component that is missing.	Intermediate	Difficult
Deployment server			
	In a distributed Splunk Enterprise environment, deployment server distributes apps and their configuration to deployment clients.	Trivial	Easy
Configuration management system			
	If you build a continuous deployment/ delivery pipeline (with tools like Chef, Puppet, or Ansible), you can define plugins, modules, and recipes for deploying and upgrading your app's .tar files to the designated Splunk leaf nodes.	Intermediate	Easy

Other packaging recommendations to ensure a clean app installation include,

- Removing any hidden files in the app, such as OS X .DS_Store files.
- Disable inputs by default in the `inputs.conf` file, if they're not needed.
- Remove any files in the `$SPLUNK_HOME/etc/apps/`*<app>*`/local` or `$SPLUNK_HOME/etc/apps/`*<app>*`/metadata/local.meta` directories.

- Remove lookup directory files that are not static, such as generated saved searches files that are specific to the environment.
- Ensure all XML files are valid. (See how to use the Splunk Enterprise XML validation tool.)
- Include any third-party software licenses for libraries you might have used.

Set up the app for first run

Most apps need to be set up when they are first run to initialize user-configurable app parameters. These parameters are global in scope and need to be specified to get the app to work the first time. They usually relate to different runtime environments or custom usage requirements that are not known until the app is installed. If your app has these kinds of parameters, the app should provide a setup panel that permits the user to modify configurable settings without having to edit configuration (.conf) files.

The setup panel is implemented using the Splunk Enterprise REST API to access configuration parameters. You can use existing REST endpoints, but you can also define custom endpoints for your app. The configuration parameters can be stored in either .conf files or by using the app key value store.

When initial setup is complete, the app should be ready to run, but users should be able to return to the setup panel at any time to change the configuration parameters as needed.

You can find detailed information about how to implement a set up panel in "Step 7: Configure a setup screen" in the Splunk app building tutorial.

Additional setup activities and cautions that can make your app easier to install and use include:

- Include a `README.txt` file in the root directory of your application with basic instructions.
- Include detailed instructions on a dashboard within the application.
- Encrypt passwords, and warn the user not to store passwords anywhere in cleartext.

The application name, version, ID, and other housekeeping information are stored in the **`app.conf`** file. The value for the ID in **`app.conf`** must match your app folder name in **`$SPLUNK_HOME/etc/apps`**, and cannot be changed. The version value can include trailing text, such as "beta."

Read Step 8: Package your app or add-on in the Splunk app building tutorial to learn more about how to package your app for distribution.

You must follow certain naming conventions, as described in Naming conventions for apps and add-ons on Splunkbase.

Now that you've fully implemented your app and made it ready for distribution, don't forget to test it one more time on a clean system.

PUBLISHING YOUR APP

You can make your app available to everyone in the Splunk community by publishing it on Splunkbase, or distribute the app directly to your customers. You can even redirect users to your own hosting site by simply listing your app on Splunkbase without hosting it there. You can show off anything you have done to make Splunk Enterprise easier or more universal—not just views, dashboards, and saved searches, but also modular inputs, field extractions, workflow actions, lookups, custom alert actions, event types, and more. Just place your work in a dedicated directory, make sure everything is clean of personally identifiable information (such as internal server names), and works outside your unique environment (Test your app!). Then add or update your **app.conf** file, icon, and screenshot to show off your extension in Launcher.

> BUS
>
> **Consider submitting your finished app for Splunk app certification. Certified app developers receive more prominent positioning on Splunkbase, prerelease builds of new versions of Splunk Enterprise, and lists of contact information for users who have downloaded an app (and opted in to have their information released). Learn more in the** App Certification **documentation.**

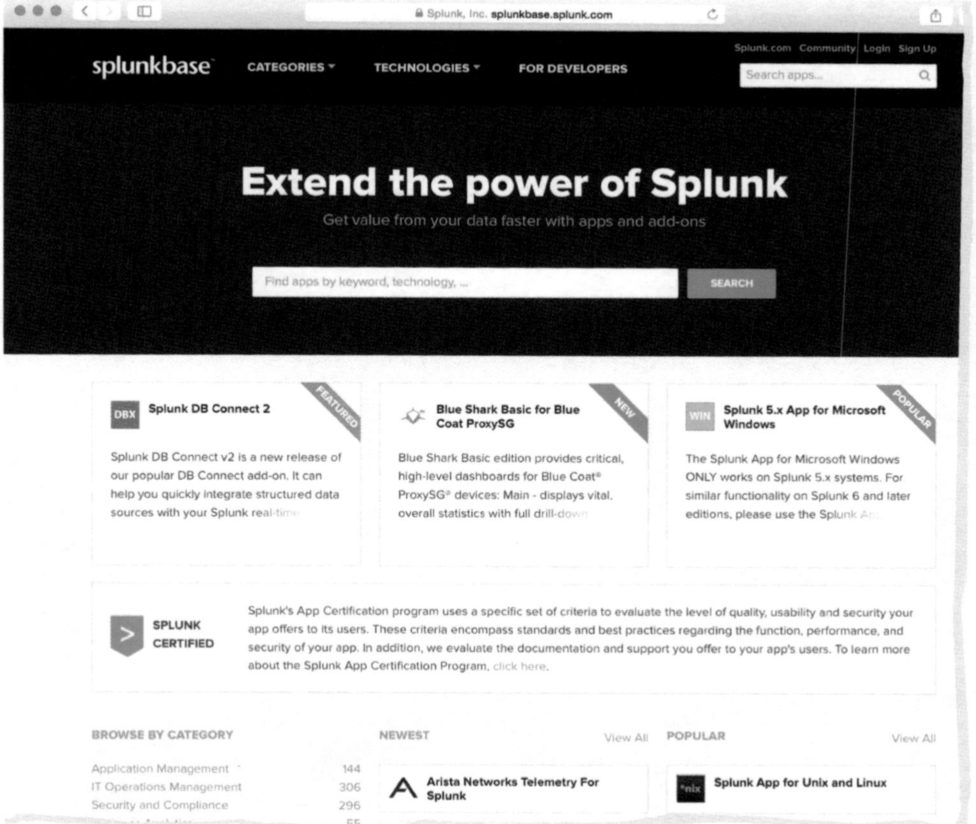

You might also consider uploading your app code to GitHub to open source your work and reap the benefits of community collaboration.

BUS

To manage your app on Splunkbase, add `/edit` **to the URL of your app on Splunkbase. There you can hide and share versions, update release notes and manage editors for your app. To upload a new version, go to** splunkbase.splunk.com/new. **Remember to bump the version number in** `app.conf` **as Splunkbase will not accept another submission with the same version number.**

BUS

Once published, you can see usage stats by adding `/stats` **to the URL of your app on Splunkbase. The analytics view gives you not only the number of app downloads and distribution by app versions, Splunk Enterprise versions, OS versions and geographic regions. It also provides an important metric of active installments.**

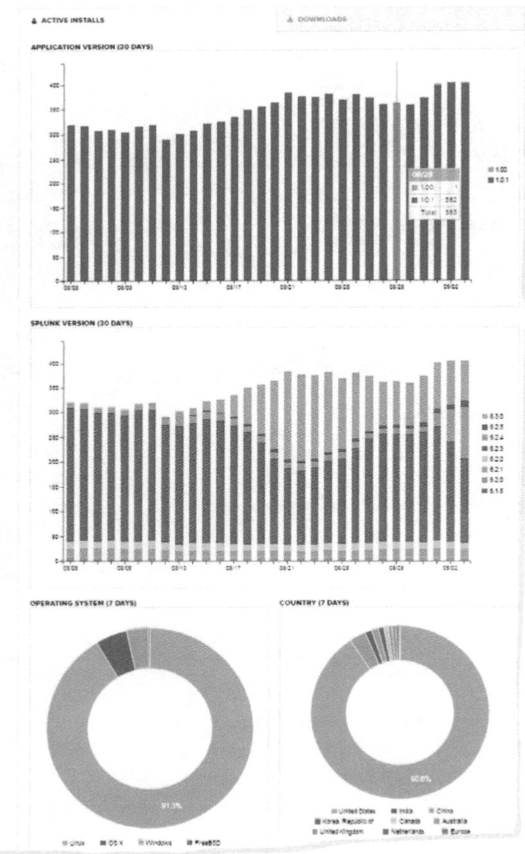

MORE INFORMATION

For information on defining the Splunk web navigation for your app, including panel ordering and specifying menu options, see the "Step 6: Build navigation for your app" in the Splunk app building tutorial at: dev.splunk.com/goto/buildnav.

For information on how to store the configuration parameters by using the app key value store at: dev.splunk.com/goto/appkvstore.

For detailed information about how to implement a set up panel, see the "Step 7: Configure a setup screen" in the Splunk app building tutorial at: dev.splunk.com/goto/setupapp.

To make your app available to everyone in the Splunk community, publish it on Splunkbase at: base.splunk.com.

To open source your work and get the benefits of community collaboration, upload your app code to: github.com.

To learn how to package your app for distribution, see the "Step 8: Package your app or add-on" in the Splunk app building tutorial at: dev.splunk.com/goto/packageapp.

To learn about the naming conventions that must be followed, see "Naming conventions for apps and add-ons on Splunkbase" at: dev.splunk.com/goto/namingguide.

Learn more about app certification at: dev.splunk.com/goto/aboutappcert.

Learn how to use the Splunk Enterprise XML validation tool at:
dev.splunk.com/goto/schemavalidation.

Learn how to create a deployment app, which can be downloaded to a set of deployment clients in a distributed Splunk Enterprise environment:
dev.splunk.com/goto/createdeployapps.

Appendix A

List of PAS knowledge objects

The following table is a list of all of the Splunk knowledge objects that exist in the PAS app. The location specifies where the *Journey* discusses the particular knowledge object.

SPLUNK KNOWLEDGE OBJECT	DEFINED IN $APP_HOME/...	TYPE	LOCATION IN JOURNEY
PAS Data Model	default/data/models/ ri_pas_datamodel.json	Data Model	Working with data: where it comes from and how we manage it Defining a custom Data Model
ri-pas-application	appserver/addons/ pas_simulated_application_addon/ default/eventtypes.conf	Event type	Working with data: where it comes from and how we manage it Tagging our events
ri-pas-application-change-permissions	"	Event type	Working with data: where it comes from and how we manage it Tagging our events
ri-pas-application-delete	"	Event type	Working with data: where it comes from and how we manage it Tagging our events
ri-pas-application-read	"	Event type	Working with data: where it comes from and how we manage it Tagging our events
ri-pas-application-update	"	Event type	Working with data: where it comes from and how we manage it Tagging our events

SPLUNK KNOWLEDGE OBJECT	DEFINED IN $APP_HOME/...	TYPE	LOCATION IN JOURNEY
`ri-pas-database`	`appserver/addons/pas_simulated_database_addon/default/eventtypes.conf`	Event type	Working with data: where it comes from and how we manage it Tagging our events
`ri-pas-database-change-permissions`	"	Event type	Working with data: where it comes from and how we manage it Tagging our events
`ri-pas-database-delete`	"	Event type	Working with data: where it comes from and how we manage it Tagging our events
`ri-pas-database-read`	"	Event type	Working with data: where it comes from and how we manage it Tagging our events
`ri-pas-database-update`	"	Event type	Working with data: where it comes from and how we manage it Tagging our events
`ri-pas-file`	`appserver/addons/pas_simulated_database_addon/default/eventtypes.conf`	Event type	Working with data: where it comes from and how we manage it Tagging our events
`ri-pas-file-change-permissions`	"	Event type	Working with data: where it comes from and how we manage it Tagging our events
`ri-pas-file-delete`	"	Event type	Working with data: where it comes from and how we manage it Tagging our events
`ri-pas-file-read`	"	Event type	Working with data: where it comes from and how we manage it Tagging our events
`ri-pas-file-update`	"	Event type	Working with data: where it comes from and how we manage it Tagging our events
`google-drive`	`appserver/addons/googledrive_addon/default/eventtypes.conf`	Event type	Adding code: using JavaScript and Search Processing Language **Example:** Adding a new provider add-on app
`google-drive-change-permissions`	"	Event type	Adding code: using JavaScript and Search Processing Language **Example:** Adding a new provider add-on app

SPLUNK KNOWLEDGE OBJECT	DEFINED IN $APP_HOME/...	TYPE	LOCATION IN JOURNEY
google-drive-delete	appserver/addons/googledrive_addon/default/eventtypes.conf	Event type	Adding code: using JavaScript and Search Processing Language Example: Adding a new provider add-on app
google-drive-read	"	Event type	Adding code: using JavaScript and Search Processing Language Example: Adding a new provider add-on app
google-drive-update	"	Event type	Adding code: using JavaScript and Search Processing Language Example: Adding a new provider add-on app
audit	appserver/addons/googledrive_addon/default/tags.conf appserver/addons/googledrive_addon/default/tags.conf appserver/addons/pas_simulated_database_addon/default/tags.conf appserver/addons/pas_simulated_application_addon/default/tags.conf Also inside ../Splunk_SA_CIM/default/tags.conf	Tag	Working with data: where it comes from and how we manage it Tagging our events
change	"	Tag	Working with data: where it comes from and how we manage it Tagging our events
change-permissions	"	Tag	Working with data: where it comes from and how we manage it Tagging our events
cloudstorage	appserver/addons/googledrive_addon/default/tags.conf appserver/addons/googledrive_addon/default/tags.conf appserver/addons/pas_simulated_database_addon/default/tags.conf appserver/addons/pas_simulated_application_addon/default/tags.conf	Tag	Working with data: where it comes from and how we manage it Tagging our events
delete	"	Tag	Working with data: where it comes from and how we manage it Tagging our events

SPLUNK KNOWLEDGE OBJECT	DEFINED IN $APP_HOME/...	TYPE	LOCATION IN JOURNEY
pas	appserver/addons/googledrive_addon/default/tags.conf appserver/addons/googledrive_addon/default/etags.conf appserver/addons/pas_simulated_database_addon/default/etags.conf appserver/addons/pas_simulated_application_addon/default/tags.conf	Tag	Working with data: where it comes from and how we manage it Tagging our events
read	"	Tag	Working with data: where it comes from and how we manage it Tagging our events
update	"	Tag	Working with data: where it comes from and how we manage it Tagging our events
FIELDALIAS-command	appserver/addons/googledrive_addon/default/props.conf appserver/addons/pas_simulated_application_addon/default/props.conf appserver/addons/pas_simulated_database_addon/default/props.conf	Field alias	Working with data: where it comes from and how we manage it Mapping to a Splunk Common Information Model
FIELDALIAS-object	appserver/addons/googledrive_addon/default/props.conf appserver/addons/pas_simulated_application_addon/default/props.conf appserver/addons/pas_simulated_database_addon/default/props.conf	Field alias	Working with data: where it comes from and how we manage it Mapping to a Splunk Common Information Model
FIELDALIAS-event_id	appserver/addons/pas_simulated_application_addon/default/props.conf	Field alias	Working with data: where it comes from and how we manage it Defining our mappings in separate add-on apps
FIELDALIAS-object_attrs	appserver/addons/pas_simulated_application_addon/default/props.conf	Field alias	Working with data: where it comes from and how we manage it Defining our mappings in separate add-on apps
FIELDALIAS-src	appserver/addons/pas_simulated_application_addon/default/props.conf appserver/addons/pas_simulated_database_addon/default/props.conf	Field alias	Working with data: where it comes from and how we manage it Defining our mappings in separate add-on apps

SPLUNK KNOWLEDGE OBJECT	DEFINED IN $APP_HOME/...	TYPE	LOCATION IN JOURNEY
`FIELDALIAS-user`	`appserver/addons/pas_simulated_application_addon/default/props.conf` `appserver/addons/pas_simulated_database_addon/default/props.conf`	Field alias	Working with data: where it comes from and how we manage it Defining our mappings in separate add-on apps
`FIELDALIAS-action`	`appserver/addons/pas_simulated_database_addon/default/props.conf`	Field alias	Working with data: where it comes from and how we manage it Defining our mappings in separate add-on apps
`FIELDALIAS-object_id`	`appserver/addons/pas_simulated_database_addon/default/props.conf` `appserver/addons/pas_simulated_files_addon/default/props.conf`	Field alias	Working with data: where it comes from and how we manage it Defining our mappings in separate add-on apps
`FIELDALIAS-user_id`	`appserver/addons/pas_simulated_database_addon/default/props.conf` `appserver/addons/pas_simulated_files_addon/default/props.conf`	Field alias	Working with data: where it comes from and how we manage it Defining our mappings in separate add-on apps
`change-type`	`appserver/addons/googledrive_addon/default/props.conf` `appserver/addons/pas_simulated_application_addon/default/props.conf`	Calculated field	Working with data: where it comes from and how we manage it Defining our mappings in separate add-on apps
`EXTRACT-user`	`appserver/addons/googledrive_addon/default/props.conf`	Field extraction	Working with data: where it comes from and how we manage it Defining our mappings in separate add-on apps
`EXTRACT-fields`	`appserver/addons/pas_simulated_files_addon/default/props.conf`	Field extraction	Working with data: where it comes from and how we manage it Defining our mappings in separate add-on apps
`EXTRACT-fields2`	`appserver/addons/pas_simulated_files_addon/default/props.conf`	Field extraction	Working with data: where it comes from and how we manage it Defining our mappings in separate add-on apps
`employee_details.csv`	`appserver/pas_hr_info/lookups/employee_details.csv`	Lookup table file	Adding code: using JavaScript and Search Processing Language Case study: Building a complex query with lookups and time data overlays

SPLUNK KNOWLEDGE OBJECT	DEFINED IN $APP_HOME/...	TYPE	LOCATION IN JOURNEY
employee_details	appserver/addons/pas_hr_info/default/transforms.conf	Lookup definition	Adding code: using JavaScript and Search Processing Language Case study: Building a complex query with lookups and time data overlays
ri_setup	default/transforms.conf	Lookup definition	Working with data: where it comes from and how we manage it Using stateful configuration data in the PAS app
violation_types	default/transforms.conf	Lookup definition	Adding code: using JavaScript and Search Processing Language Example: Combining multiple searches
about	default/data/ui/views/about.xml	View	N/A
anomalous_activity	default/data/ui/views/anomalous_activity.xml	View	Adding code: using JavaScript and Search Processing Language How we work #2: Pairing between the stakeholders
customer_monitor	default/data/ui/views/customer_monitor.xml	View	UI and visualizations: what our apps look like A simple example using the D3 third-party visualization library
offhours_document_access	default/data/ui/views/offhours_document_access.xml	View	Adding code: using JavaScript and Search Processing Language Case study: Building a complex query with lookups and time data overlays
setup	default/data/ui/views/setup.xml	View	Working with data: where it comes from and how we manage it Using stateful configuration data in the PAS app
summary	default/data/ui/views/summary.xml	View	UI and visualizations: what our apps look like
terminated_employee_document_access	default/data/ui/views/terminated_employee_document_access.xml	View	Working with data: where it comes from and how we manage it Modifying the data model to support additional queries

SPLUNK KNOWLEDGE OBJECT	DEFINED IN $APP_HOME/...	TYPE	LOCATION IN JOURNEY
user_activity	default/data/ui/views/user_activity.xml	View	Working with data: where it comes from and how we manage it Integrating with a third-party system
default	default/data/ui/nav/default.xml	Navigation menu	UI and visualizations: what our apps look like Adding colors and logos
pas	default/indexes.conf	Index	Packaging and deployment: reaching our destination Tips and useful resources
pasadmin	default/authorize.conf	Role	Packaging and deployment: reaching our destination Managing authorization and permissions
pasuser	default/authorize.conf	Role	Packaging and deployment: reaching our destination Managing authorization and permissions
jira_alerts	default/alert_actions.conf default/savedsearches.conf bin/jira.py	Alert action	New adventures require new tools: alerting

Appendix B

Eventgen troubleshooting tips

Here are some troubleshooting tips to help you make the best use of the Eventgen data generation tool. These tips are intended to show you how to use various Eventgen features in ways that give you greater insight into your code. Dive deeper into how to use the tips suggested here by reading the Eventgen documentation on the GitHub splunk/eventgen repository.

SETTING PERMISSIONS

To verify that you have permissions set correctly by viewing the <host><managementPort>/services/configs/eventgen endpoint. There, you should see every sample that you've configured and their parameters. If you don't see a sample listed, either permissions are not set correctly or **eventgen.conf** is not installed correctly.

Permissions apply to modular input mode.

USING THE COMMAND LINE

Eventgen can be run either manually from the command line or as a modular input.

Running Eventgen from the command line can be useful for quickly debugging your eventgen configuration:

```
python bin/eventgen.py -s <sample>
```

This runs Eventgen using the **sample** configuration file and outputs the results to **stdout**. Use the **-v** (verbose) argument to output autogenerated events and **-d** (debug) option to output debug information.

REPLAY MODE AND TIMESTAMP EXTRACTION

You can choose to run in *replay* mode or *sample* mode to generate samples. An advantage of replay mode is that it allows you to take an export of existing data and replay it in the current time. Replay mode gives you more flexibility than sample mode, which is necessarily random. Generally, you'll find that it is usually sufficient to run in sample mode.

Replay mode is single-threaded because it depends on timestamp extraction to generate events in their correct sequence. You can encounter two undesirable effects, that you might not expect: 1) because replay mode is single-threaded, event throughput is significantly slower than in sample mode, and 2) it's possible that timestamps are not always recognized so events can be missed.

FLUSHING EVENT QUEUES

To improve performance, you can specify the number of events to queue before flushing the queue. Set the `[global] MaxIntervalsBeforeFlush` parameter to the number of events to be queued before flushing the queue. (An event interval is the *interval* you defined an event to be.)

TROUBLESHOOTING CSV SAMPLES

If you are using a CSV file to specify event samples, use Microsoft Excel to produce/test a well-formed CSV file.

TEST

Did you know you can use Eventgen to do performance testing?

PERFORMANCE TESTING

To learn how to do performance testing with Eventgen, read the Performance documentation, on the **dev** branch.

A quick way to see if there might be performance issues is to observe queue sizes in your debug output. If your queue sizes and throughput values are stuck at zero or unusually high, it might indicate performance problems.

MORE INFORMATION

Dive deeper into how to use the tips suggested here by reading the Eventgen documentation on the GitHub splunk/eventgen repository at: dev.splunk.com/goto/eventgenreadme.

To learn how to do performance testing with Eventgen, read the Performance documentation, on the **dev** branch at: dev.splunk.com/goto/performancereadme.

Appendix C

Splunk app configuration

A **configuration file** (or **.conf file**) contains configuration information for Splunk Enterprise and apps. You can configure settings and processes by editing stanzas within copies of the default configuration files. **Stanzas** begin with a text string enclosed in brackets and contain one or more configuration parameters defined by key-value pairs.

Global configuration files for Splunk Enterprise are stored at `$SPLUNK_HOME/etc/system/`, with default files stored in the **default** folder, and editable local files in the **local** folder. You store your app's .conf files as follows, where *<your_app>* indicates your app's directory:

- Default settings that are not to be edited by users: `$SPLUNK_HOME/etc/apps/`*<your_app>*`/default/`
- Local settings, where user-modified settings are stored. Ideally, your app will include UI that obfuscates these .conf files from users and prevents them from having to edit them manually. Local files are located at `$SPLUNK_HOME/etc/apps/`*<your_app>*`/local/`

To learn more about configuration files, including how settings precedence is determined based on file placement, see "About configuration files" in the Splunk Enterprise Admin Manual. Every .conf file has a corresponding .spec file, which contains a comprehensive listing of every possible .conf file setting, along with an explanation of each possible value. Global .spec files are located at `$SPLUNK_HOME/etc/system/README/`, and in the "Configuration file reference." You should include .spec files for each of your app's .conf files inside a **README** folder at the root level of your app's folder.

The following table lists some common .conf files that are applicable to app development.

.CONF FILE	DESCRIPTION
`alert_actions.conf`	Configures global alert actions and saved search actions.
`app.conf`	Maintains the state of an app in Splunk Enterprise and customizes an app's settings. This file only exists within individual app folders, not in the global Splunk Enterprise settings location.
`authorize.conf`	Roles and granular access controls.
`collections.conf`	Configures the App Key Value Store (KV Store) collections for a given app in Splunk Enterprise.
`commands.conf`	Search commands for any custom search scripts created. You add your custom search script to $SPLUNK_HOME/etc/searchscripts/ or to $SPLUNK_HOME/etc/apps/*<your_app>*/bin/. For the latter, put a custom `commands.conf` file in $SPLUNK_HOME/etc/apps/*<your_app>*. For the former, put the custom `commands.conf` in $SPLUNK_HOME/etc/system/local/.
`datamodels.conf`	Configures data models. To configure a data model for your app, put the custom `datamodels.conf` file in your app's **local** folder.
`default.meta.conf`	*.meta files contain ownership information, access controls, and export settings for Splunk Enterprise objects like saved searches, event types, and views. Every app has its own `default.meta` file.
`eventtypes.conf`	Configures event types and their properties. You can also pipe any search to the `typelearner` search command to create event types. Event types created this way will be written to $SPLUNK_HOME/etc/systems/local/eventtypes.conf.
`inputs.conf`	Configures inputs, distributed inputs such as forwarders, and file system monitoring.
`macros.conf`	Search language macros.
`props.conf`	Configures Splunk's processing properties.
`savedsearches.conf`	Saved search entries. Each saved search is its own stanza.
`tags.conf`	Configures tags. Set any number of tags for indexed or extracted fields.
`transforms.conf`	Configures data transformations and event signing.
`ui-prefs.conf`	UI preferences for a view. A view is a UI that uses Simple XML as the underlying code, such as the search app, dashboards, and forms.

Index

E

O

P

Q

R

S

T

U

V

50919359R00190

Made in the USA
Charleston, SC
06 January 2016